Russian-American Dialogue on Cultural Relations, 1776–1914

Russian-American Dialogues on United States History

Volume 3

General Editors

Eugene F. Yazkov

Louis W. Potts

Russian-American Dialogue on Cultural Relations 1776–1914

Edited by Norman E. Saul
and Richard D. McKinzie

University of Missouri Press • Columbia and London

Copyright © 1997 by
The Curators of the University of Missouri
University of Missouri Press, Columbia, Missouri 65201
Printed and bound in the United States of America
All rights reserved
5 4 3 2 1   01 00 99 98 97

Library of Congress Cataloging-in-Publication Data

Russian-American dialogue on cultural relations, 1776–1914 / edited by Norman E.
    Saul and Richard D. McKinzie.
        p.   cm.—(Russian-American dialogues on United States history ; v. 3)
    Includes bibliographical references (p.   ) and index.
    ISBN 0-8262-1097-X (alk. paper)
    1. United States—Relations—Russia.   2. Russia—Relations—United States.
3. Russia—Foreign relations—1801–1917.   I. Saul, Norman E.   II. McKinzie,
Richard D.   III. Series.
E183.8.R9R89   1996
303.48'247073—DC20   96-31075
                                                                                    CIP

∞™ This paper meets the requirements of the
American National Standard for Permanence of Paper
for Printed Library Materials, Z39.48, 1984.

Designer: Mindy Shouse
Typesetter: BOOKCOMP
Printer and binder: Thomson-Shore, Inc.
Typefaces: Industria and Times

Contents

	Joint Preface	vii
	Editor's Preface	ix
	Acknowledgments	xi
	Editorial Notes	xiii
1.	Russian-American Cultural Relations An Overview, *by N. N. Bolkhovitinov*	1
2.	Enlighteners and Revolutions of the Eighteenth Century, *by V. I. Moriakov*	26
	Comment, *by John T. Alexander*	42
3.	The American Theme on the Pages of *Dukh Zhurnalov* (Spirit of Journals), *by N. N. Bolkhovitinov*	45
4.	The Development of Culture and Literature in the U.S.A. during Jacksonian Democracy in the Assessment of Russian Periodicals, *by I. A. Ivanchenko*	77
	Comment, *by J. Dane Hartgrove*	89

5.	Russia and the U.S. Civil War, *by N. S. Kiniapina*	93
6.	Ivan Turchaninov and the American Civil War, *by A. I. Startsev*	107
7.	Russians in the United States: Social, Cultural, and Scientific Contacts in the 1870s, *by G. P. Kuropiatnik*	128
	Comment, *by Ronald J. Jensen*	166
8.	Leo Tolstoy and Social Critics in the United States at the Turn of the Century, *by I. P. Dement'ev*	170
9.	American History and Policy on the Pages of *Delo* (Cause) and *Slovo* (Word), *by I. K. Mal'kova*	192
10.	Chekhov and America, *by A. N. Nikoliukin*	212
	Comment, *by Richard M. Abrams*	222
11.	Some Questions on American Foreign Policy in 1898–1914 in the Russian Bourgeois Press, *by A. F. Tsvirkun*	227
	Comment, *by Norman E. Saul*	241
	Postscript: Past, Present, and Future, *by N. N. Bolkhovitinov and Norman E. Saul*	243
	Contributors	249
	Select Bibliography	251
	Index	255

Joint Preface

This is the third published volume in a series originally conceived by historians in Russia and the United States in 1986. It is an outgrowth of the Fulbright faculty position hosted for now two and a half decades at Moscow State University. Dr. Richard McKinzie, so vital to originating and sustaining the joint intellectual venture, sought to create a dialogue among scholars in the Soviet Union and America who shared interest in the study of America's heritage. Soviet scholarship was then flourishing, most especially in journals published in the U.S.S.R. The initial volume, edited by Otis L. Graham, Jr., appeared in 1989. This featured eleven essays on the New Deal translated into English and critiqued by American experts. Following the political upheavals of 1989–1991 and subsequent intellectual reverberations, the series was continued in 1995 with Gordon and Louise Wood's edition of a volume focusing on the American Revolution.

We are pleased that this third volume, which the late Professor McKinzie initially edited, is now completed. These original Russian essays were translated into English by Professor Richard Tempest of the Department of Slavic Languages and Literatures at the University of Illinois at Urbana-Champaign. Translation assistance for the initial Bolkhovitinov piece was provided by Howard Solomon of the Department of Slavic Languages and Literatures at the University of Kansas. As explained in Dr. Norman Saul's editorial note, these translations were subsequently polished by the volume and series editors and approved by the original essayists.

This volume provides a distinctiveness to the series. The eleven essays offer deep insights into the mind-sets of the Soviet academic community at the height of the contentious Cold War. As Professor Norman Saul points out in his appraisal of the cultural relations of the two countries, "Despite the many limitations, Soviet/Russian historians have been more interested in, and have accomplished more on, this topic than their 'freer' colleagues in the West."

Future volumes are envisioned. The two-party system in America, the particular focus of Americanists at Moscow State University's Department of Modern and Contemporary History, will be the basis of our next publication. We are pleased to acknowledge the cooperation and sustenance of scholars and academic administrators in both countries. Critical aid at the University of Missouri–Kansas City was provided by Executive Dean Marvin Querry, College Dean James Durig, and the University of Missouri Research Board.

We trust that this volume, and this series, further establish scholarly dialogue between specialists in both lands with common intellectual interests. It is worth renewing the pledge of our initial volume that it "may facilitate a new kind of political thinking that is so necessary for both scholars and politicians and, more generally, for all people in these complicated and crucial times."

Eugene F. Yazkov
Louis W. Potts

Editorial Board

Russian Members

Eugene F. Yazkov, Moscow State University
Igor P. Dement'ev, Moscow State University
Alexander S. Manykin, Moscow State University
August Mishin, Moscow State University
Yuri N. Rogulev, Moscow State University
Grigori N. Sevastyanov, Institute of General History, Russian Academy of Sciences
G. A. Trofimenko, Institute of U.S. and Canadian Studies, Russian Academy of Sciences

American Members

E. David Cronon, University of Wisconsin–Madison
George M. Fredrickson, Stanford University
Leon F. Litwack, University of California–Berkeley
Richard K. McKinzie, University of Missouri–Kansas City
Louis W. Potts, University of Missouri–Kansas City
E. B. Smith, University of Maryland
Eugene P. Trani, Virginia Commonwealth University
Peter F. Walker, University of North Carolina–Chapel Hill

Editor's Preface

The purpose of this volume in the Dialogues series is to provide in English translation some of the best Russian scholarship on Russian-American relations before 1914 that first appeared in article form in the U.S.S.R./Russia. The selections focus primarily on cultural relations: the contributions that each country made to the cultural life of the other; correspondence and interactions of writers, scientists, journalists, and ordinary citizens of each country with those of the other; the development of public perceptions and how these changed over time; the "American focus" in Russian periodicals in the nineteenth century; and the significant roles that Russians and the Russian presence played in American history. This material is far from being comprehensive, since, as the postscript demonstrates, many topics are left untouched; it is, rather, a sampling of what has been done over the past twenty-five years, a scratching of the surface that, hopefully, will be more thoroughly explored in the future.

Obviously, much of the work represented here is dated, handicapped by restrictions in access to information in the United States, and even to Russian archival sources, and tinged more or less by unavoidable ideological trappings. Yet it is important that this work be made available to show what could actually be done in the Soviet period in terms of professional research and analysis, and to provide a foundation for future study. Almost all of these authors at least had the opportunity to study in the United States through the exchange of scholars programs that began in the 1950s.

Despite the many limitations, Soviet/Russian historians have been more interested in, and have accomplished more on, this topic than their "freer" colleagues in the West. These were pioneer efforts, undertaken with considerable professional risk, that kept study of the West, and of the United States in particular, alive in the former Soviet Union through the ups and downs of the Cold War.

Unlike most of the articles in the other volumes in the Dialogues series, these extensively use and cite Russian archives and publications, thus providing new and less readily accessible information for American readers. In addition, the results may offer new material for Western historians of Russia as well as of the United States; for example, on the extent to which Russian liberals and radicals used American examples in their pursuit of liberalizing-reform or revolutionary goals at home. Much can be found here to fill niches and provoke thought in comparative international studies.

The authors of these articles in general faced countervailing problems. The cultural relations between the two countries were indeed extensive and loom larger than one might expect; yet very little professional work had been done. Similarly, the interest in America in the Soviet Union, especially in American literature and music, was quite high throughout the twentieth century. To devote part or all of one's career to this study was somewhat risky, even during the eras of peaceful coexistence and détente. These soft spots in the Cold War, however, provided the critically important base in the form of more fruitful cultural exchanges and opportunities for study and travel abroad.

Fortunately, the authors of these articles did not have to start from scratch but, in fact, were nurtured by a previous generation of professional historians who maintained an international and even an American focus, and who managed to survive the Stalin era with their academic credentials more or less intact: Evgenyi Tarle, Aleksei Efimov, Aleksandr Narochnitskii, and Lev Zubok, to name a few. As in the case of Russian studies in the United States, American studies in the U.S.S.R. was given a decided boost by the Cold War and the need "to know the enemy." And also as in America, much of this effort was extended back into the study of the "irrelevant" past. Credit definitely must go to able leaders, administrators, and protectors with a degree of political clout, such as Georgii Arbatov and Grigorii Sevost'ianov, for the expansion of the Institutes of General History and of the U.S.A. and Canada of the Academy of Sciences, and for providing a base for a new generation of professional researchers.

Fortunately for American studies in Russia, a number of members of this postwar generation devoted their careers to the study of the earlier history of the United States and Russian-American relations. They included Nikolai Sivachev of the University of Moscow, Aleksandr Chubarian and Nikolai Bolkhovitinov of the Academy of Sciences in Moscow, and Aleksandr Fursenko in Leningrad/St. Petersburg. With the assistance of a cadre of distinguished scholars such as Irina Beliavskaia, Igor Dement'ev, Robert Ivanov, Boris Shiraev, Aleksandr Nikoliukin, Evgenyi Iaz'kov, Gennadii Kuropiatnik, Viktor Furaev, Boris Marushkin, and Viktor Mal'kov (some of whom are represented in this volume), they laid the foundation for decades to come. Under their tutelage, promising young scholars have emerged. Ironically, new opportunities for archival investigations and absence of topical restraints are accompanied by severe economic limitations and sharply reduced relevance for the post-Soviet historical profession.

This volume especially, as well as the whole Dialogues project, owes its existence to a friend and colleague of many years, Richard McKinzie, whose dedication to improving mutual professional understanding and contacts of American and Soviet/Russian historians and students was nurtured in his own teaching and research at the University of Missouri–Kansas City, and especially by his experiences as a Fulbright professor at Moscow State University. To him we all owe a great debt of gratitude.

Norman E. Saul

Acknowledgments

The editors wish to acknowledge the valuable assistance of the Word Processing Center of the College of Liberal Arts and Sciences of the University of Kansas, the professional service of the production staff of the University of Missouri Press, the advice and contributions of the commentators, and the helpful suggestions and corrections of Professors Basil Dmytryshyn and Walter LaFeber.

Editorial Notes

The guiding principle in presenting these articles has been to intrude as little as possible so that they may stand on their own merits. It has been necessary to check, smooth, and correct the professional translation to fit the times and historical material. Since the Russian language tends to be more verbose than English, repetitious phrasing and wording has been cut in a number of places. Emissions that exceed one manuscript line are indicated by "[number of lines]". Some of these were required in the interests of brevity and conservation of space without, however, in any way changing the interpretation or flavor of the original. All translations were rechecked with the original Russian texts by the editors.

One big problem has been quotations from English sources being retranslated from Russian to English. In most cases these have not been restored to the original. The general reputation of Russian translations from English is excellent and reliable, but ideological bias in wording is possible, especially those that deal with revolutionary thought and action. Invariably, Russian authors use Russian editions of major sources, such as the works of Marx and Engels, which are rarely found in the West for the obvious reason that English translations or originals readily exist. They will thus vary in wording from available English-language editions.

A case in point is in the article by Moriakov, who quotes a number of passages from Thomas Paine's works from Russian editions. To put these back into the original might, in fact, distort the context, but would be a small research project in itself—determining how Russians interpret or misinterpret Paine through the different or varying meanings of Russian words. So Moriakov's Paine appears here in double translation, neither of which are his responsibility. Though primary texts such as *Common Sense* are readily available, other sources, for example, quotations from the writings of General Turchaninov (in the article by Startsev), are quite rare and difficult to find even in the United States.

All authors have had the opportunity to check and verify the translations, and some have made, mostly minor, corrections. Nikoliukin, in an exception to the above, provided the original English passages quoted in his article, and these replace the retranslations. All authors let stand their ideological references, though they might have preferred to change or omit them under present conditions of Russian scholarship. They all know and expect the reader to appreciate the circumstances under which they were originally written, edited, and published.

Russian scholarly practice is to spell foreign names phonetically, which, when transliterated by a translator, can become practically unrecognizable. Almost all of these, however, have been correctly identified and put into proper English spelling. It took some searching, for example, to identify "Harlebat" (Garlbat in Russian) as the minor Civil War General Hurlbut. Fortunately, Russian scholars cite foreign texts in the original in notes, though in some cases these were misspelled or inaccurate. A greater challenge was the translation of Russian sources into English. These have been restored to the Russian transliteration form in initial footnote citations, using the modified Library of Congress system that is standard for most American research libraries and scholarly journals such as the *American Historical Review*. In this way those who wish may readily locate these sources in the *National Union Catalogue* or elsewhere.

The texts of the articles have been altered from Russian standard practice in one other respect. In the original Russian names of people, both Russian and foreign, are usually rendered with initials only, as in "V. I. Lenin" or "K. Marx." When known, first names have been inserted in the first references and initials omitted in subsequent ones. Also, the more common Russian names are rendered in standard English form—such as Herzen rather than Hertsen, Leo Tolstoy for Lev Tolstoi (but Dmitrii Tolstoi)—in the text, while direct transliteration is retained in the Russian citations of authors and titles in the notes.

Since Russian dates varied from American by eleven, twelve, or thirteen days in the successive centuries represented, readers should exercise caution. Where provided in the original article, the two dates are given as follows: Russian (Julian or "old style")/Western (Gregorian). If only one date is available, one can assume that if the context is Russian it is old style, if American, new style. Fortunately for students of the twentieth century, the Bolsheviks shifted Russia to the Western calendar in February 1918.

Russian-American Dialogue on
Cultural Relations, 1776–1914

1

Russian-American Cultural Relations: An Overview, by N. N. Bolkhovitinov

1. Initial Contacts

The earliest information on America in Russian sources is from the sixteenth century. Maksim Grek (Mikhail Trivolis, ca. 1475–1556) mentions the Europeans' discovery of the "New World," in particular Cuba, "whose inhabitants know not the end." In Martin Bel'skii's translated manuscript "Chronicles of the Whole World" (1584), the word "America" is first used in Russian as the name of a "Great Island," discovered during the voyage of "Ammericus Vespucia."[1]

Even before Captain John Smith, one of the founders of Jamestown, set out in 1607 for North America, he spent some time on the Russian steppe. Smith found shelter in a fortress in the Don region after escaping from Turkish captivity. From there his journey proceeded west, apparently through Donkov, and then through Dorogobuzh and Ostrog to Galich. Never in his life, he claimed, had he encountered "such hospitality, kindness, warm welcome, and friendship" as he had during his stay in these places. "It is amazing," he wrote, "that this country, constantly devastated by attacks and raids from nomads and neighbors, has so many envious of it as well as enemies. Settlements are few and far between. The houses of the residents consist of pine logs bunched together, joined at the ends with wooden reinforcements." Smith had a more negative view of the division of Muscovite society into rich and poor, masters and slaves, which in his opinion hid "the true reason for the weakness and all the misfortunes of this

---

1. N. Lazarev, "Pervye svedeniia russkikh o Novom svete" (The First Russian News of the New World), *Istoricheskii Zhurnal* 1 (1943): 72–75; N. Polevoi, "Povestvovanie ob otkrytii Ameriki, pomeshchenoe v russkikh khronografakh" (Tales of the Discovery of America in Russian Chronographies), *Moskovskii Telegraf* [hereafter *MT*] 43, no. 4 (1832), 594–99; A. Yarmolinsky, *Russian Americana* (New York, 1943), 11. This article by N. N. Bolkhovitinov was first published in *Istoriia SShA* (History of the U.S.A.), vol. 1 (1607–1877) (Moscow, 1983), 607–33.

country." Smith later used his knowledge of Don fortifications to defend Jamestown. "Not one of the English colonies attempting to solidify their position on the American coast could withstand raids by Native Americans until Smith, who had assimilated and applied the Russian method for quickly raising fortifications."[2]

But if John Smith had contact mainly with inhabitants of Russian lands, then the founder of another English colony in America, William Penn, had the opportunity to exchange opinions with Peter the Great. The fact of the matter is that the tsar, visiting England in 1698, conversed with a group of Quakers, and Penn even addressed a special epistle to him containing his views.[3] Penn's religious views and those of his friends did not apparently influence the young Peter outright. Only many years later, in 1790, was Penn's book, *Fruits of Solitude,* published in Moscow, and during the reign of Alexander I Quakers had an opportunity to visit Russia.[4]

The first colonial newspaper, *News Letter,* which was first issued in Boston in 1704, occasionally printed short informational pieces on the war between Russia and Sweden. News on events in distant Russia became even more varied and frequent with the appearance of new weekly newspapers, the *Boston Gazette,* the *New England Courant,* the *American Weekly Mercury,* and the *New York Gazette.* Colonial publications reported on Peter the Great's interest in archaeology and agronomy, on his correspondence with the Paris Academy, and his organization of the Kunstkammer in St. Petersburg. Evaluating Peter's efforts, the *Boston News Letter* of August 5, 1725, gave him credit for establishing trade with other countries, "for developing craft and science, about which earlier nothing was known in the country, prohibiting many outdated customs, and introducing military discipline."[5]

From time to time news about America would appear in Russian publications, Peter's *Vedomosti* (Herald), *Rossiiskie Vedomosti* (Russian Herald), and *Istoricheskie, genealogicheskie i Geograficheskie Preimechanie* (Historical, Genealogical, and Geographical Notes), and finally *S.-Peterburgskie Vedomosti* (St. Petersburg Herald). Of special interest was "News of the Present English and French Settlements in America," published in the *St. Petersburg Herald* on November 25/December 6, 1750, during the time when the foreign section of the newspaper was edited by Mikhail Lomonosov. The analytic character of this article and vast breadth of historical information distinguished

---

2. Ekaterina Dvoichenko-Markova, "Dzhon Smit v Rossii" (John Smith in Russia), *Novaia i Noveishaia Istoriia* 3 (1976), 160.

3. Ekaterina Dvoichenko-Markov, "William Penn and Peter the Great," *Proceedings of the American Philosophical Society* 97, no. 1 (1953), 16–17.

4. William Allen (England) and Stephen Grellet (United States) visited charitable and penal institutions in St. Petersburg, Moscow, Novgorod, and Tver and presented critical comments to the Russian government. Alexander I gave an order "to inform all concerned about these comments by the Quakers and under the authority of the public inspector to direct the administration's special attention to the situation in boarding schools in Novgorod and Tver, where only 35 out of 285 children had survived over the course of a year." A. N. Golitsyn to S. K. Viazmitinov, May 15/27, 1819, f. (record group) 1282, op. (inventory) 2, d. (list) 2099, TsGIA (Central State Historical Archive, St. Petersburg).

5. R. A. Mohl, "America Discovers Russia and Peter the Great," *Journalism Quarterly* 44, no. 4 (winter 1967), 66.

it from other materials on America, printed earlier in the Russian press. The author of the article (most likely Lomonosov himself), taking account of the disputes between England and France, gave his readers a description of Canada, Virginia, the Carolinas, Maryland, Pennsylvania, New York, and New England. On the latter it was reported: "New England is the main province and mercantile storehouse from where all the settlements in America draw their supplies." The article noted also that "in the middle of the land are many American tribes who are often used by the French and English to quell various disturbances—on the English side the Iroquois, on the French the Huron."[6]

Several years later, on March 5, 1754, Benjamin Franklin's *Pennsylvania Gazette* printed an "excerpt from a letter from Moscow of 23 August," in which the circumstances were related surrounding the death of Georg Richmann during experiments on atmospheric electrical charges. The "consultant Lomonosov" was cited as a participant in the experiment, which was in all likelihood the first mention of the Russian scholar in the American press.[7]

On the basis of various documentary materials, the history of Russo-American relations properly begins in the middle of the eighteenth century with the direct and indirect contacts between Franklin and other American scientists and their St. Petersburg colleagues Lomonosov, Richmann, Aepinus, and Braun.[8] Franklin's famous "Experiments and Observations on Electricity" had already become well known in Russia by the middle of the eighteenth century and were developed further in the work of Russian scientists like Lomonosov, Richmann, Aepinus, and Dmitri Golitsyn.

In a major treatise, "Experiment on the Theory of Electricity and Magnetism" (1759), Aepinus wrote, "The inherent body of force, called electricity, discovered only recently, has hardly been adequately studied. . . . I am pleased to the highest degree by the theory on this force proposed by Franklin. . . . I have found several deficiencies in this theory; therefore I devoted my efforts to rectifying them, and with the help of these corrections thus to adapt this theory so that it is in complete agreement with phenomena."[9]

Aepinus himself sent this work to Franklin, who gave it high marks and acquainted his colleagues, Ezra Stiles and John Winthrop, with it. Finally, in June 1766, as a sign of acknowledgment for the contributions by the St. Petersburg academician, Franklin

---

6. A. N. Nikoliukin, *Literaturnye sviazi Rossii i SShA: Stanovlenie literaturnykh kontaktov* (Literary Connections of Russia and the U.S.A.: Establishing Literary Contacts) (Moscow, 1981), 17–22, appendix, 386–87.

7. L. W. Labaree and W. B. Willcox, eds., *The Papers of Benjamin Franklin*, vols. 1–21 (New Haven, 1959), vol. 5, 219–21.

8. Bolkhovitinov, *Stanovlenie russko-amerikanskikh otnoshenii, 1775–1815* (The Beginnings of Russo-American Relations, 1775–1815) [American edition, Harvard, 1975] (Moscow, 1966), 220–31; *Rossiia i SShA: stanovlenie otnoshenie, 1765–1815* (Russia and the U.S.A.: Establishment of Relations, 1765–1815) (Moscow, 1980) [American edition: *The United States and Russia: The Beginning of Relations, 1765–1815*], 15, 16, 18, 21, passim.

9. F. U. T. Epinus, *Teoriia elektrichestva i magnetizma* (Theory of Electricity and Magnetism) (Leningrad, 1951), 10–11. Only two centuries later did the scholarly treatise of the St. Petersburg physicist receive real recognition. In 1979 Princeton University Press published an English translation of Aepinus's work with scholarly commentary and a valuable introduction by Melbourne University professor R. W. Home.

sent him his own work on physical and meteorological observations, which was to appear in a volume of the "Transactions of the Royal Society."[10]

Stiles's letter of February 20, 1765, to the "esteemed Mr. Lomonosov" is now well known. In it he elaborates a detailed program for joint studies (expressing interest in the polar expeditions and temperature measurements from various regions in the Russian empire planned by Lomonosov).[11] His address to academician Joseph-Adam Braun is no less significant. He informs Braun of American attempts to repeat the famous experiments on freezing mercury, carried out in St. Petersburg in 1759.[12] Although initially Stiles did not manage to repeat the brilliant experiments of Braun and Lomonosov, ultimately the persistent American did manage to freeze mercury in Salem in February 1786.[13]

When the American Academy of Arts and Sciences was established in Boston in 1780, one of its most worthy members from abroad was the famous Leonard Euler, whose official election is dated January 30, 1782, but in all likelihood took place earlier. In any event the protocols (February 28/March 11, 1782) of the St. Petersburg Academy of Sciences mention a letter from "the Academy of Arts and Sciences, recently established in Boston, America," of June 1, 1781, with news of Euler's selection, and also an "Act for establishing and managing a society of cooperation and encouraging arts and sciences." American scientists no doubt were well informed about the scientific contributions of Euler, and in the library of the Boston Academy, judging from its first manuscript catalogue, there were eleven works (17 volumes) of the great scientist.[14]

Even earlier, at the beginning of the 1770s, official ties between the American Philosophical Society in Philadelphia and the Academy of Sciences in St. Petersburg had been established. Thanks to Franklin and one of the founders of the Free Economic Society, Timotheus Klingstadt, the first volume of the *Transactions of the American Philosophical Society* was received in St. Petersburg, the primary contents of which found subsequent reflection in *Akademicheskie Izvestii* (Academic News) (1779, part 2).

The vice president of the American Philosophical Society, Thomas Bond, touted the achievements of Russian science in his 1782 speech and strongly recommended that members of the scientific institution in the United States collaborate with scholars from a country that promoted the development of science and literature, and that "has risen to a greatness commensurate with the morning sun."[15]

Important and fruitful scientific contacts between the young Republic and the Russian Empire developed in the second half of the 1780s. With the help of George

---

10. *Ameerikanskii Ezhegodnik 1971* (Moscow, 1971), 330–31; *Physical and Meteorological Observations, Conjectures and Suppositions,* Philosophical Transactions of the Royal Society (London, 1766), 182–92.

11. Bolkhovitinov, *Russia and the U.S.A.,* 16–18.

12. Stiles to I. A. Braun, May 15, 1765, Stiles Papers, Yale University, Beinecke Library.

13. Stiles, *Thermometrical Register,* vol. 1; *Literary Diary,* vol. 12, February 3, 1786.

14. Boston Athenaeum, American Academy of Arts and Sciences, Records, vol. 1, 51; *Protokoly zasedaniia konferentsii imp. Akademii nauk s 1725 to 1803* (Protocols of the meeting of the Imperial Academy of Sciences from 1725 to 1803) (St. Petersburg, 1900), 3, 577; American Academy of Arts and Sciences, Catalogue.

15. Bond, *Anniversary Oration . . . printed by J. Dunlap* (Philadelphia, 1782), 31–32.

Washington, Franklin, and the Marquis de Lafayette, Catherine the Great received valuable information from America on the languages of Native Americans that was used in the preparation of a general comparative dictionary.[16] Gathering material for this dictionary, Americans were themselves drawn into comparative study of these languages. Later, following the example of the Russian dictionary, Benjamin Barton, John Heckewelder, Theodore Schultz, and several others prepared dictionaries of languages of various Native American peoples. Both Barton and Heckewelder felt that the similarity between the languages of Native Americans, Tatars, and several other Asiatic peoples could probably be explained by their common origin. In a letter to Andrei Nartov, Heckewelder expounded upon this proposition, stating that American tribes had originated from Asia and the majority of them were related to the Tatars.[17]

The stormy events of the American Revolution greatly increased the interest toward the United States by figures associated with Russian science, literature, and education. It is noteworthy that as soon as Russia received news of the preliminary peace agreement signed in Paris, Aepinus sent Franklin a special note of congratulations in which he greeted his American colleague as not only a famous natural scientist but also a brilliant politician who had secured for his country freedom and independence.[18]

Progressive representatives of Russian society did not wish to be thought of as having the monarchist sympathies of the court, and openly expressed their support and sympathy for the cause of the American Revolution. If the official *St. Petersburg Herald* in the capital published only a brief report on the "peace preliminaries," the *Moscow Herald*, edited by Nikolai Novikov, printed texts of the relevant documents "in their entirety" in March 1783.[19] "Oh steadfast warrior, you are and were invincible, your authority is freedom, Washington," wrote Alexander Radishchev, greeting the victory of the American revolutionaries. The well-known Latin verses, inscribed under Franklin's portrait *(Eripuit coelo fulmen screptrumque tyrannis)* were translated by Radishchev in witty antimonarchist form ("This savior storm from the heavens, which swept the scepter out of the hands of tsars," although it would probably be better to say "out of the hands of tyrants"), and he thought that this was the most exquisite inscription "that a person can have beneath his portrait."[20] Catherine the Great, on her part, called Radishchev a revolutionary worse than Pugachev, emphasizing that he praised Franklin. But, not long before this, in November 1789, the St. Petersburg Academy of Sciences had elected the great American an honorary member.[21]

In the 1770s and 1780s the first personal contacts between Russian cultural figures and citizens of the young Republic took place. While in Paris, Denis Fonvizin (known

---

16. *Sravnitel'nyi slovar' vsekh iazykov i narechii, po azbuchnomu poriadku raspolozhennyi* (Comparative Dictionary of All Languages and Dialects, in Alphabetical Order), 4 vols. (St. Petersburg, 1790–1791).

17. Bolkhovitinov, *Russia and the U.S.A.*, 206.

18. Ibid., 117–18.

19. *Moskovskie Vedomosti* 19 (March 8/19, 1783): 146–49; 20 (March 11/22, 1783): 154–55.

20. Radishchev, *Poln. Sobr. Soch.* (Complete Collected Works), 3 vols. (Moscow-Leningrad, 1938–1952), vol. 1, 391.

21. For more details, see Bolkhovitinov, *Rossiia i voina SShA za nezavisimost', 1775–1783* (Russia and the U.S. War of Independence, 1775–1783) (Moscow, 1976) [American edition: *Russia and the American Revolution* (Tallahassee, 1976)], 126–31, 164–75.

for his erudite letters) met Franklin and English physicist John Magellan in August 1778, and this was reported in the press. "A representative of the young enlightenment in Russia was conversant with a representative of young America," Petr Viazemskii subsequently wrote.[22] It is quite possible that Fonvizin's personal acquaintance with Franklin influenced his characterization of Starodum in his comedy *The Minor* (Nedorosl'). The first exchange of letters and meetings between Franklin and Princess Ekaterina Dashkova took place in Paris in the winter of 1781. Finally Fedor Karzhavin visited the United States during these stormy revolutionary years.

Immediately after his sojourn in Virginia from the island of Martinique during the spring of 1777, Karzhavin offered his services to the Continental Congress in the capacity of a translator.[23] Apparently not receiving a reply, the Russian traveler practiced medicine and engaged in commerce, and as a result established friendly relations with members of the faculty of the College of William and Mary in Williamsburg, including Carlo Bellini, George Wythe, and Bishop James Madison (a cousin of the future president—ed). After Karzhavin returned to Russia in 1788, his rich impressions of America were included in many published articles, letters, diary entries, and an autobiographical "fairy tale," all of which served as objects of careful study.[24] In such manner the prerequisites were created and the initial foundation was put in place for developing systematic scientific and literary contacts between Russia and the United States during the nineteenth century.

2. Scientific Ties

The breadth and range of these connections can be judged from the election of a significant number of Russians as members of the American Philosophical Society in Philadelphia and of the American Academy of Arts and Sciences in Boston. From the end of the eighteenth century up to the 1870s, twenty-six Russians were selected as members to the Philosophical Society, including Dashkova (April 17, 1789), Peter Pallas (October 21, 1791), Friedrich Adelung (January 16, 1818), Nicholas Fuss and Gotthelf Fischer (April 17, 1818), V. G. Tilezius (April 16, 1819), Ia. V. Bilie and Ivan Kruzenshtern (April 16, 1824), Adolph Kupffer (April 16, 1847), and Wilhelm Struve (October 21, 1853).

Twelve Russians were elected to the ranks of the Academy in Boston between 1782 and 1872. On November 22, 1812, academicians Fuss, Fischer, and Friedrich Schubert became foreign members of the American Academy of Arts and Sciences. Well-known scientists inducted in 1834 included Struve, mathematician Mikhail Ostrogradskii, and

---

22. Viazemskii, *Poln. Sobr. Soch.* (Complete Collected Works), 12 vols. (St. Petersburg, 1878–1896), vol. 5, 91.

23. Karzhavin to J. Hancock, June 15, 1777, in Bolkhovitinov, *Russia and the U.S.A.,* 40.

24. Bolkhovitinov, *Russia and the U.S. War for Independence,* 209–23. Relatively recently in the manuscript division of the Saltykov-Shchedrin State Public Library (OR GPB) Soviet researcher S. R. Dolgova discovered a portion of Karzhavin's diary for 1777–1778 that he kept during his travels in Virginia. Record group 1000, l. (page) 76–101, OR GPB. The basic contents of the diary are reflected in Karzhavin's letter to his French friend, [J. C.] Barr, dated April 15, 1780, in Bolkhovitinov, *Russia and the U.S.A.,* 61–64.

the grandson of Euler, mathematician Edward Collins, followed by the founder of embryology, Karl Baer (1849), and Otto Struve (1864).[25]

In turn the St. Petersburg Academy of Sciences elected, in addition to Franklin, physicist John Churchman (1795), meteorologist Matthew Maury (1855), physicist Alexander Bache (1861), historian George Bancroft (1867), astronomers Simon Newcomb (1875) and Benjamin Gould (1875), and other American scientists to their ranks.[26]

A simple enumeration of these authoritative scientists shows the diversity and importance of the ties that existed between Russian and American scientists. The Philosophical Society in Philadelphia and the Academy in Boston promoted contacts during the nineteenth century with not only the Imperial Academy of Sciences but also the Moscow Society of Natural Scientists, the Pulkovo Observatory, the Corps of Mining Engineers, and many other scientific institutions in Russia. John Quincy Adams transferred a collection of minerals to the Moscow Society of Natural Scientists.[27] Informing Adams about his selection as a member of the Society, Fischer expressed the hope that the American envoy would direct the attention of Moscow scientists "to the faraway realms which are little-known and the gifts of nature that we have in very small quantities."[28] In the spring of 1810 Adams, Joseph Willard, and John Davis were also selected as members of the Moscow Society of Natural Scientists. The number of American members of the society subsequently continued to grow, reaching twenty-eight by 1857.[29] As early as 1810, Fischer began sending the transactions of the society and his own scientific publications to the United States.

There was significant interest on the part of Russians in the system of agriculture in the United States and in cultivating the best varieties of American tobacco and cotton. The Moscow Agricultural Society and its publication, *Zemledel'cheskii Zhurnal* (Farming Journal) emerged as an active proponent of American practices. In one of its first issues (1821, no. 3) the journal contained an article, "On Encouraging Agriculture in the States of North America," and in 1828 the society obtained several types of American tobacco, which were sent to the Caucasus, Ukraine, and Crimea. *Farming Journal* later published "Practical Notes on Sowing and Cultivating American Tobacco" and regularly provided information on the results of its cultivation in Russia.[30]

---

25. Dvoichenko-Markov, "The American Philosophical Society and Early Russian-American Relations," *Proceedings of the American Philosophical Society* 94, no. 5 (1950): 610; and "The Russian Members of the American Academy of Arts and Sciences," *Proceedings of the American Philosophical Society* 109, no. 1 (1965): 56.

26. M. I. Radovskii, "Iz istorii russko-amerkanskikh nauchnykh sviazei: protokol'nye bumagi arkhiva AN SSSR XVIII vv." (From the History of Russo-American Scientific Ties), *Vestnik AN SSSR* 11, 1956.

27. Davis to J. Q. Adams, August 1, 1809, pt. 4, reel 408, Adams Papers, Massachusetts Historical Society.

28. Fischer to Adams, February 3/15, 1810, in Bolkhovitinov, *Russia and the U.S.A.,* 402.

29. Record group 418, inventory 28, list 3, 44, TsGA g. Moskvy (Central State Archive, Moscow).

30. *Zemledel'cheskii Zhurnal* 2 (1834): 295–300; 5 (1837), 249–84. See also: Ia. A. Ivanchenko, "Amerikanskaia problematika v russkoi periodicheskoi pechati (1825–1841)," (American

These activities of the society received government support and cooperation. In May 1837 Minister of Finance Egor Kankrin sent to the president of the Moscow Agricultural Society, Dmitrii Golitsyn, American tobacco seeds of the best varieties received from New York.[31] These seeds were distributed to various people in the Crimea, Kherson, Saratov, Belgrade, and even Siberia, primarily to those who had earlier cultivated "American tobacco and received rewards for their efforts." As is clear from a letter in response written by one of them, a Crimean landowner, F. Zommerfel'd, of all tobaccos "Havana and Maryland varieties are preferred and for harvesting ability are . . . of the highest quality."[32]

Of special interest is the trip to the United States in 1853–1854 by Viktor Mochul'skii, a member of the Free Economic Society in St. Petersburg, to see a world exhibition in New York and familiarize himself with American agriculture and industry. Mochul'skii was entrusted with obtaining such works of the New World, "which could be applied successfully to the climate and needs of Russia." Having traveled through almost all of the American states east of the Mississippi, Mochul'skii collected "a multitude of curiosities," including a large and varied collection of American plant seeds—"vegetables, grains, and hay" (around 190 varieties). In the collection were various types of wheat, corn, beans, fruit, and berries. In his specially printed catalogue attention was directed to "Sea Islands Cotton that sold at a much higher price than the normal variety and was often used mixed with silk. It most likely could be cultivated successfully on the islands and shores of the Caspian and Black seas."[33] Connecticut tobacco and sugar maples were also recommended for cultivation in Russia. If any farmers or gardeners desired seeds in a large quantity, Mochul'skii offered to order them from America. One of Mochul'skii's collections was sent by the Free Economic Society in the fall of 1854 to the Moscow Agricultural Society.[34]

The trip to America in 1839 by army engineers Pavel Mel'nikov and Nikolai Kraft, who acquainted themselves thoroughly with the state of railroads, was of great significance in hastening technological progress in Russia. Returning to Russia in the summer of 1840, they presented strong arguments in favor of building railroads as soon as possible. Experienced specialists from the United States, George Whistler, William L. Winans, and Joseph Harrison, were invited to Russia, and a contract was signed to construct locomotives and transportation equipment. Begun in 1842, the construction of the line from St. Petersburg to Moscow, a distance of 656 kilometers, continued until the end of 1851 and cost 66.8 million rubles.[35]

Issues in the Russian Periodical Press [1825–1841]), Moscow University diss., 1983, 58–64 [see excerpt herein].

31. Record group 419, inventory 1, list 310, 1, TsGA g. Moskvy.

32. "F. Zommerfel'd to the Moscow Agricultural Society," February 1839, ibid., 4.

33. V. I. Mochul'skii, *Katalog semian: derev, kustarnikov ovoshchei, khlebov, kormovykh trav i drugikh rastenii, privezennykh v 1854 godu iz Severnoi Ameriki* . . . (Catalogue of Seeds: Trees, Bushes, Vegetables, Grains, Feed Grasses, and Other Plants, Brought from North America in 1854 . . .) (St. Petersburg, 1854?), 9.

34. Record group 419, inventory 1, list 1255, 1–2, TsGA g. Moskvy.

35. N. S. Kiniapina, *Politika russkogo samoderzhaviia v oblasti promyshlennosti* (Policies of the Russian Autocracy in the Area of Industry) (Moscow, 1968), 188–89; Richard M. Haywood,

Important, and previously completely unknown, materials on Russo-American scientific ties were discovered in the archives of the Smithsonian Institution in Washington. When, in May 1840, the National Institution for the Promotion of Science was established in the American capital, its constitution and other administrative documents were sent to various foreign scientific organizations, including the St. Petersburg Academy of Sciences, the Medical-Surgical Academy, the Mineralogical Society, the Botanical Gardens, Pedagogical Institute, Society of Natural Scientists, and the Lovers of Russian Letters in Moscow. Many of these Russian institutions responded eagerly to the Smithsonian and established systematic working contacts with it. By the summer of 1842 among the foreign members of the National Institute were ten Russian representatives, including Sergei Uvarov, minister of education and president of the St. Petersburg Academy; Wilhelm Struve, director of the Pulkovo Observatory; famous sea-voyager and scientist Admiral Fedor Litke; and tireless voyager and geographer Platon Chikhachev.[36]

Responding to an inquiry by the secretary of the Smithsonian, Professor F. B. Fischer in the spring of 1841 sent to Washington a collection of cereal grains and a large number of scientific publications. Consisting of 109 packages coded to a printed pamphlet, several catalogues of seeds sent by the Botanical Gardens in exchange, and a series of scientific papers on botany in Russian, German, French, and Latin, the collection was received and officially registered by the Smithsonian on August 8, 1842. Later, on May 3/15, 1843, with the assistance of Charles S. Todd, the American minister in St. Petersburg, Fischer sent the Smithsonian a collection of seeds from the northern part of Central Asia and specimens of seedlings of new plants found by Leopold Shrenck in Kirghizia.[37]

Subsequently, ties between the Smithsonian and Russian scientific organizations and societies became even more extensive. In 1852, through Professor Johann Flugel (Leipzig), the Smithsonian Institution sent thirty-two packages to fifteen different places in Russia. Among its regular correspondents were many provincial scientific institutions, including the University of Kazan, the Society of Literature and Art in Mittau, and the observatory and scientific society in Dorpat. Several years later, in 1859, through Flugel 112 packages were sent to various addresses in Russia.[38] Among the active correspondents with the Smithsonian Institution were many outstanding Russian scientists, notably the director of the Botanical Gardens in St. Petersburg, Fischer, and the established scientist-encyclopedist and director of the Zoological Museum, Johann Brandt.

The Beginnings of Railway Development in Russia in the Reign of Nicholas I, 1835–1842 (Durham, 1969).

36. Second Bulletin, *Proceedings of the National Institution for the Promotion of Science* (Washington, 1842), 142–43; Third Bulletin, ibid. (Washington, 1843), 395–414, 417; National Institution, misc., 112 (List of Members 1840–1842), Smithsonian Institution Archives (SIA).

37. National Institution, misc., 99, SIA; Third Bulletin, *Proceedings . . .* , 245–46, 320, 327; Fourth Bulletin, ibid. (Washington, 1844), 492.

38. Smithsonian Institution, *Annual Report of the Board of Regents . . . for the Year 1859* (Washington, 1860), 57.

Of particular interest is the correspondence over many years between Brandt and the assistant secretary of the Smithsonian Institution, Spencer F. Baird, beginning in 1856. In one of his first letters to Baird, dated February 12/24, 1857, Brandt expressed his interest in receiving samples of various mammals, fish, and amphibians from America and on his part expressed his readiness to send the Institution specimens of Russian fauna [2].[39] As Baird noted, the collection sent by Brandt turned out to be "acceptable to the highest degree" for the Institution. Simultaneously he elaborated a broad and concrete program for cooperation. "What the St. Petersburg Academy would like to do for Russia," emphasized Baird, "the Smithsonian Institution is striving to achieve for North America, and the interests of both institutions are being fostered by close contacts, correspondence, and cooperation." Having noted the interest of the Institution in receiving a complete set of the scholarly publications of the Russian Academy, Baird, in turn, expressed his readiness to "in addition to our own publications to send all works of a scientific character, published by the American government."[40]

The scientific ties between Russian and American scientists in the area of astronomy warrants special attention. It is significant that when the construction of the Harvard observatory began in Cambridge, it was decided to equip it with a telescope fitted with a lens of the same quality as that which was installed earlier in the Pulkovo Observatory in Russia. A comparable lens was prepared by the German firm Mertz and Maler in Munich, and as a result, with the opening in 1847 of the Harvard observatory, the Pulkovo telescope had a duplicate.

For a host of astronomers from the United States, the observatory at Pulkovo became in the middle of the nineteenth century a convenient place for studying methods of practical astronomy. It was there that George Bond, son of the founder of the Harvard Observatory, was sent in 1851, so that he could receive information "from the original source of stellar astronomy." Another American astronomer, Cleveland Abbe, who subsequently became the director of the observatory in Cincinnati, spent two years at Pulkovo (1864–1866).[41]

Over the course of many years American astronomers maintained systematic contacts with their Russian colleagues, exchanging results of their observations and participating in joint scientific projects. In the archives of the Russian Academy of Sciences are preserved, in particular, correspondence between academician Kupffer and Matthew Maury for 1850–1855 and that of astronomer Otto Struve with Asaph Hall between 1873 and 1890. Ties between Russian astronomers and Gould and Newcomb continued for more than four decades. The Americans' work received the highest esteem and recognition in Russia. In turn, Newcomb, learning of his election as a corresponding member of the Academy of Sciences, wrote on February 9, 1876, to Struve: "I value

---

39. *Amerikanskii Ezhegodnik 1971*, 335–36.
40. Baird to Brandt, March (?), 1857, S. F. B., vol. 16, Letters written, March–December 1857, 23–27, SIA.
41. For details, see Bolkhovitinov, "Iz istorii russko-amerikanskikh nauchnykh sviazei v XVIII–XIX vv" (From the History of Russo-American Scientific Ties during the Eighteenth to Nineteenth Centuries), *SShA—Ekonomika, Politika, Ideologiia* 4 (1974): 23–24.

to the utmost the title bestowed upon me by such a famous institution, whose works play such an important role in contemporary science."[42]

An even brighter reflection of scientific relations are found in the voyages to the United States by the geographer Aleksandr Voeikov, the chemist Dmitrii Mendeleev, and Otto Struve, and also Russia's participation in the 1876 Centennial Exhibition in Philadelphia.[43] During his stay in the United States in 1873, Voeikov became well acquainted with the state of American meteorology and, in particular, was interested in the organization of the international system of telegraphic weather warnings. The Smithsonian Institution published in 1873 his scientific paper on "Meteorology in Russia," printed subsequently in Russian.[44] On the instructions of Joseph Henry [secretary of the Smithsonian], Voeikov added his own discussion and analysis to the work of American professor John Coffin, "Winds of the Globe."[45]

The trip to America in 1876 by Mendeleev, who became well acquainted with the American oil industry, was of great scientific and practical significance. "Everything is done and explained simply," wrote the Russian scientist, "without a shadow of empty pretense. These are English traits at their best, and it is impossible not to compliment the Americans for it." In addition, Mendeleev expressed some critical remarks: "If such an original and rich industry like the oil industry were to be in another country, a multitude of people would be working on the scientific side of it. In America they are only concerned with extracting oil in large quantities, not worrying about the past and the future." The Russian scientist was clearly dismayed by societal relations: "In the New World the established order has remained the same for the past hundred years as that of the old world. . . . They simply are repeating in a new form the same Latin history on which Western thought was nourished."[46] [3]

Along with Mendeleev a large group of Russian scientists, engineers, tradesmen, sailors, and merchants were present at the Centennial Exhibition, headed by the

42. Record group 2, inventory 17, list 6, 341; record group 32, inventory 2, list 110; record group 286, inventory 1, list 181, 209, 424–26, and others, Leningrad Divison (LO) of Archives of Academy of Sciences. G. Iu. Perel' and M. I. Radovskii, "Iz istorii nauchnykh sviazei russkikh i amerkanskikh astronomov" (From the History of Scientific Ties between Russian and American Astronomers), *Istoriko-astronomicheskie issledovaniia* (Moscow, 1960) 6: 227.

43. For details, see G. P. Kuropiatnik, *Rossiia i SShA: ekonomicheskie, kul'turnye i diplomaticheskie sviazi, 1867–1881* (Russia and the U.S.A.: Economic, Cultural and Diplomatic Ties, 1867–1881) (Moscow, 1981), 163–91 [and article herein].

44. Voeikov, *Meteorologiia v Rossii* (Meteorology in Russia) (St. Petersburg, 1874).

45. Coffin, *The Winds of the Globe . . . with a Discussion and Analysis of the Tables and Charts by Dr. Alexander Woeikof* (Washington, 1875); G. K. Tsverava, "Iz istorii russko-amerikanskikh nauchnykh sviazei v XIX v.: Dzhozef Genri i Aleksandr Ivanovich Voeikov" (From the History of Russo-American Scientific Ties during the Nineteenth Century: Joseph Henry and Aleksandr Voeikov), *Priroda* 7 (1979), 84–85.

46. Mendeleev, "Poezdka v Ameriku" (Journey to America), *Sobr. Soch.* (Collected Works), 25 vols. (Moscow-Leningrad, 1939–1959), vol. 10, 26, 96, 97; Kuropiatnik, *Russia and the U.S.A. . . . Ties,* 184–89. On Mendeleev's relations with American scientists, see G. D. Kaufman, "Perepiska Mendeleeva s khimikami SShA" (Correspondence between Mendeleev and U.S. Chemists), *Voprosy istorii estestvoznaniia i tekhniki* (Problems of History of Natural Science and Technology) 4, 29 (1969).

mining engineer Konstantin Skal'kovskii; N. N. Petrov, founder of the theory of hydrodynamic friction in machines; and metallurgist N. A. Ioss.[47] The Russian section of the exhibition, although opening very late, immediately attracted much attention. The *Boston Evening Journal* on July 23, 1876, reported: "The opening of the Russian section created a sensation. Visitors enthusiastically acquainted themselves with the exquisite exposition that had suddenly appeared, as if by the wave of a magic wand, in the machine pavilion."[48] The display by the artillery department of the Ministry of the Navy made quite an impression on visitors, including the products of the Demidov factories, the Skazikov plant, and the Ovchinnikov foundry. In the American press it was noted that Russia overshadowed all the other participants by the magnificence of her fabrics, furs, handicrafts, and gems.[49]

In Russia, American inventions and machines enjoyed an excellent reputation. Thus, during the fall of 1872 at the Moscow polytechnical exposition, gold and silver medals were awarded to several American inventors and firms. The grand gold medal, in particular, was won by the inventor of the sewing machine, Elias Howe. The Singer company received the same award as well as a host of other people for the sewing machine system presented by them.[50] Scientific and technical ties increasingly began to take on a practical significance.

3. Literary Relations

Russo-American rapprochement and the exchange of diplomatic and consular representatives in 1809 could only help strengthen and broaden literary contacts. In addition, in the ranks of the official missions of both countries were several individuals whose interests closely concerned literature, journalism, and art: Aleksei Evstaf'ev, Pavel Svin'in, Petr Poletika, Alexander Hill Everett.

While in Moscow in September 1810, Everett ecstatically wrote that the ancient capital "overshadows poets' descriptions and compares to the glory of Mexico and Quito."[51] Upon returning to America the young diplomat attended the celebrations in Boston on March 25, 1813, in connection with Russian victories over Napoleon. For this occasion he composed an ode to the sons of Russia who arose "out of the temples and huts" to battle for "the freedom of Russia and the rights of humanity." Curiously this

---

47. Upon leaving for America, each of the Russian participants tried to acquaint themselves personally with the achievements of their American colleagues in their respective areas. Thus two university medical professors asked for leave of absence from May 1 to September 1876 to go to the World Exhibition in Philadelphia to study the contemporary state of "practical medicine and social hygiene" (V. S. Bogoslovskii) and "gynecology and obstetrics" (V. F. Snegirev). Record group 418, inventory 45, list 54, 3–5, 16, TsGA g. Moskvy.

48. Cited from Kuropiatnik, *Russia and the U.S.A. . . . Ties,* 176.

49. Dvoichenko-Markova, "Uchenye Rossii na mezhdunarodnoi vystavke v Filadel'fii v 1876 g." (Scientists of Russia at the 1876 International Exhibition in Philadelphia), *Novaia i Noveishaia Istoriia* (Recent and Contemporary History), (1975, no. 4), 153.

50. Record group 227, inventory 1, list 43, 22–23, TsGA g. Moskvy.

51. Bolkhovitinov, *Russia and the U.S.A.,* 435. While in Russia from 1809 to 1811, Everett kept a diary, preserved by the Massachusetts Historical Society. See Noble Papers, A. H. Everett, 1809–1811, MHS.

ode was written on the model of "Anacreon in Heaven," which subsequently became the basis for the American anthem "Star Spangled Banner."[52]

Evstaf'ev and Svin'in maintained active and varied literary activities in the United States. Among the numerous books and brochures published by Evstaf'ev in the United States, we can name in particular "Collection of Anecdotes" about Peter the Great and the tragic end of Tsarevich Aleksei, an epic poem about Dmitrii Donskoi (*Demetrius, The Hero of the Don*), and a drama, "Cossacks on their way to Paris," based on articles written by the Russian consul for American newspapers.[53]

Svin'in left not only interesting and original articles and books on the United States but also an exceptionally valuable collection of watercolors, a pictorial encyclopedia of American life at the beginning of the nineteenth century.[54] His detailed essay on Russian-American trade deserves special attention, as does his "Letters of a Russian Traveler in North America," and especially his "A View of Free Art in the United States of America," in which he gives a very informed view of American painting, sculpture, architecture, and engineering.[55]

Finally, of particular interest is a book on the United States written by Petr Poletika, first published in French in London, and then translated in Baltimore in 1826. In the foreword the American publisher noted the phenomenal familiarity of the author with the situation in the United States, its laws and customs, and his objectivity in evaluating the merits and inadequacies of life in the United States.[56] This essay received a favorable evaluation on the pages of the influential *North American Review* in October 1826. Unfortunately, this book was never printed in its complete form in Russia, although a small essay, "The Social Condition in the Regions of the United States," appeared in *Literaturnaia Gazeta* (Literary Gazette) in August 1830.

Russian newspapers and journals manifested an ever-growing interest in American topics from the beginning of the nineteenth century. American themes occupied a

---

52. *Sketch of the Church Solemnities at the Stone Chapel and Festival at the Exchange, Thursday, March 25, 1813 in Honour of Russian Achievements* (Boston, 1813).

53. The literary activities of A. G. Evstaf'ev already attracted the attention of a number of researchers, including Leo Wiener and M. P. Alekseev. See Wiener, "The First Russian Consul at Boston," *Russian Review* 1, 3 (April 1916); Alekseev, "A. G. Evstaf'ev—Russko-Amerikanskii pisatel' nachala XIX v." (A. G. Evstaf'ev—Russian-American Writer of the Beginning of the Nineteenth Century), *Nauchnyi Biulleten' LGU* (Scholarly Bulletin Leningrad University) 8 (1946): 22–27; Bolkhovitinov, *Establishment of Russo-American Relations*, 570–90.

54. P. P. Svin'in, *Opyt zhivopisnogo puteshestviia po Severnoi Amerike* (The Experience of a Pictorial Journey in North America) (St. Petersburg, 1815; 2d ed., 1818). Fifty-two watercolors by P. P. Svin'in were reproduced in Avram Yarmolinsky, *Picturesque United States of America, 1811, 1812, 1813, being a Memoir on Paul Svenin* . . . (New York, 1913); Dmitri Fedotoff White, "A Russian Sketches Philadelphia, 1811–1813," *Pennsylvania Magazine of History and Biography* 75, no. 1 (January 1951), 2–24, plus 8 plates.

55. See, correspondingly, *Otechestvennye Zapiski* (Fatherland Notes) 4 (1820): 89–107; 5: 87–93, 200–209; *Nevskii Al'manakh* (Nevskii Almanac) 4 (1827); *Otechestvennyi Zapiski* 38 (1829): 145–64, 289–312; 39: 181–93. Originals are preserved in the State Archives of Kostroma oblast, record group 558, inventory 2, list 185, and in OR GBL, record group 138, 306.2, 109–30; part published in Bolkhovitinov, *Russia and the U.S.A.*, 515–16, 520–28.

56. *A Sketch of the Internal Conditions of the United States and Their Political Relations with Europe*, by a Russian (Baltimore, 1826), 2.

particularly special place on the pages of *Dukh Zhurnalov* (Spirit of Journals), published by Grigorii Iatsenkov from 1815 to 1820. [7] Studying the numerous excerpts from American publications printed by *Spirit of Journals* allows a reevaluation of this important periodical, which first dared to pose openly a number of the most pressing political problems—constitutional rule, civil rights, freedom of the press.[57]

Subsequently, American themes were developed in *Zhurnal Manufaktur i Torgovli* (Manufacturing and Trade Journal), published by Iatsenkov from 1825, and especially in *Moskovskii Telegraf* (Moscow Telegraph), 1825–1834, published by Nikolai Polevoi.[58] In general 1825 was in this respect very notable. The popular journal *Syn Otechestva* (Son of the Fatherland) published Washington Irving's famous story "Rip Van Winkle," translated by the Decembrist Nikolai Bestuzhev. In Moscow in a separate publication appeared James Fenimore Cooper's novel *The Spy*;[59] *Moscow Telegraph* called this publication pleasant news for Russian readers, who should become convinced that "it is no surprise that Cooper's work has been accepted with such approval not only in his homeland, but in England and France as well."[60]

Polevoi himself became an active proponent in Russia of Irving's and Cooper's works. On the pages of the *Moscow Telegraph* were included Irving's "Hotel in Terrachina" (1825), "Wolfer Verber, or Golden Dreams" (1826), "The Haunted House" (1827), and many other works.[61] In 1825 it published an article "On the Successes of Education and Literature in the United States," taken from the Hamburg *Political Journal,* and three years later Polevoi published his own original work on the development of American journalism and literature.[62] Finally, in 1829 on the pages of the journal appeared an article by Cooper, which acquainted the Russian public with the general state of education and literature in the United States. In this article the writer expressed certainty that in the long run American literature "would attain from all nations the glory which it deserves."[63]

Cooper had already begun to win this glory. In that same year, 1829, "the second novel of the famous American writer" (*The Prairie: A Tale*) was printed in Moscow, and Polevoi immediately responded to it with a review.[64] Following this were published translations of *The Pilot, The Red Rover,* and many other novels of Cooper. As a whole, the works of Cooper and Irving became amazingly popular during the 1820s and 1830s. "Their novellas and novels, essays and articles were read and discussed in literary salons

---

57. Bolkhovitinov, "Amerikanskaia tema na stranitsakh *Dukha Zhurnalov* (1815–1820 gg.)" (The American Theme on the Pages of Spirit of Journals, 1815–1820), *Amerikanskii Ezhegodnik 1972* (American Annual 1972) (Moscow, 1972), 266–302 [see article herein].

58. Ivanchenko, "Pozitsiia redaktsionnogo kruzhka *Moskovskogo Telegrafa* v otnoshenii Soedinennykh Shtatov" (The Position of the Editorial Circle of *Moscow Telegraph* in relation to the United States), *Amerikanskii Ezhegodnik 1980* (Moscow, 1981), 216–35.

59. For more details, see Bolkhovitinov, *Russko-amerikanskie otnosheniia, 1815–1832* (Russo-American Relations, 1815–1832) (Moscow, 1975), 555–58.

60. *MT* 7 (1825): 254–55.

61. A list of translations of Irving in Russian during the 1820s and 1830s is given by Alekseev in *Pushkin: stat'i i materialy* (Pushkin: Articles and Materials), vol. 2 (Odessa, 1926), 85.

62. *MT* 19 (1825): 11 (1828).

63. *MT* 16 (1829): 416–17.

64. Ibid., 489–90.

and circles, leafed through in the Smirdin bookstore, talked about at Zhukovskii's Friday gatherings attended by Pushkin, Viazemskii, Gogol, and Ivan Krylov, and at Nikolai Grech's Thursday salon where an entirely different crowd gathered."[65]

When at the end of the 1830s Cooper's well-known disillusionment began with several negative reviews of the translation of the novel *Bravo* (St. Petersburg, 1839), literary critic Vissarion Belinsky came out in defense of the American novelist. He was especially delighted with *The Deerslayer* and its hero Natty Bumppo or Leather Stocking. "Many scenes from *The Pathfinder*," wrote Belinsky, "would color any drama of Shakespeare. Its basic idea is one of the greatest and mysterious acts of the human spirit: self-denial, and in this respect the novel is the apotheosis of self-denial."[66]

Belinsky's attraction to the novels of Cooper was shared by writer Mikhail Lermontov. They were both prepared to place the American novelist even higher than Walter Scott. There were reasons, however, for this. The proximity to nature, glorification of simple and natural human qualities, the more democratic character of Cooper's work (as opposed to the Tory aristocratism of Scott), all of this may well have affected both Belinsky and Lermontov.

In turn, Cooper was very sympathetic toward Russians and in this regard repeatedly expressed his intention to visit Russia, which was even reported in the press in 1828. Unfortunately, he did not carry out these plans, but warm feelings for Russians stayed with him till the end of his life. "For my first introduction to European society," recalled Cooper in 1845,

> I am obliged to the Russians, because over the course of many months I lived in Paris, unknown to anyone, disdained by all, until I was welcomed with extreme politeness into the circle, which included various members of the Golitsyn family, who even to this day I remember with fondness. . . . Under all the circumstances I became convinced of the Russians' friendly disposition toward us Americans. . . . With Russians I always found friends, and I have reason to think that other Americans experienced on their part the same politeness.[67]

One of the first Americans who became well acquainted with Russian literature and made a series of original translations of poetic works into English was William D. Lewis. The young Lewis arrived in Russia in 1814 to assist his older brother John, who had established a large merchant house in St. Petersburg. The commercial affairs of his brother did not interest William very much, but he immediately began to study Russian and showed a serious interest in Russian literature.

In the Russian capital he met the publisher of *Son of the Fatherland*, Grech, who introduced him into the circle of literary figures that gathered at the home of Gavril

---

65. Nikoliukin, *Literary Connections*, 211.
66. Belinskii, *Poln. sobr. soch.* (Complete Collected Works), 13 vols. (Moscow, 1949–1955), vol. 4, 211.
67. "Cooper to D. I. Dolgorukii, 12 July 1845," in M. P. Alekseev, ed., *Neizdannye pis'ma inostrannykh pisatelei XVIII-XIX vv. iz Leningradskikh rukopisnykh sobranii* (Unpublished Letters of Foreign Writers of the Eighteenth-Nineteenth Centuries from the Leningrad Manuscript Collections) (Moscow-Leningrad, 1960), 274.

Derzhavin. Among Lewis's papers are preserved his translation of the famous ode by Derzhavin, "God," literary excerpts, translations of popular poems, and the author's own writings, in particular the poems "Description of a Petersburg Beauty," "Advice to My Friend, a Young Man in Love" (August 1815), "A Strange Feeling," and several other literary experiments by the young American. It was no accident that Lewis especially was taken by the famous sentimental poem by Ivan Dmitriev, "The Blue-Gray Dove" (1792). He copied out this poem in Russian, transliterated it into Latin letters, and then into English. As a result he not only captured the simple contents of the poem but also preserved the unity of the emotional tone and unique melodiousness of the romance.[68]

In Lewis's opinion Dmitriev's poem gave a picture of the character of the Russian language, which "by nature attains the highest degree of poesy." He emphasized the exceptional flexibility of Russian and the opportunities to create "the most magnificent sound orchestration." Despite the youth of literature in Russia, there already were, in the American's words, writers endowed with "talent and taste."[69]

After his departure from Russia in October 1819, Lewis published in the American press translations of several Russian poets. Among them, in particular, was "Folk Songs" of Iurii Neledinskii-Meletskii, which appeared on the pages of the *Philadelphia National Gazette* in January 1821. But if Lewis's first publication went almost unnoticed, then the anthology of Russian poets by the Englishman, Sir John Bowring, became a major event, prompting extended commentary in American journals. "The whole world heard the roar from her cannons, the clatter of horses' hooves, the sound of her victories, but only a few were allowed to hear the story of her heralds or the songs of her bards," one of the reviewers wrote. This publication acquainted Americans with the work of Lomonosov, Derzhavin, Karamzin, Zhukovskii, Krylov, and many others.[70]

Unfortunately, much less was known about the work of Alexander Pushkin. For the contemporary reader it might seem strange that the first Russian novel translated in America, in 1832, was not *Eugene Onegin,* nor Karamzin's *Letters of a Russian Traveler,* but the long-forgotten *Ivan Vyzhigin* by Faddei Bulgarin.[71] Even one of the

---

68. Lewis-Neilson Papers, Literary Section, Historical Society of Pennsylvania.

69. Ibid. Recently it was established that Lewis translated "Yankee Doodle" into Russian during the fall of 1815, at that time especially popular in the United States. See Norman Saul, "A Russian 'Yankee Doodle,'" *Slavic Review* 33, no. 1 (1974): 46–54. For observations on life in Russia, see Lewis's letter to Edward Cole in October 1816 in *Delaware History* 9 (October 1961): 303–40; Eugene Anschel, ed., *The American Image of Russia, 1775–1917* (New York, 1974), 65–77.

70. *Specimens of the Russian Poets: with Preliminary Remarks and Biographical Notes,* translated by John Bowring, F. L. S. (Boston, 1822); *The Christian Disciple* 3 (1822): 371–72. Although contemporaries gave overall positive marks to Bowring's "Russian Anthology," the quality of the English translation leaves much to be desired. See Alekseev, *Russko-angliiskie literaturnye sviazi (XVIII-pervaia polovina XIX v.)* (Russo-English Literary Ties [Eighteenth to the first half of the Nineteenth Century]), *Literaturnoe Nasledstvo* (Literary Heritage), vol. 91 (Moscow, 1982), 191–215.

71. *Ivan Vejeeghen, or Life in Russia* (Philadelphia, 1832). Among other early Russian novels translated in the United States were *Iurii Miloslavskii* by Mikhail Zagoskin (*The Young Musovite,*

more competent American specialists in Slavic philology, Therese Robinson (Talvj) described the great poet in 1834 only as an "imitator of Byron."[72] And this was written about the author of *Boris Godunov* and *Onegin*! In this case it is impossible to justify this by ignorance. Mrs. Robinson not only knew about the publication of *Boris Godunov* in 1831, but even called this tragedy Pushkin's poet's "most magnificent work."

Only many years later, in an essay included in a book about Slavic languages and literatures, did Robinson place Pushkin at the head of Russian poetry almost "beyond comparison." It is in all truth impossible to say that the poet's work had by that time received its completely objective and all-encompassing light. But this time she noted that his Romantic poems ("Prisoner of the Caucasus," "The Fountain of Bakhchisarai," and others) were of great worth. *Boris Godunov* was especially valued, but *Onegin* clearly did not fare as well, and by the same token neither did the work of the young Lermontov. The author lamented that "instead of freshness, power, and happiness" in representatives of a young and growing literature, she found examples of the "superfluous man" (un homme blasé), "frustration, dissatisfaction, and indifference."[73]

There is no need to polemicize these early evaluations and preferences of Mrs. Robinson. In the final analysis it is important that in 1850 she provided a fairly extensive survey of the work of Pushkin and decisively reevaluated her previous opinion. She viewed Pushkin as an entirely exceptional phenomenon and as almost the only Russian poet "who even thought in verse."[74]

The primary regret is not so much the mistaken and tendentious evaluations of the work of the Russian poet, as much as the lack of opportunity for an American reader to become acquainted with it firsthand, to read the works of the poet and form an opinion of their worth and deficiencies. For a long time it seemed that no English translation of Pushkin existed in America during the first half of the nineteenth century. Only accidentally did the Harvard University Library preserve a rare translation of "Talisman" and several verses printed in St. Petersburg in only one hundred copies.[75] More important, however, was that in 1846 in New York a translation of *The Captain's Daughter* came out,[76] and three years later, in July 1849, Lewis published "The Fountain of Bakhchisarai" together with several other works by Russian poets.[77]

---

vols. 1–2 [New York, 1834]) and *Ammalat-bek* by Aleksandr Bestuzhev (Marlinskii) (*The Tartar Chief* [New York, 1846]).

72. *The Biblical Repository* 4 (1834), 384. Therese Robinson was the daughter of a Kharkov professor, L. G. von Jacob, and took her literary pseudonym from the letters of her full maiden name: Therese-Augusta-Ludovica von Jacob.

73. Talvj, *Historical View of the Languages and Literature of Slavic Nations* (New York, 1850), 80.

74. Ibid., 97.

75. Pushkin, "The Talisman, from the Russian," translated by G. Borrow (St. Petersburg, 1835), 14 pages.

76. *The Captain's Daughter; or the Generosity of the Russian Usurper Pugatscheff, from the Russian of Alexander Pushkin,* translated by G. C. Hebbe (New York, 1846), 48 pages.

77. *The Bakchesarian Fountain by Alexander Pooshkeen, and Other Poems by Various Authors,* translated by William D. Lewis (Philadelphia, 1849). Lewis dedicated his translations

One of the first biographical articles on Pushkin appeared on February 11, 1847, in the new abolitionist newspaper *National Era* (Washington) written by the American poet John Greenleaf Whittier. Although the basic information on Pushkin came from a comprehensive article by Thomas Budd Shaw, published in Britain in the summer of 1845, the American poet interpreted it in his own way. Emphasizing that Pushkin's grandfather on his mother's side was a Negro by the name of Hannibal, Whittier used this fact in the struggle with racist stereotypes in the United States. "We refer to this famous writer in order to show the complete inappropriateness and unjustifiable nature of general stereotypes about the colored population in America."[78] It should be noted that Pushkin himself was well acquainted with American literature. In the poet's library were at least five works by Irving and the collected works of Cooper in thirteen volumes.

Soviet Pushkinists, especially academician Mikhail Alekseev, have long directed their attention to the generic similarities of *The History of New York* and *The History of the Village of Goriukhin,* although direct evidence that Irving's composition was known to Pushkin has not been established. The conception behind the latter as a parody of historical works could have come to Pushkin under the influence of Irving or some other author, considering the poet's interest in the American writer and his magnificent knowledge of Western literature and journalism. "Having received an impetus to create a similar conception," wrote Alekseev, "Pushkin, however, entirely independently and using his own material applied similar parodic devices."[79]

On the basis of astute literary analysis, [the well-known Russian poet] Anna Akhmatova proved that the literary source for Pushkin's "The Tale of the Golden Cockerel" was the "Legend of the Arab Astrologer" from the two-volume French publication of *The Alhambra* by Irving, with which the poet became acquainted in 1833.[80] Borrowing the basis of the plot, Pushkin, however, reworked it in the spirit of a Russian folktale, and most importantly, sharpened it with antimonarchial sentiments. In his own experiment Pushkin knew the true price of the tsar's word, and it was no accident that the main idea became the unfulfilled promise by the tsar.

Also well known is the fact that Pushkin referred to Irving, Cooper, Chateaubriand, and de Tocqueville in *John Tanner*:

---

to his "Russian friends" as a sign of the attention and kindness shown to him during his stay "in their exceptionally hospitable country." The book was meant for "private distribution," and immediately after its issue turned into a bibliographic rarity. The newspaper *Severnaia Pchela* (Northern Bee), July 18/30, 1851, published a special note about this book.

78. V. Aleksandrova in *Voprosy Literatury* 6 (1979): 162; Thomas Shaw, "Pushkin, The Russian Poet," *Blackwood's Edinburgh Magazine,* June–August 1845; *National Era* 6 (1847): 2. [2]

79. Alekseev, "K istorii sela Goriukhina" (On the History of the Village of Goriukhin) in *Pushkin: stat'i i materialy* (Pushkin: Articles and Materials), 70–87; Dieter Boden, *Das Amerikabild im Russischen Schriftum bis zum Ende des 19. Jahrhunderts* (Hamburg, 1968), 98, 104.

80. Akhmatova, "Posledniaia skazka Pushkina" (The Last Tale of Pushkin), *Zvezda* 1 (1933): 161–76. The characterization of the Irving's king, "the conqueror in retirement" (un conquerant retire des affaires), could not have but evoked in Pushkin associations with Alexander I, who also had communicated with prophets and clairvoyants at times. Several, although less evident, common traits were shared by the character Tsar Dadon and Nicholas I.

> The customs of the North American savages are familiar to us from the description by the famous novelists. But Chateaubriand and Cooper both showed us the Indians from their poetic side and painted the truth with colors of their imagination. "Savages, placed in novels," writes Washington Irving, "look just as much like real savages as idyllic shepherds in typical pastorals." This is what the readers suspected; and the untrustworthiness of the words of deceptive writers diminishes the pleasure of their brilliant works.[81]

In working on *John Tanner,* Pushkin relied not only on the books of Tocqueville, Thomas Hamilton, Hildebrand Bowman, and Matthew Lewis, which he possessed in his library, but also on various materials about the United States in the pages of Russian periodicals. In *Biblioteka dlia chteniia* (Reading Library), for example, in the summer of 1835 a critique of Bowman's book, *Maria, or Slavery in the United States,* appeared together with a lengthy commentary by the editor.[82] The form of the publication itself (an exposition of the book with commentary and citations), and also separate concrete notes ("tyranny of the popular will," passion for practicality, and toward money) are reflected in several ideas found in Pushkin's Tanner.

But of course the main source for Pushkin were the notes of John Tanner himself. These writings did not have, it goes without saying, special literary value, but for the poet they were "valuable in all respects" as a good source and true eyewitness account of events. Pushkin emerged not only as a literary figure but also as a historian, carrying out a careful analysis of primary sources, of Tanner's notes on life among the Indians.

> They are the most complete and perhaps the last document of the life of the people of whom there soon will not be a trace. . . . The authenticity of these "Notes" is beyond doubt. John Tanner is still alive; many people . . . saw him and bought from him his book. In their opinion, it cannot be a forgery. And it is worth reading several pages in order to confirm this: the lack of any art and the meek simplicity of narration vouches for this truth.[83]

In contrast to Irving and Cooper, Russian readers became acquainted with the works of Edgar Allan Poe after some delay, only in 1847, when, as Joan Grossman has established, Poe's famous story "The Gold Bug," about finding a treasure hidden by pirates, was published in the journal *Novaia Biblioteka dlia Vospitaniia* (New Educational Library). This fascinating story was clearly enjoyed by Russian readers, a fact confirmed by repeated printings in journals and anthologies.[84]

---

81. Pushkin, *Poln. sobr. soch.* (Complete Collected Works), 4th ed., 10 vols. (Leningrad, 1977–1979), vol. 7, 299. Alekseev, "K stat'e Pushkina 'Dzhon Tenner' " (On Pushkin's Article "John Tanner") *Vremennik Pushkinskoi komissii 1966* (Leningrad, 1969), 50–56.
82. *Biblioteka dlia Chteniia* 2, no. 2 (1835): 51–66.
83. Pushkin, *Works,* vol. 7, 299.
84. *Biblioteka dlia Chteniia* 89 (1848): 186–208; *Zhurnal dlia chteniia vospitannikam voenno-uchebnykh Zavenenii* 74 (1848), 231–51, 346–71; "Zolotoi zhuk" (The Gold Bug) (St. Petersburg, 1858); *Skazki dlia detei* (Stories for Children) (St. Petersburg, 1859), 41–104; J. D. Grossman, *Edgar Allen Poe in Russia: A Study in Legend and Literary Influence* (Wurzburg, 1973), 191–93.

Even critics such as Belinsky did not immediately recognize the value of the work of this pioneer of the mystery genre. Fedor Dostoevsky was the first to really appreciate Poe's work. He published several of the writer's stories in his journal *Vremia* (Time): "The Tell-Tale Heart," "Black Cat," "Devil in City Hall," accompanied by a foreword. With amazing acumen Dostoevsky managed to perceive in the American literary figure a kindred spirit, simultaneously a visionary and a realist. "Edgar Poe," wrote Dostoevsky,

> has one particular quality that distinguishes him sharply from all the other writers and shapes his striking peculiarity: that is the power of imagination. It is not that he has exceeded the imagination of other writers; but in the scope of his imagination is a uniqueness that we have never seen in anyone else: the power of detail.... In Poe if there is fantasy, it is grounded in the material world.... It is evident that he is completely an American, even in the most fantastic of his works.[85]

The literary manner of Poe, his acute psychologizing, and his "materialistic fantasy" are echoed in Dostoevsky's work. They might have interested Gogol, who, however, most likely did not experience the direct influence of the American writer. But Russian society as a whole in the middle of the nineteenth century was interested most of all not in purely literary plots and the nuances of artistic virtuosity, but in social and political problems, first of all the question of slavery and serfdom. That is why in the 1850s in America and in Russia, precisely those works that dealt with Negro slavery and peasant serfdom received the most resonance.

The appearance of Harriet Beecher Stowe's *Uncle Tom's Cabin* became a major event in the history of American literature. In 1851 it began to appear on the pages of *National Era,* and in 1852 was published as a separate publication. In the first year three hundred thousand copies were sold, and subsequently the book was distributed by the millions all over the world, translated into thirty-seven languages, read by adults and children, repeatedly commented upon in the press, and presented on stage. With bitter irony Alexander Herzen wrote in 1853: "America is a good country, as only the enslaved people are black; our black people are white . . . probably from the snow."[86]

Despite the obstacle of censorship, *Uncle Tom's Cabin* circulated widely in Russia. As soon as "the opportunity to translate *Uncle Tom* presented itself," Nikolai Nekrasov decided that at "any cost" he would in earnest publish it in the first issue of *Sovremennik* (Contemporary) for 1858. "As soon as this was announced, subscribers increased. One should note that there is a good reason for this: the question of our own domestic negroes is the rage."[87] The novel also appeared in the form of an appendix to the

---

85. *Vremia* (Time) 1, no. 1 (1861): 230–31. Later in the 1870s, Nikolai Shelgunov analyzed the peculiarities of the American writer's work and noted the special character of the psychologizing of Poe, whom America instilled "with their philistinism and mercantilism." See Nikoliukin, *Literary Connections,* 342–46.

86. Herzen, *Sobr. soch.* (Collected Works), 30 vols. (Moscow, 1954–1966), vol. 25, 24.

87. Nekrasov, *Poln. sobr. soch* (Complete Collected Works), 12 vols. (Moscow, 1948–1953), vol. 10, 375.

liberal *Russkii Vestnik* (Russian Herald), edited by Mikhail Katkov in Moscow, and in *Son of the Fatherland*.[88]

In the winter of 1858–1859 in St. Petersburg, [Ukrainian patriot] Taras Shevchenko became acquainted with the magnificent Negro tragedian Ira Aldridge, who was performing in the Russian capital to great acclaim. Shevchenko was completely taken by his magnificent performance in Shakespeare's tragedies *Othello* and *King Lear*, and did not miss one show. Close in their tragic fates, characters, and views, both men immediately became friends. While Aldridge became enchanted with Ukrainian folk songs, Shevchenko listened with pleasure to songs about the hard life of Negroes. As a sign of thanks and friendship Shevchenko drew a wonderful portrait of the black tragedian, and Aldridge took with him as a memento a portrait of a Ukrainian folksinger painted by Mikhail Mikeshin. Later, between 1861 and 1866, Aldridge repeatedly performed in Russia and in Ukraine three times, but Shevchenko was no longer alive (burdened by difficult experiences, the poet died in March 1861 at the age of 47).[89]

The scholarly literature has analyzed the detailed and in-depth surveys of events in America, which Nikolai Chernyshevskii regularly printed on the pages of the *Contemporary*.[90] For example, in the November issue for 1859, Chernyshevskii not only gave high marks to the raid on Harper's Ferry but also published a translation of the basic articles of the "Provisional Constitution" of John Brown.[91] Chernyshevskii in all likelihood was acquainted with articles in the *New York Tribune* on serfdom in Russia.[92] In the novel *What Is To Be Done,* Lopukhov-Beaumont describes his life in the United States: "I wrote several articles for the *Tribune* on the influence of serfdom on society in Russia. This was a relatively good and new argument for the abolitionists against slavery in the Southern states, and I was made a citizen of Massachusetts."[93]

What sort of articles about Russia were printed in the *Tribune*? An examination of a number of *Tribune* issues reveals that from August to December 1858, its pages

---

88. *Khizhina diadi Toma, ili Zhizn' negrov v nevol'nich'ikh shtatakh Severnoi Ameriki* (Uncle Tom's Cabin, or Life of the Negroes in the Slave States of North America) (Moscow, 1857), 434 pages; *Khizhina diadi Toma* (Uncle Tom's Cabin) (St. Petersburg, 1858), 476 pages; *Syn Otechestva* 1 (1858): 9–16; 2: 33–41; 3: 61–70; 4: 9–99. For more on Russian translations of Stowe's novel, see I. N. Bushkanets, "Pervye perevody *Khizhinu diadi Toma* na russkii iazyk" (The First Translations of Uncle Tom's Cabin into Russian), *Uchenye Zapiski Kazanskogo Pedagogicheskogo Instituta* (Studies of Kazan Pedagogical Institute) 66 (1969): 49–59.

89. D. M. Corbett, "Taras Shevchenko and Ira Aldridge," *Journal of Negro Education* 33 (1964): 148–49. The overall recognition of the Negro tragedian was reflected in his election as a foreign member to the Academy of the Arts in St. Petersburg.

90. R. F. Ivanov and I. Ia. Levitas, "Chernyshevskii o rabstve negrov v SShA i probleme grazhdanskikh svobod" (Chernyshevsky on Negro Slavery in the U.S.A. and on the Problem of Civic Freedoms), *Amerikanskii Ezhegodnik 1980,* 118–38.

91. I. P. Dement'ev, "Chernyshevskii i konstitutsiia Dzhona Brauna" (Chernyshevsky and John Brown's Constitution), *Voprosy istorii* (Problems of History) 12 (1959): 137–44.

92. I. Popov, "Iz amerikanskoi zhizni Dmitriia Sergeevicha Lopukhova" (From the American Life of Dmitrii Sergeevich Lopukhov), *Inostrannaia Literatura* (Foreign Literature) 2 (1981): 251–56.

93. Chernyshevskii, *Poln. sobr. soch.* (Complete Collected Works), 16 vols. (Moscow, 1939–1953), vol. 11, 325.

systematically included broad and interesting essays by the American writer Bayard Taylor, who had traveled around the European part of Russia. In several issues Taylor touched on the question of serfdom, and in the first article emphasized that Russia needed very much "a class of entrepreneurial landowners."[94] On the whole, however, the essays by the American concerned mostly the external side of Russian life, and, although he described Moscow, St. Petersburg, and Pulkovo in detail, his articles do not relate to the one mentioned by Chernyshevskii, which, of course, does not exclude their significance in Russian-American cultural ties.[95] The most probable variant would be two articles by Karl Marx, "On the Emancipation of the Serfs in Russia," published in the *Tribune* on January 17, 1859.[96]

It is true that from time to time other notes about Russia and serfdom found their way into the newspaper, but they were purely informative and factual, taken from various publications. Of interest, perhaps, is a progressive article in the *Tribune* of November 11, 1858, which basically made a detailed comparison of the system of serfdom in Russia with plantation slavery in the United States. But it should also be noted that this untitled article praises Alexander II. Chernyshevskii in all likelihood read, or at least knew about, the articles on serfdom in the *Tribune,* and these articles could have been, and most likely were, those of Marx.

As in *Moscow Telegraph* of the 1820s and 1830s, *The Contemporary* emerged as the active propagandist for the best works of American writers during the 1850s and 1860s. The journal was the first to introduce Russian readers to the work of Nathaniel Hawthorne. In it were published works by Longfellow, Taylor, Winthrop, and others. In a survey article, "American Poets and Novelists," in *The Contemporary* (no. 12, 1860) Mikhail Mikhailov noted that the "Verse on Slavery" by Longfellow "is permeated by a heated feeling of indignation and full of bitter reproaches . . . for the country, which up to this time cannot wash its hands of the black spot of slavery."

The Russian revolutionary democrat himself translated these verses and in January 1861 attempted to publish them. At first the censor forbade publication, but then "Verse on Slavery" (like "Verse on Negroes") appeared in the March issue of *The Contemporary,* the same that printed the [emancipation] manifesto of February 19, 1861, as well as an article by Vladimir Obruchev, "Slavery in North America." It is quite likely that these materials were perceived by Russian readers to be a unique call by revolutionary democrats for tsarist reforms.[97]

---

94. *New York Daily Tribune,* August 24, 1858.

95. Taylor's articles from Russia elicited interest from many readers of the *Tribune* and in 1859 were published in a separate edition. See *Greece and Russia* (New York, 1859), 303–426.

96. Marx and Engels, *Soch.* (Works), 2d ed., vol. 12, 692–701. The question on abolishing serfdom in Russia was examined in another article by Marx, and also in a survey by Engels, "Europe in 1558." In our opinion they should not be included in this group; the *Tribune* published them without any sort of title. See ibid., 605–8, 671–75, and *Inostrannaia Literatura* 2 (1981): 255–56.

97. "Iz arkhiva N. G. Chernyshevskogo (ob odnom perevode M. L. Mikhailova)" (From the Chernyshevskii Archives [on one translation by M. L. Mikhailov]), *Voprosy Literatury* (Problems of Literature) 3 (1965): 251–52 (note by M. Blinchevskaia); Iu. S. Melent'ev and L. N. Kogan, "O stat'e V. A. Obrucheva 'Nevol'nichestvo v Severnoi Amerike' " (On Obruchev's Article "Slavery

For another, earlier chronological coincidence, in 1852 when *Uncle Tom's Cabin* came out in a separate edition in the United States, Turgenev's *A Sportsman's Sketches,* previously published in *The Contemporary* (1847–1851), appeared in Russia. Turgenev's book was immediately greeted with enthusiasm not only in Russia but also in Germany, France, and England.[98] And how was it received in America? Herzen mentioned in a letter to Maria Reichel, dated September 29, 1853, that "in America the German *Revue* had translated Turgenev's *Sketches"* and that it "also was read with sympathy," but it had so far been impossible to verify this. Moreover, it has been confirmed that before 1867 the name of Turgenev appeared only once in American periodicals, "in an article by E. [T.—author] Robinson, 'Slavery in Russia,' printed in the April issue of *The North American Review* for 1856."[99]

In addition, during the fall of 1854 excerpts appeared in at least two American journals from "Khor' and Kalinych," "Two Landowners," and "The Steward" [burmistr], and several other stories by Turgenev along with a detailed introductory article, "Photograph of Russian Life," taken from *Fraser's Magazine* (London).[100] Thus almost simultaneously with European readers, Americans had the opportunity to become acquainted with the magnificent stories of Turgenev. In the introductory article it was noted that the original *Sketches* came out in Moscow in Russian two years earlier, but in 1854 it was published in Paris in translation by Ernest Charriere.[101] Curiously, Turgenev's stories were evaluated as "a Russian 'Uncle Tom's Cabin' without the blood and gunpowder."[102]

In April of the following year, 1855, a detailed survey of contemporary Russian literature, also taken from one of the English journals, appeared in *The Eclectic Magazine.* The pretext for the survey was the publication in England of a book by some "Russian nobleman," which was a distorted translation of Gogol's *Dead Souls.*[103] "Whatever page we open we find everywhere a bad translation of this novel."

Later there followed a short but precise essay on Russian literature in which Herzen's influence is clearly seen. The essay in particular recalled the tragic fate of the Decembrists and the majority of Russian poets—Pushkin, Lermontov, Griboedov, and others. The death of Pushkin, as pointed out in the article, "evoked the indignation of society,

---

in North America"), *Uchenye Zapiski Ural'skogo Universiteta* (Studies of Ural University) 13 (1955): 142–52.

98. Turgenev, *Poln. sobr. soch. i pisem* (Complete Collected Works and Letters), 30 vols. (Moscow, 1978–), vol. 3, 420–33; Alekseev, "Mirovoe znachenie *Zapisok okhotnika*" (The Global Significance of *Sportsman's Sketches*) in *Zapiski okhotnika I. S. Turgeneva: sb. st. i materialov* (Turgenev's Sportsman's Sketches: Collected Articles and Materials) (Orel, 1955), 36–117; *Tvorchestvo I. S. Turgenev* (Work of Turgenev) (Moscow, 1959), 69–180.

99. S. K. Miloslavskaia, "I. S. Turgenev v otsenke svoikh amerikanskikh sovremennikov" (Turgenev in the Estimation of His American Contemporaries), in *Literatura SShA* (Literature of the U.S.A.) (Moscow, 1973), 11.

100. *The Eclectic Magazine of Foreign Literature, Science, and Art* 33 (October 1854): 231–42; *Graham's American Monthly Magazine of Literature and Art* 45 (November 1854): 451–61.

101. *Memoirs d'un seigneur russe,* translated by Ernest Charriere (Paris, 1854).

102. *The Eclectic Magazine . . .* 33 (October 1854): 232.

103. *Home Life in Russia, by a Russian Noble,* vols. 1–2 (London, 1854).

in as much as the poet was the literary pride of his country." Also noted was the knowledge of Lermontov's famous novel, *A Hero of Our Times,* in the West thanks to German, French, and English translations. In the opinion of the journal, this novel deserved close study "not only as the major work of Russian genius, but also for its substantial expositions of various issues." Highest praise was given to Gogol's *Dead Souls,* "whose sympathy lay with the people, despite the writer's noble origins."[104]

The real triumph of Russian literature in America was, however, still to come, and proof of this triumph was the popularity of Turgenev's writings during the 1870s.[105] In 1867 Eugene Schuyler's translation of *Fathers and Sons* came out in New York, and in the 1870s about twenty more works by Turgenev were published in the United States, including *Smoke* (1872), *A Nest of Gentlefold, Rudin, Spring Floods* (1873), *Annouchka, Virgin Soil* (1877), and others.[106] William Dean Howells recalled subsequently that just at this time occurred "a recognition of the greatness of Turgenev's novels," evoking in Howells "the deepest literary attraction" to the Russian writer. "Life appeared to me in entirely different colors after I once read Turgenev."[107]

Thomas Perry, Henry James, Haljmar Boyesen, and other American writers also showed great interest in Turgenev's works. In turn, the Russian writer met several times with Schuyler, Boyesen, and Howells, praised Hawthorne, and translated Walt Whitman and others. "I sincerely am interested in all that is going on on your side of the Atlantic," noted Turgenev in a conversation with Boyesen in Paris in December 1873, "and always try to keep up with your literature. If I have missed something important, I hope that you will let me know." In this same conversation Turgenev revealed that even in his youth he had dreamed about visiting America and seeing the country with his own eyes.[108]

Examining the interconnection between sociopolitical, moral, and artistic problems, Leo Tolstoy gave a precise and deep characterization of the development of Russian and American literatures during the period discussed. "A great literature arises when a high moral feeling awakens," said Tolstoy in a conversation with his translator and biographer Aylmer Maude. "Take for example the period of liberation movements, the struggle to abolish serfdom in Russia and to emancipate the Negroes in the United States. Look at what sort of writers appeared at this time in America: Stowe, Thoreau, Emerson, Lowell, Whittier, Longfellow, William Lloyd Garrison, Theodore Parker, and others, and in Russia: Dostoevsky, Turgenev, Herzen, and others, whose influence on the educated circles of society . . . was very great."[109]

The peculiarities of the literary process in both countries exerted a significant influence on the development of Russo-American literary ties. "The factor of active

---

104. "Modern Russian Literature," *The Eclectic Magazine . . .* 34 (April 1855): 450–61.
105. For details, see Kuropiatnik, *Russia and the U.S.A. . . . Ties,* 104–11.
106. Turgenef, *Fathers and Sons: A Novel, Translated with the Approval of the Author by E. Schuyler* (New York, 1867).
107. Cited in Kuropiatnik, *Russia and the U.S.A. . . . Ties,* 108.
108. P. E. Seyersted, "Turgenev's Interest in America . . .", *Scando-Slavica* (Copenhagen, 1965) 11: 25–28; I. Chistova, "Turgenev i Uitmen" (Turgenev and Whitman), *Russkaia Literatura* 2 (1966): 196–99; Miloslavskaia, "I. S. Turgenev," 3–38.
109. *Literaturnoe Nasledstvo* 75 (Moscow, 1965), no. 1: 428.

selection directed the interest of Russian Romantics of the 1820s and 1830s toward European and American Romanticism . . . In distant overseas they found their own, and the foreign suddenly became so near: the poetry of Byron, the novels of Walter Scott, Cooper, the novellas of Irving."[110] On the other hand, American literature during the first half of the nineteenth century, oriented primarily toward its West European heritage, was not yet prepared to enrich itself with the achievements and discoveries of Russian artistic culture. Only later, in the 1870s, when there occurred a manifestation of the Realist school in the literature of the United States, did Americans look to the work of Russian writers, foremost the novels of Turgenev. Subsequently Dostoevsky, Tolstoy, and other classics of the nineteenth century became extremely popular.

110. Nikoliukin, *Literary Connections,* 6–7.

2

Enlighteners and Revolutions of the Eighteenth Century, by V. I. Moriakov

The second half of the eighteenth century was characterized by the intensive growth of capitalist relations within the dominant feudal-absolutist order. The development of capitalist structures in the economy resulted in a sharpening of antagonism within the feudal serf-based system, contributed to a rise in social antagonisms, and led to the intensification of the class struggle. The genesis and evolution of the antifeudal ideology of the Enlightenment, whose representatives subjected all laws and dogmas of the existing order to merciless criticism, was a vivid manifestation of the decay and crisis of feudalism.

The European philosophers of the 1740s to 1760s based their criticism of the feudal-absolutist system and their search for ways of bringing about its downfall on their study of the history of England and Holland, on the experiences of those two countries with revolution, and on their subsequent development. However, since the revolutions in England and Holland, considerable change had occurred in Europe. The economies of the advanced countries were now very different, and the same was true of the bourgeoisie and its aspirations. That is why the European bourgeoisie and its ideologues paid close attention to the revolutionary struggle for independence in America in the 1770s and 1780s, and studied its ideas and experience.

The war of the North American colonies for independence, in the course of which they pursued the goals of bourgeois revolution, had broad international repercussions. In the words of Karl Marx, this war gave the initial impetus to the European revolution of the eighteenth century and "sounded the tocsin for the European bourgeoisie."[1] The ideas of the American Revolution inspired the enemies of the absolutist regimes

---

1. Karl Marx and Friedrich Engels, *Soch.* (Works), vol. 23, 9. This article by V. I. Moriakov first appeared in *Vestnik Moskovskogo Universiteta* (Herald of Moscow University), Series 8 (History), 5 (1984), 63–76.

of Europe to take up the struggle and contributed to the radicalization of European enlightened thought.

One of the most important ideologues of the American Revolution was Thomas Paine. On January 10, 1776, in Philadelphia he published *Common Sense,* "which represented the supreme achievement of anticolonial thought, its apogee and which, according to contemporary testimony, effected a revolution in the outlook of the Americans."[2] Paine's pamphlet became extraordinarily popular. Within the first three months of publication it sold 120,000 copies. During the years of revolution, altogether 500,000 copies were printed,[3] which was an unprecedented figure for the period. The soldiers of the Revolutionary armies would read *Common Sense* before going into battle. The ideas expressed in it enjoyed considerable influence during the most intensive phase of the struggle of the North American colonies for independence.

> Paine was among the first to identify the revolutionary struggle for independence with the goal of bringing about the democratic transformation of America and of creating a new society in which the equality of all its members would be affirmed. Paine's ideas reflected the aspirations of the masses: the liquidation of the monarchy and of political, religious, and racial privileges and constraints.[4]

Together with the events of the American Revolution, Paine's pamphlet influenced the development of French ideas, whose exponents in the 1780s moved from criticism of the existing order to the advocacy of revolution. The most vivid expression of these revolutionary tendencies is to be found in the third edition of Abbe Guillaume Raynal's treatise *Histoire philosophique et politique des établissemens et du commerce des européens dans les deux Indes,* which appeared in 1780–1781 in Geneva.

The revolutionary events in America also attracted considerable attention in Russia, a country where the feudal-absolutist system was only beginning to enter the stage of disintegration. The spread of the ideas of the American Revolution, a growing awareness of its main events, and an increasing familiarity with the writings of radical French thinkers contributed to the shift within the Russian Enlightenment, especially effected by Alexander Radishchev, from a reformist position to a revolutionary one.

The ideas of Tom Paine played a major part in the mobilization of America's patriotic forces in the struggle for independence and helped to accelerate the course of revolutionary events in the 1770s. In the 1780s, as the revolutionary process in the United States developed further, Paine's ideas became a threat to the American bourgeoisie, which had now taken power. The year 1789 saw the start of the French Revolution, whose echoes resounded in every country in Europe. Its impact shook the thrones of the absolute monarchs. Paine, Raynal, and Radishchev witnessed, and the first two also participated in, the revolutionary events in France.

2. Vladimir Sogrin, *Ideinye techeniia v Amerikanskoi revoliutsii XVIII vega* (Ideological Currents in the American Revolution of the Eighteenth Century) (Moscow, 1980), 11.
3. Richard Morris, ed., *Encyclopedia of American History,* 6th ed. (New York, 1982), 4.
4. *Voina za nezavisimost' i obrazovanie SShA* (The War for Independence and Creation of the United States) (Moscow, 1976), 269.

The present study has a number of goals: first, to analyze the role of the ideas expressed in Paine's work in the radicalization of European Enlightenment thought (particularly in France and Russia); second, to explain why in America in the 1780s, as the Revolution there continued to unfold, Paine's ideas were increasingly forgotten; third, to attempt to describe the respective positions adopted by Paine, Raynal, and Radishchev during the period of the French Revolution.

Events in North America were followed in France with tremendous interest. The absolutist order increasingly hindered France's progressive development. The French bourgeoisie, deprived of political rights yet forced to bear the burden of ever-growing expenditures by the monarchy, wished to assume a leading role not only in the economic sphere but in the political sphere as well. The French peasantry, suffering under the weight of numerous feudal exactions and sinking deeper into poverty and pauperism, grew increasingly militant in its struggle against the feudal lords. Often its acts of resistance against oppression merged with armed actions by the city poor. The government had to exert all its strength to suppress the people's struggle for their rights.

From the 1740s to the 1760s the French philosophes, basing themselves on the philosophical, economic, and other theories they had developed, harshly criticized the existing order. But they failed to draw any revolutionary conclusions, because they still entertained illusions about the universal power of enlightenment and the decisive role an "enlightened monarch" could play in the future transformation of France. In the course of developments in France, it became clear that problems in the internal life of France could not be resolved peacefully, demonstrated by the failure of Turgot's reforms. At the same time the hopes vested in an "enlightened monarch" also collapsed.

In these circumstances French thinkers persisted in their search for ways and means of fighting the absolutist order. Consequently, they devoted particular attention to the war of the British colonies in North America for independence, as well as to the ideas of Americans. During this period the French scholar Daniel Mornet pointed out a considerable number of works in which the ideology of bourgeois liberalism was further developed were published in France.[5] In volume 9 of the third edition of *Histoire des deux Indes,* the revolutionary events in America were discussed at length, and Raynal paraphrased the content of Paine's *Common Sense,* laying particular emphasis on the American thinker's revolutionary ideas.

Common Sense was a summons to the American people to rise up against British rule. Paine published his pamphlet at a time when it had become clear that a break between the American colonies and the mother country was inevitable, but also when many in American society continued to entertain illusions about a possible reconciliation with Britain and persisted in advocating the introduction of a constitutional monarchy along British lines. The advocates of compromise claimed that the severing of the relationship with Britain would have a deleterious effect on the economic development of the colonies and that only British military power could protect America.

5. Daniel Mornet, *Les origines intellectuelles de la révolution française (1715–1787)* (Paris, 1933).

Paine was vociferous in his arguments against such views, insisting that a rupture between the American colonies and Britain was historically inevitable, that independence would guarantee America's economic development and the establishment of advantageous economic relations with the entire world, and that a separation from Britain would remove the danger of America being dragged into every future British military adventure. Paine also subjected Britain's constitutional monarchy, which was considered a model political system, to withering criticism.

Raynal and Paine were proponents of the idea that the origin of society was contractual. They held that society had appeared in response to man's needs, that it was primary, that originally it was independent and free, that the government was a creation of society; when the social situation is conducive to the public good, they said, the government must continually strive to guarantee it.[6] Both Raynal and Paine considered absolutism an evil that harms and humiliates the people. An even greater evil, however, was the monarchical principle of hereditary succession, which, they insisted, served only to deceive and insult posterity. "For all men are born equal and no one should have the innate right to bestow upon his family an advantage over all others," wrote Paine (29).

Raynal echoed Paine's ideas. "Nature," he declared, "did not create the world for the purpose of submission, nature established the laws of equality, which it obeys both in heaven and on earth" (IX, 250). Paine and Raynal believed that absolutism deprives man of his liberty and of the right to defend his person and his property. On the basis of their harsh criticism of absolute monarchy, Paine and Raynal drew the conclusion that it should be destroyed, because, as Paine put it, it was a form of government "against which we find testimony in the Word of God and which produces bloodshed" (33). Raynal, developing Paine's idea, wrote that authority was engendered either "by the consent of the governed, or by the power of the ruler" but that "in either case it may expire lawfully, for nowhere is tyranny prescribed over freedom" (IX, 21).

It is worth noting that while Paine considered the republican form of government to be ideal and argued against both absolute and constitutional monarchy, believing that this type of government "has covered not only this or that kingdom but the whole world in blood and ashes" (IX, 33), Raynal, nevertheless, felt that under certain conditions the existence of a constitutional monarchy of the British kind was permissible, even though he acknowledged that the British constitution was "not free of inappropriate elements" (IV, 347).[7] Raynal's inconsistent attitude toward the monarchical system probably reflected the fact that a segment of the French bourgeoisie was inclined to strive for an improvement in its situation by means of a compromise with the king

---

6. Guillaume Thomas François, *Histoire philosophique et politique des établissemens et du commerce des europeens dans les deux Indes,* vols. 1–10 (Geneva, 1780–1781), vol. 9, 214 [hereafter all quotations (retranslated from Russian) are from this edition, a Roman numeral in parentheses indicating the volume number, an Arabic numeral the page number]; Paine, *Izbr. soch.* (Collected Works) (Moscow, 1959), 21–23 [all quotations are cited to this Russian edition].

7. See Moriakov, *Iz istorii evoliutsii obshchestvenno-politicheskikh vzgliadov prosvetitelei kontsa XVIII veka: Reinal' i Radishchev* (Concerning the History of the Development of the Sociopolitical Views of the Enlighteners of the Late Eighteenth Century: Raynal and Radishchev) (Moscow, 1981), 136–39.

within the framework of a constitutional monarchy, a desire for which the first stage of the French Revolution offers clear evidence.[8]

But in the early 1780s the French bourgeoisie attached paramount importance to the struggle against absolutism, which is why Raynal attacked despotism in all its manifestations. One of these, in the opinion of Paine and Raynal, was Britain's domination over its American colonies. In *Common Sense* Paine sharply criticized the British constitutional monarchy, expressing the view that Britain had not left despotism far behind (25–26).

Raynal and Paine both claimed that British rule in the colonies was an example of despotism, and that the British wished to turn Americans into slaves. "The dominion of Great Britain over this continent," wrote Paine, "is a form of government that sooner or later must come to an end. . . . It is not within Britain's power to bring justice to our continent . . . for if she cannot conquer us, she cannot govern us" (38, 40). Raynal agreed with Paine's ideas and developed them further: "The English call the Americans criminals, because the latter do not wish to be their slaves. A people subjected to the will of another people is a people of slaves" (IX, 220). According to Raynal, slavery of this kind was even worse than "slavery endured under a tyrant," for the power of one nation over another must be founded either on conquest, or on agreements that had been proposed and entered into.

Yet freedom cannot be exchanged for anything, for there is nothing more precious than freedom. Paine and Raynal spoke out against the claims of the British and of those Americans who advocated a compromise between America and the colonists' motherland. "In that case her behavior is even more shameful. . . . The word 'fatherland' or 'mother country' was Jesuitically employed by the King and his sycophants with the base Papist intention of influencing our credulous and feeble minds. America's fatherland is Europe, and not England," argued Paine (36). Raynal wrote that the consolidation of British rule over America could not be viewed from the perspective of "Britain is the mother country," because "there comes a time when the authority of parents over their children ceases; this is the moment when the children are now able to govern themselves" (IX, 226).

The separation of America from Britain was necessary, Paine believed, because what was at stake was the fate of an entire continent, rather than of a county or a province. Such a separation was also required by the obligation his contemporaries owed toward future generations of Americans, for "we must undertake to care for our children and strengthen our position for several years ahead" (38). Britain could not govern the colonies, since

> a voyage of three or four thousand miles carried out for the purpose of submitting a report or petition, a four or five month wait for a response, which, in turn requires clarifications that take a further five or six months—all this in a few years will seem like reckless childishness. There was a time when such arrangements were appropriate, but now we must put an end to them. (40)

---

8. Ibid., 145–66.

Paine stated that reconciliation between America and the colonial power was impossible; he dismissed the notion that Britain wished to protect America, since "it is appropriate for small islands that are incapable of defending themselves to be placed under the protection of a government; but there is something absurd in the supposition that a continent will always be governed by an island.... Clearly, they belong to different systems. Leave Europe to England, and America to herself" (42). In *Histoire des deux Indes,* Raynal argued along the same lines (IX, 250).

Paine constantly emphasized the need for unity among the colonies and the entire people in the struggle with Britain. Raynal agreed, declaring, "If we wish to guarantee our happiness, let us unite. If we are fathers, if we love our children, let us unite. Laws and liberty—this is the legacy we leave them" (IX, 249). Paine wrote that every bloodless avenue of resistance, every means of achieving a peaceful settlement had been explored and had been found wanting; there was no possibility for reconciliation between Britain and America, which he now called "an illusory dream" (40). He insisted that compromise between Britain and America was no longer practical: "The violence that has been inflicted upon us or with which we have been threatened; the destruction of our property by force of arms; the ravaging of our country with fire and sword—this is what entitles us to use our weapons with a clear conscience.... All obedience to Britain must cease, and the first musket shot fired at her must be regarded and proclaimed as signifying the dawn of the era of American independence" (62–63).

Raynal reacted to this statement by Paine with enthusiasm, emphasizing and amplifying it. "We have the right to take up arms. Our rights are—necessity, the justifiability of our defense, our misfortunes, the misfortunes of our children, the abuses of which we have been the victims. Our rights are our sacred title as a nation.... Liberty, and complete liberty, is the only goal worthy of our endeavors and the perils that we face. From this moment it is ours" (IX, 250–51).

A comparison of the texts of Paine's *Common Sense* and the sections dealing with America in Raynal's *Histoire des deux Indes* shows that the French thinker did not simply repeat Paine's ideas about the necessity and justice of the armed struggle waged by the Americans. Raynal was in effect calling for the violent overthrow of despotism in France. As he studied the American experience of struggle against colonial rule, Raynal saw that the insurgents were able to triumph because they had achieved the unity that Paine had so persistently advocated in his essay. This idea of unity thus became part of the ideological arsenal of this intellectual spokesman of the French bourgeoisie, who repeatedly declared that only if the nation were united in its revolutionary struggle against despotism would it be assured of victory. [7]

Obviously, Raynal made wide use of the ideas of the American Enlightenment, particularly those enunciated by Paine in his famous work. The French thinker based his arguments on these ideas and drew conclusions from them that by virtue of their revolutionary orientation contributed to the further evolution of Enlightenment ideology, and to its assumption of an increasingly revolutionary character.

Raynal's *Histoire des deux Indes* was an immensely popular work. In the last years of the eighteenth century alone it was published in seventy editions; twenty-five hundred copies were sold in North America.[9] The success enjoyed by this work, in the writing of which Raynal was assisted by Diderot, Nejon, Paul Henri Holbach, and others, was because the reader could find in it sharply worded criticism of absolutism as a form of government, a condemnation of the policy of "enlightened absolutism," and a demand for the abolition of class privileges and prerogatives, slavery, the slave trade, and serfdom. But what excited the interest of Raynal's readers more than anything else was his conclusion that reforms carried out by monarchs who retained absolute power were actually harmful. From issuing calls for the enlightenment of monarchs, Raynal had moved to voicing revolutionary demands. [4]

Paine had the highest opinion of Raynal's treatise. He stated that the groundwork for the Revolution in France had been prepared by the writings of the French enlighteners.

> All these tracts, as well as many others, produced this effect, thanks to the various ways in which they treated the problem of government authority (Montesquieu, with his reasonableness and knowledge of laws, Voltaire with his keen intelligence, Rousseau and Raynal with their ardor, Quesnay and Turgot with the moral maxims and economic systems), readers of all classes were able to find in them something to their taste, and the spirit of political investigation began to be diffused throughout the country—this took place at the very moment when the quarrel between England and its former American colonies first erupted. (228–29)

Paine openly declared that in the writings of Raynal "we found, to the contrary, an exalted love of liberty, which commands respect and inspires man" (228). [5]

The ideas of the American Revolution reached even the distant land of Russia, which lay crushed under the weight of autocratic and serf-based oppression. According to Nikolai Bolkhovitinov,

> Russian society (at least its educated part) was quite adequately informed about the situation in North America and the nature of the events taking place there in the 1770s and 1780s. The Russian reader had access to a number of Russian books (not to mention a variety of foreign publications), numerous journal articles, and, finally, lengthy and varied reports about the events in America which were systematically published by *Moskovskie Vedomosti* (Moscow Gazette) and *S.-Peterburgskie Vedomosti* (St. Petersburg Gazette).[10]

---

9. Hans Wolpe, *Raynal et sa "machine de guerre": "L'Histoire des deux Indes" et ses perfectionnements* (Stanford, 1957), 9.

10. Bolkhovitinov, *Rossiia i voina SShA za nezavisimost', 1775–1783* (Russia and the U.S. War of Independence, 1775–1783) (Moscow, 1976), 335 [American edition: *Russia and the American Revolution,* translated and edited by C. Jay Smith (Tallahassee, 1976)]. See also M. N. Shprygova, "Osveshchenie v "S.-Peterburgskikh Vedomostiakh" voiny Severnoi Ameriki za nezavisimost' " (The Reporting of the War of North American Independence in *St. Petersburg Gazette)* in *Uchen. zap. MGPI im. V. I. Lenina* (Transactions of Moscow State Pedagogical Institute Named after V. I. Lenin), 286 (Moscow, 1967); Shprygova, "Voina Ameriki za nezavisimost' v osveshchenii *Moskovskikh Vedomostei*" (America's War of Independence as Reported by *Moscow Gazette*), in *Nauchnye doklady vysshsei shkoly, istoricheskie nauki* (Scholarly Papers of the Higher School of Learning: Historical Sciences) 3 (Moscow, 1961); A. I. Startsev, *Amerika i russkoe obshchestvo* (America and Russian Society) (Moscow, 1942).

A very important role in informing the Russian public about the final stages of the American War of Independence was played by Nikolai Novikov, who had been allowed to lease the Moscow University press, together with *Moscow Gazette,* for a period of ten years (1779–1789). Novikov's involvement with the latter had the result that "the tone adopted by the newspaper towards America became increasingly objective and even sympathetic."[11] In number 68 of *Moscow Gazette* the first of Novikov's "Notes on Certain Celebrated Men of the Present Century, Taken from a Newly Published French Treatise" appeared, which together with character sketches of Montesquieu, Voltaire, Rousseau, and Raynal contained memorable portraits of Benjamin Franklin and George Washington. During the same period Raynal's book enjoyed a wide circulation in Russia.

That the American Revolution attracted the interest of Russian society is understandable. As the feudal and serf-based system in Russia began to disintegrate and class antagonisms grew more acute, and as disturbances among the peasants continued even in the aftermath of the suppression of the great peasant rebellion led by Emelian Pugachev, conditions were rising in Russia—a country dominated by a harsh gentry-based dictatorship—that were propitious for the dissemination of the ideas of lovers of freedom. Representatives of the progressive part of the nobility and the emerging non-noble intelligentsia were beginning to think more and more about the fate of Russia and the methods to be employed in the struggle against the autocracy and the serf-based order. As Bolkhovitinov correctly noted, "the reports about the war in America published in Russia to a certain extent acquired, because of their objective content, a specific revolutionary political meaning."[12] This fact, together with the situation existing in the country and dissemination of the writings of advanced representatives of French thought, contributed to a shift among the Russian enlighteners from an enlightenment-reformist position to an enlightenment-revolutionary one.

Indications for this shift are evident in Novikov's works of the early 1780s. During this period he published many articles about the Revolution in America; he studied closely the revolutionary experience of England and Holland and the political systems of those two countries, believing that while Britain's constitutional monarchy was the most rational form of government, a republican order was more effective in encouraging the development of commerce, which Novikov considered one of the sources of prosperity in society, but he never reached any conclusions that might be described as revolutionary.

This was done by Alexander Radishchev, who was the first in Russia to proclaim the right of the Russian people to change the existing order by means of a popular revolution. Radishchev was familiar with the contents of Paine's pamphlet as rendered by Raynal, since he had carefully read the third Geneva edition of *Histoire des deux Indes* and had extensive knowledge of that work. Raynal's paean to the American Revolution, together with Radishchev's own analysis of that revolution and of the facts of life in Russia, provided the basis for Radishchev's final revolutionary outlook.

11. Bolkhovitinov, *Russia and the U.S. War of Independence,* 153.
12. Ibid., 163.

"Radishchev and the American Revolution" is a topic to which modern scholars have devoted considerable attention.[13] In fact, Radishchev acted as a propagandist for the American Revolution in Russia. What chiefly interested him in the events in America was the revolutionary activity of the people. He put forward the idea of a popular revolution that would bring down the hateful autocratic and serf-based order. The fact that the Revolutionary army of the United States had owed its tremendous strength to ordinary farmers confirmed Radishchev in the belief that a revolution could be successful only if it involved participation by the broad masses of the people. While hailing the Revolution in America and the political freedoms that had been established there, however, the Russian thinker did not ignore the negative aspects of life in the United States (the genocide of the Indians, Negro slavery). As Bolkhovitinov states, this was not a reflection of any ill will on Radishchev's part toward the United States; on the contrary, "it was precisely because Radishchev had such a high opinion of the American Revolution of the eighteenth century that he condemned so indignantly the presence in the new republic of the ugly legacy of the old regime."[14]

Having proclaimed the idea of a popular revolution as the only means of eliminating serfdom and autocracy, Radishchev expressed the belief that "a day chosen above all other days" would eventually come, when tyranny would collapse and, standing at his grave, a member of a new generation would say:

> This man, born under a tyrant's yoke,
> Wore gilded chains, and yet he spoke—
> The first to tell of freedom's dawn.[15]

The development of Enlightenment thought in a given country was first of all determined by that country's level of socioeconomic development and the sharpness of the class antagonisms there. As the feudal-absolutist order tried to obstruct the growth of the productive forces and the new social relations that were taking shape deep within feudal society and developing into more or less advanced capitalist structures, social antagonisms became more acute and the class struggle intensified. As a result certain aspects of the most egregious flaws in the existing order became the subject of increasingly severe criticism. Of course the enlighteners were inconsistent in the conclusions they drew from their criticism of the feudal system; they continued to believe in the omnipotence of enlightenment and in the possibility that reforms could be implemented by a "sage on a throne." Their criticism, however, laid the ground for an ideological frontal assault on the old order in an era of progressive disintegration

---

13. See also Startsev, "O Zapadnykh sviaziakh Radishcheva" (Concerning Radishchev's Western Contacts), *Internatsional'naia Literatura* (International Literature) 7/8 (1940); Iurii Kariakin, Evgenyi Plimak, *Zapretnaia mysl' obretaet svobodu* (Forbidden Thought Gains Its Freedom) (Moscow, 1966); K. S. Rukshina, "Radishchev i amerikanskaia revoliutsiia," in *Izvestiia AN SSSR, Ser. Literatury i iazyka* (Proceedings of the U.S.S.R. Academy of Sciences, Series on Literature and Language) 35, no. 3 (1976).

14. Bolkhovitinov, *Russia and the U.S. War of Independence*, 174.

15. Radishchev, *Poln. sobr. soch.* (Complete Collected Works) (Moscow-Leningrad, 1938–1952), vol. 1, 15.

of the absolutist system and the deepening of class antagonisms. During this stage in the evolution of Enlightenment ideology, its representatives were vociferous in their denunciation of the feudal system in all its manifestations. They now expressed skepticism about the benign intentions of the "enlightened monarchs" and began to criticize their actions. The attention of the enlighteners was increasingly drawn to instances of revolutionary action against despotic rule.

Such were the stages of development experienced by French Enlightenment thought in the 1740s–1760s and by its counterpart in Russia in the 1760s–1780s. This evolution may be described as a process that embraced the whole of Europe. In France in the 1770s and 1780s the feudal order was in a state of crisis and a revolutionary situation developed in that country, while in Russia in the 1780s and 1790s the feudal order began to unravel and the antagonisms between serfs and landowners grew particularly acute. During this period the French and Russian enlighteners abandoned the hopes they had vested in the figure of an "enlightened monarch" and embarked on a search for a different way of bringing about the transformation of society—one that would take account of the revolutionary events in America in the mid-1770s, when in the course of the War for Independence, Enlightenment thought took an important step forward. In *Common Sense* Paine showed that the existing order could be changed not by the reforming actions of a monarch, but only by means of revolution.

Therefore, when discussing the evolution of Enlightenment thought, it is not enough to consider the level of a particular country's socioeconomic development. It is impossible to analyze Enlightenment ideologies in France and Russia, as well as in any other European country, outside the context of the development of sociopolitical and revolutionary ideas elsewhere in Europe and America. Radical thinkers in a given country were influenced by the revolutionary theories enunciated in the more advanced countries that were on the verge of a revolution or indeed had already carried one out. The experience of such revolutions was also a factor in the radicalization of Enlightenment thought.

In the late eighteenth century in those countries where the problem of eliminating the feudal-absolutist order was at the top of the political agenda, the ideas propounded by Paine in his essay retained their relevance, were used in the struggle against the existing order, and contributed to the radicalizing of Enlightenment thought. In Britain, however, the fate of these ideas was different.

With the growth of capitalist relations, the social importance of the bourgeoisie increased, and in the second half of the eighteenth century they assumed leadership of the antifeudal forces, rallying and guiding them in the struggle with absolutism. On the eve of the American Revolution the manifestations of antagonisms between the bourgeoisie and the democratic strata of the population were not as visible as during the Revolution itself. The two groups were united in the pursuit of a single goal: the destruction of the feudal-absolutist regime. Because of its maturity and high political consciousness, the bourgeoisie in England and America was able to lead the revolution. The victory was made possible by the participation in it of broad democratically minded sections of the population. Yet even as the revolution unfolded, the existence of sharp antagonisms between the bourgeoisie and the masses of the people became apparent. [. . .] It is precisely in the course of the class struggle that "the deep gulf between the interests of the different classes, which demand different economic and political measures in the name of the same 'democracy,' is laid bare."[16]

The war with Britain won America its independence. In the course of the war a bloc of bourgeoisie and planters came into being that grew rich during the war and continued to accumulate capital after it had ended. The burden of the economic difficulties in the country fell on the shoulders of the working people. Inflation and the rise in the cost of living increased their indebtedness, and the growth of private debt in turn caused a major increase in the national debt. All these factors created discontent among the masses of the people. The early 1780s were thus marked by large-scale disturbances among the poor.

The most important of these was Shays's Rebellion, in the course of which the insurgents put forward demands for the equal distribution of land and wealth, the abolition of taxes, and the just application of law by the courts. The movement led by Shays aimed to give the revolution a consistently democratic character that would have led to its transformation into a bourgeois-democratic one. The upper bourgeoisie and the planters considered the insurgents' demand for an equitable distribution of wealth an encroachment on that "holy of holies" of the bourgeoisie—the right to own private property. Even while the War of Independence was still being fought, the bourgeoisie and the planters tried to restrain the growing revolutionary activism of the masses and to limit revolutionary change as much as possible; later, during the period of upsurge in the democratic movement, the bourgeois-planter bloc demanded the centralization of authority, the pursuit of a more repressive policy toward the popular masses, and the protection of private property.

After Shays's Rebellion the American bourgeoisie assumed a significantly more right-wing orientation. Slave-owning planters, usurers, real-estate speculators, merchants, industrialists, and shipowners were all represented at the Constitutional Convention of 1787. There were few radicals among the delegates; many figures who had been prominent in the Revolution were absent from the convention, including Paine, who was in Europe at the time. This body was markedly more conservative than the Congress that had adopted the Declaration of Independence. The Constitution drawn up at the convention satisfied the bourgeois-planter bloc, which desired a strong central government. After the publication of the text of the Constitution a bitter conflict erupted between the Federalists—supporters of the Constitution who stood for the interests of a large section of the upper bourgeoisie and the planters—and their opponents, who represented the interests of the broad masses of the American people. The Federalists emerged victorious, and by June 1788 the Constitution had come into force.

In a republic that provided not "a political form for the revolutionary transformation of bourgeois society, but . . . a conservative form for its existence,"[17] Paine's unshakable belief in the sovereignty of the people and his criticism of large-scale property ownership no longer reflected the interests of the victorious bourgeoisie. In the last years of the eighteenth century the American bourgeoisie attempted to consign Paine's ideas to oblivion and slighted him personally.

16. Lenin, *Works,* vol. 15, 277.
17. Marx and Engels, *Works,* vol. 8, 127.

During the upsurge in the democratic movement in America in the 1780s, however, Paine's own lack of consistency became apparent. He found it difficult to orient himself in the new situation that had risen in the country. His uncompromising republicanism did not always prove to be of much use in the debates on questions relating to the internal development of the young Republic—tariffs, financial and fiscal policy, and internal improvements. Paine, in fact, hailed the Constitution of 1787; the statements he made about it in the early 1790s are free of any criticism, because the principle of a strong central government met with his approval. "It was only in 1795," writes Vladimir Sogrin, "that Paine conceded that the federal Constitution contained a number of features that were unacceptable: he criticized the bestowal of executive authority upon a single individual—the president—and declared that the Senate's term of office was excessively long."[18] Paine had nothing to say about the articles in the Constitution that preserved Negro slavery and the slave trade.[19] As in the case of other ideologues of the bourgeoisie, the inconsistencies in Paine's worldview were a consequence of class-based limitations.

In *Common Sense* and later in his treatise *The Rights of Man,* Paine defended the right of the people to destroy the feudal order through revolution. For Paine, revolution meant a reconstitution of the entire set of principles on which government was based; it was the necessary means for the elimination of tyranny. A despotic government may be overthrown by war or rebellion. But having achieved freedom, it is necessary to find ways of preserving it. He rejected the use of violence after a revolution had taken place, believing that its gains could be protected under a system of government in which power was exercised by the majority. Thus Paine reached the conclusion that "the establishment in the country of a republican order means the realization of popular sovereignty, and, therefore, allowing the masses to continue to have the right to revolt would be equivalent to bestowing upon them the right to overthrow the government of the people."[20] After the Revolution in the United States, Paine advocated the development "of the nation along the path of commercial-industrial capitalism, freed of ulcers and contradictions by means of reforms."[21] In no way did Paine envisage the possibility of a new revolution in the United States after the establishment of the Republic.

Paine's lack of consistency was evident during the Revolution in France, which he greeted with great enthusiasm. He followed its development closely, and beginning in 1792 participated in it. Together with other prominent foreign revolutionary figures like Washington, Joseph Priestly, Anacharsis Cloots, and Pestalozzi, Paine was granted French citizenship by a decree of the Legislative Assembly of August 1792. He was elected to the Convention and took an active part in it. He greeted the establishment of a republic in France with enthusiasm and, as a member of the committee charged with drawing up a new constitution, produced his own constitutional project (which, unfortunately, did not survive).

18. Sogrin, *Ideological Currents,* 196.
19. Ibid., 256.
20. Ibid., 291.
21. Ibid.

One of the major questions facing the Convention was the fate of the deposed king, which was debated from November 1792 until January 1793. Paine declared his opposition to the Jacobin demands that the king be executed. "Fearing England's intervention and remembering that Louis XVI had given America succor he said that vengeance should not be taken on the king; instead his trial must be used to demonstrate the existence of an international conspiracy against the revolution, thereby providing a stimulus for revolutionary upsurge in other countries."[22] In effect the American thinker had joined the Girondins, who as representatives of the merchant-industrial bourgeoisie strove to limit the further development of the revolutionary process, and as a result were increasingly moving to a position in support of counterrevolution.

Soon Paine was speaking out against the revolutionary terror of the Jacobins. He believed that now that France was a republic, the government should act within the constitution and in accordance with the principles established by the Revolution. He thought that the Jacobins were governing the country as they saw fit, guided by circumstances rather than principles—a practice that would lead to the destruction of freedom, because not everyone was capable of changing his opinion immediately and assimilating the principles of the Revolution.

> There has never been any truth of any principle that was so absolutely self-evident that all people immediately embraced it. Time and reason must act together in order to bring about the final affirmation of a principle. Therefore, those who were immediately able to become convinced supporters of this principle do not have the right to persecute others for becoming convinced of its truth more slowly. The moral principle of revolutions is to instruct, and not to destroy.[23]

Moreover, Paine was unable to comprehend fully the complex situation, the distribution of class forces, and the nature of the party strife that emerged in France during the last period of the Revolution. This was because the Revolution in America differed in a number of significant ways from the French Revolution.[24] The feudal order in France had taken shape as a result of a centuries-long process, and its destruction required an immense application of force, provided by the merciless Jacobin dictatorship.

Nothing like this occurred during the Revolution in America. It is true that the American Revolutionaries waged a struggle against the Loyalists, but the measures taken against the latter could in no way be compared to the revolutionary-democratic dictatorship of the Jacobins.

> America did not witness either a conflict of such bitterness or a revolutionary struggle on such a scale. The lines separating the classes fluctuated, while class antagonisms

---

22. Nikolai Gol'dberg, *Tomas Pein* (Thomas Paine) (Moscow, 1969), 47.
23. B. S. Gromakov, *Politicheskie i pravovye vzgliady Tomasa Peina* (The Political and Legal Views of Thomas Paine) (Moscow, 1960), 42.
24. For a comparison of the American and French Revolutions of the eighteenth century and an analysis of the differences between them, see Aleksandr Fursenko, "Amerikanskaia i frantsuzskie revoliutsii XVIII veka" (The American and French Revolutions of the Eighteenth Century), *Voprosy Istorii* (Problems of History) 11 (1972).

had not yet acquired the same intensity as in Europe. One of the main reasons for this was the existence of a fund of free land in the West which, despite the prohibition of the British authorities, attracted a continuous stream of colonists. This was in effect an escape route, which even during later periods in American history fulfilled the role of a kind of safety-valve that reduced the intensity of class conflicts.[25]

From the moment the French Revolution broke out the French people were its main actor. Their participation guaranteed its continuing development, which forced the bourgeoisie to advance further and further along the path of revolutionary change. The popular disturbances and the growing strength of the democratic movement, however, frightened the bourgeoisie and caused it to search for ways of limiting the participation of the masses in the Revolution.

Raynal's letters to the National Assembly show that as the Revolution continued to unfold, he spoke out against its further development. When he had advocated revolution as a means of waging the struggle against absolutism, Raynal, like the ideologues of the bourgeoisie, had argued that the future social order should be founded on the principle of property. In the course of the Revolution, as the indigent masses began to encroach upon the principle of property and to demand the systematic implementation of the principle of equality, the movement of these masses, which had given the Revolution its power and impetus, became a threat to the bourgeoisie. Fear of the growing strength of the people's movement prompted Raynal to search for alternative ways in which the Revolution could be carried forward and, as the Revolution continued, to develop new theories in order to justify his conclusion that the activity of the people must be curtailed. At a time when the Revolution was rising but the final defeat of feudalism was still a long way away, Raynal was already arguing that the Revolution should be brought to an end on the basis of a compromise between the leaders of the bourgeoisie and those very same feudal lords whom he had recently attacked so bitterly.[26]

In Russia the French Revolution attracted the closest attention of both the representatives of the advanced elements in Russian society and of the feudal reactionaries.[27] Radishchev closely followed the progress of the Revolution. This is shown by the post-censorship insertions he added to the text of his *Journey from St. Petersburg to Moscow* and by the note in his "Letter to a Friend Resident in Tobolsk." During the climactic stage of the French Revolution, Radishchev lived in exile but continued, insofar as possible, to follow events in France. To this day, however, the question of Radishchev's attitude toward the French Revolution continues to be the subject of lively debate.[28]

The post-censorship insertions in Radishchev's *Journey* and the note in "Letter to a Friend" indicate that the events in France, coming as they did after the events in

---

25. Ibid., 74.
26. For a fuller discussion of Raynal's position during the French Revolution, see Moriakov, 145–66.
27. See M. M. Shtrange, *Russkoe obshchesvo i frantsuzskaia revoliutsiia, 1789–1794 gg.* (Russian Society and the French Revolution of 1789–1794) (Moscow, 1956).
28. For more on Radishchev's attitude to the Revolution in France and the debate among historians concerning this issue, see Moriakov, *Development*, 167–87.

America, led the Russian thinker to conclude that the people could achieve their full liberation only by mounting their own movement, by waging their own struggle, by becoming active themselves. Far from moderating the revolutionary conclusions drawn in the *Journey,* the post-censorship insertions actually strengthened them. Living as he did in a country where at the time a revolutionary situation did not exist, and indeed could not have existed, Radishchev did not and could not know the form that a revolution in Russia would take. That is why the experience of America and France, which convinced him that only the revolutionary impulse of the masses could guarantee the success of the revolution, meant so much to the author of the *Journey.*

It would appear that Radishchev expected a great deal from the Revolution in France, since the American Revolution had preserved both Negro slavery and the slave trade. Yet in Radishchev's opinion the French Revolution ended with the establishment of a new despotism. Of course, he did not—and could not—understand that the victory of the bourgeoisie in France signified the victory of capitalism over feudalism, representing another stage on the path of social progress. Radishchev saw only that the Revolution was unable to free the masses of the working people from poverty and oppression— whereas the result of a revolution, he held, must be precisely the opposite, as he had declared in 1783 in his "Ode to Liberty."

Radishchev acted as a spokesman for the oppressed Russian peasantry, which is why his works contain a condemnation of oppression and the denial of civil rights in every form. Ultimately, the revolutions in America and France produced results that proved to be far removed from the ideal goal—the creation of a society where reason and justice reigned—which had been proclaimed on the eve of each revolution by the Western enlighteners.

Radishchev had dreamed of and written about the same goal. The revolutions in America and France convinced him that only a popular revolution could bring down tyranny; but at the same time these two events, together with the peasant revolution in Russia led by Pugachev, showed that in the eighteenth century "there was not enough strength to expel all the spirits of hell" and to bring about freedom and happiness on this earth; at this point in history the common people were unable to achieve their liberation, lacking as they did the strength and opportunity to do so. This does not mean, however, that Radishchev rejected revolution as a weapon in the fight against tyranny; on the contrary, he believed in the inevitability of revolution in the future, "saw an entire century ahead," and, therefore, spoke of the need to prepare the people for it by spreading "the word of freedom."

In the 1780s the enlightened writers of France and Russia moved from a belief in an "enlightened monarch" as the main instrument for the transformation of society to the advocacy of revolution as the only possible means of fighting absolutism. This evolution was determined by the socioeconomic development of those two countries and the intensity of the class struggle there. The American Revolution and the ideas expounded by Paine in *Common Sense* played a crucial role in the radicalization of French Enlightenment thought. The shift to a position in support of revolution effected by its representatives accelerated the process that led to the emergence of a revolutionary situation in France. The experience of the American Revolution, its ideas, and the radical writings of the French philosophes helped the writers of the Russian Enlightenment to formulate the idea of a popular revolution.

During the period when the struggle against the feudal system took place and the groundwork for revolution was being laid, the enlighteners acted in a revolutionary manner, speaking in the name of the entire nation and showing the difference between the existing order and a society that would be based on the principles of reason and justice. After the victory of the bourgeois revolutions in America and France, however, it became clear that "in reality a state founded on reason . . . turned out to be—and could not but turn out to be—merely a bourgeois democratic republic." In a sense the revolutions were the crucible of the ideas of the Enlightenment, in which they underwent a test by revolutionary practice. [3] "The great thinkers of the eighteenth century," Engels continued, "like all their predecessors, were unable to break out of the bounds within which they had been placed by their age."[29] In a situation where society was evolving peacefully it would have taken years before the contradictions and weaknesses in the ideology of the Enlightenment would have been revealed. In the conditions of a revolution, when a theory is tested by revolutionary practice, its contradictions and flaws manifest themselves very quickly. As the revolutionary struggle unfolded, Paine's lack of consistency, Raynal's desire for a compromise with the monarchy, and Radishchev's dissatisfaction with the results of the revolutions in America and France all became clear.

---

29. Marx and Engels, *Works,* vol. 19, 190.

Comment
by John T. Alexander

These two essays may be seen as representing different periods and styles of Russian/Soviet historiography on Russo-American relations in the era of the American War for Independence and the early national period. Because of the rapid changes in the U.S.S.R. and its abrupt disintegration, the political and cultural spectrums have become discombobulated with the result that the two essays may look a little old-fashioned. Marxist categories loom large in Moriakov's essay while lurking in the background of Bolkhovitinov's paper.

Vasilii Moriakov, a student of the late M. T. Beliavskii at Moscow State University in the 1970s, offers a sweeping comparison and contrast of the revolutionary writings of Thomas Paine and Alexander Radishchev in the context of what some scholars have termed "The Atlantic Revolution" of the late eighteenth century. Raynal's influence on both Paine and Radishchev is explicated as evidence of the French Enlightenment's impact on the intellectual ferment preceding and accompanying the revolutionary upheavals. Marxist categories form the basis of Moriakov's discussion; hence the stark contrast between "bourgeois" and "republican" North America versus Russia, "long crushed under the weight of autocratic and serf-based oppression." Indeed, the very title of Moriakov's essay sounds rather vague and dogmatic as he uses the term "enlightener" quite narrowly (presumably excluding thinkers with religious orientations), just as his concepts of "enlightenment" and "revolution" seem either strangely indefinite or so all-inclusive as to mask important differences in national context and social structure. His treatment of Nikolai Novikov, for example, labels this Russian nobleman entrepreneur-publisher-freemason a republican while denying that he ever reached any "revolutionary conclusions."

Moriakov's discussion exhibits no familiarity with the revisionist biography of Novikov by W. Gareth Jones (Cambridge, 1984), which emphasizes Catherine II's patronage of his many publishing ventures and Novikov's varied interests and activities.

Moriakov speaks of "the American Enlightenment" and also assumes there was a somewhat similar "Russian Enlightenment," though his discussion of the printing and circulation of Paine's and Radishchev's most famous works may just as easily suggest the great contrasts between the reading publics in late-eighteenth-century North America and Russia. Surely it is a considerable oversimplification to see the Enlightenment as any sort of monolithic "movement," or to focus on the supposedly "main trend" as a simple progression from reform to revolution. It is equally surprising to see no sign of Robert Darnton's revisionist views of publishing and reading in late-eighteenth-century France or Marc Raeff's essay, "The Enlightenment in Russia and Russian Thought in the Enlightenment," in J. G. Garrard, ed., *The Eighteenth Century in Russia* (Cambridge, 1973), which stresses the impact of German social and religious thought, Pietism in particular, on Russian notions of enlightenment.

In like manner, Moriakov shows no appreciation of Anglo-American scholarship on Radishchev and his ambivalent and ambiguous relations with Catherine II. In fact, the Russian philosopher (if one may provisionally use this term for him) and the enlightened empress held many ideas in common as regards their faith in law and education as sources of gradual and fruitful social change. The commonalities in their thinking have been deftly explored by Allen McConnell, "The Autocrat and the Open Critic," reprinted in Marc Raeff, ed., *Catherine the Great: A Profile* (New York, 1972). Their reactions to the French Revolution once it entered its violent and bloody phases also exhibited many similarities, as Moriakov implicitly acknowledges in mentioning Radishchev's concern about a new despotism in France—something Catherine II had predicted years earlier. He might have extended his remarks about the inconsistency of "the enlighteners" to Radishchev specifically. I was astounded by Moriakov's references to the "tremendous strength" of the American Revolutionary army and his contention that the upper bourgeoisie and the planters "grew rich during the war and continued to accumulate capital after it ended." Similar unthinking dogmatism seems to underlie his mention of "the great peasant rebellion led by Pugachev"—a complicated phenomenon that hardly fits into the procrustean bed borrowed from Engels by Soviet scholarship. Truly these are at best half-truths if not misguided assertions.

Academician Nikolai Bolkhovitinov's essay, by contrast, provides a broad survey based on research in both Russian and U.S. archives and libraries. His brief treatment of scientific ties inevitably highlights transnational themes inasmuch as science had become an international enterprise by the mid to late eighteenth century. In that regard, it jars slightly to encounter the term "Russian science," while the German names of many "Russian" scientific figures well into the nineteenth century hint at the multinational and multiethnic composition of the scientific community in Russia, especially that concentrated at the Imperial Russian Academy of Sciences. The academy's scholars and the academy's press published in various languages, Aepinus's work on electricity first appearing for example in Latin, then still a significant international medium of science. Even so, it is refreshing to see Catherine II's linguistic interests cited approvingly, for her intellectual concerns used to be disparaged in the U.S.S.R. Yet Bolkhovitinov's discussion of Stiles's letter to Lomonosov may mislead U.S. readers concerning the sporadic nature of Russo-American scientific contacts, for Lomonosov died barely a year later and left no direct disciples to carry on his diverse (and sometimes sketchy) activities. Bolkhovitinov's enthusiastic discussion of the "Russian books" sent to the American Philosophical Society presumably includes many publications in languages other than Russian, and one wonders how much and by whom these publications were actually used.

It does not seem surprising that early Russian and American literary contacts were sporadic and shallow, for the reading public in both countries must have been quite limited albeit steadily growing. And it has been well established that many English works of literature came to Russia via French or German translations and abridgements, a circuitous route that probably was followed by American works as well and by Russian works in the other direction. Bolkhovitinov's focus on bilateral relations may therefore result in some distortion or at least oversimplification of the nature of Russo-American literary interrelationships. I am somewhat surprised at his slightly indignant discussion of Americans' slow discovery of Pushkin. Surely it is hard to imagine many Americans of the time learning Russian sufficiently to read sophisticated poetry like Pushkin's, or that anyone should produce an English translation of such a complex work as *Evgenii Onegin,* Pushkin's famous novel in verse. Nor should we wonder that Pushkin became better known for prose works such as *The Captain's Daughter* than for his verse or drama. In short, the hit-or-miss pattern of Russo-American literary relations may well have repeated the slightly earlier experience of Anglo-Russian borrowings and translations via intermediaries, with sometimes bizarre results on all sides as in the appearance and popularity of Daniel Defoe's *Robinson Crusoe* and its many European imitations. See the discussion by Iu. D. Levin, "The English Novel in 18th-Century Russia," in A. G. Cross and G. S. Smith, eds., *Literature, Lives, and Legality in Catherine's Russia* (Nottingham, 1994), 143–67, especially 147–50.

3

The American Theme on the Pages of *Dukh Zhurnalov* (Spirit of Journals), by N. N. Bolkhovitinov

In 1820 a detailed summary of the American political system was published in several issues of the periodical *Spirit of Journals*.[1] Today's reader might not attach particular significance to this fact. In order to fully understand its importance, one should recall that until then only Alexander Radishchev had dared openly to express approval of the constitutions of the American states and to publish some of their articles in his *Journey from St. Petersburg to Moscow* (1790). "He praises Franklin—he's worse than Pugachev," was the sentence pronounced on the great Russian revolutionary of the eighteenth century by the "enlightened" Catherine II. And yet, thirty years later a summary of a republican constitution appeared on the pages of a periodical published in the capital of Russia, not during the period that Alexander Pushkin had called "the beautiful flowering of Alexander's days," but at a time when the iron grip of Aleksei Arakcheev was stifling the country and the Holy Alliance was being consolidated. So what was this? An absurd fluke? A censor's oversight? An inexplicable mistake—or the result of a deliberate, considered, and logical decision by the publisher?

Some scholars have noted that *Spirit of Journals* published many interesting materials relating to America, of which the most important was a summary of the American Constitution.[2] Unfortunately, this has not been the subject of detailed study. To answer these questions, it is necessary to consider all the relevant facts and to analyze the circumstances surrounding the founding and subsequent history of *Spirit of Journals*, as well as the articles it published and the polemics it conducted with other Russian

---

1. "The Constitution of the North American Provinces," *Dukh Zhurnalov* (Spirit of Journals) 32 (1820), no. 2: 73–78; no. 3: 97–116; no. 4: 157–64. This article by N. N. Bolkhovitinov was first published in *Amerikanskii ezhegodnik* (Annual of American Studies) in 1972.

2. A. I. Startsev, *Amerika i russkoe obshchestvo* (Russian Society and America) (Moscow, 1942), 11–12; D. Boden, *Das Amerikabild im russischen Schriftum bis zum Ende des 19. Jahrhunderts* (Hamburg, 1968), 76–78.

periodicals. It is essential to establish the character of the relationship that existed between this journal and its publisher on the one hand, and the authorities, above all the tsarist censors, on the other. Finally, it is very important to identify and analyze those articles that were specifically devoted to American subjects and establish their place and significance in the history of Russian social thought.

From the very start there were unexpected developments. Even the founding of *Spirit of Journals,* which began publication in January 1815, took place in unusual circumstances, involved unforeseen difficulties, and led to heated polemics in the Russian press. The new journal was announced in the newspapers on November 17/29, 1814, without the knowledge and approval of "higher authority." Sergei Uvarov, the administrator of the St. Petersburg Department of Education, was quick to address an inquiry about the matter to the city's censorship committee:

> In the 92nd issue of the St. Petersburg *Gazette* there was published an announcement concerning the projected appearance in 1815 of a periodical entitled *Spirit of Journals, or a Collection of all the Best . . . in the Field of History, Politics and Other Subjects.* However, no instructions from higher authority in the Ministry of Education authorizing such a publication were received.[3]

Minister of Police Sergei Viazmitinov was particularly concerned about the plans to establish a new periodical. Having learned that the journal intended to publish articles about the internal situation in Russia and even discuss shortcomings and abuses, he immediately addressed a letter to Count Aleksei Razumovskii, the minister of education, in which he stressed that these subjects "relate to the competence of the Government itself and cannot be publicly discussed by private persons."[4] In response to this letter Razumovskii requested that Censor Grigorii Iatsenkov be reprimanded for allowing the announcement about *Spirit of Journals* to appear in print, while Uvarov ordered that the publication of "the said journal" be forbidden pending "a special decree by His Excellency the Minister of Education authorizing this."[5] In addition, on December 9/21, 1814, he asked that the identity of the publisher of the new journal be revealed.[6] This resulted in the discovery that the publisher was none other than the same Iatsenkov who had allowed the announcement to appear in *St. Petersburg Gazette.*[7]

---

3. *S. Peterburgskie Vedomosti* (St. Petersburg Gazette), November 17/29, 1814; S. S. Uvarov to the St. Petersburg Censorship Committee, November 19/December 1, 1814, Central State Historical Archive (TsGIA), record group 777, inventory 1, list 181, 1.

4. P. K. Shchebalskii, "Materialy dlia istorii russkoi tsensury, 1803–1825" (Materials for a History of Russian Censorship between 1803–1825) in *Besedy v obshchestve liubitelei rossisskoi slovesnosti pri im. Moskovskom universitete* (Proceedings of the Society of Lovers of Russian Literature of the University of Moscow) [henceforth *Proceedings*], vol. 3 (Moscow, 1871), 16 (S. K. Viazmitinov to A. K. Razumovskii, November 23/December 5, 1814).

5. Razumovskii to Uvarov, November 30/December 12, 1814, TsGIA, record group 777, inventory 1, list 181, 3; Uvarov to the St. Petersburg Censorship Committee, December 3/15, 1814, ibid., 6.

6. Ibid., 8.

7. Initially the publisher tried to hide his true role, stating that the announcement about *Spirit of Journals* had been submitted to the censors by Collegiate Assessor V. F. Veliaminov-Zernov

The tsarist authorities found themselves in a difficult position. To close *Spirit of Journals* before it commenced publication, and after a special announcement had been printed in the government newspaper, meant creating a public scandal without the presence of a corpus delicti, for nothing reprehensible had yet been published. True, no official permission for the new periodical had been issued, but the chief culprit was a member of the "old boy network," a censor, state councillor, and holder of an imperial order.

After considering all the circumstances of the affair, the minister of education decided not to resort to extreme measures and in the end agreed to the appearance of the new periodical on the condition that it would be subject to strict control by the censors. On December 13, 1814/January 4, 1815, Razumovskii wrote Uvarov, "Having received the necessary intelligence regarding the planned periodical entitled *Spirit of Journals*, I do not find it necessary to ban this publication, and I request Your Excellency to make arrangements for the committee of censorship to permit the publication of this journal." The letter specifically referred to a prohibition on the publication of newspaper articles, as well as "comments about the internal situation in Russia." The police minister asked Uvarov to instruct the censorship committee to "examine this periodical most carefully," and to assign this duty to Censor Ivan Timkovskii.[8]

On January 2/14, 1815, Timkovskii sanctioned the appearance of the first issue of "the new periodical for 1815." The complete name on the title page was: *Spirit of Journals, or a Collection of All that Is Best and Most Curious in All Other Journals in the Fields of History, Politics, the National Economy, Belles-Lettres, the Various Arts, Estate Management, Etc.* Explaining the goals of the new periodical, its publisher wrote:

> *Spirit of Journals* is not a compendium of journals: it will not partake of anyone's property, but, like the bee that extracts fragrant juices from thousands of flowers, which do not lose thereby either their freshness, or their beauty, it will extract from all the flowers of literature their strength and, in a manner of speaking, their spirit; or, like the artist who paints enchanting scenes of picturesque landscapes, *Spirit of Journals* will present its readers with a panorama of the best periodicals, merely pointing to those items in them that are, among all the others, particularly worthy of attention.[9]

---

and that other participants in the project, who were "respected by the public because of their rank and erudition," had wished to remain anonymous. *Proceedings,* vol. 3, 17.

Little is known about Iatsenkov's earlier activities. In 1804, before he joined the censorship committee, he was a teacher of ancient Greek and Latin, later becoming an adjunct professor of "Philosophy and the Liberal Sciences" at Moscow University. He had been a translator, publishing at the end of the eighteenth and beginning of the nineteenth century many books by French and German authors. In addition to *Spirit of Journals* (1815–1820), in 1825–1834 he was the first publisher of *Zhurnal manufactur i torgovli* (Journal of Manufacturing and Trade). See S. D. Poltoratskii, "Bibliographical Notes," Manuscript Division, Lenin (Russian National) Library, 67, 35; 54, 9; A. P. Piatkovskii, *Iz istorii nashego literaturnogo i obshchestvennogo rasvitiia* (From the History of the Literary and Social Development of Our Country), 2 vols. (St. Petersburg, 1889), vol. 2, 196.

8. Razumovskii to Uvarov, December 23, 1814/January 4, 1815, TsGIA, record group 777, inventory 1, list 181, 12; *Proceedings,* vol. 3, 18.

9. *Spirit of Journals* 1 (1815), no. 1: vii. To fulfill this task, sixteen foreign publications were ordered "for a special reason" through the "newspaper dispatch office." These included

But, of course, it turned out that "to present a panorama of the best periodicals," to determine what was the most important and interesting that they had to offer, was not an easy task. Not all the articles that appeared in the journal interested the reading public, and not all of them are of importance for the researcher. Compared with *Syn Otechestva* (Son of the Fatherland) or *Vestnik Evropy* (European Herald), the journal's literary section was undistinguished and obviously unsuccessful. However, the "Historical and Political Archive," "Observer of the Fatherland," and the section entitled "Most Recent Travels" clearly made a favorable impression on readers. It is important to note that as early as in its first year of publication, *Spirit of Journals* began systematically to devote attention to American subjects, publishing information on major events in the United States, statistical data about economic development, a variety of official documents, as well as a biographical series entitled "A Description of the Most Famous Persons in North America." In part 1 of the journal appeared a "Statistical Survey of North America" and a brief biography of Thomas Jefferson, extracted from the book by John Lambert.[10] Noteworthy also was the article "On the Negro Trade," which contained a sharp condemnation of the "shameful commerce, in which all European nations took part" (with the exception of Russia, added the publisher, who went on to tell his readers that "according to the latest intelligence from Vienna," it had finally been decided to "liquidate" the slave trade).[11]

Two weeks later a second article on the subject, "On the Slave Trade," appeared. It emphasized that "in this matter no notions concerning the dignity of human nature are respected.... The whole business is founded solely on greed."[12] Somewhat later the journal published President James Monroe's message to Congress of February 25,[13] as well as a brief note about the new tariff adopted by the United States at the beginning of March 1815. "It is clear that this law, which in its essence is most just and most simple, will multiply the fortune and the prosperity of this happy land, whereas a system of barriers would only have served to impoverish and ruin the State."[14]

The fascinating series of "Letters from Philadelphia," which contained an open defense of constitutions, democratic freedoms, religious tolerance, etc., occupied a special place on the pages of *Spirit of Journals* and in the Russian press for 1815 as a whole. It is clear that the owner of the journal could not have published articles such as these under his own name. The "Letters from Philadelphia" were presented as a translation of letters written by a "certain German"—a not uncommon device—but their contents and tone left no doubt as to the political sympathies of the publisher.

---

the *Journal des Débats, Mercure de France, Hamburgischer Correspondent, Moniteur,* and the *Edinburgh Review.* Subsequently the list of these publications was somewhat changed, and it came to include the *Times,* the *Courier de l'Europe,* the *Morning Chronicle, Esprit des Journaux,* and others. See *Spirit of Journals* 1 (1815), no. 1: vi; 7 (1815), no. 44: 951.

10. *Spirit of Journals* 1 (1815), no. 4: 227–29, 230–34, from John Lambert, *Travels through Canada and the United States of North America in the Years 1806, 7, 8,* 3 vols. (London, 1810).
11. *Spirit of Journals* 1 (1815), no. 8: 453–56.
12. *Spirit of Journals* 2 (1815), no. 10: 558.
13. *Spirit of Journals* 2 (1815), no. 18: 985–86.
14. *Spirit of Journals* 4 (1815), no. 23: 1266.

The first Letter, of December 14, 1814, published in issue 31 of 1815, began with a highly romanticized description of life in republican America: "At last, I am in the land where a man can boast that he enjoys all possible political liberty and respects nothing but the law.... There are no titles, ranks, nor orders here, and yet everything takes its normal course in the greatest order and prosperity."[15] These Letters were published at regular intervals throughout August, September, and October 1815 (issues 31, 32, 33, 35, 36, 37, 41, 42, 43). They constantly praised the constitution, government, and way of life of the American people. "The general prosperity of the people of these United Provinces is undoubtedly to be ascribed to the existence of a free government and an excellent constitution that guards the rights of every and all individuals," read the Letter in issue 36.[16]

The American Constitution was judged to be greatly superior to those of many European countries, including Great Britain.

> The Constitution of the United American Provinces has all the advantages of the English constitution, without, however, possessing its flaws. Among these advantages are, undoubtedly, the unlimited freedom to think, speak and write. Nowhere do people speak, opine, and write as freely as in Great Britain and America.... The journals and newspapers, of which there are a great many here and in which everyone may freely express his ideas, do much to make public opinion and the voice of the people known.[17]

The advocacy by *Spirit of Journals* of the constitutional system of government and its open defense of freedom of the press could not of course remain unnoticed. It is revealing that in their first "Message to Our Readers," appearing in February 1815, the publishers of the new journal expressed their "most sincere gratitude to the esteemed public" for its "generous approbation."[18] They spoke of their "special feeling of gratitude" to the "gentleman of the city of Arzamas for his excellent suggestions which, however, cannot be published for reasons that will be plain to him. His opinion of our publication is all the more flattering since it reflects a way of thinking that reveals a judgment founded on common sense and experience." Although the identity of "the gentleman of Arzamas" remains a mystery, this was probably a member of the literary society of that name, which existed in 1815–1818 and included a number of Decembrists and writers who later became famous.[19]

Iatsenkov's comments about the readers' reaction to the "Letters from Philadelphia" in his "Report of the Society of Publishers of *Spirit of Journals* for 1815," dated December 29, 1815 (o.s.), are also of great interest. "In particular, we had occasion to learn of the public's enjoyment of the curious 'Letters from Philadelphia.' How many exceedingly pleasant feelings they have inspired in the hearts of all those who treasure

---

15. *Spirit of Journals* 5 (1815), no. 31: 217–18.
16. *Spirit of Journals* 6 (1815), no. 36: 488.
17. *Spirit of Journals* 5 (1815), no. 31: 222–23.
18. *Spirit of Journals* 1 (1815), no. 8: 479.
19. Ibid., 480; *Istoriia russkoi literatury* (History of Russian Literature) (Moscow-Leningrad, 1941), vol. 5, 327–38.

the happiness of the people!"[20] Iatsenkov did not elaborate, but, even so, this brief statement is extraordinarily revealing; these Letters, containing a passionate defense of the constitutional system of government, were bound to inspire "exceedingly pleasant feelings" among the circles of freethinkers in Russian society.

However, the journal received not only praise from the progressive section of the Russian reading public; it was subjected to malicious attacks by reactionaries, criticism on the part of conservative and moderately conservative publications, and, finally, met with the clear disapproval of the tsarist authorities. For example, in February 1815 Mikhail Kachenovskii's *European Herald,* one of the most respected and influential Russian publications of the period, published a scathing review of *Spirit of Journals* in the form of a letter from a "Smolensk landowner" who said he regretted that he no longer subscribed to *European Herald* and criticized the new journal from a reactionary and pseudopatriotic position. The "Smolensk landowner" was particularly exercised by "Letters from Foreign Lands of a Russian Traveler," which compared the conditions of life in Russia and Britain and concluded that "the constancy and honesty of Englishmen, as well as their superiority in all fields, make it advisable that we adopt them as an example for ourselves."[21]

Of course, the article by the "Russian traveler" was far from being perfect either in its factual content or in its general conclusions. Still, the refutation that the *European Herald* published in response was shamelessly obscurantist: "Let this reprobate son of Russia, newly ensconced in England, admire the legions of professional beggars, thiefs, and robbers who live there; our journals should not print such ravings, or should print them only with a suitable commentary."[22]

Responding to the criticism, Iatsenkov in a "Message to the Readers" stated his guiding principles in these emotional terms: "Publishers are disinclined to exclaim on every page, like some others, 'O, beloved Fatherland! O, sacred truth! We wish to die for you!' Such enthusiasms are ridiculous, and often suspect. Nonetheless, publishers love their fatherland and seek the truth, and—above all else—justice."[23] Explaining the difference between true love of country and ostentatious patriotism, he wrote: "Love of the fatherland means respect for everything in it that is good and contributes to its prosperity; but an excessive partiality for all that is native sees in the very flaws of the fatherland proof of its superiority, thus preventing it from becoming more prosperous."[24]

In order to understand fully the difficulties facing the publisher of *Spirit of Journals,* one must bear in mind that, although the journal had been officially permitted to appear, it continued to be subjected to close supervision by tsarist authorities, thus experiencing "the burden of a double censorship—that of the Ministry of Police and that of the Ministry of National Education."[25]

20. *Spirit of Journals* 8 (1815), no. 52: 1351.
21. *Spirit of Journals* 1 (1815), no. 2: 111.
22. *Vestnik Evropy* (European Herald) 89, no. 3 (February 1815): 217.
23. *Spirit of Journals* 1 (1815), no. 8: 485 (here and henceforth all italics are Iatsenkov's).
24. Ibid.
25. Piatkovskii, *From the History of the Literary and Social Development of Our Country,* vol. 2, 195.

In the spring of 1815 Viazmitinov discovered in the new journal what he felt were blatantly seditious statements. The minister of police declared that an article "Concerning the Endeavors of Empress Catherine II to Guarantee Low Prices for the Necessities of Life" contained "ideas which are not only senseless and absurd, but also impermissible and impudent, and which might have a deleterious effect on the opinion of the people." According to the journal, Catherine II "endeavored to grant the freedom to trade to the largest number of merchants . . . which would have resulted in the disappearance of monopolies, which the Empress did not tolerate in anything."[26]

Viazmitinov was particularly angered by a comparison made between the situation in Russia in 1815 and the condition of the country in the reign of Catherine II: "Then things were different!" the minister wrote, "This expression may be explained only by stupidity, for otherwise it would be a crime, and a crime of the utmost gravity."[27] A few days later Razumovskii sent Uvarov a secret instruction, in which he spoke of the "absurd ideas and impudent comments concerning the present government of Russia" contained in the article and demanded that "special attention" be paid to the new journal.[28]

The intensity of the press campaign against *Spirit of the Journals* also increased. Another harshly critical article full of fulminations against it appeared in the September issue of *European Herald*. Its author, a certain Str-vich, declared that "the public would experience no loss if this journal were to cease to exist altogether." In support of his contention, he wrote: "The publishers have tried to distinguish themselves by employing a certain tone . . . that is entirely inappropriate for a Russian journal. . . . Its style wants elegance and refinement. . . . [2] The publishers are foreign to the spirit of belles-lettres."[29] Iatsenkov, apparently at the end of his tether, printed an article that stated his belief in the existence of a "conspiracy" against him.[30]

Nikolai Grech, the editor of *Son of the Fatherland*, thought the references to a "conspiracy" were aimed at him, and on October 30/November 11, 1815, publicly demanded that "evidence should be provided to support all this."[31] Aleksandr Izmailov published a spirited defense of the aforementioned article in *European Herald* and categorically denied the possibility of a plot against *Spirit of Journals* organized by the editors of the *Son of the Fatherland* and *Russian Invalid*.[32] *Spirit of Journals* was

26. *Spirit of Journals* 3 (1815), no. 16: 875–78.
27. Viazmitinov to Razumovskii, April 29/May 11, 1815, in *Proceedings*, vol. 3, 19.
28. Razumovskii to Uvarov, May 3/15, 1815, TsGIA, record group 777, inventory 1, list 181, 7. Because the censorship committee had failed to adopt the necessary measures concerning *Spirit of Journals,* Razumovskii wrote to Uvarov again, this time about an excerpt "from the writings of Bentham, entitled 'On the Suppression of Manufactories,' which the publisher prefaced with his own ideas." The education minister told Uvarov "that this warning would be the last one, and next time no leniency will be shown to the censors responsible, who will be dismissed from their positions." Razumovskii to Uvarov, July 1/13, 1815, in N. D[ubrovin], "K istorii russkoi tsenzury (1814–1820)" (Toward a History of Russian Censorship [1814–1820]), *Russkaia Starina* (Russian Antiquity) 12 (1900): 649.
29. *European Herald* 83, no. 18 (September 1815): 131–43.
30. *Spirit of Journals* 7 (1815), no. 42: 845.
31. *Son of the Fatherland* 25 (1815): 281–82 (correspondence with journals).
32. *European Herald* 84, no. 22 (1815): 142–48.

able to refrain from further bickering with its rivals. Even though the editors received a number of letters complaining about *Son of the Fatherland,* Iatsenkov refused to print them. Responding to one of these, he wrote, "The board of editors . . . wishing to refrain from provoking the animosity of other journalists, particularly those like the publisher of *Son of the Fatherland,* will not print this letter."[33]

Moreover, having begun to publish a *Review of Russian Journals* in 1816, Iatsenkov adopted an attitude to his colleagues that was fair and objective.

> *Son of the Fatherland* commenced publication at the end of 1812. In that year and the one that followed it contained much that was interesting, and was without a doubt the best of our journals. In subsequent years it changed so much that one could be led to suppose that it is being published by persons other than those whom the public quite rightly held in the highest esteem.[34]

Son of the Fatherland was founded during Napoleon's invasion of Russia as a historical and political review whose aim was to describe the struggle against the foreign invaders and the heroism of the people. For example, the first issue of the journal for 1812 included Aleksandr Kunitsyn's article, "An Epistle to the Russians," and Ivan Krylov's famous fables, "The Wolf in the Doghouse" and "The Chicken and the Crow." Beginning in 1814, the journal's character started to change, and it eventually became a largely literary publication. Iatsenkov, whose main interests were clearly political, may have disapproved of this.

Nevertheless, Iatsenkov, after carefully examining the first ten issues of *Son of the Fatherland* for 1816, spoke favorably of them: "We have read all the issues . . . that were published this year with pleasure, and we were able to find articles of interest in every one of them."[35] He was especially impressed by the works of Krylov that had appeared: "The fable 'The Monkey and the Glass' by Mr. Krylov, like all his fables, is beyond all praise," wrote Iatsenkov. He went on to say that "the words, he is *not made, but born,* apply to writers of fables as much as to poets in general."[36]

The irony with which Iatsenkov's review greeted the reprinting of the "sorrowful reminiscences" and expressions of "the most terrible remorse," which had been published in France in connection with the anniversary of the execution of King Louis XVI, says much about the journal's political orientation: "All these declarations are nothing but words learned by rote, a mere *comedy.* And that is why we do not wish to inflict upon the readers a repetition of this miserable *comedy.*"[37] [3]

Of special interest is the review of an article by American merchant Peter Dobell (*Son of the Fatherland,* 1816, no. 1), describing his journey through Kamchatka and Siberia. "We should be grateful to this distinguished foreign traveler for his ideas, which promise to benefit our country," wrote Iatsenkov, concluding that Siberia lacked "two

33. *Spirit of Journals* 9 (1816), no. 1: 29 (from the Publishers).
34. Ibid., 45 (published anonymously).
35. *Spirit of Journals* 10 (1816), no. 13: 631.
36. *Spirit of Journals* 9 (1816), no. 2: 94–95; no. 3: 135.
37. *Spirit of Journals* 10 (1816), no. 13: 647.

main resources, *population* and *capital*. Time, rather than force, will increase both of them. It appears that Mr. Dobell would like to see Russians settle in Kamchatka, so that they would be closer to Japan and the Philippine Islands. Let us allow time to bring about that which force alone cannot accomplish."[38]

Iatsenkov also spoke out against the tempting "advice" to dispatch an expedition against Japan for the purpose of making it "pay tribute to Russia and maintain commercial relations with her." Responding to a letter by Dobell published in *Son of the Fatherland* (1816, no. 3), he wrote:

> We know that the Russian government ... has no intention of conquering Japan, but would rather establish amicable relations with that country and trade with it. Should the Japanese have the smallest suspicion that we intend to conquer them, they will forever break off all intercourse with Russia, and then it would be much more difficult for the two countries to establish relations with each other.[39]

Iatsenkov combined the desire not to exacerbate his journal's relationship with other periodicals and even to find common ground with the most progressive among them (especially *Son of the Fatherland*) with a willingness to defend the principles for which *Spirit of Journals* stood as an organ that had the right to express its views on political matters. In an editorial statement that appeared in March 1816, Iatsenkov again stressed that "a true patriot is not someone who finds everything in his country admirable ... but one who, by discovering its shortcomings, shows how it may be further improved."[40]

The publisher of *Spirit of Journals* was particularly forceful and consistent in defending his views on the United States. As had been the case earlier, Iatsenkov used the theme of America (which he often described in an abstract and idealized way) as a convenient pretext for engaging in a veiled discussion of critical political and economic questions. Beginning early in 1816, *Spirit of Journals* resumed the serialization of "Letters from Philadelphia" (nos. 3, 6). These were followed by "Letters from Baltimore" (nos. 9, 10, 11), "Letters from a Certain German in North America" (no. 13), "Letters from Washington" (nos. 16, 18, 20), "The American Congress" (letters from Washington, nos. 29, 33, 34, 35), "A Description of North and South America" (no. 37), etc.

In "A Gallery of Famous Men," *Spirit of Journals* published eulogistic biographical sketches of Washington, Madison, and General Moreau. The article about Washington (presented as "a translation from the French, by V. K-ov of Tobolsk") emphasized the great American hero's lack of ambition and the manner in which he faithfully observed the laws of his country. "He accepted the reins of power only in order to secure the happiness of his country; and he gave up power, when he saw that it no longer needed his services.... The name of *Washington* shall forever remain the most celebrated in America."[41] The author of "Letter from Washington" also observed that "Washington,

---

38. *Spirit of Journals* 9 (1816), no. 2: 92.
39. *Spirit of Journals* 9 (1816), no. 4: 204.
40. *Spirit of Journals* 9 (1816), no. 9: 436.
41. *Spirit of Journals* 10 (1816), no. 42: 718.

Adams, Jefferson, and Madison are all men who are above praise and who shall forever be remembered with gratitude by Americans."[42] Particularly interesting was the open defense of the representative system of government.

> Such a system of government has the advantage that it naturally elevates the spirit and fills every citizen [with] a noble ambition that inspires patriotism. . . . All these decrees by the great founders of the constitution of the United American Provinces were the result of careful thought and careful planning, so that even today America sees in them the true palladium of its liberty.[43]

Never before had the pages of the censored Russian press contained so many detailed articles about the internal situation of the United States, their system of government, and their success in developing their commerce and industry.[44]

A special place among the materials published in *Spirit of Journals* in 1816 is occupied by the lengthy "Notes about Agriculture, Manufactories, and Trade in Russia" written by a "citizen of the United American Provinces," who, on the basis of the experience of the United States and the countries of Western Europe, sought to show that Russia had to develop its trade and industry and create its own merchant marine. "Neglect of manufactories and trade is frequently the cause of the people's decline, weakens and reduces it to primeval barbarism."[45] At the same time "American citizen" drew attention to the character of Russian agriculture and the low productivity of Russian farmers. He stressed the need for a transition to the cultivation and fertilizing of only the most productive and advantageously located plots. "When I was in Russia, I was frequently surprised to see endless fields of poor land, which had not been in any way fertilized, sown with corn [grain]. . . . , the corn grew to be so weak, sparse and stunted that it almost seemed not worth threshing." A reduction in the area under crops with a simultaneous improvement in cultivation and fertilizing would not only produce better harvests, but would also free "many persons, no longer needed for agriculture, who could be employed in the manufactories."[46]

Using his personal observations, the author exposed the tendentiousness and incompetence of Western travelers who had written about Russia. He spoke with great sympathy and warmth about the country and its people, their national traits and abilities. It is interesting that the toiling and oppressed masses did not escape the attention of "American citizen":

> One need only look carefully at the lowest class of the people to see that it possess a natural intelligence and understanding of which none of the nations of Europe can offer

---

42. *Spirit of Journals* 10 (1816), no. 20: 940.
43. *Spirit of Journals* 10 (1816), no. 18: 842, 848.
44. Many articles about America appeared also in the oldest Russian journal devoted to international affairs, published by professors of the University of Moscow: *Istoricheskii, statisticheskii i geograficheskii zhuranal, ili sovremennaia istoria sveta, 1790–1830* (Historical, Statistical and Geographical Journal, Or Modern History of the World, 1790–1830). Although Iatsenkov's periodical was to a certain extent devoted to the same subjects as this *Historical . . . Journal,* it was more radical and polemical in character.
45. *Spirit of Journals* 10 (1816), no. 21: 981.
46. Ibid., 1014–15.

superior examples. . . . I confess that I found them to be not barbarians, but, rather, a people capable of acquiring an excellent moral and civil education.[47]

The central idea of these "Notes" concerned the advantages of a close alliance between Russia and America, the strongest powers in the two hemispheres, who had the capacity to put an end to Great Britain's pernicious domination of the seas. As a "true friend of Russia," the author declared that the United States was

> without a doubt the most stable and best-organized of all states . . . [they] will probably become one of the strongest naval powers in the world. These considerations, together with the present interests of the two nations, should lead to the creation of an alliance between Russia and America, which would be based on close ties of friendship and concord . . . [4], so that together they might curb the dangerous ambition of the nation [Britain] that would like to hold undisputed sway over the seas that Providence intended for the free and equal use of the whole of mankind.[48]

The ideas developed by this "citizen of the United American Provinces" found some support, producing sympathetic reactions from several writers. For example, "A Russian's Opinion about the Notes by an American," in issues 21 and 22 of *Spirit of Journals,* offered detailed arguments in favor of the creation of a Russian merchant marine. The author had been a sailor and knew from experience the importance of sea navigation.

> Wishing to render justice to the views of the esteemed American, and having discerned the true reasons for the increase in the strength of the navies of the foreign powers, I venture to state positively that, until Russia is able to provide useful practical training for her sailors and naval officers by conducting sea trade on her own ships, her navy will be of no use to her.[49]

The writer devoted particular attention to the "natural situation of the Amur River," whose estuary was suitable for the construction of a seaport that would be "the greatest in the world," "the high road for Russia's trade with Asia and America."[50] This "Russian" concluded by expressing his sincere hope that the prophecy of the "esteemed American" would be realized as soon as possible, "and these two nations—America and Russia—would form a close alliance."[51]

The annual report of the publishers of *Spirit of Journals* for 1816 stated that the reading public had been "particularly impressed" by "Thoughts Concerning Trade and Manufactories" by "Mr. Straight-thinker," "Notes about Manufactories and Trade in Russia" by "the esteemed American citizen," "A Russian's Opinion about the Notes by an American," "On Russian Trade" by Mr. Arsen'ev,[52] among others. Iatsenkov

---

47. Ibid., 1026–27.
48. Ibid., 986–87.
49. *Spirit of Journals* 10 (1816), no. 23: 1115.
50. Ibid., 1109.
51. Ibid., 1116.
52. This was probably Konstantin Arsen'ev. The very fact of his collaboration with the journal is revealing. Arsen'ev's book, *Nachertanie statistiki Rossiiskogo gosudarstva* (An Outline of the

wrote that "it would seem that the main question—what is the benefit to be derived from free trade and a free industry?—has been irrefutably resolved. And soon, after the new tariff was introduced, we had the pleasure of seeing the triumph of the free system in practice."[53]

Judging by the publishers' report for 1816, articles specifically devoted to American themes had also met with the approval of the reading public. "Our readers will in particular recall the excellent 'Letters from Philadelphia, Baltimore and Washington,' that were read with the greatest pleasure by all those who consider highly the well-being of peoples," wrote Iatsenkov.[54]

But if all these articles provoked the interest and sympathy of the progressive circles of Russian society, the reaction of the tsarist authorities was very different, particularly since the political situation in the country continued to deteriorate. In August 1816 Alexander Golitsyn, the head of the Russian Bible Society and the former Chief Procurator of the Holy Synod, became minister of education. Soon after his appointment he sent a letter to Uvarov about the articles systematically being published in *Spirit of Journals*.

> Many of the political articles do not conform to the ideas of the Government. The letters from America, for example, contain remarks that are most improper, which compare the government there with other governments . . . [and] some of the poetry is suggestive. Moreover, the censor who examined and licensed some of the issues of this journal (34, 35) was Iatsenkov himself, who should not have been a judge of his own case.[55]

It is difficult to say which verses Golitsyn thought "suggestive," but as for "improper remarks" in the letters from America, the minister was able to find more than enough

---

Statistics of the Russian State), 2 vols. (St. Petersburg, 1818–1819), contained a bold attack on serfdom and despotism. Some time later he was dismissed from his position at the University of St. Petersburg and together with three of his colleagues was tried at the instigation of D[mitrii] P. Runich (see A. V. Predtechenskii, *Ocherki obshchestvenno-politicheskoi istorii Rossii v pervoi chetverti XIX veke* [Studies in the Sociopolitical History of Russia in the First Quarter of the Nineteenth Century] [Moscow-Leningrad, 1957], 338).

53. *Spirit of Journals* (1816), no. 52: 1183. For a detailed account of the vigorous campaign by *Spirit of Journals* against protectionism and its enormous success among the public, see Mikhail Tugan-Baranovskii, *Russkaia fabrika* (The Russian Factory), 6th ed. (Moscow-Leningrad, 1934), 214–19.

The tariffs of 1816 and especially 1819 amounted to a significant retreat from protectionism. It soon transpired, however, that Russian factories were unable to match foreign competition and were being forced to close. Contemporaries began to regard the tariff of 1819 as the second "destruction" of Russia after Napoleon's invasion. This led *Spirit of Journals* to change its position on the issue. See N. S. Kiniapina, *Politika russkogo samoderzhaviia v oblasti promyshlennosti (20–50-e gody XIX v.)* (Russian Autocratic Industrial Policy, 1820s to 1850s) (Moscow, 1968), 96–97; *Moskovskii telegraf* (Moscow Telegraph) 9 (1829): 47; William Blackwell, *The Beginnings of Russian Industrialization 1800–1860* (Princeton, 1968), 124, 172–73.

54. *Spirit of Journals* (1816), no. 52: 1186–87.

55. Golitsyn to Uvarov, September 6/18, 1816, TsGIA, record group 777, inventory 1, list 221, 4; *Russian Antiquity* 12 (1900): 651–52.

like them in the texts published in *Spirit of Journals*. Apparently Golitsyn deemed clearly "improper" any defense of the advantages of the representative, democratic form of government, freedom of the press, etc. The minister of education concluded his letter by demanding that "special attention be paid to this journal; its publisher should be advised to give his journal a different, more appropriate spirit." Otherwise, threatened Golitsyn, "the journal would be closed."[56]

In accordance with Golitsyn's instructions and Uvarov's letter, the St. Petersburg censorship committee confirmed its decision to forbid Iatsenkov to act as the censor of his own journal and issued a strongly worded decree that all the articles in it should be reviewed by Censor Timkovskii.[57] The committee "reprimanded" the publisher of *Spirit of Journals* for printing articles that the minister of education had found reprehensible, and decided "henceforth to subject this journal to the strictest supervision, lest it cause the displeasure of the higher authorities."[58]

Iatsenkov, however, acting in strict conformity with existing laws and the "Censorship Regulations" of 1804, which combined rules that were reactionary and conservative in spirit with vaguely liberal principles, tried to defend his right to publish critical articles.[59] In his "Report of the Society of Publishers for 1816" he wrote, "Here we cannot refrain from mentioning our gratitude to the magnanimous tolerance of our enlightened Government. The opinions we expressed may have differed from the opinions of some members of the Government but, having been stated with the required modesty, they were not only not suppressed, but indeed were in no way criticized by the Government."[60] Iatsenkov was clearly putting the best face on things. By doing this he probably hoped to be able to continue to defend critical views on the pages of his journal. [8]

Trying to recruit allies even among the members of the tsarist government, Iatsenkov referred to the official newspaper, *Severnaia Pochta* (Northern Post), published under the supervision of Osip Kozodavlev, Minister of Internal Affairs.[61] "We were particularly happy to read in *Northern Post* a strong defense of a judiciously practiced freedom of book-printing at the very time when we so freely and frankly had stated our views concerning the manufactories, the industry in our country, and the deficiencies in the postal system." Iatsenkov went on to express his "firm conviction" that the authorities would continue to extend "magnanimous tolerance to our

---

56. Ibid.

57. Uvarov to St. Petersburg Censorship Committee, August 30/September 11, 1816, TsGIA, record group 777, inventory 1, list 221, 1; decree of the committee of September 1/13, 1816, ibid., 2.

58. Decree of committee of September 16/28, 1816, ibid., 5.

59. *Sbornik postanovlennii i rasporiazhenii po tsenzure s 1720 po 1861 g.* (Collection of Decrees and Instructions Relating to Censorship Issued between 1720 and 1861) (St. Petersburg, 1862), 81–96; *Russian Antiquity* 7 (1901): 154.

60. *Spirit of Journals* (1816), no. 52: 1183–84.

61. According to Anatolii Predtechenskii, who studied Kozodavlev's views and economic policies, he belonged "to the group of liberal statesmen of the reign of Alexander I." The historian based his conclusion in part on the report of the society of publishers of *Spirit of Journals* for 1816. Predtechenskii, *Studies in the Sociopolitical History of Russia*, 326–27.

opinions concerning the various requirements and reforms of the political system inside the country, which we propose freely and frankly to describe in this publication, without, however, leaving the bounds of modesty and due respect for the Government."[62]

But Iatsenkov failed to circumvent the vigilance of the authorities. In February 1817, *Spirit of Journals* was strictly forbidden to print any articles discussing the actions of the government.[63] The St. Petersburg censorship committee watched the journal closely, lest it publish the kind of articles about America that had caused "governmental displeasure" in 1816. It is, therefore, not surprising that throughout 1817 and part of 1818 almost no materials concerning America were published.[64] Information about the revolutionary events in Spanish America also occupied only a modest place in the journal. Nevertheless, even under these conditions the publisher-in-chief could express satisfaction that his journal had provided a relatively detailed "picture of the revolutions in South America, which is now attracting the close attention of statesmen. While not concerning ourselves with daily news, which belongs in the realm of the newspapers, we fully described the most important acts that served as the foundation for the new system of government in those countries."[65]

In the summer of 1817 *Spirit of Journals* reported that the rich Spanish colonies "have almost all seceded and declared themselves independent," and that Spanish ships were being intercepted by privateers. The journal suggested that "Spain's struggle with the rebelling colonies is in vain."[66] In February 1818, in "The Most Recent Political News," the journal printed a detailed summary, with commentary, of President Monroe's annual Message to the Congress of December 2, 1817, and, what is particularly important, a long and appropriately annotated "Review of the Revolutions in Spain's American Possessions (from the Notes of a Direct Observer)."[67] The conclusion was a credit to his perspicacity:

> Among all the Spanish provinces in South America only the lower section of Peru still clearly continues to recognize the rule of Spain . . . for the reason that it is inhabited by a large number of landowners who own many slaves and, consequently, fear losing their property because of popular revolts and popular rule; for ownership of land is the best guarantee of the landowner's loyalty to the existing order of things.[68]

---

62. *Spirit of Journals* 16 (1816), no. 52: 1184–85, signed "Chief Publisher, State Councillor Ia—, St. Petersburg, 26 December 1816."
63. February 8–16/20–28, 1817, "Concerning the Strict Prohibition on the Publication in *Spirit of Journals* of Articles on the Actions of the Government and the Reprimand Issued to Censor G. M. Iatsenkov for Permitting the Publication of *O vinnom otkupe* (On the Wine Trade)," TsGIA, record group 777, inventory 1, list 243. Arsen'ev's article, "On the Wine Trade," which appeared in *Spirit of Journals* at the beginning of 1817, received a special mention in the annual report of the society of publishers. *Spirit of Journals* (1817), no. 52: 1218.
64. One exception was the informative section entitled "The United Provinces of America" in the "Review of the Political Events of 1816," *Spirit of Journals* 24 (1817), no. 51: 1093–1104.
65. *Spirit of Journals* 31 (1818), no. 52: 677–78.
66. *Spirit of Journals* 20 (1817), no. 26: 242–43, 246–47.
67. *Spirit of Journals* 26 (1818), no. 8: 245–70.
68. Ibid., 262.

Of course *Spirit of Journals* could only publish a few reports of this kind, but it is significant that even during this time the periodical was able to maintain its earlier orientation. Also, it is interesting that on occasion the journal continued to promote the advantages to be gained from the development of direct trade links with the United States. Thus, an account of "the foreign trade conducted through the port of St. Petersburg in 1817" included this important argument: "Let us congratulate our country on the prospects . . . of a most profitable trade which close links with Americans will enable it to conduct. This industrial nation brings us colonial goods from the source, which means that they are cheaper, and as it needs many of our own products, trade with it will be most profitable for Russia."[69]

A researcher analyzing the contents of *Spirit of Journals* faces the greatest difficulty when trying to interpret correctly its position on the peasant question. At the end of 1817 the journal published an article by a certain "Pravdin, a Russian Nobleman" (perhaps one of the "gentlemen of noble birth" whose support Iatsenkov sought),[70] who argued that "liberty" was an "empty" and "pernicious" word and that the Russian serfs were living "in clover."[71] Some time later another article by Pravdin appeared defending the corvée (1818, 25, no. 6). In response, *Son of the Fatherland* published an article by Kunitsyn, "On the Condition of Foreign Peasants," which was harshly—and justly— critical of this advocate of serfdom who, moreover, had used "a name inappropriate for him."[72] In its next issue the journal published another article by Kunitsyn, "On the Constitution," which subsequently became famous, as it contained a reference to Alexander I's speech at the opening of the Polish Seim in March 1818.[73] This scenario is often adduced as evidence of the conservative character of *Spirit of Journals* and, above all, of its openly reactionary and pro-serfdom position on the peasant question.[74]

[1] It is true that the journal printed the articles by Pravdin, but does this mean that Iatsenkov was in full agreement with the opinions of the "Russian nobleman"? Pravdin was just one of many authors whose articles were published in *Spirit of Journals*. Many that appeared, such as the article entitled "On the Wine Trade" (1817, no. 3) by Arsen'ev and the essay "On the Guardian Classes" (1819, no. 2), were entirely different in character. In 1818 alone the journal published a whole series on slavery and serfdom, among them: "On the Main Advantages Enjoyed by Peasants Performing the Corvée

---

69. *Spirit of Journals* 25 (1818), no. 4: 128.
70. Piatkovskii, *From the History of the Literary and Social Development of Our Country*, vol. 2, 203.
71. *Spirit of Journals* 24 (1817), no. 49: 981–1008.
72. *Son of the Fatherland* 17 (1818): 162–86.
73. *Son of the Fatherland* 18: 202–11.
74. I. G. Bliumin, *Ocherki ekonomicheskoi mysli v Rossii v pervoi polovine XIX veka* (Essays on Economic Thought in Russia in the First Half of the Nineteenth Century) (Moscow-Leningrad, 1940), 88–90, 106; *Istoriia russkoi ekonomicheskoi mysli* (History of Russian Economic Thought), vol. 1, pt. 2 (Moscow, 1958), 19, 27–28, 38–39; *Russkaia periodicheskaia pechat' (1702–1894)* (The Russian Periodical Press [1702–1894]), edited by A. G. Dement'ev, A. V. Zapadov, M. S. Cherepakhov (Moscow, 1959), 140–43, 149–51; *Istoriia russkoi zhurnalistiki, XVIII-XIX vv.* (History of Russian Journalism in the Eighteenth and Nineteenth Centuries), edited by A. V. Zapadov, 2d ed. (Moscow, 1966), 137; Boden, *Das Amerikabild im russischen Schrifttum bis zum Ende des 19. Jahrhunderts*, 76.

over Those on Quit-rent, an Essay by Mr. Pravdin"; "On the State Peasants"; "On Slavery in the Foreign Countries of Europe"; "On the Meaning of the Word 'Slave.' " [2] An objective evaluation of the journal's position can only be made if not just Pravdin's essays, but the sum of all these articles is considered.

Moreover, even the articles by Pravdin should not be seen in a wholly negative light; one must take into account the author's motives in writing and publishing them, and the circumstances in which they appeared. Historian Vasilii Semevskii pointed out that they contained an important idea "about the undesirability of emancipation without land."[75] Let us also note that Pravdin himself was in some cases unable to conceal the parlous condition of the Russian serfs, who were at the mercy of the uncontrolled tyranny of the landowners. Iatsenkov drew attention to this very fact: "When reading this, aware as one is of more than one such example, one is moved to exclaim, 'How terribly the poor peasants are oppressed . . . !' "[76] In response Pravdin wrote, "Your observations about the unjust actions of many of the landowners toward those of their peasants who owe the corvée are, unfortunately, valid not only in the case of the provinces of St. Petersburg and Novgorod, but also in the case of all the others, particularly those in Great Russia and White Russia."[77] It is interesting that even Pravdin, a supporter of serfdom, was forced to concede that the authority exercised by the landowners and their bailiffs over the peasants should be somewhat restricted. [3] However, he also stipulated that "this would require the greatest prudence, lest grave difficulties ensue," and suggested that the "intelligent" and "humane" governors be entrusted with supervising the landowners' conduct.[78]

Partial reforms aimed at improving the condition of the peasants were proposed by many other writers. A certain B., author of "On the State Peasants," discussed the causes of "the increasing poverty of the people" and suggested ways of "reducing that poverty." B. proposed that special officials whose task would be "to defend the peasants during lawsuits and in court cases, as well as during army recruitment" be appointed in every province.[79] And Iatsenkov added that the government was aware of "the improvement that will take place in the condition of the state-owned peasants when they are given their own local protectors." He voiced the hope that "the time will soon come when this useful and urgently needed institution will be newly established."[80]

The journal's position on the peasant question is best characterized by Iatsenkov's own editorial comments and insertions. When the author of one article spoke of the necessity for landowners to supervise "their country farms" personally, the publisher added a most revealing parenthetical comment that amounted to an almost open attack on serfdom: "Here the author should have inquired whether our landowners are actually capable of supervising agriculture. Do they possess the necessary knowledge? Are they

75. V. I. Semevskii, *Krest'ianskii vopros v Rossii v XVIII i pervoi polovina XIX v.* (The Peasant Question in Russia in the Eighteenth and First Half of the Nineteenth Centuries), 2 vols. (St. Petersburg, 1888), vol. 1, 400.
76. *Spirit of Journals* 25 (1818), no. 6: 188.
77. Ibid., 184.
78. Ibid., 192.
79. *Spirit of Journals* 26 (1818), no. 10: 341.
80. Ibid., 342.

trying to acquire it? Do they bring up their children to be good managers? Otherwise their personal superintendence would do no good."[81] In another comment about the same article Iatsenkov directly linked the bread shortage in Russia to the government's "restrictive measures."[82]

Subject as it was to strict censorship, *Spirit of Journals* was not in a position to propose radical reforms. But even the most discreet and seemingly innocuous references to the peasants' difficult lot and to the need for reforms that would improve it angered the authorities. In a letter to Uvarov of May 25/June 5, 1818, Golitsyn wrote, "I have noticed . . . that the publisher of *Spirit of Journals* prints articles that discuss the liberty and slavery of peasants, the actions of the Government, and much else that is improper." He went on to draw Uvarov's attention to issue 20 for 1818 and to an article "concerning which there had earlier . . . been issued a general instruction to the censors that it should not be published."[83]

Golitsyn was referring to Prince Nikolai Repnin's speech at the opening of the assemblies of the nobility in Poltava and Chernigov in January 1818, in which he gave his audience the unexceptional advice to look for ways of ensuring the peasants' well-being by "defining their obligations," yet without severing the "beneficial link" between landowners and serfs. Repnin had suggested that they should somewhat moderate their appetites and refrain from "attempting to extract from the peasant everything he is capable of giving you" in favor of receiving from him "that which you may demand from him without affecting his well-being."[84]

Golitsyn "required" the administrator of the St. Petersburg District of Education

> to draw the censors' attention to the journals and other books being published in order to make sure that they do not advance any arguments either in the defense of, or against, the liberty or slavery of peasants, whether Russian or foreign, or in general discuss any matters pertaining to the decisions of the Government, as was done in the article "On Deeds of Purchase for Houses in District Towns," of the same 20th issue of *The Spirit of Journals,* in which improper references were also to be found in "On Audiences for the Entire People" in "Miscellany."[85]

In addition, Uvarov was instructed to demand appropriate explanations from the publisher and the owner of the press where the periodical had been printed.[86]

---

81. *Spirit of Journals* 12 (1816), no. 22: 1080.

82. Ibid., 1074. Many years later Iatsenkov published, "at the expense of" the Free Economic Society, a special brochure in which he harshly criticized the backwardness of farming in Russia (Iatsenkov, *Na kakoi stepeni nakhoditsia semledelie v Rossii* [What Is the Level of Agriculture in Russia?]) (St. Petersburg, 1841).

83. Golitsyn to Uvarov, May 24/June 5, 1818, TsGIA, record group 777, inventory 1, list 266, 2; *Russian Antiquity* 12 (1900): 655.

84. *Spirit of Journals* 27 (1818), no. 20: 599–600; Semevskii, *Peasant Question,* vol. 1, 404–6.

85. The reference was to a letter to the chief publisher, in which measures to facilitate the sale of houses to peasants were proposed, and to a short piece about the people's right to public audiences with, and free access to, the emperor (*Spirit of Journals* 27 [1818], no. 20: 603–6, 619–22).

86. Golitsyn to Uvarov, May 24/June 5, 1818, TsGIA, record group 777, inventory 1, list 266, 2–3; *Russian Antiquity* 12 (1900): 656.

Golitsyn's letter to Uvarov was chiefly prompted, however, by the appearance in issue 12 of *Spirit of Journals* of a long article, "On Slavery in the Foreign Countries of Europe," written in the form of a reply to a question addressed to the editor and ostensibly meant to demonstrate the superiority of serfdom as compared with full slavery. [1] "I read in the foreign newspapers that some German rulers are abolishing slavery in their states. I had thought that slavery only existed in our country."[87] The reply of Iatsenkov was cunningly worded: "The condition of serfdom of our peasants, as defined on the basis of our laws, does not amount to slavery (and the abuse of power is not lawful)."[88]

Note the curious phrase in the parentheses! In the light of the numerous "abuses" uncovered on the pages of the journal, it had a particularly resonant ring. The publisher went on to argue strongly against the "misconception" that "slavery supposedly exists only in Russia, whereas the whole of Europe is free of it." "How long ago was slavery abolished there, and was it abolished everywhere?" asked Iatsenkov, and answered, "In the Polish provinces of Austria, as well as in Hungary, peasant serfdom remains in full force.... In Mecklenburg the government not only has no thought of abolishing slavery but actually forbids discussion of it."[89]

And most important, *Spirit of Journals* openly hailed the abolition of serfdom in a number of German states, for example Württemberg.[90] Iatsenkov concluded with an indignant denunciation of the shameful institution of slavery in the United States and cited American newspaper advertisements that were amazing in their cruelty and cynicism. "Sir, have you ever heard of serfs—not criminals or convicts—being *branded* with a hot iron in Russia, just for the purpose of identification? Or of our Government selling *a free man into slavery* (even if he were a vagrant) to cover the cost of his imprisonment? Yet this is done in *free* America!" exclaimed Iatsenkov. "The laws of the United American Provinces relating to slaves may be the most inhumane that have ever existed."[91]

A nominal argument in support of the superiority of "the institution of serfdom" in Russia in effect took on an opposite meaning, becoming a passionate indictment of slavery and serfdom throughout the world, including the United States. It is, therefore, not surprising that the tsarist authorities were quick to find evidence of dangerous sedition and "many other improprieties" in *Spirit of Journals*. In order to make sure that such articles would never again appear, Golitsyn prudently ordered a ban on the publication of any articles "either in defense of, or against, the liberty or slavery of peasants, whether local or foreign."

In addition, the "minister of religious affairs and popular education" demanded that the publisher of *Spirit of Journals* and the owner of the printing house explain their actions. As a "loyal subject," Karl Krai did not hesitate to promise solemnly never to allow his press to print anything "without the approval of the appropriate censorship."[92]

---

87. *Spirit of Journals* 26 (1818), no. 12: 359.
88. Ibid.
89. Ibid., 361–63.
90. Ibid., 368.
91. Ibid., 374.
92. See "Statement by Karl Krai, Printing-press Owner," June 11/23, 1818, TsGIA, record group 777, inventory 1, list 266, 10.

Iatsenkov's "explanation" testifies not only to the publisher's courage but also to his outstanding diplomatic skills. Citing the articles of Pravdin and other writings, he strongly denied the existence of a "corpus delicti" and even insisted that his journal was only trying "to defend the order of things that now exists in law." As for "On Slavery in Foreign Countries," Iatsenkov stated that

> it largely concerns foreigners, and relates to Russians only because it offers a comparison, and also because it is not an original piece, but a translation from foreign journals,[93] and therefore had been already read both abroad and in our country long before it was published in *Spirit of Journals*. . . . Indeed, when in the 19th number of *Son of the Fatherland* an article about foreign peasants was published in refutation of *Spirit of Journals*, the Government found nothing reprehensible in a scholarly polemic on this subject.[94] [8]

Iatsenkov was particularly persistent in defense of the journal's right to discuss the policies of the government, citing the relevant article of the "censorship regulations which have been approved by His Imperial Majesty," as well as *Severnaia Pochta* (Northern Post), an official newspaper. "The repeated statements about the benefits the Government itself derives from unrestricted book-printing, which may be read in *Northern Post* . . . made it clear that this policy, the responsibility for which is borne by a well-constituted censorship, had not changed."[95]

We can begin to understand not only the nature of the views and activities of Iatsenkov as a liberal, a reformer, and a believer in constitutional government, but also the objective factors that enabled him to publish his political journal for almost six years. Until the early 1820s the Russian government displayed not only an open preference for reactionary solutions but also some vaguely liberal tendencies. Historians have written about the "duality" of Alexander I, a tsar who was both a liberal reformer and an extreme reactionary. Fedor Martens observed,

> In Russia the tsar was a convinced autocrat; in Poland, a defender of the constitutional system of government; in Germany, Austria, Italy, and Spain he was a bulwark of the principles of unrestricted royal authority and absolute government; finally, in France he was among the most enthusiastic supporters of the constitutional system and a resolute enemy of absolutism.[96]

Alexander I no longer intended to carry out the far-reaching program of reforms that he and his advisers had drawn up in the first years of his reign. Yet even after 1815 the tsar did not exclude the possibility that circumstances might lead him to return to his

---

93. The article's contents clearly indicate that this was an original piece, although the facts it documented had been taken from foreign sources.

94. Iatsenkov to the St. Petersburg censorship committee, "-June 1818," original bearing the office inscription "7 June 1818," TsGIA, record group 777, inventory 1, list 266, 5; *Russian Antiquity* 12 (1900): 657–58.

95. For the full text of Iatsenkov's "statement," see TsGIA, record group 777, inventory 1, list 266, 4–5; *Russian Antiquity* 12 (1900): 657–58.

96. Quoted in S. B. Okun, *Ocherki istorii SSSR* (Essays on the History of the U.S.S.R.) (Leningrad, 1956), 303.

earlier "liberalism." In utmost secrecy Nikolai Novosiltsev was working on a Legal Charter, a document that would be Russia's constitution. "In March 1818, at a time when all progressive thought was mercilessly persecuted in Russia, when the censors had even forbidden the use of the word 'constitution,' at the opening of the Polish Seim Alexander continued to proclaim his attachment to constitutional forms of government and hinted at the possibility of introducing them in Russia," wrote Semen Okun.[97]

It is not surprising that in these circumstances the publisher of *Spirit of Journals* pinned his hopes on the "beneficent" intentions of the government and, first of all, of the emperor. He was happy to print "The Speech Given by His Imperial Majesty at the Opening of the Seim of the Kingdom of Poland" of March 15/27, 1818 (no. 14, 423–30), as well as "The State Code of the Kingdom of Bavaria." "The year 1818 will forever remain in the annals of Bavaria," wrote Iatsenkov, "for on 27 May of that year the Bavarians received from their King a State Code (constitution) founded on the principles of lawful political and civil liberty. This act is of such importance that we feel it necessary to communicate it to our readers in full."[98]

Finally, in the beginning of 1819 the editors of *Spirit of Journals* published an appeal addressed directly to Alexander I. Its form was unusual. The first article in the issue, "The Genius of the Nineteenth Century" extolled the actions of the Russian tsar.[99] Next came a piece by Iatsenkov, "What Does the Spirit of the Age Demand? What Do the Peoples Require?" that contained proposals for an extensive program of liberal and constitutional reforms. *Spirit of the Age,* the author declared, "is the general voice of the people, which is not always heard, but which an observant mind perceives quite clearly. . . . The peoples wish for the *rule* of law!—for laws that are fundamental, immutable, and define the rights and duties of everyone; laws that are equally binding on the government and on the governed; laws that would make autocracy impossible."[100] He added that people expected "the throne" to promulgate such laws, and mentioned France in this connection: "The kings themselves understood the importance of placing the *rule of law* on an unshakable foundation," and therefore granted a "government code of laws," that is, a constitution. But to guarantee this *code of laws,* "popular representatives" are necessary. "They are the faithful guardians of its sanctity, they persecute its violators, advise the King, and participate with him in promulgating legislation. . . . Through them the people have their own voice, which then is truly a *vox dei.*"[101]

A. V. Predtechenskii, a scholar with a uniquely profound knowledge of the reign of Alexander I, ascribed particular significance to the year 1818. "That memorable year" saw the appearance of several important articles by Kunitsyn, as well as the publication of the treatises "An Outline of the Statistics of the Russian State" by Arsen'ev and "An Attempt at a Theory of Taxes" by Nikolai Turgenev. "The first issue of *Spirit of Journals* for 1819 included 'Spirit of the Age,' which received wide publicity.

97. Ibid., 305.
98. *Spirit of Journals* 31 (1818), no. 50: 525; text of constitution, 525–72.
99. *Spirit of Journals* 32 (1819), no. 1: 8.
100. Ibid., 10, 13.
101. Ibid., 15–16.

The article spoke in clear and firm tones about the superiority of the parliamentary system over absolutism. . . . All these events," concluded the author, "could happen only because of the manifest indulgence of the censors or because of the equally manifest support of the tsar."[102]

The hopes inspired by the "august peacemaker" were not realized. Neither in 1819, nor later, did he grant the Russian people a constitution. The journal's position grew even more precarious. In February 1819 Golitsyn sent Uvarov an angry letter in connection with the article "On the Guardian Classes" (1819, no. 2), which argued that civil institutions in Russia served the interests of only those persons "whom fate has already favored. . . . The wealthy shall have and shall wax richer, and the poor shall be deprived." The minister declared that "these statements are impermissible" and threatened that if the publisher had the temerity to discuss the government's actions again, "this journal will be closed."[103]

To Iatsenkov's credit, even in these difficult conditions he did not abandon the struggle and continued to speak out about the need for constitutional reforms, the freedom of the press, etc. Because it had become impossible to discuss the situation in Russia openly, however, the publisher now began increasingly to turn to his favorite American themes. In March 1819 a description of the Philadelphia city jail was published in *Spirit of Journals*. The article noted that the declaration of independence in the Pennsylvania constitution was followed by a promise "to examine and amend criminal laws, abolish cruel and painful punishments, and introduce in their stead statutes that are as humane and as lenient as possible."[104] Iatsenkov promised to provide his readers with a detailed explanation of "the advantages of public legal procedure over one that is secret, the superiority of jurymen" in one of the next year's issues and to give examples of actual court cases.[105]

A speech "by the former President of the United States of America concerning the improvement of agriculture" was published in the two May issues of 1819. Iatsenkov wrote that "the importance of the subject . . . as well as the fame of the speaker" made this speech worthy "of special public attention in our country."[106] The most important article on an American topic to appear in the journal in 1819, however, was one entitled "Picture of America (from a Journey by Mr. Fearon to that Country in 1817 and 1818)."[107] The author had gone to North America at the request of a group of English families who planned to settle there.

"Of all the accounts of that fascinating country," wrote Iatsenkov in his introduction, "Mr. Fearon's treatise appears to us to be the most objective and reliable. As the attention of the enlightened public is now in large measure drawn to that blessed land, we shall

---

102. Predtechenskii, *Studies in the Sociopolitical History of Russia*, 378.

103. Golitsyn to Uvarov, February 3/15, 1819, *Proceedings*, vol. 3, 23–24; *Russian Antiquity* 7 (1901): 158–59.

104. See "The Philadelphia Town Jail," in Lt. Francis Hall, *Travels in Canada and the United States in 1816 and 1817* (London, 1818); *Spirit of Journals* 33 (1819), no. 5: 239–40.

105. *Spirit of Journals* 37 (1819), no. 24: 527–28.

106. *Spirit of Journals* 34 (1819), no. 9: 442.

107. The book was Henry Bradshaw Fearon, *Sketches of America: A Narrative of a Journey of Five Thousand Miles Through the Eastern and Western States of America* (London, 1818).

excerpt from Mr. Fearon's letters the most interesting articles about the character and way of life of the Americans and the institutions they have created to serve the public good."[108] "This enlightened traveler," wrote Iatsenkov, "looked at everything with an observant eye and presented the current condition of America in an accurate light, showing all her achievements, yet without concealing her shortcomings."[109]

"Picture of America" was serialized in the summer of 1819 in three numbers of *Spirit of Journals* (13: 23–38; 15: 127–34; 16: 143–58). Today not all of Fearon's conclusions appear valid, for the English traveler displayed a certain bias against the former British colony. His statement, "Politically they are a great people; but science and enlightenment are quite alien to them,"[110] seems too categorical. Yet it is impossible to deny the justice of his harshly critical comments about the cruel treatment of blacks and Indians, as well as the pernicious effect of slavery on the whole of American society:

> The slavery that exists in the United Provinces has the most unfortunate consequences for their inhabitants. It dulls the mind, stifles the sense of justice and humanity, and severs the link between theory and practice.... However much some writers, particularly Mr. Monroe, philosophize about the advantages of supplanting the hordes of savages with an enlightened people, there can be no doubt that despite the peace treaties they sign, the Americans, by waging war and committing various other depredations, are forcing the native inhabitants to retreat more and more and are taking away their land.[111]

In the series of articles on American themes that appeared in *Spirit of Journals,* a special place is occupied by an essay entitled "About Russia's American Colonies," reprinted from an 1818 issue of the respected Boston journal *North American Review.* "Our American Company," wrote Iatsenkov,

> may have its reasons for preventing the public from learning about the conditions of these territories, the success of the local enterprises and of local trade, the socially useful institutions that have been established there, and other matters, but the public, which is interested in everything that pertains to Russia, has its own reasons for wishing to learn more about this subject.[112]

On the whole the article gave a reasonably objective picture of the state of the Russian colonies in America, their economies, and relations with the United States and China. Everything indicates that the Russians have "a far-reaching goal," the article stated.

> In many of the colonies forts have been erected, and these have been provided with guns and the requisite artillery munitions, armories have been constructed, spare powder

---

108. *Spirit of Journals* 35 (1819), no. 13: 24.
109. *Spirit of Journals* 37 (1819), no. 24: 532–33.
110. *Spirit of Journals* 35 (1819), no. 15: 134.
111. *Spirit of Journals* 35 (1819), no. 16: 156–57.
112. *Spirit of Journals* 37 (1819), no. 23: 492.

stores, hospitals, schools, courthouses, etc. built—in a word, what is being created there is the nucleus of a state, a state which will eventually grow and spread. Mr. Baranov governs these colonies in a most sensible manner, particularly with regard to the interests of the Company; in recent years the shareholders' profit amounted to 15% per share.[113]

The overall conclusion reached by this journal is interesting:

> The English and the Americans cast a covetous eye on the great achievements of the Russians in that country, and since with every year fur-bearing animals are becoming rarer, while the demand for furs in Canton increases, it is not difficult to foresee that soon the proximity in which the three different nations—Russians, Americans, and English—find themselves will engender competition and open enmity; then force will decide who will control this important trade.[114]

The enormous amount of journalistic work carried out by the editors of *Spirit of Journals* in the first five years of its existence represented, in a sense, merely a prologue to the key events of 1820. The fate of the journal was inseparably linked to the general political development of Russia and, partly, to that of Europe as a whole. Iatsenkov was aware of this, for in his report for 1819 he wrote: "The struggle between liberty, and absolutism and despotism has begun. The coming year of 1820 is fraught with important changes, which must decide the destiny of our children."[115]

The entire thrust of Iatsenkov's activities until then clearly showed where his true sympathies lay. Of course, he was not a revolutionary, a second Radishchev, but he was an honest, intelligent journalist, a consistent advocate of a constitutional system of government, and a fighter for the freedom of "book-printing" and for bourgeois-liberal reforms that were progressive for the time. In the beginning of 1820 the die was finally cast—*Spirit of Journals* openly and defiantly raised the question of a constitution. And the periodical not only raised it, but indeed was the first to publish in Russian a full account of the republican constitution and system of government in the United States of America.

In his report for 1819 Iatsenkov informed his readers that he had received a foreign journal, *Picture of America.* "This new journal is in some ways a 'Spirit of the American Journals,' " wrote Iatsenkov. "We have decided to use this felicitous idea and, starting next year, to compose a special collection of interesting reports from that country bearing the title 'Picture of America.' "[116] In the foreword to "Picture of America" in the first issue of 1820, he declared enthusiastically, "When one wishes to name a country where the people enjoy all the fruits of a wise and freedom-loving government founded on immutable laws, one names North America!" A proponent of liberal reforms and constitutions, the publisher drew his readers' attention to the fact that North America

---

113. Ibid., 487.
114. Ibid., 491–92.
115. *Spirit of Journals* 37 (1819), no. 24: 527.
116. Ibid., 533.

was flourishing "under the aegis of the rule of law."[117] The keen enthusiasm for the system of government and political life of the United States expressed by *Spirit of Journals* may strike the modern reader as naive and idyllic. Indeed, the journal showed America in a romantic light, depicting it more as an ideal to be admired than as a real country. One must bear in mind, however, the time when these articles appeared, the situation then prevailing in Imperial Russia, and the views of the publisher. It is easy to understand how in a country suffering under the yoke of the autocracy, the tyranny of the censors, and the outrages inflicted by Alexander's reactionary favorite Arakcheev, the republican constitution and bourgeois-democratic freedoms of the United States could seem ideal.

The publisher intended his "'Picture of America, Drawn from the Original,'[118] That Is from Her Own Sources" to provide a detailed and comprehensive description of the United States—their territory, population, system of government, constitution, economic and political state, army, navy, social life, etc. In the foreword, Iatsenkov sketched out the general form the articles would take.

> [They] will be published in serial form throughout this year, and perhaps later. . . . All these materials are ready; they will be conjoined with the "Newest Political Events in North and South America," and we hope that such a varied picture of that part of the world will be of interest to every one of our readers.[119]

The first issue of *Spirit of Journals* for 1820 included a curious "historiographical" introduction that offered a critical analysis of earlier accounts of life in America.[120]

> The learned English critics, having gone up in arms against our country and its constitution, tell us Americans things that are akin to slumberous reveries; but simple-hearted foreigners take them to be the literal truth. Other writers, on the contrary, describe our country as a paradise, and its inhabitants as angels. Reading their accounts, one might think that America is the Promised Land, flowing with milk and honey, where the air is full of aromatic fragrance and eternal spring scatters flowers with a generous hand. . . . This is the resplendent picture of America painted by Gilbert Imlay and St. Jean de Crèvecoeur. . . . [121] Necromancers like Parkinson,[122] Ashe,[123] Janson,[124] and their friends say something entirely different. According to them, America is an accursed, savage and barren land. . . . The government is weak, autocratic and corrupt; the people are the dregs of Europe.

---

117. *Spirit of Journals* 38 (1820), no. 1: 3.
118. The title of the journal published by the Society of Learned Men in Germany and the source of materials printed in *Spirit of Journals*.
119. *Spirit of Journals* 38 (1820), no. 1: 4.
120. Ibid., 9–13.
121. M. G. St. Jean de Crèvecoeur, *Letters from an American Farmer (1770–1781)* (London, 1782). In subsequent years this book appeared in numerous editions and remains in print.
122. Richard Parkinson, *Tour in America* (London, 1805, rev. and extended, 1807).
123. Thomas Ashe, *Travels in America Performed in 1806* (London, 1808).
124. Charles W. Janson, *The Stranger in America* (London, 1807).

The introduction recommended "Volney's Essays on the Soil of the Land and the Climate of the United States,[125] Schultz's Travels," and also the travel writings of Melitt [sic],[126] Bradbury,[127] and Birkbeck.[128]

Clearly, the authors of "Picture of America" were fervent admirers of the United States. "There is no doubt," the foreword declared, "that the Republic of the United Provinces of North America will soon be numbered among the greatest and most powerful countries in the world. . . . This vast country is inhabited by people who are free as air, a people who are strong, industrious, enterprising, temperate, brave, and endowed with all the qualities of body and spirit necessary to make a nation happy and great."[129] They described the situation of the working people in America in glowing terms. "Day laborers receive twice as much as in England and four times as much as in France. Arable but as yet uncultivated land may be bought most cheaply, for between $2 and $5 an acre."[130]

However, the most important feature of the series was not all these extravagantly enthusiastic statements, but a documented description of the new political system in the form of five letters from Philadelphia, entitled "The Constitution of the United Provinces of North America."[131] To protect himself and avoid drawing attention of censors, Iatsenkov stated in a special note that the American Constitution was described

> such as it is, without being in any way judged and without being contrasted with those of other countries. It is obvious that a republican constitution would be different from the constitution of a monarchy, and a system of government that is most suitable for one people may be quite inappropriate for another. This proviso should be sufficient to prevent any misunderstanding.[132]

Yet it is doubtful that such a "note" could have misled the authorities, for the basic principles of the Constitution of the American Republic had too radical and revolutionary a ring in the conditions of autocratic Russia. "Government should be founded on a social contract, with the consent of the governed. . . . The people are the fount of all laws and institutions, which must be adopted and approved by them. . . . The powers—legislative, executive, and judicial—depend on the will of the citizens that are governed by them, or on that of their representatives. The people are the source of all power in the state."[133] In a summary of the Constitution, particular attention was

---

125. C. F. C., comte de Volney, *Tableau du climat et du sol des Etats-Unis,* 2 vols. (Paris, 1803).
126. This seems to be a reference to the travel writings of cartographer John Melish, *Travels in the United States* [1806–1807; 1809–1811], 2 vols. (Philadelphia, 1812).
127. John Bradbury, *Travels in the Interior of America* (Liverpool, 1817).
128. Morris Birkbeck, *Notes on a Journey in America, from Virginia to Illinois* (Philadelphia, 1817); and *Letters from Illinois* (Philadelphia, 1818).
129. *Spirit of Journals* 38 (1820), no. 1: 15–16.
130. Ibid., 20–21.
131. *Spirit of Journals* 38 (1820), no. 2: 73–88; no. 3: 97–116; no. 4: 157–64, signature (161) reads "T.S."
132. *Spirit of Journals* 38 (1820), no. 2: 73.
133. Ibid., 75–77.

paid to the "rights and liberties of the people," such as "the equality of all before the law," the officials' answerability and subordination to the people, the public character of legal procedure, "freedom of religion," "freedom of opinion," etc. When explaining the principle of the responsibility of government officials, the author noted that "any official may be accused of violating his office, tried, and punished according to the law."[134]

After describing the contents of the American constitution, *Spirit of Journals* implemented the next part of its program, publishing several articles full of praise for the United States: "On the Internal Industry of the United Provinces of North America" (40, no. 7: 287–302), "The Mores, Customs, Way of Life, and National Character of the North Americans" (41, no. 10: 355–76), "On the Banks and the Balance of Trade of the United Provinces of North America" (41, no. 12: 497–508). A short essay, "The City of New Orleans," also appeared in this last issue. Within the context of an autocratic state where the institution of serfdom continued to exist, these materials acquired a special meaning, and sometimes even had a revolutionary tone. "The United Provinces of America know no distinctions based on rank and title; here there are no orders, nor ranks outside government service; the people's representatives, governors, and the president hold their positions for only a short time, after which everyone reverts to the condition of an ordinary citizen."[135] The reader was further informed that numerous newspapers and journals were published in America, and that complete freedom of the press existed in that country. Special attention was drawn to the wide prevalence in America of the "mercantile spirit"—the desire for profit and rapid enrichment.

In order to provide balance to "Picture of America," in the summer of 1820 Iatsenkov published the "Notes of a Traveler about the United States of North America." In his commentaries to this travelogue he wrote: "Until this time almost everything written about North America has been filled with such extraordinary praise that the skeptical reader could not but doubt its justice.... We do not presume to decide which picture is closer to the truth, but in order to avoid being accused of bias, we submit a contrary description to the judgement of the public."[136] When printing the critical statements by a German traveler about the factories and commerce of the United States, Iatsenkov made, however, a point of observing that "this author is himself guilty of the same bias for which he condemns others."[137]

It is difficult to say whether Iatsenkov foresaw all the consequences of his decision to publish articles on American themes in *Spirit of Journals*. Yet having begun in January 1820 the publication of "Picture of America," he continued to pursue his goal with extraordinary consistency and determination, and did not change his plans even after being dismissed from his position as censor.[138]

In the autumn of 1820, he published another important document, "The Calendar of Government of the United States of America for 1819," which contained an exhaustive

---

134. *Spirit of Journals* 38 (1820), no. 3: 112.
135. *Spirit of Journals* 41 (1820), no. 9: 355.
136. *Spirit of Journals* 42 (1820), no. 14: 65.
137. Ibid., 69.
138. See documents relating to the dismissal of Censor Iatsenkov, April 10–June 20, 1820, TsGIA, record group 777, inventory 1, list 340.

yet clear and concise description of the political system and the general structure of the executive, legislative, and judicial branches of power in America.[139] The same issue included an article about the composition and activities of the U.S. Navy,[140] "Low Prices in North America,"[141] and a satirical story ("No Work, No Bread") about a young "sponger" who, after receiving a "fashionable education" in Europe, fails to find a job in the United States.[142] The issue was filled exclusively with materials about America.

This was too much for the tsarist authorities. The patience of "the minister of spiritual affairs and popular education" was exhausted, and he decided to adopt the extreme measure of closing *Spirit of Journals,* thereby putting an end to any further polemics about the superiority of the constitutional system of government. Writing to Uvarov in October 1820, Golitsyn discussed at length its systematic violations of the censorship regulations, its criticism of the government's policies, and, finally, its open defense of the republican and constitutional form of government.[143]

> I have always noticed ideas and arguments that were impermissible and contrary to the censorship regulations in . . . *Spirit of Journals.* In the past the publisher allowed himself to argue against the decrees concerning the subject of manufactories, which were issued by the ministry of internal affairs at a time when the import into Russia of foreign manufactured articles was prohibited; later, when after the introduction of the new tariff their free import was allowed, this journal dared to criticize that measure as well; one can therefore conclude with certainty that the publisher, driven solely by a desire to revile the Government in everything it does, is attempting to convince the readers that all its decisions, whatever they are, are rash and contrary to the general good. This journal has violated the provisions of the Regulations and even the rules of propriety. [10]

After this lengthy and threatening preamble, the minister stated the main charge against the publisher.

> Finally, numbers 17 and 18 of this journal again clearly criticized the monarchical system of government in a way that made it abundantly clear that this publication was committed to acting against the interests and aims of the Government, which would not be allowed or tolerated in any country.
> Taken together, all these considerations lead me to request Your Excellency to issue the appropriate instructions to the censorship committee that from the beginning of the coming year of 1821 this journal should be discontinued.

---

139. *Spirit of Journals* 42 (1820), no. 18: 175–87.
140. Ibid., 188–202.
141. Ibid., 203–5.
142. Ibid., 205–6.
143. Golitsyn to Uvarov, October 6/18, 1820, TsGIA, record group 777, inventory 1, list 328, 5–6; *Russian Antiquity* 12 (1900): 663–64. [5] When publishing in 1871 an excerpt from Golitsyn's letter, Shchebalskii was unable to determine "precisely to which articles" the minister referred in his comments (*Procedings,* vol. 3, 24), while Piatkovskii mistakenly linked the banning of the journal with the publication of "On the Guardian Classes" (Piatkovskii, *From the History of the Literary and Social Development of Our Country,* vol. 2, 205).

An examination of the materials published in these issues shows that the noble prince had reason to be angry. As noted above, the whole of number 18 was devoted to American subjects. As for 17, it contained a panegyrical biography of Charles Fox, the brilliant orator and leader of the Whig opposition. In particular, the author quoted Fox's passionate speeches condemning King George III and the conservative government of Lord North. Fox described this reign as "an unending chain of unprecedented disasters and misfortunes," comparing it to that of Charles I, who was overthrown by a victorious revolution in the middle of the seventeenth century. "In general all the speeches he made in the lower house during the American war exuded a revolutionary spirit. . . . The King regarded him as an instigator of the rebellion, and the more he respected his talents, the more he felt himself insulted."[144]

As was to be expected, Uvarov hastened to obey the "request" of the minister of education, and forwarded a copy of Golitsyn's letter to the censorship committee "for faithful execution and observation."[145] It had earlier received Golitsyn's letter of October 1/13, 1820, which referred to certain pages of the journal that had particularly angered him. On October 4/16, 1820, the acting administrator of the St. Petersburg district of education informed the committee that "the minister of religious affairs and popular education states in his circular of 1 October of this year that pages 187 and 188 in number 17 and number 18 of *Spirit of Journals* contain ideas and expressions that are clearly directed against monarchical governments, which is a clear violation of the censorship regulations."[146]

Golitsyn's reference to specific pages leaves no doubt as to the real reasons why the periodical was suppressed. These pages contained the introduction to "The Calendar of Government of the United States of America." Judging from its contents, the "foreword" may have been composed by the publisher himself, although his name was not mentioned anywhere, let alone set in bold print (leading one to suppose that Iatsenkov had probably used the introduction from the German journal where "Picture of America" was first published). Be that as it may, when presenting the American "Calendar of Government" to the Russian reader, *Spirit of Journals* provided this explanation:

> Before us is the Government Calendar of the United States of America for 1819. It shows the entire structure of the government of that republic, including its division into different departments, with a detailed list of the titles, positions, and salaries of all officials. It is most interesting to see how small is the number of those who conduct all affairs there, whereas in some states a whole army of functionaries, permanent officials, and supernumeraries would be required for this purpose.

He emphasized one point in particular: "Here there is no court and no guard—two important institutions which are necessary in monarchical states and which require large expenditures."[147] [6]

---

144. *Spirit of Journals* 42 (1820), no. 17: 167–81.
145. Uvarov to censorship committee, October 9/23, 1820, TsGIA, record group 777, inventory 1, list 328, 3.
146. Fus to the St. Petersburg censorship committee, October 4/16, 1820, ibid., 1.
147. *Spirit of Journals* 42 (1820), no. 18: 175–76.

This time it proved impossible to trick the irate authorities with a phrase like "a translation from the German." In precise conformity with Golitsyn's letter, the St. Petersburg censorship committee on October 12/24, 1820, officially decreed that *Spirit of Journals* should be closed as of the beginning of the following year.

> The instructions issued by the Minister of Religious Affairs and Popular Education concerning *Spirit of Journals* are to be carried out in the appropriate manner; the publisher is to be informed of this in strict accordance with these instructions, after the censor with responsibility for reading this journal decides to do so. The Administrator [of the education district] is to be informed when these instructions are carried out.[148]

On November 2/14, 1820, an official letter reporting that this indeed had been done was sent to Uvarov.[149]

The days of *Spirit of Journals* were numbered. On September 21/October 3, 1820, Censor Timkovskii authorized the publication of number 19 of the journal. In effect this was the last issue of the journal to appear before the decision to close the journal was made. Dated October 4/16, 1820, its contents fully correspond to the plans the editors had outlined earlier. It included a biography of Edmund Burke as part of the continuing series, "The Characters of the Most Famous Statesmen in the Reign of George III."[150] The remaining pages were devoted to the chapter, "The Land Forces of the United States of America," accompanied by tables and quotations from documents that formed part of "Pictures of America."[151]

After the decision to ban *Spirit of Journals*, only two more issues were published before the end of 1820 (instead of five): number 20, dated November 1/13, and 21, the last one, on December 13/25, 1820. Even in terms of size there is a great difference between these two issues and the earlier ones, and it would have been obvious to the more observant among the readers that the censors had made drastic deletions. Nonetheless, with the exception of one item, "A Traveler's Notes about London,"[152] the two last issues were devoted to American subjects and contained materials about both North and South America. Among them were the articles "The Present Structure of the Militia of the United States of America,"[153] "Concerning the Mails in the United States of America (Taken from an American Journal),"[154] "Mail Steamships in the United States of North America,"[155] a short piece entitled "The City of Buenos Aires (Taken from an American Journal),"[156] and an "Extract from a Letter from a Traveler in the Provinces of South America (Taken from *Morgenblatt*)."[157] The promise contained

---

148. Excerpt from minute book of the St. Petersburg censorship committee, October 12/24, 1820, TsGIA, record group 777, inventory 1, list 328, 4.
149. Censorship committee to Uvarov, November 2/14, 1820, ibid., 7.
150. *Spirit of Journals* 43 (1820), no. 19: 225.
151. Ibid., 231–54.
152. *Spirit of Journals* 43 (1820), no. 20: 287–94; no. 21: 303–18.
153. *Spirit of Journals* 43, no. 20: 261–70.
154. *Spirit of Journals* 43, no. 21: 287–301.
155. Ibid., 300–302.
156. *Spirit of Journals* 43, no. 20: 255–60.
157. Ibid., 271–85.

in the words "to be continued" was left unfulfilled. With the publication of number 21 of the truncated part 43, *Spirit of Journals* ceased to exist.

A brief "obituary" of *Spirit of Journals* was printed in *Son of the Fatherland* as part of its "Historical and Critical Review of the Russian Journals Published in the Previous Year of 1820," serialized throughout 1821. The author of the "Review" referred to the seditious periodical in a few carefully chosen phrases:

> *Spirit of Journals* (*de mortuis aut bene aut nihil!*), which was discontinued at the end of last year, had its own character and many virtues: this journal was more political than literary; it discussed the system of government in various countries and the laws, finances, trade, tariffs, and prosperity of nations, as well as the reasons for their greatness and well-being, drawing conclusions which were frequently correct, but equally frequently were erroneous and suffered from a kind of inappropriate forcefulness.[158]

Son of the Fatherland was not of course in a position to offer a detailed and constructive analysis of the contents of *Spirit of Journals,* as it did in the case of all the other journals published in 1820, including some that were far less important. By quoting the Latin saying, "The dead should be spoken of well, or not spoken of at all," it seemed to be justifying its refusal to provide a detailed critique of *Spirit of Journals*. At the same time, the passage from "Review" cited above is revealing. *Spirit of Journals* did indeed have "its own character and many virtues."

Of course, not all the articles that appeared in *Spirit of Journals* are still of importance and interest to a scholar. The journal printed a number of flawed and even intellectually frivolous pieces, as well as some articles that were written from a conservative perspective (for instance, the essays by Pravdin, the "Russian gentleman" who defended serfdom and the corvée). On the whole, however, after examining all forty-three volumes, it can be stated with some confidence that this was one of the best political journals of the age. And despite the reference in early 1821 by *Son of the Fatherland* to the "inappropriate forcefulness" of *Spirit of Journals,* the modern reader has every right to say that the publisher's assertiveness was not only appropriate, but necessary. This journalistic "forcefulness" in the dark age of tyranny and reaction was a credit to the Russian press.

Iatsenkov was not, of course, a revolutionary. He repeatedly proclaimed his allegiance to Alexander I and his support of the tsar's actions and policies. That he placed his hopes in the emperor may be seen from a program of constitutional and liberal reforms entitled "What Does the Spirit of the Age Demand? What Do the Peoples Require?" published at the beginning of 1819. But Iatsenkov was much more than just a loyal subject. *Spirit of Journals* entered into an unequal struggle with the tsarist authorities and the censors. Among the journal's enemies were some of the most influential tsarist officials—Golitsyn, Viazmitinov, Razumovskii, Uvarov, and others.

The question naturally arises, how was the obscure Iatsenkov able to persevere for six difficult years and bring out forty-three volumes of his journal? His opponents

---

158. *Son of the Fatherland* 12 (1821), pt. 68: 208.

had more than enough power to silence *Spirit of Journals* from the very start, at the time it first began publication, or indeed even earlier, when Iatsenkov had the audacity to publish at his own initiative an announcement about a new periodical without the permission of higher authority.

The publisher was apparently helped by his official connections, his skill at concealing his views and intentions, and also by his close familiarity with the workings of the government. He received some help from colleagues and friends, but historians have yet to establish the identities of the members of the "Society of Publishers" of *Spirit of Journals* and of the "influential persons" to whose support Iatsenkov alluded. There can be no doubt, however, that of the factors that made the existence of the journal possible, the most important one was the "ambivalence" of Alexander I. Even after 1815 the Russian emperor still believed that in certain circumstances he might be forced to abandon the methods of open reaction and police tyranny in favor of some semblance of liberal reform.

The revolutions of 1820 in Europe buried once and for all the vague "constitutional designs" in Russia. Alexander I now doubted the efficacy of liberal reforms, for he saw that the introduction of constitutions in Europe had not prevented a revolutionary explosion there. In October 1820 there was a mutiny in the Semenovsky regiment of the Imperial Guard. This spontaneous protest by the soldiers, who had been reduced to despair, was cruelly suppressed. The tsarist satraps now relied exclusively on the stick and completely forgot about the carrot. *Spirit of Journals* could not have been allowed to exist in these circumstances, and it is no accident that it was officially banned at this very time, in the autumn of 1820.

Did this mean that the efforts by Grigorii Iatsenkov and his collaborators were in vain? Of course not. When discussing the role *Spirit of Journals* played in the history of Russian journalism, one must bear in mind the fact that this was in effect the first publication in the country that dared openly to tackle a number of the most urgent political issues, including those of constitutional government, civil rights, and freedom of the press. And we have not even mentioned the journal's comments on specific government measures and the attention it devoted to issues such as the freedom of trade and the development of manufactories.[159] Finally, as may be seen from what was

---

159. Further research will certainly uncover other areas where *Spirit of Journals* also played a significant role, for example, "in Russia in the first half of the nineteenth century the conditions for the development of the genre of the political review did not exist, because among the privately published journals only Grech's *Son of the Fatherland* was occasionally permitted (and even then only under the strictest supervision) to publish political information from abroad." V. G. Berezina, "Zhanr godovogo obozreniia literatury v russkoi zhurnalistike pervoi poloviny XIX veka" (The Genre of the Annual Review of Literature in Russian Journalism in the First Half of the Nineteenth Century) in *Russkaia zhurnalistika XVIII-XIX vv: Is istorii zhanrov* (Russian Journalism in the Eighteenth–Nineteenth Centuries: From the History of Its Genres) (Leningrad, 1969), 43. It is true that these conditions did not exist, and yet such surveys appeared in *Spirit of Journals* on a fairly regular basis. It also systematically published political news from abroad. The first issues of the new journal contained a long article entitled "The Age of Renewal of the European States." In later years Iatsenkov continued to publish various surveys, including those of the journals.

said above, it was only the articles on American themes that occupy an independent and, perhaps, even exceptional place in the history of Russian social thought. No other Russian journal before had published such extensive and interesting information about the various aspects of life in the United States, their system of government, and economic development. It was these articles, and particularly the introductory comments to the "Calendar of Government of the United States of America," that led to the suppression of *Spirit of Journals* by the tsarist authorities.

4

The Development of Culture and Literature in the U.S.A. during Jacksonian Democracy in the Assessment of Russian Periodicals, by I. A. Ivanchenko

In the late 1820s and 1830s Russians showed great interest in the events taking place in the United States. This was due to the considerable achievements of that country in the economic and cultural spheres, as well as to the fact of its activist foreign policy. The late 1820s saw relations between Russia and the United States grow somewhat closer, a development reflected in the [Russian-American] commercial treaty of 1832.

Thanks to Count Alexis de Tocqueville, a French traveler who visited the United States, the period of the presidencies of Andrew Jackson and Martin Van Buren (1829–1841) became associated with the term "Jacksonian Democracy." At the time much was said and written in Russia and other European countries about the "flourishing republic" and the "equality of social conditions" in the land beyond the ocean. Foreign observers described the rapid growth of manufacturing in America as an "extraordinary and amazing industrial miracle." The United States was increasingly regarded as "the rival of England" and "one of the leading countries of the world."

Russian observers were particularly impressed by the young Republic's advances in the field of education.[1] Technological progress and the development of capitalist relations in the United States had given an impetus to the development of science and culture, and had led to an improvement in the educational system. Numerous scientific societies, universities, engineering colleges, and secondary schools were being established throughout the country. More newspapers and journals were published in

---

1. By the term "education" we mean the diffusion of knowledge and culture, the sum of the educational and pedagogical activities in the country. This article first appeared in *Vestnik Moskovskogo Universiteta* (Herald of Moscow University), series 8 (History), 5 (1984), 63–76.

the United States than in any other country. American literature and art were gaining worldwide recognition.

In Russia, where the genesis and development of bourgeois relations clearly conflicted with a feudal and serfdom-based social order, discussion of a "free and strong society" in the United States was not conducted solely on the level of theory. During the period of severe reaction inaugurated by the regime of Nicholas I, following the defeat of the Decembrist uprising [1825—ed], the process of sociopolitical and cultural change assumed a new direction. In these circumstances, the propagation of the idea of bourgeois development reflected the influence of the country's emerging democratic movement. Indeed, many contemporary thinkers believed that education and the diffusion of knowledge played a decisive role in the democratic transformation of society.

The press, particularly periodicals, did much to popularize bourgeois ideals and values. It exercised increasing influence on the debate on social issues that was beginning to take place in Russia, newspapers and journals frequently serving as a forum for the emerging sociopolitical struggle. One may agree with the British scholar Ronald Hingley, who wrote that "despite the fact that many types of publications were subjected to censorship, the press provided the fullest, and at times the only, opportunity for public debate and struggle between the forces of imperial 'law,' and those of liberal revolutionary 'disorder'."[2]

No other Russian periodical published as many articles about literature and education in the United States as *Moskovskii Telegraf* (Moscow Telegraph), an organ of the Russian middle class that appeared in 1825–1834. The articles in *Moscow Telegraph* revealed the bourgeois approach to the subject. The journal's editor, Nikolai Polevoi, was an advocate of the idea of the indissoluble connection and unity between the industrial and cultural development of the people. "A national industry," declared *Moscow Telegraph,* "is the only means of maintaining and increasing the might of the state. . . . Industry engenders both affluence and enlightenment, for the one cannot exist without the other."[3] The journal held up the successes of the United States in the fields of industry and education as examples to Russia.

In August 1829 *Moscow Telegraph* published an article by American writer James Fenimore Cooper, entitled "A Survey of the Condition of Literature and Education in the United States of America."[4] In this article that took the form of a letter to an Italian, Cooper wrote about the achievements of the educational system in the United States and the development of American literature. He discussed American writers of the early nineteenth century, the freedom of book printing in the United States, and expressed his belief that the social system existing in that country contributed to the diffusion of knowledge.

> With regard to advances in education and learning, Americans were in a completely different position from that of other nations. They have always enjoyed the fruits of enlightenment. Paintings, books, statues, in a word everything that contributes to the

2. Ronald Hingley, *Russian Writers and Society, 1825–1904* (New York–Toronto, 1967), 221.
3. *Moskovskii Telegraf* [hereafter *MT*] 18 (1828): 246.
4. *MT* 16 (1829): 387–417.

joy of living, was made available to anyone who wished only to make some sacrifice to satisfy his taste. Books, purchased at a moderate price, were certain to be in greater demand than works of art, and the people acquired a certain penchant for learning. I believe there is no house so poor in North America that does not have a book.[5]

Further in the article he described America's schools and universities, and "the lessons of experience, the struggle of opinions, the continuous intellectual activity" of Americans. He emphasized, "What is most important, the laws themselves become fused with contemporary mores," and that these laws "corresponding to the exigencies of society, shall make the people more intelligent and more prosperous." In Russia, where a tyrannical censorship had suppressed numerous books, journals, and individual articles, the following passage from Cooper's essay had a particularly resonant ring:

> Where any subject relating to politics is concerned, printing presses in the United States enjoy the widest freedom. An official has no protection from the journals other than a trial by jury in an independent court. . . . Moreover, if the publisher of a journal or some other person were to accuse the President himself of committing a crime (however grave), and could offer proof of this, he would be able to proceed in the certainty that he would not be punished, as if it were he who was in authority.[6]

In 1828 *Moscow Telegraph* published a long article about the development of literature and journalism in the United States.[7] Its author wrote,

> After less than fifty years North American literature is flourishing; that is why in every one of its genres we find writers who are worthy of attention, even though in the sphere of literature America has not yet produced names as celebrated as the names of Washington and Jefferson are in the sphere of politics.[8] This appears to be the result of the political structure and social orientation of the United States. North Americans strove to organize their civil existence and strengthen the material power of their country, and until now did not have the time to devote themselves to the fine arts. However, even if America is yet to enter the age of poetry, it may be said that her forces are in a state of continuous and successful development.[9]

Political statements like these were found quite frequently in the articles on literature that appeared in *Moscow Telegraph.*

On one occasion *Moscow Telegraph* expressed its regret about "the distant relations" between Russia and America, which, it believed, had prevented Russians from obtaining reliable information about that country. "France and Germany are more familiar

---

5. Ibid., 387–88.
6. Ibid., 394; 404–5.
7. *MT* 11 (1828): 395–402.
8. Compare this with George Sand's statement that in the field of literature America owed Cooper as much as it owed Franklin and Washington in the field of science and politics. And in 1825 *Moscow Telegraph* itself noted: "Having devoted themselves to the literature of North America, Irving Washington [sic] and Cooper did more to influence Europe than the statesmen of their country" (4: 297).
9. *MT* 11 (1828): 398.

with the United States than we are," wrote the author. "They have already seen many examples of North American literature that are worthy of interest, and the journals of North America are now becoming an important source for those of Europe."[10]

Characterizing the American press, *Moscow Telegraph* dwelled in particular on *North American Review*, a journal that had been the first to gain "the attention of its compatriots and the respect of Europeans."

> This journal may be regarded as the ambassador of American literature; it informs its readers of the condition and tenor of American literature, the resources that support it, and the means that it employs.... It is important to note that all the articles in the *American Review* relate to America, for in addition to acting as a court of literary criticism, this journal is the organ by means of which the Government addresses political opinion and guides the public mood in a desirable direction; among its contributors are some of the highest officials, and advertisements for the journal openly state this.[11]

Moscow Telegraph wrote about the layout and contents of *North American Review* and, in the belief that "a description of this publication may provide an idea of the subjects that interest American authors and the American public,"[12] published a list of the articles that had appeared in the American journal in 1821–1824. Most of these articles dealt with the laws and the foreign and domestic policies of the United States, England, France, and other countries—subjects that most Russian journalists were forbidden to discuss. It is worth noting that in 1822 *North American Review* published an article entitled "Communications between the United States and Russia Concerning Russia's American Possessions."[13]

Moscow Telegraph informed its readers that "Europe is believed to have 227,000,000 inhabitants; 2142 newspapers and journals are published there: 490 in France, 483 in England, 84 in Russia." The journal added, "America is believed to have up to 40,000,000 inhabitants and 978 newspapers and journals! Of these 840 are in the United States (of which 137 are in the province of New York, 110 in Pennsylvania, 48 in Vermont, 35 in Virginia, 35 in Massachusetts, 23 in Connecticut, 22 in Maryland, 18 in New Jersey, 18 in Kentucky)..."[14]

The readers of *Moscow Telegraph* were thus in a position to make a clear comparison between the achievements of the press in the United States and its condition in Russia. "Are there many journals in Russia?" asked Polevoi in the *Telegraph* in 1833. His answer was: "There are altogether ten journals in the whole of Russia. Ten journals, some of them good, some mediocre, some bad.... But is it really possible to draw any distinctions? One must admit that this is a superb illustration of what it is like to be a writer in our country and of the esteem in which it holds the press!"[15]

10. Ibid., 396–97.
11. *MT* 11 (1828): 398. *North American Review*, one of the best journals of the age, was published in Boston from 1815 to 1840. See Sidney Kobre, *Foundations of American Journalism* (Tallahassee, 1958), 211–12.
12. *MT* 11 (1828): 398.
13. Ibid., 400.
14. *MT* 8 (1828): 519–20.
15. *MT* 2 (1833): 343, 346.

In 1835 *Teleskop* (Telescope) published an article about the rise in the number of periodicals in the United States stating that in the years that had passed since the War of Independence, Americans had achieved considerable success in this field. *Telescope* offered a detailed description of the character, orientation, and contents of some of the American journals, and stressed that they were published in very large editions.[16]

In Russia in the 1820s little was known about American literature. There were very few translations of works by American authors, and the original texts were frequently unavailable in the bookshops owing to the stringent censorship regulations. *Moscow Telegraph* wrote in this connection,

> It is said that sometimes journalists write about foreign books that the readers will never see, for example, books from India, Persia, and North America. But if we have no knowledge of some subject, why shouldn't we try to learn about it? The more variety there is in a journal, the better. . . . Intelligence about any literature, any important book, even if the reader is ignorant of that literature and will never see that book, is useful and interesting.[17]

For that reason Polevoi's journal regularly published articles about the young literature of the United States, as well as works by Fenimore Cooper and Washington Irving. The two celebrated romantics, the most prominent representatives of American literature at the time, were far from being the only American writers with whom the Russian reading public was familiar.

In 1831 a moral tale, *What Is Good Form?* by Mrs. Harrison-Smith [sic], was published in a Russian translation in St. Petersburg.[18] *Moscow Telegraph* described this work as an "ethical dissertation, in which the characters play the part of syllogisms." It praised the quality of the Russian text and stated that Harrison-Smith's novel was "of interest" above all "in its portrayal of the character of the society of the United States, this character being a subject about which until now we knew little."[19] In January 1831 an excerpt from this novel appeared in *Literaturnaia Gazeta* (Literary Gazette), and in February that journal published a review. The critic, Orest Somov, also praised Konstantin Masal'skii's translation and wrote that "the lady who is the author of the novel, Mrs. Harrison-Smith, the wife of a well-known Washington journalist and a native North American, was familiar with local society and the exigencies of the fashionable world." Somov mentioned the novel's "incredible success" in the United States and the favorable reviews it had received in the French press.[20]

16. *Teleskop* [hereafter *T*] 27 (1835): 415–18.
17. *MT* 9 (1828): 130–31.
18. *What Is Good Form? A Novel of North America,* translated by Konstantin Masal'skii, 4 pts. (St. Petersburg, 1831), printed at the press of the Department of Medicine of the Ministry of Internal Affairs and the Imperial Academy. [The reference here is apparently to Margaret Bayard Smith and her Washington society novel, *What Is Gentility?* published in 1828. She was married to *National Intelligencer* editor Samuel Harrison Smith.—ed].
19. *MT* 3 (1831): 395.
20. *Literaturnaia Gazeta* [hereafter *LG*] 5 (1831): 35–38; 10: 81–82.

In August 1830 the *Literary Gazette* published an article by Petr Poletika, a prominent diplomat who had been [1817–1822] Russian minister to Washington. The article, entitled "The Condition of Society in the United Provinces of America," appeared in two successive issues.[21] We know exactly when the article was written because it was dated "Washington, 16–22 February 1822." The editors of *Literary Gazette* thanked Poletika for offering them the article and informed their readers of the forthcoming publication of an "interesting book" by him, *A Short Survey of the Internal Situation in the United Provinces of America and Their Political Relations with Europe.* This had already appeared in French in London and in an English edition in Boston in 1826, enthusiastically received by the American press.[22]

Moscow Telegraph, keeping its readers informed about new books on the United States published abroad, reviewed many of them even before they appeared in Russian translation and received the imprimatur of the tsarist censorship. For example, in 1832 *A Moral and Political Sketch of the United States of North America* was published in Paris by Achille Murat, a citizen of the United States and son of famous French marshal Joachim Murat. In its review, *Telegraph* stated: "The book would be of interest even if the author's name, which inspires special curiosity, were different. The preface is nobly and intelligently written; the entire work is full of sensible ideas that are expressed passionately, with heart-felt ardor. It explains much of what travelers and geographers and Cooper and Irving failed to notice."[23] The reviewer was impressed by the wealth of information in Murat's book, which consisted of ten letters on the political system of the United States, American laws, the history of the Republic and its political parties, freedom of religion, Negro slavery, the economic development of the United States, and its scientific and literary achievements.[24]

It should be remembered that at this time the reactionary press of Europe, including the Russian press, was doing its best to belittle the progress made by the United States in industry and culture and to depict the republican system of government as a source of "ignorance," "backwardness," and "rude manners." The progressive periodicals, on the other hand, denounced such views and never ceased to extol the development of the young Republic on the other side of the Atlantic. "Just a few data are sufficient to paint a picture of the gigantic successes of the United Provinces," observed *Istoricheskii . . . Zhurnal* (Historical . . . Journal). "They boast 3,000 students, 2,700 seminarians, 10,000 physicians, 6,000 lawyers, 5,000 clergymen, 9,000 churches and chapels. Every year 4,500 patents for new discoveries and inventions are issued, and $2,000,000 to $3,000,000 worth of books is published; there are 596 newspapers. . . ."[25]

---

21. *LG* 45 (1830): 65–68; 46: 73–77.

22. See Nikolai Bolkhovitinov, *Russko-amerikanskie otnosheniia, 1815–1832* (Russian-American Relations, 1815–1832) (Moscow, 1975), 534–36. [the book by Poletika, published in Baltimore rather than Boston and translated from the French original, was entitled *A Sketch of the Internal Condition of the United States of America and of Their Political Relations with Europe by a Russian*—ed].

23. *MT* 15 (1832): 422. [French title, *Equisse morale et politique des Etats-Unis de l'Amerique du Nord.*]

24. Ibid., 422–23.

25. *Istoricheskii . . . Zhurnal* 3, no. 2 (1826): 95–96.

Telescope devoted much attention to the development of the system of education in the United States. In 1832 it reprinted from *Revue Britannique* an article by Balbee entitled "Education in America in Ancient Times and Today." *Telescope* declared that there was no other country in the world "where institutions of education are more numerous than in this part of America."[26]

> Every citizen wishes to learn, and in particular wants to be informed about the workings of the body politic, of which he is a part; and the more than 800 periodicals—a number almost equal to a third of the almanacs of this kind that are published in the entire civilized world—endeavor to help him achieve this double goal; they constitute the main part of the flourishing book trade, where the amount turned over is almost equal to that of the book trade in the whole of Southern Europe.[27]

That same year *Telescope* reprinted another article from *Revue Britannique*, the title of which was "A Statistical Description of Popular Education in England, France, and the United States." Its author argued that the United States had "greatly surpassed all the states of Europe in regard to the diffusion of knowledge."[28] The piece is of interest because it included a table showing the proportion of students in the general population of several countries. In the United States there was one student for every four people, in Prussia one for every seven, in Bavaria one for every ten, in England one for every eleven, in Austria one for every thirteen, and in France one for every twenty. According to the article, Russia had the lowest proportion of students, one student for every 367 people. *Telescope* thus enabled its readers to draw their own conclusions about the state of the educational system in the United States, where the number of students was more than ninety times larger, proportionately, than in Russia.

The editors wrote that, owing to the lack of statistical data, they were not in a position to provide a comprehensive survey of popular education in the United States. This was why they had published an article that only described the level of education in the Province of New York, which "is undoubtedly the most prosperous part of the entire North American Union," and gave the figures for government spending on education. The journal drew attention to a "strange discrepancy": in 1830–1832 in New York State the number of schoolchildren exceeded the total number of children, which suggested that "every year many families with children, almost all of whom are unschooled, arrive in the United States from Europe, and the parents send them to the local schools."[29]

During this period there was a growing movement in the United States for free education and the teaching of manual labor in schools (the first free school was opened in New York in 1809).[30] The *Journal of the Ministry of Public Education* described in one of its issues the structure of these schools and the extent to which they had become common in the United States. It observed that originally such schools had

---

26. *T* 10 (1832): 224–25.
27. Ibid., 226.
28. *T* 21 (1832): 142.
29. Ibid., 143–44.
30. See Lev Goncharov, *Shkola i pedagogika SShA do vtoroi mirovoi voiny* (Schools and Pedagogy in the U.S.A. before World War II) (Moscow, 1972), 56–60.

been established for the benefit of the lower classes, in order "to ease the lot of those poor mothers who are engaged in trade," and that their pupils were not subjected to harsh treatment or corporal punishment.

> Such schools for the children of the poor were to be found in almost every area of the larger North American cities, and because parents who were rich or well-to-do were displeased to learn that children from humble and poor families leave these institutions better-educated and better-informed than their own children of the same age, who had been taught at home, a large number of boarding-schools based on the same principles and employing the same rules as the schools we have described were established by private individuals. These boarding-schools educate the children of the wealthy for a certain fee.[31]

Russian journalists of progressive views, while in every way extolling the success of the educational system in the United States, defended the cruel and predatory policy of American capitalism toward Native Americans. Their attitude reflected the influence of great-power chauvinism, which for centuries had been the ideology of the Russian autocracy, and revealed the bourgeois limitations of the worldview of even the most open-minded Russian journalists. *Historical Journal* wrote that "the Indians carried out violent attacks on the colonists, and it became necessary to repel them with armed force. However, with the spread of enlightenment, the natives are increasingly dying out, and their number is now quite small."[32]

Telescope used similar language when it declared that in the United States "civil education and the force of law flourish" and thus overcome "the barbarism and superstition of the primordial inhabitants."[33] *Moscow Telegraph* on the one hand noted the advances made by the American Indians, particularly the Cherokees, in the field of education (even reporting that the Cherokees were publishing a newspaper, *The Phoenix*),[34] but on the other hand wrote,

> The unenlightened peoples are forced to cede their place to those that are enlightened; let us recall the savage neighbors of the Anglo-Americans. How many areas of the globe, which Nature originally allotted to the *colored* generations of mankind for their settlement, are now occupied by the *white* generation, which is the most enlightened, and therefore the strongest![35]

In the early nineteenth century American writers were hardly known in Europe and did not enjoy much success with the reading public even at home. Often the literature of the United States was regarded as a branch of English literature. "Because it owes its existence to English literature," wrote *Moscow Telegraph*, "American literature not only still shows signs of its origin, but indeed has found it advantageous not to separate

---

31. *Zhurnal Ministerstva Narodnago Prosveshcheniia*, pt. 7 (1835), 9: 539–43.
32. *Istoricheskii . . . Zhurnal* 3, no. 2 (1825): 96–97.
33. *T* 10 (1832): 224.
34. *MT* 1 (1831): 162–63.
35. See Iastrebtsov on education, *MT* 12 (1832): 431.

itself from the mother whose child it is.... That is why, despite the enmity of the two peoples and their political rivalry, American literature continues to experience the strong and irresistible influence of English literature."[36]

American literature came of age and acquired an international reputation with the appearance of two major writers, Washington Irving and James Fenimore Cooper. Dieter Boden, a German scholar who is the author of a study of American themes in eighteenth- and nineteenth-century Russian literature, is correct in his belief that after a period when "the concept of 'American literature' was ignored or remained subsumed within the concept of English literature, the influence of these two writers helped to reveal the unique style of American literature. In 1825 Russian critics began to realize the importance of the national literature of America. The first critic to make this discovery and embark on a determined effort to popularize it was Nikolai Polevoi."[37]

It is not surprising that Polevoi admired the works of Irving and Cooper, for the editor of *Telegraph* was one of the most prominent representatives of the romantic school in Russian literature. His journal regarded romanticism as a component of the bourgeois-democratic movement,[38] published a large number of articles about developments in the literatures of various nations, and introduced Russian readers to the best works of West European and American writers.

Scholars have already noted that American romanticism manifested certain strong sociopolitical features connected, on the one hand, with the romantics' advocacy of the ideas of the American Revolution and the American War of Independence and, on the other, with their subsequent criticism of the capitalist way of life in America.[39] The publication of the works of the American romantics in Russia had, therefore, a special significance. When in 1831 Cooper's novel *The Spy*, which extolled freedom and glorified George Washington, was adapted as a play for performance on the Russian stage, the censors refused to give it their approval, "fearing the possibility of an analogy with the political situation that currently exists."[40]

Russian and foreign authors have published a number of studies offering a detailed analysis of the various aspects of the treatment by Russian critics and, in particular, by *Moscow Telegraph*, of the works of Irving and Cooper,[41] but several issues relating to the critical reception of their works in Russia require further consideration and

36. *MT* 11 (1828): 396.
37. Boden, *Das Amerikabild im Russischen Schriftum bis zum Ende des 19. Jahrhunderts* (Hamburg, 1968), 205.
38. See *Russkii romantizm* (Russian Romanticism) (Moscow, 1974), 51–52; E. A. Maikin, *O Russkom romantizme* (On Russian Romanticism) (Moscow, 1975), 22–23; *Istoriia romantizma v russkoi literature: romantizm v rus. lit. 20–30-kh XIX v.* (The History of Romanticism in Russian Literature: Romanticism in Russian Literature in the 1820s and 1830s) (Moscow, 1979), 251–55.
39. See M. N. Bobrova, *Romantizm v amerikanskoi literature XIX veka* (Romanticism in Nineteenth Century American Literature) (Moscow, 1972), 4–10; Vernon Parrington, *Main Currents of American Thought*, 2 vols. (Moscow, 1962), vol. 2, 5–8.
40. From N. V. Drizen, *Dramaticheskaia tsenzura dvukh epokh 1825–1881 gg.* (Two Eras of Theatre Censorship, 1825–1881) (Petrograd, 1917), 67.
41. See Bolkhovitinov, *Russian-American Relations,* 555–68; Aleksandr Nikoliukin, *Literaturnye sviazi Rossii i SShA: stanovlenie literaturnykh kontaktov* (Literary Relations between Russia and the United States: The Establishment of Literary Contacts) (Moscow, 1981); Boden,

elucidation. They include the question of the influence of these American writers on Russian literature, which at times is either ignored or, on the contrary, exaggerated. In considering this question an analysis of the Russian press could be most useful.

Scholars have already commented on the fact that the first work of Russian literature translated and published in America was the novel *Ivan Vyzhigan* by Faddei Bulgarin. This rather mediocre book had already been translated into English and French and had enjoyed success with Western readers, when in 1831 a new translation of it by George Ross appeared in American bookshops.[42] Bulgarin's novel was also very popular in Russian. The *Telegraph* wrote that "it attracted a degree of attention that no other book had ever enjoyed in Russia" and compared it to the works of the "inimitable" Washington Irving.[43]

Immediately after the publication of Alexander Pushkin's *Tales of Belkin,* Polevoi compared it to the works of Irving, but he also noted: "Belkin clearly wanted to follow in the footsteps of Irving. But just as Eugene Onegin is different from Don Juan, so *Tales of Belkin* is different from the creations of Irving."[44] *Moscow Telegraph* also claimed to discern signs of Irving's influence in a collection of stories, *Evenings on a Farm Near Dikanka,* by Nikolai Gogol.[45] The influence of Cooper and Irving on Pushkin has been noted by a number of scholars.[46] Indeed, Pushkin mentions Cooper's name in some of his literary works, such as the poem "My Fate Is Decided" and in the early drafts of "Journey to Arzrum."

Moscow Telegraph regarded Mikhail Zagoskin's novel, *Iurii Miloslavskii,* as belonging to the same tradition as the novels of Cooper. It suggested that Zagoskin's hero "is similar to *The Last of the Mohicans* of Cooper."[47] Aleksandr Bestuzhev-Marlinskii also spoke of the inspiration the Russian writer had drawn from Cooper. He saw in the character of Zagoskin's Zariad'ev a captain from Cooper's novels.[48] A number of contemporaries also wrote about the influence exercised by Cooper, particularly *The Spy,* on Polevoi's *The Oath before the Holy Sepulchre.*[49] However, in its review of *The Oath* and *Askold's Grave* by Zagoskin, *Moscow Telegraph* stated:

87–112; Zofia Dziechciaruk, *Estetyka i literatura romantyczna w crasopisme Mikolaja Polewoja Moskowskij Tielegraf (1825–1834)* (Esthetics and Literary Romanticism in the Writings of Nikolai Polevoi's *Moscow Telegraph*) (Wroclaw, 1975).

42. See Gilbert Phelps, *The Russian Novel in English Fiction* (London, 1956), 16, and Aleksander Rogalski, *Rosjua-Europea* (Warsaw, 1960), 645.

43. *MT* 7 (1829): 346.

44. *MT* 22 (1831): 254–56.

45. *MT* 20 (1831): 208.

46. See M. P. Alekseev, "Concerning 'The History of the Village of Goriukhino,'" in *Pushkin: Articles and Documents* 2 (Odessa, 1926); N. N. Bolkhovitinov, *Russian-American Relations,* 560–66; M. Eremin, *Pushkin—publitsist* (Pushkin the Publicist), 2d ed. (Moscow, 1976); N. F. Preobrazhenskii, "The Magic Little Soldiers (Pushkin and Washington Irving)," *The Belgrade International Slavic Conference (September 15–21, 1995)* (Belgrade, 1957), 645.

47. *MT* 24 (1829): 462–67; *T* 3 (1831): 588.

48. Bestuzhev-Marlinskii, *Sochineniia v dyukh tomakh* (Collected Works in Two Volumes) (Moscow, 1958), vol. 1, 596. Bestuzhev-Marlinskii also wrote about the influence of Irving's *The Salamander* on his own *Frigate "Nadezhda"* (ibid., 667).

49. See *Neizdannye pis'ma inostrannykh pisatelei XVIII-XIX vekov* (Unpublished Letters of Foreign Writers of the Eighteenth and Nineteenth Centuries) (Leningrad, 1960), 265–66;

Some critics mistakenly thought that its inspiration (or model) was Cooper's *The Spy*. Cooper portrays a loyal son of his country who, endeavoring to bring about its liberation, employs all his strength and all means at his disposal to save it and to destroy its enemies, does not fear death or humiliation, does not seek honor or glory, and thinks only of saving the fatherland and defeating its foes.... But Polevoi's Ivan Gudoshnik and the character of Blud in Zagoskin's novel are entirely different: these are men who have sworn to avenge the fatherland, which has already been lost. They wish to see it restored.[50]

In order to study successfully the literary connections between Russia and the United States and to understand the character of the social movements of the period, it is necessary to establish the extent to which the literature of Russia was influenced by that of America. Russian journalists clearly did much to introduce the Russian reader to American writers. Indeed, Polevoi once declared, "The journals are the most faithful and intimate of literary intermediaries."[51]

An analysis of the critical reaction in the Russian periodical press of the 1820s and 1830s to developments in the American system of education and in American literature shows that the Russian periodicals did much to acquaint their readers with the dynamics of social life in the United States and, at the same time, objectively contributed to the evolution of progressive Russian social thought in the post-Decembrist period.

Of course, the circumstances in which the development of social thought in Russia and the United States occurred were very different. Yet one must not ignore the fact that, even though in general Russian observers had a positive view of the development of American education, some of them were harshly critical of the character of that process. It seems that such attitudes were linked to the belief, widespread even among progressive circles in Russia, that American capitalism with its "materialism" and "materialistic pragmatism" was not a congenial environment for literature and the arts. Even the fame that Cooper and Irving clearly enjoyed in Russia did nothing to change this view. The *Journal of the Ministry of Education* claimed, for example, that "it is almost considered an axiom that in industrial America there are no, nor can there be any, belles-lettres, particularly poetry, and that the two American novelists who are known in our country are merely an exception to the rule."[52]

Such beliefs about the excessive practicality and artistic ineptitude of Americans were undoubtedly exaggerated, parochial, and in many ways even mistaken. But it cannot be denied that there was much in America's corrupt and flawed bourgeois society that could be used as evidence to support these views. The age of Jacksonian democracy, like all the other periods in American history, was characterized by class inequality, the cruel exploitation of the working masses, and racial oppression. This was essentially a bourgeois democracy, a democracy in quotation marks, so to speak.

Bestuzhev-Marlinskii, "On the Novel *An Oath before the Holy Sepulchre* by Polevoi," in *Collected Works,* vol. 2, 610.

50. *MT* 1 (1834): 170.

51. Quoted from V. I. Kuleshov, *Literaturnye sviazi Rossii i Zapadnoi Evropy v XIX veke: pervaia polovina* (Literary Relations between Russia and Western Europe in the First Half of the Nineteenth Century) (Moscow, 1977), 11.

52. *Zhurnal... proveshcheniia* 16 (1837): 480.

Progressive thinkers in Russia knew about the vices and flaws in American society. For a number of reasons, they decided to express their rejection of the unattractive aspects of American life by directing their criticism at the developments in the field of literature and education in the United States. In his article, "Naught about Naught," that appeared in *Telescope* in 1836, Vissarion Belinsky wrote:

> The esthetic sense is the foundation of good, the foundation of morality. Civil prosperity may flourish in the United States of North America, civilization there may have reached the ultimate degree, the jails may be empty, the courtrooms quiet: but if, as we are told, that country has no art and no love of beauty, I scorn that prosperity, I refuse to respect that civilization, I do not trust that morality, because such prosperity is artificial, such a civilization is arid, such morality is suspect. Where art does not hold sway, men are not virtuous, but merely sensible; they are not moral, but merely prudent: they do not fight evil, but avoid it, not because they hate it, but because they calculate that this would be to their advantage. Therefore, civilization is only worthy of respect when it contributes to enlightenment and, hence, to virtue—the only goal of man's being, of the life of nations, of the progress of humanity.[53]

---

53. *T* 31 (1836): 658.

Comment
by J. Dane Hartgrove

The articles under consideration are N. N. Bolkhovitinov's "American Theme on the Pages of *Dukh Zhurnalov*" and Ia. A. Ivanchenko's "The Development of Culture and Literature in the U.S.A. during Jacksonian Democracy in the Assessment of Russian Periodicals." While there are similarities between the two efforts, these are heavily outweighed by the differences.

Bolkhovitinov's paper, the longer and meatier of the two, is also the earlier chronologically. In 1814, Censor Grigorii Maksimovich Iatsenkov announced plans to publish a new journal, the subtitle of which, a "Collection of All That Is Best and Most Curious in All Other Journals in the Fields of History, Politics, the National Economy, Belles-Lettres, the Various Arts, Estate Management, Etc.," pretty much summed up his editorial stance. But *Dukh Zhurnalov* was not destined to become the *Reader's Digest* of Alexander I's Russia. As Bolkhovitinov points out, not all the articles that appeared in the journal were particularly interesting to the contemporary Russian reader, nor are they important to the modern researcher. *Dukh Zhurnalov* attempted to provide accounts of what was happening outside Russia that would be of interest to the Russian reading public, and it was this coverage, and the journal's analysis thereof, that aroused the Russian government's concern and ultimately caused it to close down the publication.

From its first issue, which appeared in early 1815, *Dukh Zhurnalov* made American subjects a specific object of attention. Part one included a statistical survey of North America and a short biography of Thomas Jefferson, plus an article on the slave trade that condemned the practice in no uncertain terms. Later articles would praise the abolition of serfdom in other European countries and comment favorably on foreign experiments with constitutions and fundamental laws. As Bolkhovitinov notes, it was a series of articles under the general title "Picture of America," viewed by the tsarist censors as an attack on the monarchical system of government, that led to the journal's demise in late 1820.

The closing of the journal coincided with Alexander I's shift away from constitutional possibilities for Russia in the wake of disorders in Europe, which the introduction of constitutions there had not prevented. The October 1820 mutiny of the Semenovskii Guards Regiment came too late to affect the decision to close down *Dukh Zhurnalov*, but may have confirmed Russian authorities in their intention of eliminating any other perceived threats to the country's public safety.

All things considered, Bolkhovitinov's paper explores an important aspect of Russian history during Alexander I's reign. It does so with a minimal amount of Soviet-era political cant, although the "progressive" emphasis throughout marks it as a Soviet production. This is not to say that the work displayed and the ideas expressed here are anything but impressive—Bolkhovitinov is nothing less than a world-class historian, and his membership in the Russian Academy of Sciences is well deserved.

Bolkhovitinov identifies *Dukh Zhurnalov* as the first Russian periodical publication that dared to discuss such matters as constitutional government, civil rights, freedom of the press, and free trade. But while it was the journal's interest in things American that ultimately brought down upon it the condemnation of the tsarist censors, the American themes it treated were a means of drawing attention to Russia's own plight, of bringing to bear alternative ways of thinking, however obliquely, on the Russian status quo. The American themes covered by *Dukh Zhurnalov*, then, have far less to do with the appreciation of conditions in far-off America than with conditions at home in Alexander I's Russia. If there is a weakness in this otherwise excellent paper, it would lie in Bolkhovitinov, the Americanist's, tendency to view *Dukh Zhurnalov*'s coverage of things American too fixedly, perhaps paying less attention than he should to the journal's coverage to equally important developments in Western and Central Europe.

Would that it were possible to consider Ivanchenko's effort in so favorable a light. Alas, into every life a little rain must fall, and in this case an apt comparison would be to a cold, fitful shower that has umbrellas going up or coming down every ten minutes or so. Ivanchenko's paper, which deals with Russian perceptions of American literature and culture in the period 1829–1841, also attempts to study the impact of American literary themes on Russian literature in this period.

Less than ten years after the demise of *Dukh Zhurnalov*, the United States was looked upon in Europe as the land of social equality and industrial miracles. America's impressive technological progress and burgeoning industry went hand in hand with scientific and cultural developments and improvements in the nation's educational system.

To a considerable extent, Ivanchenko focuses upon coverage of American events in Nikolai Polevoi's *Moskovskii Telegraf*. An 1828 article compared the number of newspapers and journals published in the major European countries and in America (there were 84 in Russia, 840 in the United States). Polevoi's journal praised the first American literary efforts, observing that the young Republic's citizens had previously been too busy organizing their government and creating a national economy to spend much time on the fine arts. The author of the 1828 article devoted particular attention to the journal *North American Review*, noted that the publication dealt entirely with American themes, and included a list of its articles for the years 1821–1824.

Moskovskii Telegraf regularly published the works of James Fenimore Cooper and Washington Irving, in addition to articles about American literature. The journal *Literaturnaia Gazeta* followed suit with works by Mrs. Samuel Harrison Smith and Petr Poletika, Russia's Minister Plenipotentiary to the United States. *Moskovskii Telegraf* frequently printed reviews of books about the United States published in Europe, and other journals printed articles that chronicled American intellectual and economic triumphs. An 1832 article in the journal *Teleskop* noted that there was one student for every four people in the United States and one student for every 367 Russians. The Russian press clearly was impressed with the rapid growth of the American periodical press and American education.

Ivanchenko is far more of a practitioner of Soviet-speak than Bolkhovitinov, with his talk of "the cruel and predatory policy of American capitalism toward native Americans" that Russian journalists "of progressive views" nevertheless extol under the influence of "great-power chauvinism." In 1831 *Moskovskii Telegraf,* while praising Cherokee accomplishments in formulating a written language and publishing a newspaper, nevertheless observed approvingly that "the white generation, which is the most enlightened," now occupied "many areas of the globe, which Nature originally allotted to the colored generations of mankind." How difficult our Soviet colleagues must have found it to portray these standard nineteenth-century modes of thinking as progressive and advanced!

By 1825, Russian men of letters had made the discovery, common to their contemporaries in Western Europe, that America indeed possessed a literature distinct from that of her mother country. The two American authors most widely recognized in Europe were Washington Irving and James Fenimore Cooper. As previously noted, Nikolai Polevoi printed the works of both Americans in *Moskovskii Telegraf.* Ivanchenko claims that the publication of the works of these American romantics in Russia had "a special significance," but neglects to tell us what works were published, and when. We learn that Cooper's *The Spy* was adapted for production on the Russian stage in 1831, but that the censors refused to approve it. Did Polevoi incur any trouble from the censors for publishing Cooper's works? Ivanchenko does not tell us, nor does he assess the impact of these works on the Russian reading public.

Ivanchenko informs us that the first Russian novel translated and published in America was Faddei Bulgarin's *Ivan Vyzhigin,* which appeared in 1831. *Moskovskii Teleqraf* compared Bulgarin's novel to the works of Washington Irving, and claimed to see Irving's influence in Pushkin's *Tales of Belkin* and Gogol's *Evenings on a Farm Near Dikanka.* Novels by Mikhail Zagoskin and Nikolai Polevoi were said to contain characters modeled on those of Cooper in the Leatherstocking tales. Not that one expects a deconstructionist analysis of Russian literature in the 1830s here, but a little more effort is required to prove the point than Ivanchenko has made. Jacksonian America was "a bourgeois democracy, a democracy in quotation marks." Ivanchenko asserts that Russia's progressive thinkers saw the "vices and flaws in American society" and signaled their rejection of them "by directing their criticism at developments in the field of literature and education in the United States." The paper concludes with a lengthy quotation from Vissarion Belinsky, that bellwether of political consciousness, to the effect that American prosperity and morality were suspect because "that country has no art and no love of beauty."

Ivanchenko's paper lacks focus, displays flaws in conceptualization, and adds little to what was previously known about Russian-American cultural and literary relations in the Jacksonian era. What holds it together is the author's ideological stance, summed up in such statements as: "The age of Jacksonian democracy, like all the other periods in U.S. history, was characterized by class inequality, the cruel exploitation of the working masses, and racial oppression."

As Ivanchenko reminds us, "it cannot be denied that there was much in America's corrupt and flawed bourgeois society that could be used as evidence to support these views." No American historian would deny that there were inequalities between social classes in the America of the 1830s. The stories told of the mess Jackson's supporters made in the White House public rooms during his first inaugural celebration carry that frisson of disapproval signifying an awareness of class differences between the old and new administrations. Workers in the United States still claim to be oppressed (although it's difficult to sympathize with a strike by baseball players who make more in one year than the average college professor makes in a lifetime), and many undoubtedly were until the 1950s. As for racial oppression, one can only say that it was easier to define when one race was largely enslaved than it is today.

The point is, could "progressive" Russian thinkers of the 1830s have had so lofty an understanding of class inequality, worker exploitation, and racial oppression that they consciously chose to condemn American society through their criticism of American literature and educational advances? Or is this a backward projection of what passed for Marxist-Leninist ideology, in effect an effort to strap Polevoi, Belinsky, et al. to a Procrustean bed of Ivanchenko's construction?

With the demise of the Soviet Union, Russian historians are now free to present historical events in any manner they choose. It's a fairly safe bet that Nikolai Bolkhovitinov would change very little about his paper if given the chance. Regrettably, the same bet regarding Ivanchenko's paper would find few takers.

5

Russia and the U.S. Civil War, by N. S. Kiniapina

The founders of Marxism-Leninism were among the first to offer a scientific analysis of the causes and character of the American Civil War. Karl Marx and Friedrich Engels saw this conflict resulting from a struggle between two systems—that of slavery and that of free hired labor. Marx wrote that the conflict that had brought about civil war in the United States "rests on the problem of slavery."[1] Referring to the events of the Civil War, V. I. Lenin spoke of its "tremendous world-historical, progressive and revolutionary significance."[2]

The American historiography of the Civil War is extensive. It has been comprehensively analyzed in the works of Igor Dement'ev.[3] Nikolai Bolkhovitinov has written on the goals and results of the research into modern American history that have been carried out by Soviet historians.[4] The best-researched work on the history of Russian-American relations in the 1860s is a book by M. M. Malkin published in 1939.[5] Malkin used a variety of historical materials, including documents from the Archive of the

---

1. Marx and Engels, *Soch.* (Works), vol. 15, 355, 347. This article by N. S. Kiniapina was first published in *Vestnik Moskovskogo Universiteta* (Herald of Moscow University) History, 2 (1980).

2. Lenin, *Polnoe Sobranie Sochineniia* (Complete Collected Works), 5th ed., 55 vols. (Moscow, 1960–1964), vol. 37, 58.

3. I. P. Dement'ev, "Evolutsiia amerikanskoi burzhuaznoi istoriografii i grazhdanskoi voiny, 1861–1865 gg." (The Evolution of the American Bourgeois Historiography of the Civil War of 1861–1865), *Voprosy Istorii* (Problems of History) 9 (1958), and *Amerikanskaia istoriografiia grazhdanskoi voiny v SShA 1861–1865 gg.* (The American Historiography of the U.S. Civil War of 1861–1865) (Moscow, 1963).

4. See Bolkhovitinov, "Nekotorye itogi i zadachi izucheniia novoi istorii SShA v Sovetskom Soiuze" (Some Results and Goals of the Study of Modern U.S. History in the Soviet Union), *Novaia i Noveishaia Istoriia* (Modern and Contemporary History) 2 (1969): 39–54.

5. Malkin, *Grazhdanskaia voina v SShA i tsarskaia Rossiia* (The Civil War in the United States and Tsarist Russia) (Moscow-Leningrad, 1939).

Foreign Policy of Russia. He showed that Russia steadfastly supported the Union and that the countries of Western Europe, particularly Britain, were hostile to it. However, some of the author's basic propositions offer opportunity for challenge. Thus, it would appear that he exaggerated the dynamism of Russian foreign policy during the period in question. We know that in the 1860s the Russian government was incapable of engaging in large-scale foreign conquests. Its main goal was to achieve the abrogation of the limiting clauses of the Paris Peace Treaty of 1856. The imperial bureaucracy had not yet begun to develop plans for the seizure of the Dardanelles. And yet Malkin argues that the policy of the tsarist government toward the United States was equivocal and contradictory throughout the Civil War,[6] for its attitude to the political system in the United States was unsympathetic. The very documents the author cites serve, however, to undermine the approach he adopts at the beginning of the book.

The mounting tensions between Russia and Great Britain and the military threat posed to the United States by certain Western European powers led the governments of Russia and the United States to regard the social differences between their countries as a matter of secondary importance. Moreover, the Russian government, which had just abolished serfdom (1861), could not have openly come to the defense of slavery and the Southern insurrectionaries without discrediting itself in the eyes of Russian public opinion. Malkin discusses the causes that led the Russian government to dispatch two naval squadrons to America in 1863, but he fails to devote sufficient attention to the part played by this event in improving the international position of the United States. In addition to Malkin's monograph and his article on Russian-American relations,[7] several other contributions by Soviet historians that examine the attitude of the Russian revolutionary democrats to the events of the American Civil War stand out.[8]

The works by American historians that discuss the problem of Russian-American relations during the Civil War fall into two groups. Some who study this subject do not believe that the friendly relations between Russia and the United States throughout the nineteenth century were the result of the operation of certain internal factors. They ignore the common economic interests of Russia and America and fail to see that the problems confronting the two countries in the 1860s, namely the abolition of serfdom in Russia and the liquidation of slavery in the United States, were to some degree similar

---

6. Ibid., 13, 16, 23–24, 241.
7. See Malkin, "Russko-amerikanskie otnosheniia v period grazhdanskoi voiny" (Russian-American Relations in the Period of the Civil War) in *K stoletiiu grazhdanskoi voiny v SShA: Sbornik statei* (Collection of Articles Marking the Centenary of the Civil War in the United States) (Moscow, 1961).
8. I. Ia. Razumnikova, "N. G. Chernyshevskii o grazhdanskoi voine v Soedennykh Shtatakh Ameriki 1861–1865 gg. (N. G. Chernyshevsky on the Civil War in the United States of America of 1861–1865), in *Trudy Voronezhsk. gos. un-ta* (Transactions of Voronezh State University) 47 (1955); Iu. S. Melent'ev and M. N. Kogan, "O stat'e V. A. Obrucheva, 'Nevol'nichestvo v Severnoi Amerike'" (Concerning Vladimir Obruchev's Article "Bondage in North America"), *Uchen. zap Ural'sk. gos. un-ta im. A. M. Gor'kogo* (Transactions of the A. M. Gorky State University of the Western Urals) 13 (1955); I. Ia. Levitas, "Grazhdanskaia voina v SShA i russkie revoliutsionery-demokraty" (The Civil War in the United States and the Russian Revolutionary Democrats), *Prepodavanie istorii v shkole* (The Teaching of History in Schools) 3 (1962).

in nature. In their opinion, the main reason for the help given by Russia to the Union was the hostility of the two governments to Britain. When the hostile attitude of the two countries toward Britain changed, these historians say, the "tradition of friendship" between Russia and America came to an end. This view found its fullest expression in Albert Woldman's *Lincoln and the Russians,* which treats official relations between Russia and America. The author claims that the support extended by Russia to the Union was a "historical curiosity." Woldman believes that the European powers, including Russia, viewed the United States as a source of revolutionary peril, while the Americans regarded Russia as a classic example of tyranny and absolutism. Nevertheless, the author concedes that the alliance that existed between Russia and America during the Civil War was of considerable benefit to both sides. "This strange alliance," Woldman writes, "was decisive in preventing European intervention in the American Civil War; moreover, it destroyed the Anglo-French alliance, which was directed against Russia's position in the Polish Question." In the author's view, the visit by a Russian naval squadron to New York represented the high point of Russian-American cooperation; this, he says, was due to a number of factors: Russia's intention to prevent British and French military interference in the affairs of the United States; Russia's need to restore its international position, which had been undermined by the Crimean War; and Russia's desire to take revenge on Britain for its defeat in the Crimean War. Woldman suggests, however, that the significance of this friendly act was greatly exaggerated by the Americans, who were to remember it as one of the events that saved their country.[9]

In his article "The Russian Fleet and the American Civil War," Howard Kushner offers an analysis of the relations between Russia and America during the Civil War period that is similar to Woldman's.[10] He examines the "equivocal nature" of Russian-American relations throughout history and sees the reason for the peculiar character of the relationship between the two countries in the differences between their social and political systems. Like Woldman, Kushner concedes that the appearance of Russian naval vessels off the American coast represented a positive development from the point of view of the Union side, but again like his colleague, he believes that the Americans attached too much significance to that event.

As well as studying the official relations between America and Russia, in recent years American scholars have devoted considerable attention to the attitude of the various groups in Russian society toward the events that took place in the United States during the Civil War. Thus, Hans Rogger has studied the views of the representatives of the three different currents—revolutionary, liberal, and official—of Russian political thought, the influence of these figures on American society, and the impact of the American Civil War on individual Russian thinkers. Rogger analyzes the views of Alexander Herzen, Nicholas Chernyshevsky, and Nikolai Ogarev on the one hand, and of Mikhail Katkov and Konstantin Pobedonostsev on the other. He writes about the two

---

9. Albert A. Woldman, *Lincoln and the Russians* (Cleveland and New York, 1952), viii, 131, 135–36, 149.
10. "The Russian Fleet and the American Civil War: Another View," *The Historian* 34, no. 4 (August 1972), 633–49, especially 642. See also V. N. Ponomarev's review of this article in *Problems of History* 3 (1973).

Russias that existed at the time—tsarist Russia and democratic Russia—the second of which looked to the United States with hope, seeing in the events taking place in that country a model for its own internal development.[11]

A brief survey of the literature on this subject shows that after the publication of Malkin's book, Soviet historians did not produce studies specifically devoted to an analysis of the position adopted by the Russian government toward the United States during the Civil War. As for American scholars specializing in this field, most of them were insufficiently familiar with Russian sources, and as a result their work suffered from a certain one-sidedness.

The Civil War was preceded by a bitter presidential contest between the governing Democrats and the opposition Republicans. The Republican Party nominated Abraham Lincoln for the presidency. Coming from a family of middle-income farmers, Lincoln represented the interests of the broad sections of the American bourgeoisie. In 1860 he was elected President of the United States. The victory of the Republican Party greatly influenced the subsequent course of American history. As president, Lincoln attempted to implement policies that reflected certain key demands by the working masses.[12]

Unable to accept their electoral defeat, the Southern planters resolved to leave the Union. They tried to induce those states that wavered between North and South, particularly those in the West, to follow them in breaking away from the rest of the country. By destroying the Union the Southern planters hoped to weaken the North and regain the dominant position in national affairs they had lost. In late 1860 and early 1861 eleven states, which together occupied some 40 percent of the territory of the United States, seceded from the Union.[13] In February 1861, in the city of Montgomery, Alabama, the slaveholding aristocracy proclaimed the establishment of a new republic, the Confederate States of America. A Confederate Congress was formed that approved a constitution that made slavery legal and elected Jefferson Davis, a rich slave-owner, President of the Confederacy. The Civil War began on April 12, 1861, when the Southern secessionists shelled Fort Sumter, which had remained loyal to the Lincoln government. On April 15 Lincoln declared the slave-owning states to be in a state of rebellion and called for seventy-five thousand volunteers for the army.

The governments of Western Europe had an interest in seeing the United States dismembered and weakened. In their struggle with the North, the insurrectionaries placed special hopes on Britain, which was the chief rival of the young capitalist Republic. Despite its wish to see the North weakened, the British cabinet was wary of the South's desire to control the American cotton trade. The cabinet was prepared to maintain trade relations with the Northern states and was anxious to ensure Britain's

---

11. Rogger, "Russia and the Civil War," in *Heard Around the World: The Impact Abroad of the Civil War,* edited by Harold Hyman (New York, 1969), 178.

12. See D. B. Petrov, *Avraam Linkol'n* (Abraham Lincoln) (Moscow, 1959).

13. For more on the Civil War in the United States, see A. V. Efimov, *Ocherki po istorii SShA* (Studies in the History of the United States) (Moscow, 1958) and *SShA—puti razvitiia kapitalizma* (The United States of America: The Path of Capitalist Development) (Moscow, 1959); Robert F. Ivanov, *Grazhdanskaia voina v SShA, 1861–1865 gg.* (The Civil War in the United States of 1861–1865) (Moscow, 1960); Gennadii P. Kuropiatnik, *Vtoraia amerikanskaia revoliutsiia* (The Second American Revolution) (Moscow, 1961).

continued ability to purchase grain from the United States. Moreover, Britain had invested considerable capital in American industry. The British government was quite happy to see the United States break up into two rival republics, for this would have allowed Britain to continue to dominate world markets.[14]

The British bourgeoisie, however, was afraid of incurring the condemnation of world public opinion by openly supporting the slave-owning South. These factors determined Britain's decision to adopt an official attitude of neutrality in the conflict between the states, although it gave the Confederacy material assistance. In 1861–1862 alone Britain sold to the Southern states $9 million worth of arms and military supplies.[15] Describing the policy of the Western powers, Russian foreign minister Alexander Gorchakov wrote, "In relation to America, England and France have adopted an attitude of non-intervention. But England's traditional antipathy towards the Americans continues. The attitude of France to America is hardly much more favorable."[16]

In early June 1861 the British government sent three infantry regiments to Canada under the pretext of protecting its colony from attack. The cabinet in London was well aware that the North had no intention of invading Canada but by mounting this demonstration Britain wished to show its support for the South and force the North to make concessions to its adversary.[17] The British turned Canada into a base of supply for the Confederacy. Arms shipments were sent from there to the South; vessels for the Confederate navy were constructed in British shipyards. Britain acted in complete accord with France and Spain. In October 1861 in London, the three powers signed an agreement providing for a joint intervention in Mexico. Acting on behalf of the three allies, France landed an expeditionary force in an area of Mexico that bordered the rebel states. The leaders of the Confederacy were able to establish direct contact with the French army of occupation.

For its part, in 1862 Lincoln's government took a number of important political steps: it adopted the Homestead Act and issued a proclamation abolishing slavery throughout the country.[18] These measures were a sign that the North was now prepared to conduct the struggle against the South in a more decisive manner. The forces of world reaction were alarmed. The British press criticized Lincoln's proclamation as a violation of the laws of the Confederacy and as an incitement for the slaves to revolt. British newspapers expressed concern about the fate of the Southern insurrectionaries, thereby demonstrating their sympathy for the slave-owners.

The Civil War in America fascinated contemporaries by its very scale. Marx and Engels described it as a "spectacle that has no equal in the annals of military history."[19] From the start the attitude of the Russian government toward the North was sympathetic.

14. See Malkin, *Grazhdanskaia voina,* 19–22.
15. *Vestnik Evropy* (European Herald) 3, no. 5 (1872): 399.
16. AVPR (Archive of the Foreign Policy of Russia), record group kants. (Chancellery), Report of the Minister of Foreign Affairs for 1864, 166–67.
17. Malkin, *Grazhdanskaia voina,* 54.
18. Under the Homestead Act every citizen of the United States who paid a ten-dollar registration fee received a 160-acre plot of land.
19. Marx and Engels, *Works,* vol. 15, 498.

This was in keeping with the tradition of friendly relations between the two countries that went back to the American War of Independence. At that time Catherine II rejected George III's official request for help, citing her preoccupation with the internal problems of her empire and the "uncertainty of the affairs of Poland and the obscurity of those of Sweden."[20] Russia also supported the United States during the Anglo-American War of 1812–1814.[21] During the Crimean War, when a joint British-French naval squadron was preparing to attack the Russian Far East, the American government informed Russia of the hostile intentions of the Allies. As a result of this warning Russia was able to adopt timely measures that repulsed the attack by the Allied fleet.

The good relations between Russia and the United States were due to several factors, chief among which was the common attitude of the two countries toward Britain. Both governments viewed Great Britain as their chief rival. In the 1860s, with the consolidation of capitalist structures in Russia's economy, British-Russian tensions in Central Asia and in the Middle and Far East became particularly acute. The same period witnessed an intensification of the rivalry between Britain and the United States. The American navy posed a threat to Britain's world hegemony, while American-made industrial goods were beginning to reduce Britain's share of the world market. As for Russia and the United States, there were no major disagreements between them. William H. Seward, the American secretary of state, believed that the amicable nature of the relationship between the two countries was due to the abolition of serfdom in Russia, the decision of the Russian government to pursue the bourgeois path of development, and their common goal of pursuing the struggle against Britain. Prince Gorchakov referred to the shared destiny of Russia and America: "Both countries carried out a struggle for emancipation, both had to face disagreements and foreign intrigues."[22] In his instructions of June 28, 1861, to Stoeckl, the Russian minister to Washington, Gorchakov expressed his regret at the outbreak of civil war in America, referred to Russia's "lively interest" in the events in that country, and spoke of his hope that the government in Washington would come to an agreement with the South "in spite of the differences in their interests and constitutions." "Russia," wrote Gorchakov, "has the friendliest interests in America, because during the preceding period it was in a sense foreordained that the two countries, which lie at the ends of two worlds, would manifest a natural solidarity of interests and sympathies, of which they have now given evidence." He spoke of his hope that the American nation would show political wisdom in its search for the possibility of a general agreement among the states.[23]

Lincoln's government was grateful to Russia for its position in the conflict. "The President and the Secretary of State informed me that of all the communications they had received from the Governments of Europe ours was the most amicable and the most sympathetic," reported Stoeckl to Gorchakov.[24]

20. *Sbornik RIO* (Collection of the Russian Historical Society) 19: 500–502.
21. See Bolkhovitinov and S. I. Divil'kovskii, "Russkaia diplomatiia i anglo-amerikanskaia voina 1812–1814 godov," (Russian Diplomacy and the Anglo-American War of 1812–1814), *Modern and Contemporary History* 4: 1961.
22. AVPR, record group kants., Report of the Minister of Foreign Affairs for 1863, 109.
23. *Krasnyi Arkhiv* (The Red Archive) 94 (1939): 115–16.
24. Ibid., 118.

The Russian government wished to see the Civil War speedily concluded and the Union restored. It viewed the United States as a counterweight to "the power of England," as an element in the "world balance." Russia would have liked to see the North and the South come to an agreement, whatever its conditions, and was prepared to countenance concessions by the North to the South. "There is no North and no South for us, but only the Federal Union, the dissolution of which we view with regret," Gorchakov informed Stoeckl. Nevertheless, the tsarist government disapproved of many of the Union's legislative structures. As Stoeckl observed,

> If the ultra-democratic regime has shown itself to be unsound, we need not feel any regret about this, but we cannot remain indifferent to the dangers that threaten the nation itself. Its existence is of greater importance to us than to any other state. We must protect our interests and strengthen our influence in the area of the Pacific Ocean. In that region we have already encountered, and in all probability, shall continue to encounter obstacles put in our way by England, and the help of the Americans will always be useful to us.[25]

It is clear that the cabinet in St. Petersburg drew a distinction between the international role of the United States as a sovereign state and its political system. Although it disagreed with Lincoln's policies inside the country, the Russian government regarded America as a future ally in the solution of the political problems of Europe and the Far East.

For its part, the United States saw Russia as a power capable of supporting its struggle with Britain and France on the American continent and in the Pacific. The two governments intended to establish economic and political links, primarily through the Far East, where the shortest route between the two countries lay. Washington, aware of the weakness of Russia's position in the Far East, hoped to avail itself of that weakness for its own purposes. But officially the two cabinets continued to insist that there were no disagreements between their countries. In 1862–1863 plans for the laying of a telegraph line between America and Russia were drawn up. It would have run from San Francisco through Alaska, the Bering Sea, and Siberia.[26]

The outbreak of the Civil War coincided with the intensification of class antagonisms and the ideological struggle in Russia. This development had been brought about by the emancipation of the serfs. In their attacks on serfdom and landlord property rights, the Russian revolutionary democrats had often turned to American history, finding in it some examples worthy of emulation and others that deserved criticism. In 1858, in a series of articles entitled "Russian Questions," Ogarev referred to the "desperate situation of the Russian peasant" under serfdom and spoke of the pernicious impact of slavery in the United States. "While the application of science to agriculture has reached a high degree of development in the Northern States, something very different

---

25. Ibid., 125–26.
26. *Mezhdunarodnye otnosheniia na Dal'nem Vostoke* (International Relations in the Far East) (Moscow, 1973) 2: 115–16.

is happening in the Southern States, where the labor of slaves is used," he wrote.[27] Chernyshevsky rightly believed that the struggle against "bondage" was the chief cause of the American Civil War, which he described as the struggle of opposing interests and forces: "The enmity of the South towards the North, the hostility among the estates, the hatred of the patricians for the lowly plebeians, the upper classes' detestation of the republican system."[28]

The military setbacks suffered by the North in the early stages of the conflict did not shake the belief of democratically minded Russians that the Union would eventually emerge victorious. "The triumph of the North over the planters is inevitable," wrote Chernyshevsky, "A mistake made by the commander of the advance guard is of no consequence, except that it will serve to strengthen the determination of that side."[29] In his articles Chernyshevsky convincingly argued that slavery was not viable economically or politically. "In that part [of the United States] where bondage has been preserved, public opinion, which is dominated by the planters, refuses to countenance a single word sympathetic to abolitionism; those persons who speak out against bondage are robbed, banished, or punished as criminals."[30] He believed that the North should be vigorous in prosecuting the war against the Southern planters and he commented on the growing prestige of the Union. "The majority of the population of the Southern States does not wish to secede from the union; the insurgents are a minority which even in the South is only capable of keeping the power it has captured by resorting to violence."[31]

In order to acquaint its readers with life inside America and with the literature of that country, the journal *Sovremennik* (Contemporary) published articles by travelers who had visited the United States, the writings of Harriet Beecher Stowe and Bayard Taylor, and essays about the works of these writers and the development of American culture. The March issue of 1861 included an "Extract" from the statute of February 19, 1861, Longfellow's "Poems of Slavery," and an article by a prominent revolutionary democrat, Vladimir Obruchev, entitled "Bondage in North America." The editors intended that the contents of this issue should emphasize the similarity in the problems confronting the two countries.

In describing the indignities visited upon the slave population of the Southern states and the stagnation and even decline of the slave-based economy there, Obruchev appeared to invite the Russian reader to ponder the situation of the common people in tsarist Russia. "The planter's whip always, everywhere, and for everything—these are the conditions in which the slaves must labor." Obruchev condemned racism, declaring that one must "abandon the obsequious worship of the genius of this or that race."[32]

27. Ogarev, *Izbrannye sotsial'no-politicheskie i filosofskie proizvediia* (Selected Sociopolitical and Philosophical Writings) (Moscow, 1952), 166.
28. Chernyshevskii, *Poln. sobr. soch.* (Complete Collected Works), 16 vols. (Moscow, 1939–1953), vol. 7, 317.
29. Chernyshevskii, *Works,* vol. 8, 545.
30. Chernyshevskii, *Works,* vol. 7, 228. Abolitionism—a movement that aimed to secure the emancipation of slaves.
31. Chernyshevskii, *Works,* vol. 8, 629.
32. *Sovremennik* (Contemporary) 3 (1861): 279, 291.

Not only the revolutionary democrats, but even liberals and government supporters were sympathetic to the events taking place in the United States. *Moskovskie Vedomosti* (Moscow Gazette), which during this period was still a liberal organ, hailed the emancipation of the Negroes, describing this act as "one of the greatest political events in history."[33] But the liberals differed from the democrats in their views on what the North's ultimate war aims should be. Although they welcomed the emancipation of the slaves, they did not call for a decisive struggle against the planters, unlike *Contemporary*.[34] The liberals wished to see a reconciliation between the North and the South and the reestablishment of a single American state. Their attitude to the events in the United States was close to that of the tsarist government.

A number of Russians joined the ranks of the Union army. Colonel Ivan Turchaninov, formerly an officer of the Russian General Staff, commanded a regiment of Illinois volunteers. [6] During the Civil War he proved to be an exemplary officer: the 19th Regiment, which he commanded, was considered to be one of the best in the Union army. President Lincoln rewarded his success in the field and his ability to plan daring military operations by promoting him to the rank of general.[35] For their part, Americans became interested in Russia. *Moscow Gazette* quoted a report from the Washington correspondent of another Russian periodical, *Severnaia Pchela* (Northern Bee), which had written that poems about the emancipation of the Russian peasants were being disseminated in the United States and were being recited in the streets of the American capital.[36]

In November 1861 the Union authorities detained a group of Confederate diplomats who were sailing on board the British ship *Trent* to London. This incident almost led to a war between Britain and the United States. The British used it to begin a violent campaign of denunciation against the North. Referring to the *Trent* affair, Marx wrote: "The importance of this event lies in its moral impact on the English people and in the fact that the secessionists' English friends—the cotton merchants—can easily make political capital out of it."[37] The London newspapers declared that the government in Washington should give Britain "satisfaction," failing which Britain should declare war against the North.[38] Herzen, who was then living in London, wrote, "Everyone here speaks of war with America."[39] The Russian press observed with some justice, however, that Britain did not really intend to go to war but rather wished to make use of the affair to help the Confederacy by forcing the North to recognize the secession of the Southern states.[40]

Progressive figures in Russian society condemned the brouhaha in the West surrounding the *Trent* affair and denounced Britain's plans to wage war on the North.

---

33. *Moskovskie Vedomosti*, May 2, 1862.
34. *Otechestvennye Zapiski* (Fatherland Notes) 2 (1862): 500.
35. For more on Turchaninov, see Dim Petrov (Biriuk), *Ivan Turchaninov* (Moscow, 1973), 117–18, 188–89 [and the article by Startsev that follows].
36. *Moskovskie Vedomosti*, March 25, 1862.
37. Marx and Engels, *Works*, vol. 15, 402.
38. Ibid., 406.
39. Herzen, *Sobr. soch.* (Collected Works) (Petrograd, 1919), vol. 11, 362.
40. *S.-Peterburgskie Vedomosti* (St. Petersburg Gazette), February 9, 1862.

Chernyshevsky believed that the incident was of itself insignificant and that the British and French bourgeoisie were using it as an excuse, in order to conceal their elaborate schemes aimed at perpetuating the breakup of the Union and weakening the American Republic. He revealed the hidden economic and political motives behind the policies of Lord Palmerston and Napoleon III.[41] Nikolai Shelgunov suggested that the supporters of the South were attempting to present the North in an unflattering light so that it would be compromised in the eyes of the "English hucksters and magnates."[42] His views on the policy of the English bourgeoisie were close to the opinions expressed by Marx in regard to the *Trent* affair. "Palmerston wants war," Marx wrote, "[but] the English people do not want war. Events will show who will emerge victorious in this duel—Palmerston, or the people."[43]

The cabinet in Petersburg did not offer the North particularly strong support in the *Trent* affair, but it viewed with disfavor the efforts by political figures in Britain and France to spread war fever in those countries. Indeed, Gorchakov told Stoeckl that the Russian government did not wish to pressure the American government to ratify the convention on maritime rights, signed between the United States and Russia on August 24, 1861, leaving it to the Americans to decide when to do this.[44]

This démarche by the Russian government enabled the Americans to employ privateers on the high seas. The Lincoln administration thanked St. Petersburg for its position in the matter of the convention, viewing it as a sign of its friendly attitude toward the United States.[45] The refusal of the Russian government to support Palmerston's bellicose intentions against the North contributed to the peaceful resolution of the Anglo-American conflict. After the *Trent* affair had ended peacefully, Gorchakov in his instructions to Stoeckl reiterated his preference for a policy of moderation designed to bring about a reconciliation between the North and the South. Nevertheless, he included this unequivocal statement: "The only government in the United States we recognize is the one that has its seat in Washington."[46]

There was growing concern among the merchants and industrialists of Western Europe that the Civil War in the United States would turn into a prolonged conflict. Responding to this concern, in 1862 the French government suggested that Britain and Russia should join it in intervening diplomatically in the struggle between the North and the South. According to the plan drawn up by Napoleon III, the North was to be persuaded to conclude a six-month armistice with the South and lift its blockade of the Confederacy. This would open the South's ports for commercial shipping from

---

41. Chernyshevskii, *Works,* vol. 8, 582.
42. *Russkoe Slovo* (Russian Word) 5 (1863): 23.
43. Marx and Engels, *Works,* vol. 15, 444.
44. The convention of August 24, 1861, elaborated on the principles of international maritime law contained in the Declaration of April 16, 1856, which had been signed by the participants in the Paris peace conference. The Declaration had outlawed privateering, that is, attacks by armed, privately owned vessels on the merchant shipping of an enemy country or on that of neutral states. The agreement of 1861, concluded after the start of the Civil War, was directed against the rebel states of the South and those Western European countries that supported them.
45. *Red Archive* 94 (1939): 121.
46. Ibid., 126.

Europe. Acceptance of this plan by the European powers would have amounted to a recognition by them of the Confederacy as a belligerent and would have provided a legal basis for the help it received from the West. Britain supported the proposal by the French emperor, and the London press grew more vociferous in its advocacy of measures that would guarantee the "protection" of British commercial interests. This, it declared, required "decisive action."[47]

The Russian government, however, believed that foreign intervention would complicate, rather than improve, the situation in the United States. It declined to support the French initiative, although it formulated its refusal cautiously. In his instructions to Stoeckl, Gorchakov wrote of Russia's desire to act in concert with the governments of the Western powers with a view to putting an end to the "tragic struggle," although he noted that the Russian government "did not find it possible" to take part in such an undertaking "officially."[48] Yet without the support of St. Petersburg the plan had only a dubious chance of success, and this was understood in Europe. British ruling circles feared that hostile action by the European powers against the North might lead to a Russian-American alliance that would be directed chiefly against Britain. "At the present time," wrote John Russell to Palmerston, "we should not act without Russia."[49] Thus St. Petersburg's refusal to support Britain and France once again prevented the governments of Western Europe from intervening in the civil war in America.

The government in Washington was highly appreciative of Russia's helpful attitude. In his instructions to Cassius Clay, the American minister to Russia, Seward wrote that the North believed that "friendship with Russia is preferable to friendship with other European powers, precisely because she constantly wishes for us success and allows us to manage our affairs in the manner we find most advantageous."[50]

In 1863 the conflict between the North and the South entered a new stage. The Union now began to employ revolutionary methods in its prosecution of the war. During this period the danger of military intervention by the Western powers again increased. The sums spent by the British and French governments on the construction of naval vessels for the South rose. On January 28, 1863, in Richmond an agreement was signed for a $3 million "cotton loan" at 7 percent interest, cotton to be the security. The Confederacy concluded the agreement with a German firm in Frankfurt, but in reality the loan had been provided by English bankers.[51] This was important to the South not only economically, but politically, for its leaders saw the loan as a means of restoring the Confederacy's shaken prestige. The likelihood of foreign intervention in the Civil War grew.

The Polish uprising of 1863 for a time drew the attention of the European powers away from the events in America. This was in the Union's interest. None of the governments in Western Europe actually desired Polish independence, but they offered

---

47. *St. Petersburg Gazette* 79, 1862.
48. Gorchakov to Stoeckl, November 8/October 27, 1862, *Red Archive* 94 (1939): 130.
49. Ibid., 105.
50. Division of Manuscripts, Lenin (Russian National) Library, record group 169 ("D. A. Miliutin"), inventory 10, list 8, 332.
51. Malkin, *Grazhdanskaia voina,* 209.

the insurgents verbal support. Western European powers tried to involve the United States in their anti-Russian policy, but the American government rejected a proposal by Napoleon III for joint intervention in the affairs of Poland. In its official response to the French initiative the Lincoln administration referred to the traditional principles of U.S. policy and to the friendly position Russia had adopted toward the Union during the Civil War.[52] Washington's declaration was warmly greeted by the Russian government. "A statement like this," wrote Gorchakov to Seward, "serves to strengthen the ties of mutual sympathy that bind the two sides."[53]

Russia's decision to dispatch a number of its warships on a visit to the United States proved to be of great benefit to Lincoln's government. In July 1863, the cabinet in St. Petersburg ordered a squadron of seven ships, commanded by Rear-Admiral Stepan Lesovskii, to set sail for America. After crossing the Atlantic, the squadron dropped anchor in New York Harbor on September 24, 1863. A second squadron under Rear-Admiral Andrei Popov reached San Francisco in October 1863. On April 12, 1863, Nikolai Krabbe, director of the Ministry of Navy, wrote to Admiral Popov, whose squadron was stationed in the Pacific, about the deterioration in the international situation caused by the events in Poland. He suggested that Popov should take steps that would enable him, upon receiving news of the commencement of hostilities between the Western powers and Russia, to lead his squadron "to the vulnerable points in the enemy's possessions, as well as to raid the trade routes." Arguing that information about events in Europe reached the Far East only belatedly and that his ships lacked provisions and instruments for effecting repairs, Popov proposed that the Russian squadrons sail to San Francisco, which he regarded as the port "best guaranteeing communications with Petersburg."[54]

It was decided that the Russian warships would patrol the high seas and attack the sea trade and colonies of Britain and France, should war between them and Russia break out. In addition, Popov was entrusted with the defense of San Francisco in case of an enemy attack. Admiral Lesovskii received similar orders. The instructions the Ministry of Navy issued to Lesovskii on July 11, 1863, read: "In case of the expected war with the Western powers you are to use all possible and available means to attack our enemies."[55] Lesovskii's squadron was also directed to carry out naval reconnaissance, to gather information "about the major trade routes along which goods are carried across the oceans, noting the nature and country of provenance of the cargo sent along them." The admiral was also ordered to compile "a full description of the colonial possessions of the Western powers, which would include your views concerning the possibility of mounting an attack upon them, the direction and strength of such an attack, their defenses, their military and commercial importance, etc."[56]

It is doubtful whether at that time the Russian government really believed that war with the Western powers was imminent, and, indeed, the two naval squadrons were too

---

52. E. A. Adamov, "Soedinennye Shtaty v epokhu Grazhdanskoi voiny i Rossiia" (Russia and the United States in the Period of the Civil War), Introduction, *Red Archive* 38 (1930): 149–50.
53. Stoeckl to Gorchakov, May 11/April 29, 1893, *Red Archive* 94: 133–34.
54. *Red Archive* 38: 156.
55. Ibid., 159.
56. Ibid., 161.

weak to threaten them seriously. Russia mounted this naval demonstration in order to distract the attention of the governments of Europe from the events in Poland and to demonstrate publicly Russian-American unity. Gorchakov later wrote: "The concentration of our naval forces off North America proved to be a fortunate decision in the political sense, and was carried out in an exemplary fashion."[57]

In July 1863, as the Russian ships sailed off to America, the authorities in St. Petersburg sent a diplomatic dispatch to Washington to inquire of the American government how it would react to the appearance of Russian naval vessels in American ports. In his reply Gideon Welles, secretary of the navy, stated that the presence of a squadron "belonging to His Majesty's navy can only be a source of joy and happiness for our compatriots." Naval yards were placed at the disposal of the Russian squadron in New York, and local authorities were instructed to render the Russian sailors "any service that they may require."[58] When reporting the arrival of the Russian warships in American ports, most of the Russian press did not comment on the event. An exception was *Moscow Gazette,* which argued that the decision to dispatch the naval squadrons had been made because their presence off the coast of the United States would weaken France, whose "ambitions in Mexico" would suffer "a most telling blow" in the event of war.[59]

Although Russia's decision to send a naval force into American waters was based on a desire to protect Russian interests, it also provided moral support to the government in Washington and contributed to the strengthening of Russian-American ties. There was speculation in Western countries about the existence of a secret Russian-American alliance. This theory was particularly popular with the British press.[60] Although rumors of such an alliance were unfounded, the governments of Western Europe, anxious about Russia's position, for a time moderated their support for the South.

In every American port they visited the officers and sailors of the crews of the Russian ships met with a warm reception. To honor them banquets were held, speeches given, and articles extolling the idea of a Russian-American rapprochement published. "The appearance of our fleet off the coast of the United States caused a sensation in that country, and particularly in New York," wrote Stoeckl to Gorchakov. ". . . The municipal authorities of New York officially offered the city's hospitality to our sailors."[61] He separately reported, "Scientific and charitable societies, indeed all the sections of the population compete with one another in their efforts to be agreeable to the sailors."[62]

At the invitation of Lincoln the officers of Lesovskii's squadron visited Washington, where they were received by the president in the White House. In a dispatch to Stoeckl, Gorchakov commented on the treatment of the Russian naval crews in the United

57. Quoted in Malkin, *Grazhdanskaia voina,* 259.
58. *Red Archive* 38: 157.
59. *Moskovskie Vedomosti,* November 5, 1863.
60. Division of Manuscripts, Lenin Library, record group 169, inventory 10, list 11, 536.
61. *Red Archive* 94: 136.
62. "Grazhdanskaia voina v SShA i Rossii: K prebyvaniiu russkikh voennykh korablei v SShA: publikatsiia dokumentov" (The Civil War in the United States and Russia: Concerning the Visit to the United States by Russian Naval Vessels: a Selection of Documents), introduction. S. I. Poval'nikov, *Novaia i Noveishaia Istoriia* 6 (1973): 89–90.

States: "Such an unconstrained expression of amicable feeling is proof indeed of the friendly relations that exist between the two countries."[63]

While they were moored in American ports, the Russian squadrons attempted to assist the North in every way they could. In late 1863 or early 1864 Rear-Admiral Popov, the commander of the Russian naval force that had been sent to San Francisco, reported to Stoeckl that he thought it advisable to help the city in defending itself against Southern raiders.[64] Popov's declaration, which was published in the newspapers, was hailed by the local population. The Confederate pirates were intimidated, and refrained from attacking the port, guarded by Russian warships. In his reply to Popov, however, Stoeckl counselled prudence, warning him against aggravating the situation in the country.

The Russian warships spent some nine months in American waters. In July 1864, when the danger of Western intervention in the affairs of Poland had passed and the Union army embarked on a general offensive against the forces of the Confederacy, the Russian naval squadrons left the United States. Bidding farewell to the warships, the mayor of Boston spoke of international brotherhood and the moral support America had received, which had been of particular importance to the United States at a time when Western Europe behaved toward it in an unfriendly fashion.[65] Upon their return to Russia the officers of the two naval squadrons were received by Clay. In his speech he described Russia and America as two great powers, one of which was of the East and the other of the West; they entertained no hostile designs against each another.

As already noted, the relations between the two countries were determined by their political and economic interests. The Russian government saw in the United States a power that could "counteract the superiority of England" and weaken the position of the Western countries.[66] For its part, Washington viewed Russia as a counterweight to the Anglo-French coalition in not only Europe but also the Americas and the Far East. The tradition of friendship between Russia and America was due also to other factors, such as the absence of significant disagreements between the two countries and their mutual interest in developing political and commercial ties. All this explains the sympathetic position adopted by Russia toward the Union during the American Civil War. While the Western powers strove to perpetuate the division of the United States and assisted the rebels, Russia made an effort to contribute to the victory of the Union side. Indeed, Russia was the only country to help the North.

In a letter to American workers in 1918, Lenin declared: "The American people possess a revolutionary tradition, which has been continued by the foremost representatives of the American proletariat, who on several occasions have expressed their full sympathy with us, the Bolsheviks. This tradition was formed in the war of liberation against England of the eighteenth century and later in the civil war of the nineteenth century."[67]

63. Ibid., 138.
64. *Red Archive* 94: 139.
65. *Voennaia Entsiklopediia* (The Military Encyclopedia), vol. 2 (1911), 365.
66. *Red Archive* 94: 144. Undated memorandum to Gorchakov from Katakazi, special assistant to Vice-Chancellor.
67. Lenin, *Works,* vol. 37, 58.

6

Ivan Turchaninov and the American Civil War, by A. I. Startsev

In 1859 Alexander Herzen, then exiled in London, received a letter from Ivan Vasilevich Turchaninov, a Russian living in the United States, that gave a vivid description of the social atmosphere and private mores in the American bourgeois republic.

> Some three years ago, in the first days of June, if I am not mistaken, at a time when the Crimean War had just ended and His Majesty was pleased to begin the preparations for his Coronation, you were visited in London by a Colonel Turchaninov of the General Staff of the Imperial Guards. That was . . . I told you I was leaving for the United States, and I recall your remark: "America is a boring country!" . . . I confess that I rather doubted your words, for my transatlantic dreams were loftier and purer than mundane reality.[1]

Next Turchaninov offered a summary of negative impressions he had accumulated during his stay in the United States.

> This republic is a paradise for the rich, for here they are truly independent; the most dastardly crimes and the basest intrigues may be a source of monetary gain for them. Here the appellation smart man (what we would call a "trickster" or "slicker") is a mark of distinction: whether one is a millionaire or a porter, a senator or a tax-collector, a manufacturer of counterfeit banknotes or a daylight robber, smartness is a definite *sine qua non*. A man may be the greatest of scoundrels, but if he has managed to dodge the scaffold and is "smart," he is respected, whatever his class or station: everyone

---

1. *Literaturnoe Nasledstvo* (Literary Heritage), vol. 62, *Herzen and Ogarev*, pt. 2 (Moscow, 1955), 599 (Turchaninov and wife to Herzen, commentary by D. I. Zaslavskii). This article by A. I. Startsev was first published in *Nov. 1919: Novaia i Noveishaia Istoriia* (Modern and Contemporary History), 1974; reprinted in *Russko-Amerikskie etiudy* (Russian-American Studies) (Moscow, 1995), 99–142.

courts him, his opinions are valued above all others in all matters his judgements and decisions are trusted more than the Bible; he controls the circle in which he moves. The governing class, which holds power in every sphere, is composed of such tricksters and slickers; the rest of the population are their subjects. The capitalist trickster is an American prince, whose dignity it is no more permissible to attack than the dignity of the Russian tsar; the person of the former employs soldiers and gendarmes to crush his enemies, the latter uses dollars and the criminals under his command to the same end.[2]

We are familiar with the harsh criticism of American bourgeois democracy advanced by conservative European writers in the first half of the nineteenth century. But a close reading of Turchaninov's letter clearly shows that he offered a critique of the American bourgeois republic from the left. The author of the letter to Herzen was an enemy of the autocratic serf-based system, but he was equally opposed to the tyranny of capital. "Even in Russia the establishment of something like a social republic is more possible than in America," he told Herzen in the same letter.[3] The term "social republic" as used here in Herzen's sense of the term, meaning a "real" or "internal" republic, provides for the economic and social equality of its citizens as opposed to an "alleged" or "formal" bourgeois republic.[4] We may, therefore, conclude that Turchaninov's critique of bourgeois rule had points in common with the utopian socialist theories of his time.

Turchaninov informed Herzen that he was sending him two articles he had written in the United States for publication in *Poliarnaia Zvezda* (Polar Star) and promised him that upon receiving a letter of reply he would send more articles, but none of these pieces appeared in print. Herzen's letter of response is not extant, and Turchaninov's original letter is at present our only source of information about his views during this period.

In the same letter, Turchaninov told Herzen that he intended to return to Europe from the United States ("back across the Atlantic") in order to establish contact with Russian revolutionary émigré circles in the Old World and to continue his literary activities on a more systematic basis. But he was unable to carry out these plans, because political events that now intervened dramatically affected Turchaninov's fate. When in the spring of 1861 civil war in the United States broke out, he decided to place his talents and military expertise in the service of President Abraham Lincoln's government.

Turchaninov's name has been preserved in the annals of the American Civil War. His generalship and personal courage won him the nickname "The Russian Thunderer" in the Union army. Throughout the Civil War he was a member of the radical group within the Union's military leadership who advocated the use of revolutionary methods in the struggle against the slaveholding South. Thanks to the publication of Turchaninov's letter to Herzen the nature of his stand as a critic of the negative aspects of American

2. *Herzen and Ogarev*, pt. 2, 599.
3. Ibid., 600.
4. Turchaninov had read Herzen's *From the Far Shore*. Apparently he was also familiar with *Letters from France and Italy*, in which Herzen had developed his concept of the "social republic" and, citing the testimony of Albert Brisbane, an American follower of Fourier, had laid special emphasis on the limited character of the bourgeois democracy of the United States.

bourgeois democracy is now known, but his views as a participant in, and commentator on, the Civil War still require investigation.

A full-scale biography of Turchaninov is yet to be written.[5] Little is known about his life in Russia before he emigrated to the United States; the extant documents are a source of only the most basic biographical information. Turchaninov was born in 1822 into the family of Major Vasilii Nikolaevich Turchaninov, "a nobleman of the Army of the Don Cossacks" and a landowner of modest means. For three years he attended a grammar school in Novocherkassk and then entered the Mikhailovskii Artillery School in St. Petersburg, from which he graduated in 1841. Upon graduation he was assigned to the 5th Battery of Horse Artillery of the Army of the Don Cossacks. In 1844 Turchaninov was transferred to the Don Battery of the Imperial Guard with the rank of ensign; in 1846 he was promoted to second lieutenant and spent the next two years with his battery in Poland, and in the autumn of 1849, upon his return to St. Petersburg, was accepted into the Nikolaevskii Academy of the General Staff. In 1852, at the age of thirty, he completed his course of studies at the academy and was recommended for promotion to the rank of staff-captain and "attached to the General Staff, with assignment to the model troops for a period of one year."[6]

Turchaninov's subsequent rapid military career is described in the "Concise Record of Service of the Divisional Quartermaster of the 2nd Guards Infantry Division, Colonel of the Guards General Staff Turchaninov," preserved in the file pertaining to his departure abroad.[7] In 1853 he was transferred to the General Staff of the Imperial Guard and, soon thereafter, promoted to captain. In 1854 he was appointed Quartermaster of

---

5. In his commentary on Turchaninov's letter to Herzen in *Literaturnoe Nasledstvo*, Zaslavskii was the first to provide biographical information concerning its author, although not all of it is accurate. For a brief characterization of Turchaninov, see A. V. Efimov, "Narodnyi pod"em i obshchestvennoe mnenie SShA v kriticheskii period Grazhdanskoi voiny," (Popular Enthusiasm and Public Opinion in the United States during the Critical Period of the Civil War), in *K stoletiiu Grazhdanskoi voiny v SShA* (Celebrating the Centennial of the Civil War in the United States) (Moscow, 1961), 115–16; and his *SShA: Puti razvitiia kapitalizma* (U.S.A.: the Paths of Capitalist Development) (Moscow, 1969), 573–75; J. Traikl, "Rossiiskii ofitser v armii Linkol'na" (A Russian Officer in Lincoln's Army), *Amerika*, 145 (1968); Albert Parry, "John B. Turchin: Russian General in the American Civil War," *Russian Review* 1, 2 (1942).

In recent years three short historical novels about Turchaninov have appeared: S. I. Semenov, *General Severa* (A General of the North) (Rostov-on-Don, 1969); D. V. Luchaninov, *Sud'ba generala Dzhona Turchina* (The Fate of General John Turchin) (Moscow, 1970); D. Petrov (Biriuk), *Ivan Turchaninov* (Moscow, 1973). In their portrayal of the protagonist, these authors follow the course of the main events in Turchaninov's life, but owing to the paucity of documentary biographical evidence, they attempt to fill the "lacunas" of fact with various suppositions, not all of which are convincing from a historical point of view. A. M. Borshchagovskii, who is currently working on a large-scale novel about Turchaninov, has promised to acquaint his readers with hitherto unknown details of the final years of Turchaninov's life in the United States—*Nedelia* (Week) 41 (1973) [apparently never published—ed]. The interest shown by Soviet writers in Turchaninov reflects the public's increasing desire to learn more about his personality and achievements.

6. See the certificate Turchaninov received upon his graduation from the academy, Central State Military Historical Archive [hereafter TsGVIA], record group 554, inventory 2, list 365, 45 (copy).

7. TsGVIA, record group 38, inventory 2, list 1115, 4 (reverse).

the 2nd Guards Infantry Division, and at the end of 1855 he was promoted to colonel "for distinguished service." The "distinguished service" Turchaninov was deemed to have rendered consisted of topographic reconnaissance of the coast of the Gulf of Finland, which he carried out at the start of the Crimean War, and the formulation of a plan for the defense of approaches to St. Petersburg against a possible landing by Anglo-French troops.

Did Turchaninov see any action during the Crimean War? The brief service record referred to above indicates that such was not the case: "Did not take part in campaigns and battles against the enemy."[8] Turchaninov's descriptions of the fortifications at Sevastopol are very precise, however. As an officer of the general staff did he ever visit the troops in Sevastopol during the siege of the city? The files of the General Staff offer no evidence of this.

Little is known about Turchaninov's intellectual evolution as a young officer. The very first biographical note about him, published in the United States after the end of the Civil War, states that he had "imbibed democratic ideas at an early age."[9] In attempting to identify the "turning points" in Turchaninov's intellectual and political development, we should bear in mind that among his fellow students at the Mikhailovskii Artillery School was [the later radical writer—ed] Peter Lavrov, who was in the class behind Turchaninov's, and that, when Turchaninov was on the Guards General Staff, one of the officers he served with was Nikolai Obruchev [later radical populist—ed]. In his published statements abroad, Turchaninov tended to be very reticent, avoiding all mention of his connections with individuals in Russia.

The next set of documents relates to Turchaninov's departure from Russia, the "Case for the Granting of a One-Year Leave of Absence to Colonel Turchaninov for the Purpose of Medical Treatment at the Waters at Marienbad." In his petition to the Emperor of April 22, 1856, Turchaninov wrote that he suffered from a "disorder of the liver and a bilious condition of the blood accompanied by strong migraines, palpitations and hypochondria" and that owing to "the exigencies of service" he had lacked the opportunity to undergo medical treatment during his years of service. He asked that he be given permission to live abroad for a year and stated that he would spend "the summer at Marienbad" and the rest of his leave, on the advice of foreign doctors, in Middle Germany, Italy, or France.[10] Turchaninov's request was granted, and he left with his wife, Nadezhda Turchaninova, who throughout their life together fully shared her husband's views.

Many years later, in an interview he gave to a Chicago newspaper, Turchaninov revealed that in the spring of 1856, after the signing of the Paris peace treaty, he was ordered to travel to Moscow in order to make arrangements for the participation of those units of the guard that were stationed in Poland in the coronation festivities. Judging the moment propitious for carrying out his plan to escape abroad, Turchaninov feigned illness and obtained a leave of absence. In Marienbad, where he promised he would spend the summer months, Turchaninov, in his own words, "eluded the vigilance of

8. Ibid.
9. Thomas M. Eddy, *The Patriotism of Illinois,* vol. 1 (Chicago, 1865), 339.
10. TsGVIA, record group 38, inventory 2, list 1115, 2 (in Turchaninov's own hand).

the Tsar's spies" and left for England.[11] By the middle of August Turchaninov and his wife were already in New York. A year later the headquarters of the Independent Corps of Guards reported to the war ministry that Turchaninov had failed to return from his trip abroad. On November 27, 1857, it was announced that Turchaninov was being "dismissed from the service for protracted failure to report to duty after a leave of absence" and "upon apprehension" he was to be "handed over to a military tribunal."[12]

Information about the first years of Turchaninov's life in the United States is to be found in the letter to Herzen, as well as in certain American sources, chief of which is the interview he gave to the *Chicago Tribune* in 1886. Upon arriving in the United States, Turchaninov bought a small farm on Long Island not far from New York City and tried to become an independent farmer. As related to Herzen, despite all his efforts he was ruined in less than a year and lost his farm. After this, the Turchaninovs moved to Philadelphia. Nadezhda Turchaninova entered a medical school for women, while her husband attended lectures at the University of Pennsylvania and wrote several articles on astronomical geodesy that attracted the attention of the local community of scholars.

In April 1858, Turchaninov traveled to Washington on the promise of an appointment to the U.S. Coastal Survey. There he was to learn much about political life in the capital and the way in which the country's legislative institutions operated, and came face to face with the bureaucratism prevailing in government. During this period, Turchaninov had discussions with Arctic explorer Isaac Hayes, who had come to Washington to seek funds for his second polar expedition. At one point a plan was mooted to put Turchaninov in charge of the expedition's astronomical and geodesical research.

With nothing to show for his visit to Washington, Turchaninov and his wife went west, settling in the town of Mattoon, Illinois. For a while Turchaninov earned a living there as an architect and builder, and it was from Mattoon that he wrote to Herzen. Later Turchaninov, now going by the name of Turchin, moved to Chicago, where he worked as a topographer-engineer at the headquarters of the Illinois Central Railroad. Two months after the start of the rebellion by the slaveholding South, Turchaninov, as Colonel John Basil Turchin, took command of the 19th Illinois Regiment of Volunteers, which had been formed in Chicago.

Official American publications and the memoirs of his contemporaries provide details of Turchaninov's service with the Union army. In the summer and autumn of 1861, his regiment was stationed in the border states of Missouri and Kentucky where the slaveholders, although not formally siding with the rebellious Confederacy, were hostile to the government in Washington. "Applying Russian military training to American patriotism," as one memorialist put it,[13] Turchaninov brought his regiment to an exemplary state of battle readiness. He attached considerable importance to the political education and ideological motivation of his men, as may be seen from the fact that in October–November 1861 he published a regimental newspaper.[14] At the end

---

11. *Chicago Tribune,* February 6, 1886.
12. TsGVIA, record group 38, inventory 2, list 1115, 27 (reverse).
13. See article on Turchaninov in *Chicago Record Herald,* January 20, 1901.
14. For Turchaninov's "Zouave Gazette," see James H. Haynie, *The Nineteenth Illinois* (Chicago, 1912), 147–48.

of 1861, Turchaninov, whom the commanders of the Army of the Ohio had come to value as a highly educated and resourceful officer, was appointed to lead a brigade composed of four regiments. Nevertheless, from the first months of his military service he continually clashed with the conservatively minded high command, which was pursuing a policy of "appeasing" the planters, to the detriment of the fundamental interests of the struggle with the slaveholding South.

Turchaninov's disagreements with his superiors concerned two main issues. During this early stage of the war, Turchaninov already believed it essential that Union troops be provisioned and provided with transport at the rebellious planters' expense; and he refused to hand over to them fugitive slaves who sought refuge in his camp. In the summer of 1861 in Missouri he had a violent falling out with Brigadier General Stephen Hurlbut who had accused him of "violating the personal and property rights of the population."[15] Soon thereafter the same complaints by the planters prompted General John Pope, head of the North Missouri Military District, to write a report critical of Turchaninov, but John Fremont, the radical Republican in charge of the Western Department of the Union's armed forces, refused to act on it and tore up Pope's report.[16] In the middle of October, when Turchaninov's regiment was stationed in Kentucky, General William T. Sherman, the commander of the Army of the Ohio, sent him a letter.

> To Colonel Turchaninov, Louisville, Kentucky, 15 Oct. 1861.
>
> Dear Sir, two gentlemen who are unknown to me but who are recommended by Mr. Guthrie, have stated that several negro slaves are hiding in your camp and that you are giving them protection. The laws of the United States and the laws of Kentucky—and we must obey both the former and the latter—stipulate that fugitive slaves must be handed over upon the demand of their owner or of a person bearing his authority. I assume that you personally have nothing to do with this case, but my orders are that all negroes must be surrendered at the first request. Indeed, it would be best if there were no negroes on the territory of your camp, with the exception of those who came with the regiment.[17]

When Major General [Don Carlos] Buell, one of the most committed appeasers (those on the Union side opposed to an intensification of the war against the slave-owning South), assumed command of the Army of the Ohio, he tried to put an end to the Russian's career. Soon after Turchaninov's troops in May 1862 carried out a strategically important offensive operation—a raid from Tennessee southward into Alabama and the successful capture of the town of Huntsville on the Memphis-Charleston

---

15. Hurlbut to Turchaninov, August 16, 1861, *The War of the Rebellion. A Compilation of the Official Records of the Union and Confederate Armies* [hereafter cited as *Official Records*], series 2, vol. 1, 774.

16. "General John Basil Turchin and Nadine, His Wife," *Illinois Central Magazine* 3 (1914): 12. The anonymous author uses the testimony of memorialists.

17. *Official Records*, vol. 1, no. 1, 307. James Guthrie, to whom Sherman refers, was the president of the Louisville-Nashville Railroad Company, a former secretary of the treasury in the administration of pro-slavery President Pierce, and a political boss in Kentucky who frequently brought pressure to bear on the Union generals.

railroad—Buell placed Turchaninov under arrest, had him tried, and sentenced him to be cashiered. Six months earlier, when Buell's patrons and supporters were calling the tune both in the army and in Washington, his actions might have been successful, but times were changing. The authorities in Washington were preparing a proclamation that was to free the slaves, and the American people were loud in their demands for a decisive shift in the conduct of the war against the rebels.

President Lincoln decided to intervene in the Turchaninov affair. Characteristically, he chose what was an indirect but, nonetheless, most effective way of doing this. Ignoring the judicial proceedings currently under way, and without in any way commenting on Buell's actions, he promoted Turchaninov, while the latter was still on trial, to the rank of brigadier general. By taking this step Lincoln implicitly sanctioned what Turchaninov had done and condemned Buell's policy of appeasement. If one is to consider Lincoln's intervention in Turchaninov's trial in the context of the other legislative and military developments of this period, one must conclude that the president's actions in this case were an early indication that the North was about to adopt revolutionary methods in its struggle with the Confederacy.

At the same time, in a purely judicial sense the tribunal was reduced to naught: a panel of colonels lacked the authority to try a general. Turchaninov left for Chicago, where in a solemn ceremony the inhabitants of the city presented him with a sword of honor. In March 1863, now a brigadier general, he was given a new posting to the Army of the Ohio (now known as the Army of the Cumberland) and, until the end of the summer of that year, commanded a division in [David Sloane] Stanley's cavalry corps.[18] Listing the generals who had come to take part in a council of war, James Gilmore, a correspondent of the *New York Daily Tribune* who in June 1863 visited in Murphreesboro the commander of the Army of the Cumberland, General [William S.] Rosecrans, wrote: "At the window, leaning against the wall, stands a portly blond general with a broad face. This is the Russian old man, Turchin."[19]

The trial of Turchaninov, which Buell had instigated, and the ignoble failure of this reactionary intrigue brought the Russian-born general national fame as a prominent representative of the radical group of military leaders in the Union army. The growth of his popularity with those who advocated revolutionary methods in the prosecution of the Civil War was accompanied by a farrago of slander emanating from the rebel camp.

Two characteristic examples may be used to illustrate Turchaninov's newly acquired prominence. One reflects the mood in the North, the other among the Southern rebels. In the late summer of 1862, as soon as the outcome of Buell's clash with Turchaninov had become clear, Senator John Sherman, who until recently had occupied a position on the right of the Republican Party, hastened to inform his brother, General William Sherman, of the policy change in Washington and suggested he should revise his opinions and conduct in accordance with these new developments. "You cannot even conceive of all the changes in the Negro question. . . . Only party differences and caste prejudice have

---

18. F. H. Dyer, *A Compendium of the War of the Rebellion*, vol. 1 (New York, 1959), 461. Additional information pertaining to Turchaninov's service in the Union army is taken from this source.

19. J. C. Andrews, *The North Reports Civil War* (University of Pittsburgh Press, 1955), 439.

prevented us until now from employing them as allies in this war. Note the popularity of Fremont, Butler, Turchin, and Cochrane, and the unpopularity of Buell, Thomas, and McClellan."[20]

At the end of 1863 Jefferson Davis, the president of the Confederacy, in his message to the Confederate Senate and House of Representatives declared: "Their commanders, Butler, MacNeil and Turchin, whose barbarous cruelty has made their names hated and has won them a sinister notoriety, are esteemed and feted in Washington."[21] In fact, neither Turchaninov nor the other two Union generals mentioned by Davis were guilty of any "barbarous cruelty," but they were all proponents of conducting the struggle against the South in a decisive fashion and for that reason were hated by the slave-owners.

During his service with the Army of the Cumberland, Turchaninov took part in the bloody fighting of that year in the western theatre. He was present at two major engagements of the campaign, the battles of Chickamauga and Chattanooga. At the Battle of Chickamauga in northern Georgia, September 19–20, 1863, Turchaninov commanded a brigade of five infantry regiments reinforced by two batteries of artillery. He led his troops on a swift bayonet assault against superior enemy forces. The success of this operation, which brought him fame and came to be known as "Turchin's attack from the rear," did much to enable General [George] Thomas's corps to break out of encirclement. At the Battle of Chattanooga, a major engagement fought near the Tennessee-Georgia state line on November 23–25, Turchaninov was in charge of an enlarged brigade of eight infantry regiments, with which he took part in the storming of the Missionary Ridge, a range of mountains southeast of the city of Chattanooga that had been fortified by the Confederate army. The capture of this position, which had been judged impregnable, determined the victory of the Union forces.

In May of 1864 Turchaninov was engaged in Sherman's invasion of Georgia almost until Sherman's troops reached Atlanta, but in July fell seriously ill and had to leave the front and return to Chicago. There, after he had regained his health, Turchaninov began to publish a monthly journal on military affairs entitled *Military Rambles,* the first issue of which appeared in February 1865. It had the dual objectives of reporting the latest news from the front and advocating the revolutionary goals of the war against the South. The prospectus stated *Military Rambles* would be published "until" the rebellion of the Southern states was "suppressed." "We spent three years at the front and now we have come home," wrote Turchaninov in a message to his readers in the first issue. "In the command we were entrusted with we endeavored within the limits of our abilities, to do everything possible to further our cause. And now we still strive to do the same."[22] Before the Confederacy capitulated, Turchaninov brought out two issues of his journal.[23]

20. *The Sherman Letters* (New York, 1969), 156–57.
21. *The Messages and Papers of Jefferson Davis* (New York, 1966), vol. 1, 379.
22. *Military Rambles,* "published monthly by John B. Turchin, late Brigadier General U.S. Volunteers, February 1865." The message to the readers was printed on the back of the cover.
23. Turchaninov's journal is available in only a few of the largest libraries in the United States. In some copies the month of issue and the conditions of subscription are not indicated; it would appear that these copies were sold as separate booklets. A holograph letter from Turchaninov to

Our knowledge about Turchaninov's life after the end of the Civil War is scanty. Until 1870 he was employed as an expert by the Office of Patents in Chicago; later he again took up his profession as a railway topographer-engineer. In 1873, together with a group of Polish immigrants, he founded the settlement of Radom [now Pulaski—ed] on land owned by the Illinois Central Railroad, some three hundred miles south of Chicago. At Radom he received an allotment of land. The author of a short entry on John Turchin that appeared in 1889 in an American biographical dictionary stated that "he currently resides on a farm at Radom" and "occasionally prints articles on military and scientific matters in the journals."[24]

In 1888 the Chicago publishing house of Fergus brought out a military-historical monograph by Turchaninov on the Battle of Chickamauga.[25] In the foreword to the book, entitled *Chickamauga,* the author analyzed the Civil War in its successive stages. An announcement at the end listed three other books by Turchaninov that Fergus planned to publish: *My Battle of Missionary Ridge* (another military-historical monograph), *My Experiences and Impressions During the Years of the Civil War,* and *Russian Sketches,* but none appeared in print. Were they ever written and, if so, what happened to the manuscripts?

Turchaninov continued to follow closely developments on the social and political scene in both America and Russia. During this period, Nadezhda Turchaninova remained his faithful companion and helpmate. In addition to Turchaninov's letter to Herzen, a letter written to Herzen by Nadezhda Turchaninova has survived that shows that her outlook was an advanced one for a Russian woman of her time. She accompanied her husband throughout his years of active service in the Civil War, and the *Civil War Dictionary* devotes several lines to her.[26] The author reports that on one occasion, when her husband's brigade wavered and began to fall back during a battle, she rushed to the front line and rallied the troops, halting the retreat.[27] The same writer, criticizing the ingratitude shown by the Americans toward the immigrants from Europe who had shed their blood for them in the Civil War, concludes his description of Turchaninova with these words: "Had she been the wife of a native-born American general as heroic as General Turchin, stories and songs about her would probably have been composed and every schoolchild in America would know about her."[28]

But with the passage of time these two Russians, whom fate had brought to the land across the ocean, came to lead an increasingly reclusive existence on their farm in the

---

John P. Nicolson of April 8, 1878, which is bound with one of the remaining copies of *Military Rambles,* suggests that a third (April) issue of the journal was published; however, so far no copies of it have been discovered. After the Great Fire of 1871 many Chicago publications of this period became bibliographical rarities or were lost completely.

24. *Appleton Encyclopedia of American Biography* (New York, 1889), vol. 6, 182.
25. Turchin, *Chickamauga: Noted Battles for the Union during the Civil War* (Chicago, 1888). The book was dedicated to the brigade commanded by Turchaninov during this battle: "This artless narrative is dedicated to the men of the Third Brigade, Fourth Division, Fourteenth Army Corps of the Army of Cumberland by their old comrade and commander John B. Turchin."
26. Mark Boatner, *The Civil War Dictionary* (New York, 1959 [rev. ed. 1988]), 853.
27. *Illinois Central Magazine* 3 (1914): 16.
28. Ibid.

American wilderness. Old-timers in Radom recalled how an aged Turchaninov, his customary cigarette in his mouth, wandered the fields surrounding the town with a hunting rifle, "always prepared to burst out with indignation at the injustices of the world."[29]

In the autumn of 1898, at the age of seventy-six, Turchaninov, now destitute, applied for a pension as a veteran of the Civil War. His request was denied. Eventually, after two state senators who had served as privates in the 19th Illinois Regiment interceded on his behalf, Turchaninov was granted a fifty-dollar annual pension. The old general had but six months to live. He died in a state asylum for the mentally ill in the town of Anna and was interred in the military cemetery at Mount [sic Mound—ed] City, Illinois. When, three years later, his wife died, the War Department, taking into account her services in the Civil War, authorized her burial next to her husband. The single tombstone that stands on their grave bears the legend: "John B. Turchin, Brigadier-General, U.S. Volunteers, December 24, 1822–June 18, 1901; Nadine, his wife, November 26, 1826–July 17, 1904."[30]

The main sources for an analysis of Turchaninov's views on the American Civil War are the speech he made in 1862 at his trial, when he was serving with the Army of the Ohio, the two issues of *Military Rambles* (1865), and the foreword to his book, *Chickamauga* (1888). As an active participant in the Civil War, as a journalist, and later as a memoirist and historian, Turchaninov always displayed intellectual integrity in his political attitudes and consistently advocated a revolutionary-democratic interpretation of the chief issues of the war.

The concept of the American Civil War as a conflict that went through two main stages, the constitutional and the revolutionary, is firmly established in Marxist-Leninist historiography. This concept was first developed by Karl Marx and Friedrich Engels in a series of studies, written while the war was still being fought, in which they analyzed the motive forces of the conflict.

> From the outbreak of hostilities the desire to retain the good will of loyal slaveholders . . . the touching concern for the interests, prejudices, and feelings of these dubious allies greatly weakened the government in the North, forcing it to conceal the principle of the war behind a veil of hypocrisy and inducing it to spare from attack the enemy's greatest vulnerability, the root of the evil—*slavery itself*[31]

declared Marx in his November 1861 article, "The Civil War in the United States." Marx foresaw that events in America would soon take "a different turn." "The North . . . will resort to revolutionary measures," he told Engels in August 1862. "A single Negro regiment would have an extraordinary effect on the nerves of the Southerners."[32] And in "Towards a Critique of the Situation in America," Marx offered an evaluation of the

---

29. Parry, "John B. Turchin," 59.
30. *Illinois Central Magazine* 3 (1914): 10.
31. Marx and Engels, *Soch.* (Works), vol. 15, 355–56.
32. Marx and Engels, *Works,* vol. 30, 222.

political and military scene in the United States. "So far we have merely witnessed the first act of the Civil War—a war that has been conducted in a *constitutional* manner. The second act—when the war will be prosecuted in a *revolutionary* manner—is yet to come."[33]

There are certain similarities between Nicholas Chernyshevsky's views on the way in which the Civil War in the United States might develop and the prediction by Marx. In his analysis of the situation in America, the leader of the Russian revolutionary-democratic movement of the 1860s also proceeded from the assumption that the clash between the slave-based system and the free-labor system was historically preordained and inevitable; he, too, believed that the slaveholding oligarchy must be defeated militarily and politically as quickly and as decisively as possible, lest it act as an obstacle to social progress in both America and Europe. In his surveys of the international scene published in 1861–1862 in *Sovremennik* (Contemporary), Chernyshevsky frequently stated that the Union's weaknesses and failures were due to the fact that "the free states started the war whilst being led by moderate men,"[34] who wished "to conduct the war against the South as mercifully as possible."[35] He noted that the masses increasingly objected to this policy and, referring to the question of the emancipation of the Negro slaves and their recruitment for the armed struggle against the South, predicted that Lincoln "will almost certainly be unable to avoid taking these decisive measures."[36]

Some of Turchaninov's statements about the American Civil War suggest that he may have been acquainted with the writings of Marx and Engels or, at least, with an account of their views. They make it possible to conclude that the consistently radical approach of this Russian "man of the Sixties" to the problems of the struggle against the slaveholding South had prompted him to consider the same key problems of the Civil War in the United States that drew the attention of Marx and Engels and were discussed by Chernyshevsky in his writings on events in America.

In the foreword to *Chickamauga*, Turchaninov, analyzing the course of the war, divided it into two distinct periods on the basis of military-political factors. He believed that the first period ended and the second began early in 1863, after the North had adopted laws providing for the confiscation of the property of rebellious slave-owners and Lincoln had issued the proclamation that freed all Negro bondsmen and made them eligible for military service:

> 1863 was notable for the remarkable change in our military policy. In 1861–62 the dominant policy, particularly on the Western front, was one which may be best described as patrolling the potato patch and which was perhaps more absurd than any other in the annals of military history.... [2] This readiness to offer concessions to the South, to coax and cajole the supporters of the rebellion so that they would remain in the Union, found its supreme expression during the first stage of the war,

---

33. Marx and Engels, *Works,* vol. 15, 542.
34. Chernyshevskii, *Poln. sobr. soch.* (Complete Collected Works), 16 vols. (Moscow, 1939–1953), vol. 8, 554.
35. Ibid., 597.
36. Ibid., 596.

in the lenity shown the insurgents on the field of battle and in the prohibition on the use of their property for the needs of our army. Our troops were told to live off their own stores of provision and to post guards to protect fields owned by the insurgent Southerners, as well as their vegetable orchards, gardens, granaries, smoking-sheds and even water wells, so that our soldiers would be unable to gain access to them. Only a complete ignorance of the art of war and the absence of basic common sense could have engendered such an idea in the minds of our leaders. And only after our officers were tried by military tribunals, after prolonged suffering by our soldiers and shameful defeats on the field of battle did the people realize the absurdity of such a policy and put an end to it through an act of the President.[37]

He continued:

The other important event of 1863, which dealt a blow to the rebellion, was President Lincoln's Proclamation of 1 January 1863, which freed the bondsmen . . . [and] led to the formation of Negro regiments, mass slave escapes and a general demoralization within the enemy's territory. By the end of the war our army included almost 150,000 Negroes. They learned to shoot as well as the white soldiers and displayed extraordinary tenacity and courage in many battles.[38]

As early as the spring of 1863, Marx and Engels, in their analysis of the causes of the North's military and political weakness during the first stage of the Civil War, rejected the general strategic approach of the Union high command, which was dominated by defeatists and proponents of a Fabian strategy. They harshly criticized the so-called Anaconda plan, which provided for the gradual smothering of the Confederacy by a ring of Federal armies. "This is pure child's play," they wrote in their treatise, *The Civil War in America.* "This is a revival of the so-called *cordon strategy,* which was invented in Austria circa 1770 and was used so obstinately and unsuccessfully against the French in 1792–1797. The French cut the 'python' in two, striking at the point where they had built up a local superiority. Then the pieces of the 'python' were chopped up one by one."[39]

At the same time, Marx and Engels argued against the idea, preached by McClellan and his entourage and popular in Washington, that capturing Richmond was the most urgent and potentially decisive aim of the war. "Countries that are populous and more or less centralized possess a center, the seizure of which by the enemy entails the cessation of national resistance. An excellent example of such a center is Paris," wrote Marx and Engels. "But the slave-holding states lack such a center. They are sparsely populated and have few large cities. . . . The capture of Richmond . . . might have an enormous impact on morale, but from a purely military point of view it would decide *nothing.*"[40]

Turchaninov [2] also criticized the plans of the Union command. "The cordon strategy, that cachectic invention of the mid-eighteenth century . . . was reborn in our celebrated 'Anaconda,'" wrote Turchaninov in *Military Rambles,*

37. Turchin, *Chickamauga,* 10–11.
38. Ibid., 11–12.
39. Marx and Engels, *Works,* vol. 15, 505–6.
40. Ibid., 506–7.

[but] the armies of the South, after concentrating at the decisive point, cut the anaconda into pieces. The Southern Confederacy is an agricultural country which has never possessed important commercial or industrial centers. . . . If an enemy army occupies Vienna, Austria would be defeated. If you storm Berlin, Prussia would be erased from the map. But what shall we have gained if we take Richmond? A certain moral advantage, but in the material sense—almost nothing."[41]

The constant desire of the conservative elements among the Northern bourgeoisie for a compromise with the slave-owners posed a major threat to the successful achievement of the revolutionary-democratic goals of the Civil War. Marx and Engels were vociferous in their support of the efforts of the radical revolutionary-democratic forces in the United States to bring about the full military and political defeat of the South. In Russia, Chernyshevsky spoke out along similar lines (insofar as this was possible under the conditions of press censorship then prevailing in the country), and in the United States Turchaninov consistently defended the revolutionary-democratic goals of the Civil War, proclaiming the need for the complete and final abolition of slavery in the economic, political, and social spheres.

"The anomaly that led the Republic to permit slavery and to endure its consolidation for so long," wrote Turchaninov, "created another anomaly—a commonwealth of slave-owners and their overseers, which in its social and political principles differs completely from a society of free men."[42] "We have had enough time to realize that . . . neither reconciliation, nor compromise is possible, that it is solely a question of complete victory by one or the other side, that . . . this race of rebel slave-owners must be swept from the continent." Turchaninov believed that a democratic resolution of the agrarian problem in the South would make victory irreversible. He listed the decisive measure he thought essential for the achievement of a speedy victory, one of which, he suggested, should be a declaration by the government that it would distribute the planters' estates among the Union soldiers and freed Negro slaves. He believed that the Republic should rid itself of the most dangerous supporters and ideologues of the slave-owners' rebellion. "The hardened killers must be executed by firing squad," wrote Turchaninov, "or put behind bars; the leaders and instigators, who are criminally guilty of plunging our country into a fratricidal war, must be hanged or banished forever. . . . If the Southerners . . . the slave-owning society, and the civilization they created must die, we will only say, 'Amen!' "[43]

The trial of Turchaninov organized by the reactionary command of the Army of the Ohio, his speech before the court, and the American public's broad response to these events show how politically charged the atmosphere in the North was prior to the Union's decision to shift from constitutional to revolutionary methods in its prosecution of the Civil War. The pretext for the trial was the property damage inflicted by Turchaninov's troops in Athens, Alabama. In response to the direct assistance given by the slave-owners to the Confederate army and the outrages perpetrated by

41. *Military Rambles,* February 1865, 9–10.
42. *Military Rambles,* March 1865, 86.
43. *Military Rambles,* February 1865, 39–40, 88.

locally recruited gangs that they had armed, soldiers from the 19th Illinois Regiment attacked several stores, as well as houses belonging to the town's wealthier residents. Turchaninov stopped the willful actions of his men but rejected the slave-owners' demand that he should post guards to protect their property and should exempt their houses and estates from use for military purposes. Buell, a defender of the planters' property interests who dealt mercilessly with fugitive Negro slaves by sending them back to their owners, accused Turchaninov of "disobeying the orders of a superior" and "conniving at robbery and looting."[44] By dealing with Turchaninov in this way he hoped to intimidate the revolutionary-minded officers in his army.

The records of Turchaninov's court case have not survived. However, his speech before the court and some of the scenes at the trial may be reconstructed from newspaper reports. The account that follows is based on articles published in the *Chicago Tribune* and the *New York Daily Tribune*.[45] Both papers borrowed liberally from reports in the *Cincinnati Gazette,* which had a correspondent at Turchaninov's trial. In addition, the *Daily Tribune* used information that had appeared in the *Louisville Journal.*

The correspondent of the *Gazette* begins by offering a critical evaluation of the panel of judges, which he describes as "quite amazing." "Almost half the judges' seats are filled by officers from Kentucky, and Kentuckians are known for their defense of the 'constitutional rights' of rebel supporters and, in some cases, for declaring that if the Government were to prosecute the war too vigorously they would go over to the enemy." The journalist believes that since the Turchaninov case affected "the common interest," regiments from other states in Buell's army, namely those recruited in Illinois, Pennsylvania, Wisconsin, and Michigan (states that were militantly antislavery), should have been represented on the panel of judges.[46]

The correspondent goes on to offer this description of Turchaninov's behavior at the trial:

> One thing may be said of the conduct of the officer who is being tried: it is fearless, dignified in every respect, and full of military rectitude. Those who have been present in the courtroom cannot conceal their admiration. He is a powerfully-built man, typically martial in bearing, whose face expresses courage and intelligence. Now, resting his head on his hand he has to listen while the next unbridled traitor vents his rage, until the clerk of the court has written down every last detail in the record of evidence, as if this were a precious revelation from above.

44. *Official Records,* vol. 1, no. 10, pt. 2: 273.
45. *Chicago Tribune,* August 8, 1862; *New York Daily Tribune,* August 8 and 11, 1862.
46. The full membership of the tribunal appointed by Buell is described in the official records. The chairman of the court was Brigadier General James Garfield (later twentieth president of the United States); six colonels were members of the court: Jacob Ammen, commander of the 26th Regiment (Ohio), Curran Pope, commander of the 15th (Kentucky), J. G. Jones, commander of the 42nd (Indiana), Mark Mandy, commander of the 23rd (Kentucky), T. D. Sedgwick, commander of the 2nd (Kentucky), John Beatty, commander of the 3rd (Ohio). The case against Turchaninov was argued by Captain R. T. Swain, a military prosecutor. *Official Records,* vol. 1, no. 10, pt. 2: 99.

"General Turchin addresses the same question of all the witnesses: 'Are you loyal to the legitimate government in Washington?'" And every time the prosecutor objects to this question," the correspondent comments,

> If such actions by the prosecutor are recognized as a precedent, every officer in our field army will henceforth have to remember that he dare not in any way insult a rebel or a traitor, for if they accuse him in court, the judges would be guided by their testimony, rather than his. The enemies of the Republic would themselves determine how much harm one of our officers may inflict upon them. . . . Such is the logical conclusion to be drawn from the prosecutor's actions at this trial.

The same point was made in a strongly worded editorial in the *Chicago Tribune*.

> The spectacle is such that all who are loyal to the Republic must blush. Rebels and traitors, who wallow in betrayal, who wish to see us crushed, who are covered in our blood, testify in court against an officer of the army who is fighting for the Republic, offering absurd tales about plundered hen-houses and burnt fences, while other officers, who also serve in our army, listen avidly to their testimony. . . . In this trial the witnesses are not asked whether they are loyal to their legitimate government. They are only asked, "Are you ready to slander Turchin?"[47]

Both the *New York Daily Tribune* and the *Chicago Tribune* printed Turchin's speech at the trial, partly as it was transcribed by the reporter from the *Cincinnati Gazette*, partly in the reporter's own rendition. Turchaninov described the situation prevailing in Athens when he arrived to render assistance to the 18th Ohio Regiment, which had been unexpectedly attacked by rebel cavalry. He named the residents of the town who had personally taken part in the skirmish with the soldiers of the 18th Regiment, and stated that the regimental camp was looted by rebel supporters from Athens. Expecting another enemy attack, he took the measures necessary to defend the town.

> My first duty was to attend to the lives and safety of the 3,000 loyal sons of the Republic entrusted to me, and I had no time to regret the inconvenience I was causing the insurgents. Yes, it is true that Mr. Donnell's property suffered damage because we were encamped on his land. But I ask you, who is Mr. Donnell? He is a man who gave active help to the rebels, he is their supporter and accomplice. His money equipped units of the rebel army. It is he who sent 70 bales of cotton to Decatur for the construction of fortifications there. The fortifications at Decatur were stormed by the same fighting men of the 24th Illinois who were now encamped on Mr. Donnell's land, and if the rebels had not been so quick to beat a retreat, our success at Decatur would have been paid for with the blood of our soldiers. Just now Mr. Donnell has proudly declared that he would not under any circumstances swear allegiance to the Government of the Republic and that he fully supports the rebel Confederacy. And this gentleman visited me demanding that I should send my soldiers to guard his plantations! Naturally, I

---

47. *Chicago Tribune,* August 8, 1862.

refused. But I admit I should have gladly ordered my men to put such an out-and-out traitor behind bars!

Next Turchaninov addressed the crucial question of the Union army's attitude toward the Negro slaves.

> I am accused here of having sheltered in my brigade a young mulatto named Joe who belonged to Mr. Vasser, a resident of Athens. Testimony has already been presented that this mulatto performed certain reconnaissance tasks for me and supplied us with valuable intelligence concerning the enemy, whereupon, in accordance with General [Ormsby] Mitchell's orders, I offered him refuge and protection. General Mitchell, after what I assume were consultations with his superiors, decided to employ Negroes for military purposes and promised to give them refuge as a reward for their services. I consider this policy to be correct in the supreme degree.[48] If we were at war with England and sent troops to occupy her territory, we should land them in Ireland because we know that the Irish people hates its oppressors and would render us assistance. Basing himself on the same considerations, Garibaldi chose to land in Sicily before undertaking his march on Naples. We have entered the Southern states, where, with a few small exceptions, the entire white population is hostile and refuses to supply us with the necessary intelligence about the enemy. In our hearts we all know that the Negroes are our only friends here, but, gripped as we are by prejudice, we are reluctant to recognize this openly. As a matter of necessity we use them, oblige them to inform us about the mood of their masters and the enemy's movements, and then, having made them hated by the white residents of the South, betray them to our foes in the shabbiest and most reprehensible way. There is no single policy in this matter. One general may be ready to offer them refuge for a while and promises them freedom. He is succeeded by another, who expels the Negroes from his camp, leaving them at their owners' mercy. And the latter mete out punishment to them at the first opportunity. When I left Tuscumbia I was told—and I have reasons to believe this—that less than a day later in Tuscumbia four or five Negro bondsmen, who had supplied us with important intelligence about the enemy, were hanged. By permitting the commission of such terrible injustices we flout the fundamental principles of humanity.

"Turchin listed the numerous advantages that their ownership of slaves gave the rebels, and described the tremendous benefits our army would derive from accepting negroes into military service," wrote the correspondent.

---

48. Turchaninov and General Mitchell, whose division during the operations in Alabama included Turchaninov's brigade, had together recruited a spy network composed of plantation slaves. Because he did not believe Buell would approve of his actions, Mitchell entered into direct contact with Secretary of War Edwin Stanton, who supported the "left wing" in the army, *Official Records,* vol. 1, no. 9: 162 (Mitchell to Stanton, May 4, 1862, concerning Negro slaves). Mitchell's decision to go over the heads of his immediate superiors illustrates the extent to which the political struggle in the Union army had intensified. Ormsby Mitchell (1809–1862), who before the war had been a mathematician and astronomer, held progressive views on the fundamental issues of the Civil War and was undoubtedly in a position to appreciate Turchaninov's political stand. Historians of the Civil War in the United States should pay special attention to the military and political aspects of the Mitchell-Turchaninov raid into Alabama of April–June 1862.

He then expressed regret that the court had given credence to the testimony of rebel supporters, in order to cast aspersions on himself and his men and in conclusion declared, "Everywhere I have fought—in Missouri, Kentucky, Tennessee, and Alabama—I was invariably hated by the rebels, and I consider this the best kind of recommendation for an officer of the Union Army. Yet I challenge you to name even one person loyal to our Republic to whom I have given the slightest cause for complaint. The greater the lenity with which we treat the supporters of the rebellion, the greater the impudence with which they will act toward us. And if we do not start to conduct this war with all possible vigor, employing all possible means against the enemy, including the freeing of slaves, our nation will inevitably perish."

The journalist ended his account of Turchaninov's speech thus:

> Addressing the judges as if he were not a defendant but a teacher conversing with his pupils, the old warrior concluded his speech with these words: "I have indicated some of the deficiencies in our conduct of the war and have suggested certain measures to correct them, and if members of the court have understood my ideas and will convey them to those holding senior positions in the chain of command, I will rest secure in the belief that this military tribunal served some purpose after all."

Even on the basis of these few excerpts from Turchaninov's speech at his Alabama trial we may conclude that there was no other general in the Union army capable of discussing with such conviction and political maturity the crucial problems presented by the need to adopt revolutionary methods in the conduct of the Civil War.

The progressive press in the North not only supported Turchaninov but also used his trial in its campaign against appeasers and secret Southern sympathizers. "Turchin is an unbending warrior in the current struggle," wrote the *New York Daily Tribune,* "an officer of the kind we need so much, and one who is deeply respected by every honest soldier and man of the people."[49] "General Turchin," declared an editorial in the *Chicago Tribune,*

> has now been placed beyond the jurisdiction of that pack of ill-wishers in epaulets, who pleased and perhaps astonished the Alabama rebels by the eagerness with which they interrupted their half-hearted struggle against the rebellion in order to devote themselves to the persecution of this officer. Their nauseating pusillanimity in the face of the enemy compounded the disgrace with which D. C. Buell has covered himself in the exercise of his command, and leads us to demand that he be now dismissed. A position of such responsibility should not be held by a man whose chief desire is to protect his standing in the drawing-rooms of the South and to preserve the sympathies of his Southern friends. We have had enough of Buell.[50]

A few months later Buell was removed from his command of the Army of the Ohio. He was obliged to appear before a commission of inquiry in Washington, and had to resign.

49. *New York Daily Tribune,* August 8, 1862.
50. *Chicago Tribune,* August 8, 1862.

In *Military Rambles,* Turchaninov devoted a great deal of attention to those internal flaws, the roots of which lay in the Union army itself. It was these flaws that were the cause of the protracted character of the Civil War, the North's defeats, and the enormous losses suffered by the Union troops. Turchaninov raised a series of questions, pointing out that the Union's professional commanders held reactionary views, and he criticized their lack of military preparedness and poor generalship. He accused generals like McClellan, Buell, and others close to them, who had led the Union army during the first stage of the Civil War, of passivity and appeasement of the enemy. These attitudes, he suggested, were due to the traditional deference shown by the professional officer corps in the U.S. Army toward the slave-owning South. Turchaninov complained of the political unreliability of this "officer caste," whose members had been educated at the West Point Military Academy in the years preceding the Civil War:

> The men who belonged to this caste were distinguished not only by their special military training but also by a tendency to assume aristocratic airs. Although the Academy at West Point accepted cadets from the North as well as the South, Southerners predominated within the Academy's walls and in the Army, and exercised a decisive influence in both. Rich men from the South, who owned hundreds of negro slaves and thousands of acres of cotton plantations . . . who cultivated aristocratic pretensions . . . who played cards without worrying if they won or lost, whose mounts were better and whose uniforms were more elegant—they were the ones who became the leaders of that military society. Everyone tried to imitate them in everything, and their influence made itself felt not only where military style and manners were concerned, but also in their comrades' political views. Professional connections and friendships made them united, and, when the rebellion broke out, many Northern officers were not sure whether they should come to the defense of the Republic or join the Southern insurgents. Some of them stayed with us not because they regarded the rebellion as criminal, but because their personal property or their wives' property happened to be in the North. Because of their old habit of looking at the Southern officer with respectful admiration, they were loath to confront him on the field of battle. . . . The constant talk among our career officers that the Southerners are invincible has died down only very recently.

Turchaninov made a special point of discussing the attitude of the West Point graduates in the Union army to the Negro slaves:

> They see in the Negro bondsman a creature that is little better than an ape, one that is suited for labor but is far inferior to a human being. When the people demanded the abolition of slavery, they were forced to comply, but their compliance was, as a rule, reluctant. . . . If some among them—those who are possessed of a greater humanity—treat the negroes decently, the majority continue to look upon them with utter contempt.[51]

Next he addressed the problem of the pernicious spread in the Union army of the dishonest methods of American politics. The tradition of political intrigue and the

---

51. *Military Rambles,* March 1865, 49–50.

scheming and infighting among competing factions were, he believed, the "national disease" of American political life. When they were transplanted into the army in the field, these phenomena, he argued, became the cause of many military defeats and failures. "The officers in the field are politically no less skillful than their civilian brethren," wrote Turchaninov.

> It is true that their field of activity is narrower and their methods have less variety, but then intrigues here are conducted with special refinement. An officer scheming against a comrade will act with jesuitical subtlety. The factions formed by military leaders are changeable in composition and their membership is small, but for all that they are extremely powerful and are merciless in their struggle for supremacy. An outsider would find it impossible to imagine how cruel and unscrupulous a military politician can be as he pursues his aims amidst the circumstances of a sanguinary war. In order to ruin the military reputation of a personal rival or of someone whom his faction opposes, the politician will, without a second thought, sacrifice him and all his men to the enemy, lest he contribute to their military success. And even after receiving a direct order to aid his rival, he will fulfill this order by performing a manoeuver so skillfull that help will only arrive after his rival is defeated, when it is certain that the latter's reputation has been irretrievably damaged. This has already been done on several occasions in so brazen and shameful a way that it became public knowledge; but more often such actions were carried out in secret and became known only to a few perspicacious observers within the army itself. A politician who climbs onto a platform to extort money for his party, who mops and mows before the public like a whirling dervish, until he is completely exhausted, is contemptible enough. But an officer-politician who pursues his dastardly designs while the cannon roar and the rifles crackle, who in order to carry out his plans is prepared to walk over the bodies of thousands of his dead or maimed comrades-in-arms, is truly monstrous.[52]

Turchaninov does not confine his criticism to the period of the outbreak of hostilities, but extends it to subsequent developments as well. Thus, he touches upon the removal in the summer of 1864 of General Benjamin Butler, an officer well known for his connections with left-wing Republicans in Washington, from his command in Grant's army.

> There was a time when General McClellan's party held sway. Now a new party has been formed, headed by Generals Grant and Sherman. Every such party needs many pliant and tractable people who will support it and strengthen it, but it will never accept a shrewd outsider into its ranks. That General Butler lacks a specialized military education is beyond dispute, but it is equally indisputable that he is a clearer thinker than ten West-Pointers put together.... [5] In this sense General Butler was unfortunate. At the same time, a man of Butler's keen intelligence and political orientation was a rather unwelcome witness of events for those who commanded the army. That is why he was dismissed.

Turchaninov also wrote about the enormous casualties suffered by the Union army in the battles of the Civil War. He placed the responsibility for these losses on the

---

52. Ibid., 50–51.

army command. If the McClellans and Buells were guilty of following a Fabian strategy and of showing a lack of resolve in the face of the enemy, some of the generals who replaced them dreamed of winning quick and dazzling victories and stormed the enemy's positions regardless of casualties, declared the author. On the basis of his extensive knowledge of military history and his analysis of recent battles, Turchaninov developed his doctrine of the tactically justified and necessary attack. He condemned "senseless and willful assaults." He noted that the public had unfortunately grown used to newspaper reports of heavy casualties and that career-minded generals unscrupulously took advantage of this.

> When both the Government and the people look upon this [long casualty lists] with indifference, the generals become too voracious. If such a general lacks ability, if he is incapable of achieving victory through the exercise of his military skills, he is ready to pay for it with a sea of blood. . . . He only thinks of cutting a dash. . . . One thousand men may be killed, or even twenty thousand—what does it matter? The appearance of success is there, and that is splendid![53]

Although he subjected the Union generals to withering criticism, Turchaninov always spoke with great warmth about the Union soldiers and the ordinary Americans—workers and farmers—who selflessly bore the burden of the sanguinary Civil War. "While our civilian and military leaders are hardly deserving of praise," he wrote, "our volunteer soldiers are true heroes." Discussing peculation in the Union armies, due to the greed of the Northern bourgeoisie, whose members waxed rich from selling supplies for the army, Turchaninov described the suffering endured by the Union volunteers because of their commanders' indifference and incompetence.

> Badly-made uniforms, which within a month turn into a beggar's rags; rotting boots that fall to pieces after a single march; knapsacks that can be worn only as a form of punishment because their straps cut into the shoulders and squeeze the chest; cartridges which contain an insufficient quantity of gunpowder or in which the gunpowder is lumpy (half of them may be considered worthless; a soldier has to carry a double supply); shells with time-fuses that make them explode in mid-air, so that they kill men in our own advance guard; guns that maim their crews because their barrels blow up as soon as they are fired for the first time; saddles that become warped after it rains and injure the horses; shirts which are so short that they do not reach the waist; socks of children's sizes, which do not fit a soldier's foot. . . . The soldier, constrained by military discipline, has been farmed out to outfitters who are little better than extortionists; some of the officers try to complain but, since their complaints must be passed up the chain of command, they are held up in divisional headquarters.

Turchaninov concludes with this encomium to the private soldier of the Northern armies:

> O, courageous and selfless patriot! The bones of your comrades-in-arms show up white on the hills of the Southern states. How many common graves are scattered throughout

---

53. Ibid., 51–52, 61–62.

the rebellious South! You lose your health, you come out of battle without an arm or a leg, you lay down your life for your country and for liberty. If we lose this war, no one will have the temerity to say that you were to blame. But if we achieve victory, an enlightened historian will knock many political generals off their pedestals and will write these words, as an eternal lesson to future generations: "The politicians brought our Republic to the edge of the abyss. The volunteer soldier saved it."[54]

Turchaninov's *Military Rambles* stand out among the mass of American writings on the Civil War. No other author in the North was able to offer a critique of the Union army that was so grounded in personal experience, so penetrating, substantive, and knowledgeable. In some respects Turchaninov's analysis shares points in common with the criticism of the conduct of the Civil War that appeared on the pages of the left-wing Republican and Abolitionist press (see, for instance, his comments on the officers trained at West Point). However, the author of *Military Rambles* was more level-headed and at the same time more principled than his American contemporaries in his discussion of the roots of the failures he condemned.

There can be little doubt that Turchaninov's generally critical attitude toward American bourgeois democracy, developed in the years before the outbreak of the armed conflict between North and South (as his letter to Herzen shows), played an important role in his analysis of the Civil War. Further research will add new and valuable insights to what we know about this figure. Of particular importance is the task of elucidating the content of Turchaninov's social views and determining the nature of his links with the progressive revolutionary circles in Russia and America. In any study of the history of the Civil War in the United States or the history of Russian-American social contacts, the importance of the figure of Ivan Turchaninov must be recognized.

54. *Military Rambles,* February 1865, 4, 33–34.

7

Russians in the United States: Social, Cultural, and Scientific Contacts in the 1870s, by G. P. Kuropiatnik

In the history of the Russian-American relations in the nineteenth century, the 1870s were on the whole a time of positive developments. There were important reasons for this. The largely constructive position adopted by those guiding the foreign policy of the North American republic, both in 1870–1871, when Russia decided to repudiate the obligation not to have a war fleet or coastal fortification on the Black Sea, and in 1877–1878, at the time of the Russian-Turkish War, was to a significant extent due to Russia's sympathetic attitude to the United States during the War of Independence, the Anglo-American War of 1812, and the Civil War of 1861–1865. These developments in the diplomatic arena were bound to influence the course of relations between the two countries in other areas, for instance in science and culture.

The 1870s saw an increase in the number of Russians traveling to the United States. The scope of the exchanges of official government publications and scientific papers—a very important measure of the level of cultural contacts between the two peoples—also grew. Russian scholars and scientists began to visit the United States more frequently, while their American colleagues traveled more and more often to the centers of learning in Russia.

The development of mutually advantageous contacts between the two countries was not limited to traditional areas, but increasingly involved other fields, including music and literature. During this period Americans and Russians attempted to set up a utopian agricultural community in Kansas, the first links between the Russian revolutionary organization "The Will of the People" and progressive political figures in America were established, and the works of Ivan Turgenev came to exercise a significant influence on American writers.

The history of Russian-American relations shows that during those periods when a mutual desire for cooperation determined the shape of the scientific and cultural contacts between the two nations, the barriers dividing the United States and Russia tended to disappear and a productive process of mutual enrichment ensued. Evidence of this will be offered in the present article, which is devoted to the history of social, cultural, and intellectual relations between Russia and the United States.

Emigration from Russia

In the mid–nineteenth century there was virtually no emigration from Russia to the United States. In 1851 America received one Russian immigrant, in 1852, two, and in 1853, three. The number of Russian subjects officially registered as immigrants reached one thousand for the first time in 1872. During the 1870s the volume of immigration from Russia continued to grow; in 1880 five thousand Russian subjects came to America as immigrants. In the ten years between 1871 and 1880, 39,284 Russian immigrants entered the American "melting pot."[1] Of the total mass of immigrants from Europe, however, only a small proportion, averaging 1.7 percent, were Russians.

People left Russia for a variety of reasons. Peasants who learned of the possibility of acquiring land dreamed of a better lot; others fled political and religious persecution or were attempting to escape compulsory military service, a reform introduced in Russia by Alexander II. Most of the foreign books about America that were translated into Russian and read by would-be émigrés, particularly young people, colored the truth about that country. Mikhail Vladimirov, who lived there more than four years, wrote that, having heard or read only about the positive aspects of American life, they "were used to seeing the United States as something close to perfection."[2] Thus the disappointment felt by a Russian stepping on American soil was all the greater. "We feel ourselves duty-bound to believe that the rivers there flow with milk and honey, and no one wishes to concede that this superior civilization encourages *the few* to amass the largest possible amount of capital in their hands," wrote Nikolai Slavinskii, reproaching his countrymen.[3]

The letters and travel writings of many Russians who, for a variety of reasons, found themselves in the United States helped to show that the myths and legends depicting America as a kind of Arcadia were false. Among these were Slavinskii, the future writer Grigorii Machtet, the populist Nikolai Tsakni, and the bankrupt landowner A. S. Kurbskii. Each of them lived in the United States for a period of time and in close contact with Russians who had settled there. In their reports from America, these authors described the ordeals and privations experienced by their countrymen in the land beyond the ocean. "Instead of finding the promised land and the happiness they had

---

1. *Historical Statistics of the United States: Colonial Times to 1970* (Washington 1975), 106. This article originally appeared in *Novaia i Noveishaia Istoriia* (Modern and Contemporary History) 4–5 (1981).
2. M. M. Vladimirov, *Russkii sredi amerikantsev: moi lichnye vpechatleniia kak tokaria, chernorabochego, plotnika i puteshestvennika, 1872–1876* (A Russian among Americans: My Personal Impressions as a Turner, Laborer, Carpenter, and Traveler, 1872–1876) (St. Petersburg, 1877), ii–iii, 305.
3. Slavinskii, *Pis'ma ob Amerike i russkikh pereselentsakh* (Letters on America and the Russian Settlers) (St. Petersburg, 1873), 237.

expected, from the very beginning they faced a bitter struggle for survival, a succession of calamities, moments of despair," wrote Slavinskii.

> Without money, without concrete information, without perfect command of the local language, sometimes without the right to seek the only help available to them—that of a representative of our government—what can they undertake, how can they live, how can they begin to make ends meet? . . . Our countrymen, like the first American pioneers, were forced to make their own way through life, without any outside help or contribution, since the sympathy of the Americans for our people is not so great as to make them forget their egoism and lend the newcomers a helping hand.[4]

Tsakni was the author of what was probably the most profound analysis of American society in the 1870s and the condition of American workers offered by a Russian observer.[5] In his articles, which bore the collective title, "A Picture of Labor in the United States," he showed with the help of official statistics that "the belief that throughout the country the American working classes live in prosperity . . . is far from correct."[6] Even Kurbskii, who had been fairly successful in America and was thus inclined to present an embellished picture of the working and living conditions in that country, from his conversations with Russian settlers was forced to conclude that "the rosy view of life in America is transformed into a kind of sombre distrust, which almost amounts to a kind of repentance."[7] The hard and hopeless life led some immigrants who had exhausted their physical and moral strength to commit suicide "and thus put an end to poverty," as happened in the case of a graduate of the University of Dorpat after he had spent ten years trying to find work in the "promised land."[8]

After experiencing failure and disappointment in the cities in the East, some Russian immigrants moved west and settled on the Pacific coast, congregating around the local Russian Orthodox Church. This eparchy was formed around Russian colonists, many of whom had moved to San Francisco after the Alaska purchase of 1867. In the early 1870s a Russian church and school were built in San Francisco.[9]

The lot of those Russian settlers who were finally able to reach the open lands of the West, where it was still possible to acquire a homestead, was also difficult.

4. Ibid., 19.
5. In the early 1870s, Tsakni was a member of the Moscow circle of "Chaikovtsy" and maintained contact with Sergei Kravchinskii (Stepniak). In 1876 he was exiled to Archangel Province for his revolutionary activities but fled to London aboard a British steamship in 1878. Thereafter he lived for a while in the United States, where he worked as a correspondent for Russian newspapers and journals, and also for underground periodicals: *Vestnik Narodnoi Voli* (Herald of the People's Will), *Kalendar' Narodnoi Voli* (Calendar of the People's Will), and *Vol'noe Slovo* (Free Word). In the late 1880s he abandoned revolutionary activity. See *Deiateli revoliutsionnogo dvizheniia v Rossii* (Figures of the Revolutionary Movement in Russia) [hereafter *DRDR*], 4 vols., 10 nos. (Moscow, 1927–1934) vol. 2, no. 4: 1894–95.
6. *Slovo* (Word) 2–3 (1880) 2: 25.
7. Kurbskii, "Russkii rabochii u amerikanskogo plantatora" (A Russian Worker for an American Planter), *Vestnik Evropy* (European Herald) 7 (1873): 21–22.
8. Vladimirov, *Russian among Americans,* 145.
9. Schuyler to Fish, February 4, 1875, Diplomatic Dispatches, Russia, vol. 27, record group 59, National Archives.

Nikolai Il'in, who spent six months in the United States before returning to Russia, reported in 1876 that the majority "of our countrymen in New York who, because of their lack of employment, lived in poverty, did their utmost to achieve the goal they had set themselves—that of starting their own farm somewhere in the interior of the country."[10] Yet many Russian settlers who were able to find the kind of jobs they liked or to start their own farm on a homestead suffered from homesickness, and sooner or later returned to Russia.[11]

The Cedar Vale Commune in Kansas

In the late 1860s and early 1870s the idea of setting up associations and communes of various kinds was quite a rage among Russian populists. But reactionary policies of the tsarist government and police persecutions forced enthusiasts of this idea "little by little to abandon the hope of establishing agricultural communes in Russia."[12] Instead they developed plans to emigrate to other countries, and above all to the United States. "At the time many Russians who dreamt of freedom and communistic experiments became attracted to the prospect of emigrating to America," wrote Vladimir Korolenko in his autobiography, *The History of My Contemporary*.[13]

In the early 1870s a group of populists in Kiev began to draw up plans to settle in the United States. The members of this group, who were known as "the Americans," were led by Ivan Debogorii-Mokrievich. "During this period," wrote his brother Vladimir, "there was a general fascination with America, American life, American free institutions; some went there, studied the local way of life, and described it in the Russian journals."[14] In 1871 Ivan Debogorii began to select individuals who were willing to join an agricultural commune, all members of which would be expected to work: there would be no hired workers and, therefore, no exploitation. Every member of the commune would be obliged to perform physical labor, for this was considered the only honest means of earning a living.

In its search for those willing to settle in the United States, the "American circle" established contacts with another set of Kiev intellectuals, who were engaged in circulating Socialist books among young people and maintained contacts with a group in St. Petersburg that later became known as the "Chaikovskii circle."[15] Soon the membership of the "American circle" in Kiev increased to twenty, but only three of its

---

10. N. D. Il'in, *Shest' mesiatsev v Severo-Amerikanskikh Soedinennykh Shtatakh* (Six Months in the United States of North America) (St. Petersburg, 1876), 171.

11. Iurii Kanovskii to Russian Legation, Washington, March 24, 1878, TsGAVMF (Central State Archive of the Navy), record group 22, inventory 1, list 73, 10; Korolenko, *Sobr. Soch.* (Collected Works), 10 vols. (Moscow, 1957), vol. 7, 334; Sh. A. Bogina, *Immigrantskoe naselenie SShA, 1865–1900 gg.* (The Immigrant Population of the United States, 1865–1900) (Leningrad, 1976), 220.

12. V. K. Debogorii-Mokrievich, *Vospominaniia* (Reminiscences) (St. Petersburg, 1906), 67.

13. Korolenko, *Works,* vol. 7, 178.

14. Debogorii-Mokrievich, *Reminiscences,* 67; see also his *Ot buntarstva k terrorizmu* (From Rebellion to Terrorism), 2 vols. (Moscow-Leningrad, 1930), vol. 1, 91–92.

15. *DRDR* 2, no. 1: 336–37, 339.

members—Machtet, Ivan Rechitskii, and Aleksandr Roman'ko-Romanovskii—were eventually able to leave for America.[16]

The members of this "American circle" had some knowledge of the United States, acquired from the Russian monthly journals. They were particularly impressed by the articles written by a "William Frey." The person hiding behind this English pseudonym was Vladimir Konstantinovich Geins [Heinz], by birth a member of the nobility of the province of Estland. He had passed through every stage of the system of military education existing in Russia at the time. After attending the Brest Litovsk Military College and the Konstantinovskii Military School, Geins joined the Finland Regiment of the Imperial Guard. Two years later he entered the Mikhailovskii Artillery Academy, graduating with honors, and, thanks to a recommendation from Colonel Peter Lavrov [future populist theoretician], who had been one of his professors there, was appointed teacher of mathematics at an artillery school.[17] His career prospects were brilliant. By the age of twenty-five he held the rank of captain, was a member of the General Staff, and had been designated to attend classes at the Pulkovo Observatory.[18]

As a cadet Geins read the works of Alexander Herzen and Nicholas Chernyshevsky, as well as the writings of the utopian socialists Charles Fourier and Robert Owen.[19] According to Geins's biographer, the future artillery officer had for a time even been a member of some kind of "secret society."[20] But Geins's involvement in the revolutionary movement, if involvement there was, was probably transitory and insignificant. Machtet, who visited him in the United States, recalled that on one occasion the conversation turned to the subject of the revolutionary movement in Russia. "In the ensuing argument [Geins] began violently to denigrate all the great heroes celebrated for their courage, selflessness, and intelligence, calling them 'egoists' who had been guided solely by an irresistible desire 'to be ringleaders' and somehow to gain popularity with the 'stupid rabble.' "[21]

Nevertheless, Geins's contacts with the representatives of progressive Russian sociopolitical thought of the mid–nineteenth century and his familiarity with the works

16. Debogorii-Mokrievich, *Reminiscences,* 78; *DRDR* 1, no. 2: 349.

17. Rukopisnyi otdel Instituta russkoi literatury (Pushkinskii dom) AN, SSSR (Manuscript Division, Institute of Russian Literature [Pushkin House] of the U.S.S.R. Academy of Sciences) [hereafter RO, PD], record group 265, inventory 2, list 580, 4, Introduction by N. V. Reingardt to the correspondence of A. K. Geins and W. Frey. [Geins first adopted the pseudonym of Wilhelm Frei (Free in German), which was Americanized to William Fry or Frey—ed].

18. *Znakomye: Al'bom M. I. Semevskogo, Kniga avtobiograficheskikh sobstvennoruchnykh zametok 850 lits, 1867–1888* (Acquaintances: An Album by M. I. Semevskii, A Book of Autobiographical Notes by 850 Persons, Penned by Their Own Hand, 1867–1888) (St. Petersburg, 1888), 247; *Russkii biograficheskii slovar'* (Russian Biographical Dictionary) (Moscow, 1896–1914), vol. 4, 355–56.

19. RO, PD, record group 265, inventory 2, list 580, 4.

20. N. V. Reingardt, *Neobyknovennaia lichnost'* (An Extraordinary Personality) (Kazan, 1889), 2.

21. Machtet, "Obshchina Freia" (The Frey Commune) in *Poln. Sobr. soch.* (Complete Collected Works), 12 vols. (Kiev, 1902), vol. 1, 203. [For an English translation, *America Through Russian Eyes, 1874–1926,* edited and translated by Olga Peters Hasty and Susanne Fusso (New Haven and London, 1988), 54–80—ed].

of the great utopian socialists affected the way in which the young officer saw the society and the world in which he lived. He proved immune to the temptations of a glittering military career or the allure of money. Moreover, he came to hate the military profession, war, and everything that war meant. As his biographer wrote, this officer of the General Staff decided to transform his life of bourgeois-aristocratic leisure into one of labor and communion with the people, hoping that he would help to bring about a future where "not only will there be no slave-owners and slaves, but also no masters and servants, so that all will be masters."[22] His interest in the projects of utopian socialists, as well as the impression made on him by a Russian translation of William Dixon's *The New America*,[23] led him to resolve to go to the United States and join one of the local communist societies that strove to improve the lives of the oppressed and suffering masses. Geins arrived in New York in 1867 accompanied by his wife, Mariia Slavinskaia, who shared his ideals. Here he officially became an American citizen and changed his name to William Frey.

But very soon the money he had brought from Russia ran out, and he was forced to look for work. A small arms firm in New England that was a supplier to the Russian government made him a most advantageous offer (at the request of a Russian officer who had discovered that the Geins family were living in abject poverty), but Frey responded by declaring that he had abandoned his military career in Russia because he hated anything that had to do with killing people. He was unable to work for an enterprise that derived its profits from war, he said. This Russian aristocrat later recalled that he was forced to perform all kinds of "backbreaking labor" in the New World. "I was a farmer, a cleaner. . . . My entire life in America was full of tremendous physical hardships," he wrote in 1886.[24]

Having learned some English, the Freys left New York for the West, where at the time communes of various kinds and political orientations were quickly sprouting up and equally quickly disappearing. They wished to find and join one of the "socialist enterprises that aim to improve life not through violence and revolution, but by offering a personal example of a better way of life."[25]

After studying the practices and goals of the "Biblical Communists" of the "Oneida," Frey chose another commune—"The Union" [better known as Reunion—ed]. According to his friend, E. S. Beasley, a professor at the University of London, Frey was

> at the time full of the kind of excessive enthusiasm that occasionally leads many upper-class Russians to renounce the advantages and privileges of their position in order to share the lot of the poor. . . . These Russian enthusiasts are inspired . . . by a burning desire to better the condition of the poor and exploited classes. Whatever one may think of the principles of these people, one cannot but marvel at their enthusiasm and sincerity.[26]

22. RO, PD, record group 265, inventory 2, list 580, 4.
23. V. Dikson [William Dixon], *Novaia Amerika* (New America), translation of 6th English ed. (St. Petersburg, 1867).
24. *Znakomye: . . . Semevskogo,* 247.
25. Ibid.
26. Reingardt, *An Extraordinary Personality,* 3–4.

Frey and his wife spent about a year with the Union, until the community broke up. He recorded his American impressions and experiences in articles and essays that he wrote mostly for *Otechestvennye Zapiski* (Fatherland Notes). He did this at the suggestion of Petr Bokov, the editor of *Nedel'ia* (Week), who was aware not only of the general tenor and character of Nekrasov's journal, but also knew that its contributors were paid more generously than was the case at some of the other periodicals.[27]

It must be noted that Frey's participation in the "communistic" experiments in America would have been impossible without the help he received from rich relatives in Russia, particularly Aleksandr Geins, his older brother,[28] who provided him with regular financial support. When the Freys' daughter Bela was born in Missouri, Aleksandr sent a large sum of money to America meant, he told Frey, "to ensure that by purchasing cows, sugar, tea, etc. you will supply little Bela with the necessary 'provisions.' "[29] "When you begin to become financially independent, take my advice—devote yourself to commerce, and make some money," added Geins.[30]

At the beginning of 1871, Frey, together with an American named [Stephen] Briggs, founded the "Progressive Commune" near Cedar Vale, Kansas, for the purpose of developing an "ideal way of life."[31] It included both Americans and Russians. The American scholar Charles Nordhoff mentions, but does not name, two Russian members: an astronomer and a "well-known sculptor" [Fedor Kamenskii—ed].[32] Machtet, a former member of the "American circle" in Kiev, spent some eight months in Frey's commune and left an interesting description of the activities, everyday life, and moral state of the Russian communalists. During his travels in the United States, Machtet learned about the hard lot of the farm laborer and unskilled worker from his own experience. He saw much and came to understand much. After undergoing all kinds of ordeals and privations, he returned to Russia together with Rechitskii.[33] After analyzing Machtet's literary works and correspondence, his biographer drew this

27. Geins to Frey, December 22, 1868/January 3, 1869, RO, PD, record group 265, inventory 2, list 579, 1.

28. Geins to Frey, August 5/17, 1869, ibid., 3. Frey's brother belonged to the upper stratum of the tsarist aristocracy. At the age of thirty he was promoted to the rank of general (1866) and appointed director of the office of the governor-general of Turkestan. In the early 1870s he directed a department of the Ministry of Communication, after which he was military governor of Turgai, governor of the city of Odessa (1878–1880), and governor of Kazan. In the 1880s he occupied high positions in the Ministry of Internal Affairs and on the General Staff. Although he expressed certain liberal views, General Geins was an ardent monarchist and an admirer of Alexander II. He was noted for his cruelty, particularly toward revolutionaries. See S. F. Kovalik, *Revoliutsionnoe dvizhenie semidesiatykh godov i protsess 193-kh* (The Revolutionary Movement of the 1870s and the Trial of the 193) (Moscow, 1928), 157.

29. Geins to Frey, August 5/17, 1869, RO, PD, record group 265, inventory 2, list 579, 3, 30, and September 11/23, 1869, ibid., 6–7.

30. Ibid.

31. Machtet, *Works*, vol. 1, 199. The regulations of the "Progressive Commune" were printed in order to attract volunteers from Europe and America and included in full in Charles Nordhoff, *The Communistic Societies of the United States from Personal Visit and Observation* (New York, 1875 [reprint New York, 1962]), 354–56.

32. Nordhoff, *Communistic Societies*, 354.

33. L. Deich, *Za polveka* (For Half a Century) (Berlin, 1923), 111; *DRDR* 1, no. 2: 349.

conclusion about the effect on the Russian writer of his two-year sojourn in the United States:

> Machtet realized that he would be unable to find the most perfect forms of communal life or implement his political and social ideals in the land of business and the all-mighty dollar. . . . He found himself irresistibly drawn back to his native country where he hoped to use his abilities in the service of his people.[34]

The members of the Progressive Commune lived in a "wretched hut with cracks in the walls. Inside it was infernally cold. There was no ceiling, only a torn roof overhead."[35] They lacked not only food but also clothes, shoes, instruments, farm tools, and tableware. Frey and his wife wore soldiers' greatcoats that they had bought for a song at a sale of surplus military stores left over from the Civil War. Inspired by the opportunity to realize his ideals, Frey stoically endured adversity and privation, but his wife found life in the commune trying and "rejected firmly and vociferously much of what it stood for."[36] In 1873 Machtet wrote to Frey's brother in St. Petersburg informing him of the needs of the Progressive Community, and soon the objects, instruments, and utensils he had requested were on their way to Kansas.[37]

While Frey and Briggs were trying to establish an "ideal way of life" in the Russian-American Progressive Commune in Kansas, a new group, composed of those wishing to found a "free commune" in America, was formed in Central Russia. Its most prominent member was Nikolai Chaikovskii. As a youth he had taken part in student political gatherings, and in the spring of 1869 he had joined a revolutionary circle led by Mark Natanson. In mid-1871 this organization, which had grown considerably in size, became known as the "Chaikovskii circle." It carried out revolutionary propaganda among the workers in St. Petersburg and took part in "going to the people." Soon thereafter this populist organization was suppressed by the authorities.

Chaikovskii went into hiding, but the police continued to look for him. During his wanderings, the twenty-four-year-old Chaikovskii met some members of revolutionary groups, who as a result of the suppression of the circle had fallen into a mood of religious fatalism. In Orel Chaikovskii met Aleksandr Malikov, a religious sectarian and God-seeker. He had been born into an ordinary peasant family in the Province of Vladimir, but thanks to his remarkable abilities he was able to graduate from the University of Moscow with a first-class degree. All those who knew him were impressed by his

---

34. D. P. Silchevskii, "Biografiia G. A. Machteta" (The Biography of G. A. Machtet) in Machtet, *Works,* vol. 12, xii. After his return in 1874 from the United States, Machtet became known as the author of sketches about life in America. He spent some nine years in exile (in the province of Archangel and Siberia) for his participation in the revolutionary movement. His poem "The Last Farewell" (1876), written on the occasion of the death of the populist medical student P. F. Chernyshev, was put to music with a new title, "Wearied by a Harsh Captivity." It became one of the most beloved songs of several generations of Russian revolutionaries. Lenin liked to listen to this song and to sing it.
35. Korolenko, *Works,* vol. 7, 178.
36. Machtet, *Works,* vol. 1, 203.
37. Geins to Frey, December 10/22, 1873, RO, PD, record group 265, inventory 2, list 579, 14.

learning and eloquence.[38] Chaikovskii became interested in Malikov's utopian plan to create a new religion, and left the revolutionary movement. As a practical step toward the establishment of the new religion, Malikov and Chaikovskii decided to go to America and find Frey's commune.[39]

They called for volunteers who would be willing to travel to America with a view to establishing a labor commune there. A number of Malikov's followers, who called themselves "avatars," as well as several members of the populist revolutionary movement who were being sought by the secret police, responded to their summons. Among these was S. L. Kliachko,[40] who had been the organizer of the Moscow branch of the "Chaikovskii circle," his wife, and two "Nechaevites" [followers of the notorious terrorist Sergei Nechaev], Vladimir and Natalia Sviatskii. Chaikovskii was the first to reach New York, arriving in the summer of 1875. In the autumn of that year he was followed across the Atlantic by Malikov, his wife and children, Kliachko and his wife, V. I. Alekseev with his family and brother, the Sviatskii couple, Bruzvich from Orel, Lidia Eigof from Samara, and Ivan Linev—fifteen persons in all.[41]

After the entire group assembled in New York, Chaikovskii (who had adopted the name N. Gray) and Malikov went to Kansas to negotiate with Frey, who was anxious that they should join his group. But the two "avatars" were discouraged by the squalid conditions in which Frey and his comrades lived and decided to organize their own commune. They invited Frey and his family to join them. When soon afterwards Frey left the Progressive Community, he did so with a light heart because of a disagreement with its American members, who wished to turn it into a commercial enterprise.[42]

On Frey's advice the Chaikovskii-Malikov group bought land near Cedar Vale [fifty miles southeast of Wichita], Kansas. After constructing their temporary quarters, they sowed their fields with wheat and corn. But soon the members of the Cedar Vale Commune began to complain about their meager and monotonous diet. This was

38. A. I. Faresov, *Semidesiatniki: Ocherki umstvennykh i politicheskikh dvizhenii v Rossii* (Men of the Seventies: Studies on the Intellectual and Political Movements in Russia) (St. Petersburg, 1905), 291–97; N. A. Charushin, *O dalikom proshlom: iz vospominanii o revoliutsionnom dvizhenii 70-kh godov XIX veka* (About the Distant Past: Excerpts from Reminiscences about the Revolutionary Movement of the 1870s) (Moscow, 1973), 154. Solely on the basis that Malikov was tried in connection with the Karakozov affair [1866 assassination attempt of Alexander II], some scholars have followed Korolenko in stating that he was a member of the Karakozov group (for example, Bogina, *Immigrant Population*, 220). First, Malikov was found not guilty (see M. F. Frolenko, *Zapiski semidesiatnika* [Notes of a Man of the Seventies] [Moscow, 1927], 115), although he was sent into administrative exile to Kholmogory. Second, greater significance should be attached to Malikov's links to Konstantin Pobedonostsev, who headed the most extreme party among the Russian reactionaries. It was thanks to him that Malikov obtained a highly paid position immediately upon graduation and, later, was quickly released from exile. After his return to Orel, Malikov waged a bitter struggle with local and exiled revolutionaries.

39. M. M. Klevenskii, "I. S. Turgenev i semidesiatniki" (I. S. Turgenev and Men of the Seventies), *Golos Minuvshego* (Voice of the Past) 1 (1914): 8.

40. N. P. Troitskii has established that Kliachko was the author of the first Russian translation of Marx's treatise "The Civil War in France," *Modern and Contemporary History* 1 (1962): 196.

41. P. L. Lavrov, *Izbr. soch. na sotsial'no-politicheskie temy* (Selected Works on Sociopolitical Themes), 4 vols. (Moscow, 1934–1935), vol. 4, 412, n. 229; *DRDR* 2, no. 4: 2091.

42. Machtet, *Works*, vol. 1, 212.

because Frey, who exercised a dominant influence on the colonists' lives, persistently preached vegetarianism. The communalists were not allowed to consume meat, alcoholic beverages, coffee, tea, sugar, or salt. Frey believed that food should be eaten in its natural state, so he even tried to ban the use of fire for cooking. He opposed the consumption of sour dough, so bread was baked without salt from plain flour that had been kneaded in water. The loaves that came out of the oven were hard and prickly, and the members of the commune nicknamed them "Frey's hygienic pine-cones."[43]

None of the communalists had training in carpentry, joinery, or metal work, and yet in the circumstances these simple skills were vitally necessary. The buildings the colonists erected were cold, uncomfortable, and impractical. They did not know how to deal with domestic animals: no one could harness a horse or milk a cow, nor did they know how and where to preserve food. Quarrels and disagreements erupted.[44] As in other American communes, the members of the Kansas commune devoted much time to spiritual self-perfection. To this end weekly meetings, at which the communalists publicly criticized each other's conduct and actions, were held. Although the colonists made an effort to keep the tone of the discussion friendly, these gatherings often led to squabbling and resentment, which in turn undermined the very foundations of the commune.[45]

The experience of living in an unfamiliar environment in a foreign country also greatly affected the mood of the communalists. Many thought of returning to Russia. Later Machtet recalled his impressions of meeting Frey in America:

> Much time had passed since he and I had last seen our country; for a long time we had lived under what were for us completely new and alien conditions, surrounded by different people; different attitudes. But when we saw each other under this new sky, in the middle of this vast expanse of freedom, our first word was "Russia." Only at a time like this do you learn how strongly, how passionately you love the land that nurtured you, raised you, educated you, and created you, the land to which you have grown accustomed, the land you have learnt to understand.[46]

Many members of the Cedar Vale Commune suffered the pangs of acute nostalgia, even though in Russia some of them could expect jail or exile for their revolutionary activities. After examining the papers and correspondence of Frey and the other members of the commune, Mark Aldanov concluded that "America proved to be a cold and reserved stepmother to them."[47]

Upon learning of the establishment of the Cedar Vale Commune, Lavrov offered an interesting critique of the utopian nature of such projects (earlier he had strongly

---

43. *Russian Biographical Dictionary,* vol. 4, 358.
44. Korolenko, *Works,* vol. 7, 179; M. Aldanov, "A Russian Commune in Kansas," *The Russian Review* 17, no. 1 (January 1957): 37–38. [The best source in English on Frey's Kansas commune is Avrahm Yarmolinsky, *A Russian's American Dream* (Lawrence, Kans., 1967); manuscripts, including Frey's diaries, are in the Manuscript Division, New York Public Library—ed].
45. Machtet, *Works,* vol. 1, 206–7; Aldanov, "A Russian Commune in Kansas," 38.
46. Machtet, *Works,* vol. 1, 197.
47. Aldanov, "A Russian Commune in Kansas," 43.

attacked Frey for his advocacy of a "positive religion of humanity)." In 1875–1876 Lavrov wrote:

> Belief in the metaphysical notion that the *socialist idea* shall win over the world as soon as it is incarnated in some phalanstery, in some Icaria or Cedar Vale Commune, that kings and millionaires will immediately come to the aid of this true idea solely because of its theoretical validity, that the *harmonious society* will appear just like that, without a bloody struggle to bring it about—removes the idea of socialism from the real world into the world of idealist philosophers.[48]

Soon the Cedar Vale Commune began to fall apart. As early as in the autumn of 1876, Il'in, who was visiting the commune at the time, saw evidence of its decline.[49] Most of its members left for Russia in the summer of 1877. Others, after experiencing further miseries in America and Europe, also sooner or later returned home. Only Frey and Chaikovskii stayed on in America. Frey, who, as he said, was to experience "the most tragic disillusionment with social activity,"[50] continued his attempts to manage the commune farmstead for another year or two. He kept the home fires burning in the belief that the defectors would inevitably return.

In 1885, Frey and his family moved to London, and in 1886, with the permission of the authorities, he came to Russia for several months as an American citizen.[51] In October 1886 he spent a week at Iasnaia Poliana, where he tried to convert Leo Tolstoy to his beliefs. Later Frey sent him a long letter in which he outlined his main principles.[52] In spite of all the privations, misfortunes, and disappointments he had experienced in the land beyond the ocean, Frey emphasized that during his eighteen years in the United States he had learned much that was useful and that he had left America with a sense of gratitude toward the country that had adopted him and the many Americans who "live not for dollars, but for other people."[53]

When in the summer of 1877 the majority of members of the Cedar Vale Commune decided to return home, Chaikovskii, who lacked the money for a train ticket, had to walk from Kansas to Philadelphia on foot. In order to avoid starvation, he worked as a common laborer in the Philadelphia shipyards and at a sugar factory, and then spent about a year in a religious commune. In 1878 he moved to Paris, and after 1880 lived for about a quarter of a century in London.[54] In 1880 Chaikovskii wrote from London to a former member of the Kansas commune: "Our disease, and the disease of

48. Lavrov, *Selected Works,* vol. 4, 381–82.
49. Il'in, *Six Months in the United States,* 172.
50. *Znakomye:* . . . *Semevskogo,* 247.
51. RO, PD, record group 265, inventory 2, list 580, 5.
52. See "L. N. Tolstoi i Vil'iam Frei: i biograficheskikh materialov" (L. N. Tolstoy and William Frey: A Selection of Biographical Materials), compiled by P. I. Biriukov, *Minuvshie Gody* (Bygone Years) 9 (1908): 68–91; excerpts from Frey to Tolstoy in Reingardt, appendix, 1–33. Tolstoy described Frey as a remarkable man of great charm, but did not adopt his religious views.
53. *Znakomye:* . . . *Semevskogo,* 247.
54. After the First Russian Revolution of 1905, Chaikovskii returned to Russia and joined the Socialist-Revolutionary Party. In 1917 he became one of the leaders of the "laborites," and then of the Workers' Popular-Socialist Party. During the civil war he presided over the White

all the Russian émigrés here is—hunger. For the last two months the five of us have lived without literally knowing if we will have anything to eat tomorrow. And my poor children? It is too painful even to speak of them. Anyway, you know all this yourself."[55]

Americans Read Turgenev

Where the political situation abroad and the history, philosophy, economics, and the arts and science of foreign countries were concerned, in the 1870s, as in earlier decades, Russian readers were mainly interested in the countries of Western Europe, particularly France, Germany, and England. But as a result of the events of the 1860s—the Civil War and the emancipation of the Negro slaves in the United States, the abolition of serfdom in Russia, reciprocal visits by naval squadrons—Russians and Americans became more interested in each other, inaugurating a new period in the cultural relations between the two nations.

The works of the great Russian writers—Turgenev, Tolstoy, and Dostoevsky—made an enormous impression throughout the entire civilized world and were the subject of constant admiration on the part of the reading public. The Victorian literary critic and publicist Arnold Bennett compiled a list of the twelve best works of the second half of the nineteenth century, and all of them without exception were by Russian authors.[56]

Until then American readers had only a superficial knowledge of Russian literature. The few works by Russian writers with which they were familiar were hardly representative of Russian literature as a whole. A number of American journals occasionally published reviews and short annotations of works by Russian writers, but few translations of Russian works of literature were available. The development of belles-lettres in America was to a significant extent influenced by English literature. In the United States in the 1850s and 1860s, Charles Dickens and William Thackeray were almost universally regarded as living classics.

The first Russian writer to attract the attention of a relatively large number of American readers was Ivan Turgenev. In the United States his works were first read in French translations and not very widely known. The first English translation of a major work by Turgenev appeared not in England, but in the United States—the novel *Fathers and Sons*. The author of this translation, which had been made from the Russian original and in part also from the French and German editions, was an American, Eugene Schuyler. The visits by Russian naval squadrons to the United States during the Civil War had filled him with a great respect for, and interest in, Russia. He completed his translation in the spring of 1867. Early in the autumn of that year in Baden-Baden, the twenty-seven-year-old American presented Turgenev with four copies of the English version of the novel. In his introduction Schuyler expressed the hope that the publication

---

government in Archangel. He was the only Russian consulted by President Woodrow Wilson at the Paris Peace Conference. Until his death in 1926 he headed a group of émigré White Guards who conspired against the U.S.S.R. See *Sovetskii entsikopedicheskii slovar'* (Soviet Encyclopedic Dictionary) (Moscow, 1980), 1492.

55. Aldanov, "A Russian Commune in Kansas," 43.
56. R. A. Gettman, *Turgenev in England and America* (Urbana, 1941), 9.

of this famous work of Russian literature in the United States "will to some extent help the two great nations learn more about each other."[57] Turgenev provided Schuyler with letters of introduction to his friends in Russia, informing them that the American translator "has a keen interest in everything Russian and knows our language."[58]

Although the 1867 English publication of *Fathers and Sons* passed almost unnoticed, interest in Turgenev's works began to grow in the early 1870s, and led to issuing new editions of the novel in New York in 1872 and 1883, and in London in 1888. In later years Turgenev's popularity in the United States continued to increase. His works were received with particular enthusiasm in America, where they enjoyed a far wider readership than in Britain. If in 1868–1879 eight of Turgenev's works of fiction, including three novels, appeared there, in the same period twenty-one were published in the United States, including *Fathers and Sons* (two editions), *Smoke* (1872), *A Nest of Gentlefolk* (which appeared as *Liza*), *Rudin, Spring Floods* (1873), *Asya, Virgin Soil* (1877).[59]

Turgenev's popularity with readers in the United States was to prove long-lasting. The critics and writers of the New World admired his skill as an artist and his realist writing technique. Many American "pilgrims" visited Turgenev at his home in Paris. Henry James recalled,

> He was the most approachable, the most benevolent genius I have ever had the good fortune to meet. He was so simple, so natural, so modest . . . Our Anglo-Saxon, Protestant, moralistic norms and conventions were alien to him, and he judged things with a freedom and ease that were always a source of inspiration to me.[60]

James emphasized that Turgenev, who was forced to spend the best years of his life abroad, never ceased to feel concern for the problems of Russia and its people and had boundless faith in the strength of the Russian nation.

> His genius is for us the Slavonic genius, his voice is the voice of a people of many millions, a people of which we have only a vague conception, but one which, as we are becoming increasingly convinced, shall in its turn enter the arena of world civilization and rise above the dark plains of the North. There is much in his works that serves to support such a belief, and there can be no doubt that he was able to express the temperament of his people with amazing vividness.[61]

The similarities in the situation and development of the two countries were noted in some critical articles in U.S. journals. An analogy between slavery and serfdom was

---

57. Turgenev, *Fathers and Sons: A Novel Translated from the Russian with the Approval of the Author by E. Schuyler* (New York, 1867), viii.

58. Turgenev, *Poln. sobr. soch. i pisem* (Complete Collected Works and Letters), 28 vols. (Moscow, 1960–1967); letters 6, 312–13. Turgenev wrote: "The translation shows that it was made from the French and that Mr. Schuyler's knowledge of the Russian language is rather limited." Ibid., 321.

59. Gettman, *Turgenev*, 187–89.

60. Quoted from N. I. Samokhvalov, *Amerikanskaia literatura XIX v.* (American Literature in the Nineteenth Century) (Moscow, 1964), 197–98.

61. James, *The Art of Fiction and Other Essays* (New York, 1946), 99–100.

often drawn. American readers were informed in this connection that Turgenev's *A Sportsman's Sketches,* directed against the institution of serfdom, was published in the same year as Harriet Beecher Stowe's abolitionist novel *Uncle Tom's Cabin.*

The works of the Russian classics acted as a creative stimulus for those American writers who were advocates of the realist method in the depiction of everyday life. In emphasizing the pioneering role of Nicholas Gogol, William Dean Howells, one of the founders of the realist tradition in the United States, wrote that Russian writers "followed Gogol and learned from him, just as the whole world today must learn from them."[62] Howells recalled,

> The greatness of Turgenev's novels was fully recognized in the mid-1870s. One after another his works . . . passed through my hands and . . . inspired in me the deepest literary admiration for their author, which has lasted all my life. . . . After I read Turgenev for the first time I saw life in a completely different way. It had become more serious, more frightening, and imposed a kind of mystic responsibility on me, which I had not known before. My happy American notions became permeated with the tremendous melancholy of the patient, trusting, and enigmatic Slav. At the same time Nature now dazzled me with new facets which until then had been invisible to me.[63]

While the great American poet Walt Whitman admired Turgenev as "a marvelous story-teller," Henry James spoke of the Russian writer's beneficial influence on literature in the United States and throughout the world and declared that he, together with a number of leading American literary critics, considered Turgenev "the foremost novelist of our age."[64]

The enormous success enjoyed by Turgenev in the United States prepared the American reading public for the works of Fedor Dostoevsky and Leo Tolstoy, and later of other Russian writers. Turgenev "increasingly took upon himself the duties of a popularizer of Russian literature in the West, acting as an intermediary between Russian culture and the culture of Western countries, including North America."[65] Turgenev was the first to try to introduce American readers to Leo Tolstoy. When he met Schuyler in Baden-Baden in 1867, Turgenev advised him to translate Tolstoy's short novel *The Cossacks,* which he considered "a most charming and perfect work of Russian literature."[66] But Schuyler's subsequent appointment to a diplomatic post in St. Petersburg meant that he could no longer devote as much energy to translation, and

---

62. Howells, *The Writings* (New York, 1910), 170.
63. Howells, *My Literary Passions* (New York, 1891 [reprint: New York, 1968]), 229, 231.
64. James, "Turgenieff," *French Poets and Novelists* (Leipzig, 1883), 211.
65. M. P. Alekseev, "I. S. Turgenev—propagandist russkoi literatury na Zapade" (I. S. Turgenev as a Popularizer of Russian Literature in the West), *Trudy otdela novoi russkoi literatury Instituta russkoi literatury AN SSSR* (Transactions of the Divison of Modern Literature of the Institute of Russian Literature of the U.S.S.R. Academy of Sciences), vol. 1 (Moscow-Lenigrad, 1948), 80.
66. "Graf L. N. Tolstoi v vospominaniiakh E. Skailera, 1867–1870 gg" (Count L. N. Tolstoy in the Recollections of E. Schuyler, 1867–1870), *Russkaia Starina* (Russian Antiquity) 9 (1890): 655. See also *L. N. Tolstoi v vospominaniiakh sovremennikov* (L. N. Tolstoy in the Recollections of His Contemporaries), vol. 1 (Moscow, 1978), 203.

it was only some ten years later, in 1878, that he completed one on *The Cossacks*.[67] However, this short novel did not enjoy much success in America[68] and failed to weaken "the cult of Turgenev, which had grown into a universal passion."[69] Only later, beginning in the mid-1880s, did Tolstoy and Dostoevsky come to exercise a dominant influence on the minds of American readers.

American Literature in the Estimation of Russian Writers

On their part, Russia's writers followed the development of the literary tradition in the New World with interest. Turgenev had a particularly high opinion of Whitman, Hawthorne, and Howells,[70] commenting especially on Howells's novel *A Chance Meeting*.[71] Tolstoy also admired the works of Howells, and he increasingly appreciated Whitman's poetry, in which he saw "something that is truly beautiful."[72] Tolstoy also read the works of Ralph Waldo Emerson, John Greenleaf Whittier, Henry Thoreau, and later Henry George and Edward Bellamy. He thought that the essay "Civil Disobedience" was Thoreau's best work, but had considerable reservations about *Walden, or a Life in the Woods,* the American writer's magnum opus, noting that it was "intentionally original, provocative, and unsettling."[73] However, Turgenev and Tolstoy both believed that the quality of most of the literary works published in the United States in the 1860s and 1870s left much to be desired, due to the American writers' tendency to imitate their English counterparts.

The artistic originality of Bret Harte and the humanistic tenor of his writings were appreciated in Russia earlier and more fully than perhaps in any other country. Gleb Uspenskii and Mikhail Saltykov-Shchedrin wrote of Harte's talent as a novelist.[74] Among the qualities that Chernyshevsky admired in the American writer was his exceptional intelligence:

> The strength of Bret Harte is that, despite all his flaws, he is a man with an innately powerful intellect, a man with an extraordinarily noble soul who, in so far as he is able

---

67. Tolstoy, *The Cossacks* (New York, 1878). Tolstoy immediately wrote to Turgenev, "Schuyler sent me the English translation of *The Cossacks*; the book seems to have been translated very well." *L. N. Tolstoi i I. S. Turgenev: perepiska* (L. N. Tolstoy and I. S. Turgenev: Correspondence) (Moscow, 1928), 82.

68. The reason for this may have been that, as Turgenev told Tolstoy, "the English translation of *The Cossacks* is accurate, but dry and *matter of fact* [in English in original], like Mr. Schuyler himself, who recently visited me when passing through." Turgenev, *Works,* vol. 12, 383.

69. Van Wyck Brooks, *New England: Indian Summer, 1865–1915* (New York, 1940), 298.

70. P. E. Seyersted, "Turgenev's Interest in America, as Seen in His Contacts with H. H. Boyesen, W. D. Howells and Other American Authors," *Scando-Slavica* 11 (1965): 25–39.

71. Samokhvalov, 214.

72. H. Wish, "Getting along with the Romanovs," *South Atlantic Quarterly* 48, no. 3 (1949): 355.

73. V. Bulgakov, *L. N. Tolstoy v poslednii god ego zhizne: dnevnik sekretaria L. N. Tolstogo* (Tolstoy in the Last Year of His Life. The Diary of the Secretary of L. N. Tolstoy) (Moscow, 1957), 261.

74. M. E. Saltykov-Shchedrin, *Poln. sobr. soch.* (Complete Collected Works), 20 vols. (Moscow, 1938–1941), vol. 19, 306.

to understand the world on the basis of the limited number of impressions and ideas at his disposal, has developed the most noble notions about it. His story "Miggles" is charming in its humanity.[75]

Having encountered indifference that bordered on hostility in his own country, Harte had to leave the United States, and ended his days abroad. Half-forgotten in America, he might rejoice at the fact that a six-volume edition of his writings had been published in Russia.[76]

The Russian revolutionary democrats were greatly interested in the American literature of the mid–nineteenth century. Lavrov had an excellent knowledge of the works of Emerson, Whittier, Lowell, Whitman, and Longfellow, and dedicated a long critical article to the latter, whom he described as "one of the best-known poets in America."[77] The revolutionary democrats found Longfellow's poems that attacked exploitation, racial oppression, and religious hypocrisy and fanaticism particularly moving. His "Poems on Slavery" were translated into Russian by the poet-revolutionary Mikhail Mikhailov. In spite of strict censorship, Nikolai Nekrasov managed to publish these in *Sovremmenik* (Contemporary). In an issue that appeared on the eve of the war between the North and the South, Mikhailov discussed the political relevance of Longfellow's poems about slavery:

> They are permeated by a burning feeling of indignation and are full of bitter reproaches to the free country which to this day has been unable to rid itself of the black stain of slavery. The scenes describing the abundant and generous nature in the midst of which the inhuman acts of injustice occur, give Longfellow's songs even greater power.[78]

By the early 1870s, Longfellow's name was well known to the Russian reading public. Many of his best poems appeared in journals and in book form, although a complete translation of his most famous poem, "The Song of Hiawatha," by Ivan Bunin, was published only in 1898, sixteen years after the poet's death. In 1873 Longfellow was elected to the Russian Academy of Sciences, the first American poet to be accorded this honor.[79]

Contemporaries noted Longfellow's great interest in Russian poetry, art, history, and nature. He even began to take Russian lessons from an Italian who had lived in Moscow, but nothing came of this project. The poet had heard much about Russia. Among his sources was a son, who had traveled to almost every country in Europe and Asia and had visited several Russian cities. "Longfellow asked me about our Russian hospitality, the clear frosty nights when you glide in a swift troika across an endless

---

75. Chernyshevskii, *Poln. sobr. soch.* (Complete Collected Works), 16 vols. (Moscow, 1939–1953), vol. 15, 240.
76. F. Bret Gart [Bret Harte], *Sobr. soch.* (Collected Works), 6 vols. (St. Petersburg, 1895).
77. Lavrov, *Etiudy o zapadnoi literature* (Essays on Western Literature) (Petrograd, 1923), 153.
78. X. [M. L. Mikhailov], "Amerikanskie poety i romanisty" (American Poets and Novelists), *Sovremennik* 11–12 (1860): 315.
79. B. B. Tomashevskii, "Genri Longfello," in Longfello, *Izbrannoe* (Works) (Moscow, 1958), xxxv.

snow-covered plain and see the cloudless winter sky studded with the constellations of the North," recalled Russian traveler Iurii Arsen'ev.[80] The thirty-one-volume anthology of poetry published by Longfellow in the late 1870s, containing verse descriptions of various corners of the globe, included a whole volume (the twentieth) entirely devoted to Russia.[81]

The article by Lavrov that dealt largely with the poetry of Longfellow included brief but very interesting references to other celebrated North American poets—Whittier, Lowell, Whitman—who in the author's opinion were "incomparably more vigorous in the expression of ideas."[82] At the time these poets were almost totally unknown to most Russian readers. In the early 1870s Turgenev had intended to introduce the Russian reading public to the works of Walt Whitman. In November 1872 he told Pavel Annenkov that he planned to send to the journal *Nedelia* (The Week) "several translated lyrical poems by the amazing American poet Walt Whitman (have you heard of him?), accompanied by a short introduction. You could not imagine anything more impressive."[83] It would appear that Turgenev only tackled the poem "Beat! Beat! Drums!" but this unfinished translation was only published almost one hundred years later.[84]

In the late 1870s or early 1880s the writer Thomas Rolleston conceived the idea of publishing a Russian edition of the *Leaves of Grass* cycle, but this plan also came to naught. Whitman, who was delighted that "the great peoples of Russia will come into emotional contact" with him, wrote his famous "Letter on Russia," intended as a preface to a Russian edition. He wrote in 1881:

> You, Russians, and we, Americans! We are so far apart from each other, so seemingly different; the social and political conditions of our existence are so different, there is such difference in the path of our moral and material development during the last one hundred years—and yet in some ways, ways that are the most important, our countries are so alike.[85]

After pointing to a number of geographical, ethnographical, and psychological elements shared by the two peoples, Whitman stressed that it was the hidden idea of his book

---

80. Iu. V. Arsen'ev, "Vospominanie o Longfello" (Recollections of Longfellow), *Moskovskie Vedomosti* (Moscow Gazette), March 16/28, 1882.

81. *Poems of Places,* 31 vols., edited by Henry W. Longfellow, vol. 20: Russia (Boston, 1878). For further details see Alekseev, "Stikhotvornaia antologiia Longfello o Rossii" (Longfellow's Anthology of Poems about Russia), *Nauchnyi biulleten' LGU* (The Scholarly Bulletin of Leningrad State University) 6 (1946): 27–28.

82. Lavrov, *Essays,* 157, 164, 166, 171–73.

83. Turgenev, *Works,* vol. 10, 18.

84. I. Chistova, "Turgenev i Yitmen" (Turgenev and Whitman), *Russkaia Literatura* (Russian Literature) 2 (1966): 196–97.

85. Whitman, "Pis'mo o Rossii" (Letter on Russia), *Izbr. proezv.* (Selected Works) (Moscow, 1970), 374. [The proposal for a Russian translation was actually that of John Lee, a friend of Rolleston's. Whitman's "Russian letter" was thus a reply to Lee, dated December 20, 1881. See Whitman, *The Correspondence,* edited by Edwin Haviland Miller, vol. 3 (New York, 1964), 259—ed].

and his cherished dream that "poems and poets should become international and bring together all the countries that exist in the world more closely and more securely than any treaties or diplomacy."[86] But a quarter of a century was to pass before the works of the great American poet were published in Russia in the excellent Russian verse translations of Konstantin Balmont and Kornei Chukovskii.

The fact that the Russian reading public was quick to notice and appreciate the true worth of the works of Mark Twain was a credit to its artistic taste. His first novel, *The Gilded Age*, was almost immediately translated into Russian (a year after its publication in the United States).[87] In later years Twain's popularity in Russia grew rapidly. By the end of the nineteenth century Twain's works were more widely read and better known in Russia than in his own country.

An American Introduction to Russian Music

In the late 1860s and early 1870s the Russian choral conductor and composer Iurii Golitsyn (the son of N. B. Golitsyn, a celebrated patron of the arts and a lover of music who commissioned Beethoven to write three string pieces known at the "Golitsyn Quartets") presented several concerts in the United States. Golitsyn's choir, formed in 1842 and first composed of serfs, is considered to have been the first concert choir in Russia, but, unfortunately, very little is known about Golitsyn's concerts in the United States.[88]

The American public's sympathy toward and interest in Russia grew as a result of an 1869–1870 tour by a choir led by Dmitri Agrenev-Slavianskii.[89] New York posters announced the first concert by a Russian folk choir in America since the day the country was discovered. The twenty members of the choir met with a rapturous reception from the three thousand New Yorkers assembled in the cavernous Steinway Hall (on the corner of Fourteenth Street and Union Square), whose eponymous owner was the well-known manufacturer of musical instruments. The singers, who wore national costume, were clearly inspired in their performances of Russian and Ukrainian folk songs and "The Cherubim" by Dmitri Bortnianskii. The following day the *New York Tribune* praised the "transatlantic visitors": "The singers have a right to be proud: the Russian choral songs are exquisite; the outpouring of poetry, spirituality, and ardent emotion,

---

86. Whitman, "Letter," 374–75.
87. *"Mishurnyi vek*: Roman Marka Tueina i Charl'za Yarnera" (*The Gilded Age*: A Novel by Mark Twain and Charles Dudley Warner), *Otechestvennye Zapiski* (Fatherland Notes) 5–10 (1874).
88. B. Shteinpress, "Khorovoi dirizher Golitsyn" (The Choral Conductor Golitsyn), *Sovetskaia Muzyka* (Soviet Music) 2 (1949): 84; D. L. Lokshina, *Zamechatel'nye russkie khory i ikh dirizhery* (Famous Russian Choirs and Their Conductors) (Moscow, 1963), 27; *Muzykal'naia entsikopediia* (Encyclopedia of Music) 1 (Moscow, 1973), 1032. See also record group Posol'stvo v Vashington, inventory 512/3 (1871), list 107, 506, AVPR (the Archive of Russian Foreign Policy).
89. In 1868 the Russian singer and choral conductor D. A. Agrenev-Slavianskii organized a small choir, the "Slavic Capella," which quickly became popular. In July 1896 Maxim Gorky, who was present at a performance by the Slavic Capella at the Nizhnii Novgorod Trade Fair, praised Agrenev-Slavianskii's choir for resurrecting the tradition of "the old folk song." Gorky, "Beglye zametki" (Brief Notes) in *Sobr. soch.*, 30 vols. (Moscow, 1949–1957) 23: 157.

together with the noble nature of the ideas expressed, is a source of complete pleasure; one listens to these songs with pure delight."[90] The choir visited a number of American cities, giving 175 concerts. This may have been the first time that audiences in Hartford, Providence, Boston, Buffalo, Chicago, and St. Louis heard professional performances of the melodious folk songs of Russia.[91]

The debut of Russian opera in the United States took place on December 15, 1869. Advance New York posters read: "The first visit to America by the Company of the Imperial Theatre of St. Petersburg. The opera 'Askold's Grave' in three acts and four scenes by A. N. Verstovskii. Magnificent costumes, music, etc.—all from Russia."[92] The hall of the French theatre in New York, which was rented by the Russians, was filled to capacity. In addition to the official concert program the orchestra played the overture to Mikhail Glinka's opera *A Life for the Tsar.* The audience was in raptures. And when the overture was followed by the performance of a Russian folk dance to the tune of the song "Kamarinskaia," the New Yorkers were beside themselves with delight. The next day the American press described the enormous success of the Russian national opera. The music critic of the *New York Sun* wrote:

> Russian opera music is not only diverting and pleasant, but indeed instructive; one hears neither roulades, nor grace-notes; everything is quiet, serene, natural, tinged with sadness, and melancholic, like Russian life itself; how pitiful all those trite French and Italian operas are, with their noisy cancan and voluptuous scenes; two hours at a Russian opera can teach one more than a whole week spent listening to the best Italian operas![93]

The great pianist and composer, Anton Rubinstein, founder of the St. Petersburg Conservatory, and the talented Polish violinist and composer Hendryk Weniawski, a professor at the Conservatory, were the next musicians from Russia to enjoy phenomenal success in the United States. Rubinstein's visit was accompanied by a publicity campaign that was conducted with magnificent, typically American panache. A month before his arrival his portraits were already displayed in the shop windows of New York, and all the newspapers announced his forthcoming concert tour.[94] The first performance by the two musicians took place in Steinway Hall, where the concert tour of Agrenev-Slavianskii's Russian folk choir had also begun. Rubinstein performed his Fourth Piano Concerto in C Minor. The next day one of the New York newspapers reported, "The hall was filled with sounds that were so melodious that even those who understood nothing were in spite of themselves entranced by the music . . . after the entire piece was performed the enthusiasm of the public was boundless."[95]

90. Quoted from Slavinskii, *Letters on America and the Russian Settlers,* 210.
91. "Vospominaniia D. A. Agreneva-Slavianskogo" (The Memoirs of D. A. Agrenev-Slavianskii), *Kievskoe Slovo* (Kiev Word), January 13, 1887; A. P. Khitrovo, *D. A. Slavianskii i ego deiatel'nost'* (D. A. Slavianskii and His Work) (Tver, 1887), 28–32.
92. Slavinskii, *Letters on America and the Russian Settlers,* 212.
93. Ibid., 213.
94. "Rubinshtein i Veniavskii v Amerike" (Rubinstein and Weniawski in America), *Muzykal'nyi Svet* (World of Music) 11 (1872): 83.
95. Ibid., 82.

After their first concert in New York the pianist and the virtuoso violinist were showered with flowers and crowned with laurel wreaths. American audiences were charmed by the magic of Rubinstein and Weniavsky's performance. "Until now New York has never known a musical week like this one," wrote one American newspaper. "The two artists have won pride of place among the musical celebrities who have visited America."[96] During the eight months of the 1872–1873 music season, Rubinstein and Weniawski performed all over America and gave a number of concerts in Canada. In 240 days the musicians appeared on stage 215 times.[97] Their performances left an indelible impression on American concert-goers. In turn, the two artists from Petersburg spoke highly of the Americans' love of music.[98]

Rubinstein and Weniawski, however, were appalled by the avarice and inhumanity of the wheeler-dealers who held the American art world in thrall. For the duration of their contracts the pianist and violinist were totally beholden to their promoter in the United States. "God forbid that I should ever again find myself so beholden!" wrote Rubinstein later.

> There is no place for art here. It is like working in a factory. One turns into a kind of automaton; the artist loses his dignity, he is done for. . . . Often it would so happen that we would play two or three concerts in one day, in different cities. . . . The performances and the box office-returns were always good, but all this was so difficult that I simply began to despise both myself and my art; I was continuously displeased with myself, so that when a few years later I was invited to go to America on another concert tour—and I was offered a honorarium of half a million marks for this musical voyage—I categorically refused.[99]

Exhausted by the almost daily concerts, Rubenstein declined to renew his contract and in the summer of 1873 returned to Russia. Weniawski continued to tour America until the middle of 1874.

The First Joint Russian-American Scientific Project

The interaction of the cultures of the Russian and American peoples in the field of literature and music was accompanied by growing cooperation between them in the scientific sphere. This cooperation, which had begun in the eighteenth century, produced tangible results in the nineteenth century.[100] Examples of such fruitful

---

96. Ibid., 82–83.
97. Manuscript Division, Leningrad State Institute of the Theatre, Music, and Cinematography, A. G. Rubinstein Papers, record group 24, inventory 1, list 41, 1–2 (Program of the American concert tour by A. G. Rubinstein and H. Weniawski, September 23, 1872–May 23, 1873).
98. *Avtobiograficheskie vospominaniia A. G. Rubinshteina, 1829–1889* (Autobiographical Reminiscences of A. G. Rubinstein, 1829–1889) (St. Petersburg, 1889), 58.
99. Ibid., 57–58.
100. See N. N. Bolkhovitinov, "Iz istorii russko-amerikanskikh nauchnykh sviazei v XVIII–XIX vekakh" (From the History of Russian-American Scientific Relations in the Eighteenth-Nineteenth centuries), *SShA: Ekonomika, Politika, Ideologiia* (U.S.A.: Economics, Politics, Ideology) 5 (1974): 17–25.

Russian-American scientific cooperation were the visits to the United States made by the geographer Aleksandr Voeikov, the chemist Dmitri Mendeleev, and other scientists for the purpose of research.

Voeikov traveled to the Western hemisphere in order to study climate and atmospheric phenomena. During the winter of 1873 he inspected the meteorological stations on the Atlantic coast of the United States—in Boston, New Haven, New York, and Philadelphia—and acquainted himself with the research being carried out. Everywhere he met with a friendly reception. In April–October 1873, Voeikov visited the central and western states and Canada.[101] When he analyzed the data collected by the Colorado meteorological station, Voeikov discovered that the climates of Colorado and Western Siberia were similar.

The widespread use of the telegraph and other new devices had led to improvements in the speed and accuracy with which meteorological observations were conducted. Voeikov wrote approvingly that "in the United States within twelve hours after measurements are made throughout the country, maps that give a clear and vivid picture of the weather are prepared and sent out; moreover, these maps are printed every eight hours."[102] In the course of his seven-month journey in North America, Voeikov collected a large quantity of meteorological data, including the records of atmospheric pressure from meteorological stations for the years 1850–1873. He established good, businesslike relations with the staff of these stations.[103] [5] Voeikov's studies of the course of the Mississippi between St. Louis and New Orleans led him to the important conclusion that the climate and river systems affect each other.

As a scientist, Voeikov had many interests. He collected statistical data about the population of the United States for a future ethnographic study, noting with approval that American "censuses are carried out with great precision."[104] Voeikov was particularly interested in the economic situation of those settlers who had decided to engage in farming. He was amazed by reports in the local press that, because of the low price of corn, farmers in several western states had burnt their crops. Until he went to Iowa, Kansas, and Nebraska, he found it difficult to believe that this had really happened, but after visiting those states he verified a newspaper article containing similar information, "Since American newspapers, to put it mildly, are not distinguished by truthfulness, I considered this story to be a common canard, but I then collected information locally, and the report turned out to be completely accurate."[105]

Voeikov completed his studies of the North American climate in Canada and then returned to Washington, where his colleagues at the Smithsonian Institution were

101. A. I. Voeikov, "Russkii puteshestvennik v Amerike" (A Russian Traveler in America), *Izvestiia Russkogo Geograficheskogo Obshchestva* (Journal of the Russian Geographical Society) 1 (1874).

102. Voeikov, *Klimaty zemnogo shara, v osobennosti Rossii* (The Climates of the World, Particularly Russia) (St. Petersburg, 1884), 1.

103. Archive of the U.S.S.R. Geographical Society, record group 17, inventory 1, list 140, 1–2, 11–13, 15–18.

104. Ibid., list 158, 9.

105. Quoted in V. V. Pokshishevskii, *Povest' o znamenitom russkom geografe A. I. Voeikove* (The Story of the Famous Russian Geographer A. I. Voeikov) (Moscow, 1955), 59.

waiting for him. In the spring of 1873 Joseph Henry, the scientific secretary of the institution, who had been impressed by Voeikov's extensive knowledge of meteorology and his "talent as an original scholar," asked the Russian geographer on behalf of the Smithsonian to complete a study on global atmospheric circulation begun by the late James Coffin, professor of mathematics and astronomy at Lafayette College in Easton, Pennsylvania.[106] Coffin had collected data from weather stations in different countries, including meteorological measurements from a number of Russian localities made by Konstantin Veselovskii and his colleagues, as well as extracts from the logs of sailing ships that spanned many years. The materials for Coffin's book, however, were in a chaotic state, as he had not had time to systematize and analyze the facts he had collected.

Voeikov appreciated the true value of these unique data and agreed to complete the whole book without compensation in the interests of science. Coffin's son Selden, who was also a professor of mathematics at Lafayette College, took charge of the technical aspects of the project (the compiling of tables and the drawing up of maps and charts). The theoretical analysis, general ideas, and conclusions were to be the responsibility of the Russian scientist. Final work on the manuscript was completed in February–March 1875, after Voeikov's return from an almost year-long journey to Central and South America. He not only reexamined Coffin's calculations but also generously added to the materials left by the American new scientific evidence he had collected in the course of his own research, as well as data from sources that for various reasons had escaped Coffin's attention. [2] The administrators of the Smithsonian Institution praised the exceptional abilities of the Russian scientist, who had completed an enormous amount of work in an exceedingly short space of time.[107] Indeed, Voeikov's commentaries to the tables and charts in *The Winds of the Globe* and his analysis of the data they contained were published as a separate book.

The Russian scientist was a strong supporter of the principle of scientific cooperation, and his activities were an example of what could be achieved in that important field. For many years Voeikov insisted on the importance of creating an international system of meteorological prediction in which weather warnings would be communicated by telegraph. He pointed to the direct practical benefits such an arrangement would produce for Russia and the United States: "Our Baltic harbors would receive word of the approach of storms from the Atlantic many days prior to their arrival, while Russian stations in the Pacific would perform the same service for Oregon and California."[108] In later years Voeikov continued to maintain the scientific contacts he had established with his American colleagues in the mid-1870s. Evidence of this is provided by not

---

106. James H. Coffin, *The Winds of the Globe: With a Discussion and Analysis of the Tables and Charts by Dr. Alexander Woeikof* (Washington, 1875). See G. K. Tserava, "Iz istorii russko-amerikanskikh nauchnykh sviazie: Dzhon [sic] Genri i A. I. Voeikov" (From the History of Russian-American Scientific Relations: John [Joseph] Henry and A. I. Voeikov), *Priroda* (Nature) 7 (1979).

107. Voeikov, *Izbr. soch.* (Selected Works), 2 vols. (Moscow-Leningrad, 1948–1949), vol. 1, 47.

108. Voeikov, *Meteorologiia v Rossii* (Meteorology in Russia) (St. Petersburg, 1874), 48.

only his correspondence but also his private library, which contained dozens of books he had received from scientific institutions and individual researchers in the United States.[109]

The Russian Pavilion at the Philadelphia Exhibition

The centenary of the independence of the United States was marked by an international exhibition in Philadelphia. Among the participants in this event was Russia. The construction of buildings for the exhibition began in 1873, employing thousands of workers from different parts of the country. On May 10, 1876, before a huge crowd of spectators the exhibition was solemnly declared open. Unfortunately, it had taken the Russian government a whole year to decide the question of Russia's participation. As a result, the Russian pavilion was ready only on July 24. Work on it had been delayed for more than two months because of the late arrival of the Russian exhibits and the necessity of repairing those that had been damaged by careless handling in transit by sea and rail. Still, it made a strong impression on the American public and was among the most popular at the exhibition, while the Russian delegation met with a warm reception and was the subject of a great deal of attention.[110]

The Russian exhibits demonstrated the country's achievements in industry, agriculture, science, and the arts. Heavy industry was represented by steam engines (the Putilov factory), rails, anchors, sheet iron (the Demidov factories), agricultural machines designed by Meshcherin, an inventor from Orel, small printing presses designed by Alisov, Vonliarovskii's loading platform, and models of ships and steamers. These models attracted the particular interest of the public. A Boston newspaper reported:

> Everyone had decided long ago that not much was to be expected from Russia's participation in the exhibition and was no longer even giving it much thought. But then in the exhibition's main building there appeared, as in the land of dreams, something amazingly beautiful—something created by the skilful hands of the workers and craftsmen from Moscow and Petersburg. Visitors to the exhibition were delighted to see the magnificent display that had suddenly, as if by magic, appeared in the mechanical engineering pavilion.[111]

Among the nautical exhibits that were shown by the leading seafaring nations, including Britain, those of Russia and the host country stood out in terms of both number and quality. The same Boston newspaper wrote that the Russian nautical section in general, and "the many models of new types of naval vessels and original inventions" in particular, "clearly demonstrate how deeply Russia has penetrated the secrets of the sea."[112]

---

109. Archive of the U.S.S.R. Geographical Society, record group 17, inventory 1, list 248, 12, 14, 16, etc.
110. E. M. Dvoichenko-Markova, "Uchenye Rossii na mezhdunarodnoi vystavke v Filadel'fii v 1876 g." (Russia's Scientists at the 1876 International Exhibition in Philadelphia), *Novaia i Noveishaia Istoriia* (Modern and Contemporary History) 4 (1975): 153.
111. *Boston Evening Journal,* July 7, 1876.
112. Ibid.

Americans were especially interested in the model of a new armor-plated ship, *Admiral Popov*, the ships of this class later becoming known as "popovkas." The representative of the Russian Ministry of Navy at the exhibition reported,

> Russia was the only country, apart from the United States, to show an extensive selection of the products of its navy and its ship-yards. The vessels built by the Kronstadt Steamship Factory were adjudged to be admirable in their elegance and quality of manufacture. The gun platforms designed by Lieutenant-General F[ilimon] V. Pestich and manufactured in the Admiralty ship-yards at Kronstadt have inspired considerable interest of the experts, owing to their new and original construction and the remarkable quality of workmanship; the experts have declared them to be excellent. The ropes produced at the Kronstadt Cable Factory were recognized as superior to all others shown at the exhibition in terms of strength. . . . The guns of the Obukhov Ordnance Factory, particularly those of 9-inch caliber, have attracted the interest of both the experts and the public.[113]

The agricultural section included a collection of cereals, nuts, berries, the seeds of a variety of vegetable crops, sugar from the factories of Leonov, Sergeev, and Apraksin, a rich collection of wines, samples of cotton, the wool of Angora goats from the Mariinskii farm near Saratov, lambskins, sheepskins and sheepskin jackets, sashes, harnesses, wooden tableware and baskets, shoes and peasant sandals made of bast. Americans admired the superb silks, furs, linen fabrics, napkins, towels, and printed cotton, as well as carved furniture and sofas, armchairs and stools made of deer antlers, and the best leather and shoes in the world.

None of the silver articles from other countries could rival the creations of the skilled craftsmen of Moscow, St. Petersburg, and Nizhnii Novgorod. The visitors to the exhibition marveled at the incomparably beautiful vases, fireplaces, and malachite coffee tables.[114] The American press emphasized that the Russian exhibits not only deserved a special mention, but were worthy of careful study.[115] Russian fine art was represented by the works of Ivan Aivazovskii and other painters. However, the American public was unable to see a broad selection of Russian paintings, because at the time the best works were being exhibited in Russia by the *Peredvizhniki* (Wanderers) group of artists.

A bust of George Washington sculpted by the peasant Semen Riabinin to celebrate the centenary of American independence was a symbol of the respect and sympathy felt by the Russian people for the people of the United States.[116] Visitors to the exhibition admired the artistry of Russian photographers, a relief map of Sevastopol, and models of two Kronstadt docks. Experts were amazed at the accuracy of scale—up to a thousandth of an inch—of the molds from which the models had been cast.

---

113. Central State Archive of the Navy, Chancellery of the Ministry of the Navy [hereafter TsGAVMF, KMM], record group 410, inventory 2, list 3713, 44.
114. K. A. Skalkovskii, *V strane iga i svobody* (In the Land of Oppression and Liberty) (St. Petersburg, 1878), 282.
115. *Boston Evening Journal*, July 23, 1876.
116. Vladimirov, 327.

The Americans were favorably impressed by the fact that among the Russians who had traveled to Philadelphia were not only sightseers and tourists but also a sizable contingent of experts, who had come to the Centennial Exhibition for professional reasons. "What an enormous number of people they have sent here!" wrote the correspondent of the *Boston Evening Journal.*

> This is perhaps the most interesting feature of their display. You see before you a group of strong and handsome men, each one of whom occupies a prominent position in his profession or trade. Moreover, almost all of those with whom we had a chance to converse speak at least one of the European languages. They all have an air of sincerity and possess a surprisingly relaxed manner.[117]

The meetings between members of the American public and the many Russians at the exhibition contributed to the growth in understanding between the citizens of the two countries and increased their interest in each other. "The Russians are as anxious to learn as much as possible about us, as we are about them," observed the Boston newspaper. "They are constantly studying the exhibits in the U.S. pavilions, undoubtedly in the hope of submitting proposals to their government for their application at home."[118] The success of the Russian exhibit in Philadelphia surpassed all expectations. Dozens of items displayed were awarded special medals and diplomas. Among the government departments, the largest number of medals (ten) went to the Ministry of Navy for the products of the Kronstadt Steamship Factory, the Admiralty factories in Izhora, the electrotype-plastic workshops of Kronstadt, and other naval works.[119]

Mendeleev Visits the United States

On the occasion of the American Centennial, Philadelphia played host to many prominent foreigners who had achieved fame in the fields of art, science, and technology. The local newspapers published the names of famous visitors to the exhibition. A new type of barometer designed by Dmitri Mendeleev was listed as item 241 in the catalogue of inventions and innovations exhibited.[120] The Russian chemist arrived in the United States in late June. He was already widely known to scientists all over the world as the discoverer of the periodic law of chemical elements, but he was not yet as famous as he would be later.

Mendeleev's scientific activities were multifarious; he called himself a "foot-soldier of Russian science." He was not only a chemist but also a geophysicist, physicist, economist, meteorologist, and specialist in technology. Mendeleev devoted much effort and energy to studying the genesis of the world's reserves of oil and devising methods for its extraction, refining, and processing. [2] In the mid-1870s the influx of American petroleum products into the market led to a fall in oil prices and a

---

117. *Boston Evening Journal,* July 23, 1876.
118. Ibid.
119. TsGAVMF, KMM, record group 410, inventory 2, list 3713, 58–59, 62–63.
120. H. M. Leicester, "Mendeleev's Visit to America," *The Journal of Chemical Education* 34, no. 7 (July 1957): 332.

reduction in the number of refineries in Baku.[121] This led to major financial losses among Russian oilmen. The Ministry of Finance and the Russian Technological Society decided to send a commission of experts to the United States to study the causes of the drop in oil prices and to gather information about the state of the American oil industry. [2]

Mendeleev was chosen as the commission's chief technical expert.[122] His task was to inspect the main oil-producing areas of the United States, examine the technology of oil extraction, refining, and processing, and discover the causes of the low price of American kerosene. He wrote in his diary that "an admiration of Americans has long drawn me to their country, and some time ago I conceived a desire to visit the United States."[123] New York in 1876 presented a very different picture from the one the members of the Russian commission had formed on the basis of stories and descriptions by earlier visitors to America. Mendeleev was disappointed: "From our very first steps in the North American States we came across the unexpected, even where trifles were concerned; we had expected to find something that would be much better planned, amazing, and beautiful than what we actually saw."[124]

Broadway, which winds its way through the whole of New York from North to South, struck him as unimpressive and even plain. Only the stretch near the southern end of Manhattan showed some life and surprised the Russians with its profusion of offices belonging to various insurance companies. "The existence of such competition in insurance and the variety of items that are insured is a striking and most commendable aspect of American life," observed Mendeleev.[125] The visitors from Russia were impressed by the recently constructed elevated railroad that had significantly improved the New York transportation system, but [2] in general the sights of the largest American city did not fill them with admiration. "We were surprised by the unprepossessing appearance of the streets of this famous city."

> They are narrow and are paved with cobble-stones, but so badly that they cannot be compared even with the worst streets in Petersburg or Moscow. The houses, which are of brick, are ugly and dirty; the streets are covered with mud. The shops and stores are reminiscent of a provincial Russian town, rather than Petersburg . . . . [3] Of course, we assumed that we were passing through the worst parts of the great city. However, later we discovered that the whole of New York, which is famous for its luxury, does not boast many attractive streets.[126]

After visiting a number of places in the Northeast, Mendeleev discovered that the condition of the streets in other cities, as well as the intercity highways and country

---

121. G. V. Smirnov, *Mendeleev* (Moscow, 1974), 148.
122. N. Kh. Reitern to N. P. Shishkin, April 22/May 4, 1876, record group posol'stva v Vashingtone, inventory 512/3 (1876), list 126, 151.
123. Mendeleev, "Poezdka v Ameriku" (Journey to America), in Mendeleev, *Sobr. soch.* (Collected Works), 25 vols. (Moscow-Leningrad, 1934–1954), vol. 10, 74.
124. Ibid., 87.
125. Ibid., 88.
126. Ibid., 87.

roads, was no better—they were rutted and bumpy. "Only the bridges are excellent," he wrote in his notebook.[127]

From New York the Russian scientists traveled to Washington, where the Russian minister, Nikolai Shishkin, and his staff gave Mendeleev valuable assistance. The concern and attention shown by the Russian embassy in Washington made Mendeleev confident that "Russia's transatlantic interests will now be properly guarded, supported, and defended."[128] In the libraries, scientific institutes, and government departments Mendeleev studied statistical data relating to the oil industry. He was pleased by the conscientious and meticulous way in which these records were kept. "The essence is in the method, in the vigor and freedom of thought and research. This is the key to civilization. In the departments and in the methods of research used here I found much that was original."[129]

After their stay in Washington the members of the commission visited the exhibition in Philadelphia to view the achievements of American manufacturing and mechanical engineering, yet they did not ignore the negative aspects of American industry.

> From my inspection of many of the items at the exhibition, as well as some of the factories here I have formed the general impression that Americans have a special penchant for mechanical devices, employing them at every opportunity, and sometimes even in cases where one could do without them with comfort and profit. The explanation for this predilection for things mechanical lies in the fact that in the past the industry here had an abundance of tasks to perform, and yet suffered from a shortage of labor. The passion for machinery in America is reflected in the invention and manufacture of sewing, harvesting and other such machines, guns and revolvers, various stamping machines, and a multitude of other mechanical devices of various kinds, some very useful, others of no use to anyone.[130]

The Russian scientists were amazed by widespread gun ownership in America. Among the carefully jotted-down observations in Mendeleev's notebook was this one: "America has found nothing better to do with its iron than to manufacture rifles and revolvers; and still they speak of 'peace and quiet.' "[131]

Before coming to America, Mendeleev had visited several international exhibitions in Europe. The Philadelphia exhibition, he found, was not as impressive as the ones he had seen in the Old World.

> In general, the stories about America, judging from what has been written about it, create the idea in one's mind of something colossal, special, practical, and original. This is what we all believed when we came here, this is what we expected from the exhibition. Reality did not conform to our expectations. The site of the exhibition is large, larger than that of other world exhibitions, but the displays are disappointing

127. The Mendeleev Museum and Archive at St. Petersburg University, Mendelev Papers [hereafter MMA], record group 1, list 21, 29.
128. Mendeleev, "Journey," 92.
129. MMA, record group 1, list 21, 17.
130. Mendeleev, "Journey," 108.
131. MMA, record group 1, list 21, 32; see also 3.

and do not match the space they occupy.... [3] This opinion of the American exhibition is not mine alone; it is shared by all those who have seen other world exhibitions."[132]

On the positive side, the presence of Mendeleev and his colleagues at the exhibition enabled them to establish contacts with American scientists, engineers, and technicians. "Every scientist and technician we dealt with was extremely obliging. We needed just a few initial contacts in order to acquire a large and varied acquaintance."[133] Mendeleev mentions meeting two American chemists, Eben Norton Horsford and Thomas Sterry Hunt, who presented him with their works on the geology and mineralogy of the oil-bearing regions of the United States. Later Mendeleev made considerable use of the records and data in these books in his own research.

The success of the visit by the Russian scientists to the United States was in large measure due to meetings with their American colleagues in Philadelphia that led to the establishment of professional contacts between the scientists of the two countries. "In this respect Americans were not only kind enough to communicate all the necessary data to us in person, but indeed went so far as to provide us with the books we needed, sent us train tickets etc."[134] Mendeleev's American colleagues valued highly his contribution to world science and later elected him an honorary member of the American Academy of Arts in Boston and the American Philosophical Society in Philadelphia.[135]

[2] Mendeleev was full of admiration for the inventiveness of Americans, reflected in the plethora of machines and mechanical devices constructed and used by them. He also praised their businesslike attitude. "The Americans are to be commended, for their calculations are simple, their replies brief; in a word, things are done quickly and without fuss."[136] At the "Atlantic" refinery, he was favorably impressed by an original solution to the problem of filling barrels and tin cans with oil. "These devices save much time," he noted.[137]

Mendeleev wrote with approval of the American desire for scientific cooperation and wide exchange of information: "Personal relations are free of empty ceremony; everything is learned quickly and easily; in one's dealings with people here one never comes across the kind of arrogance that is so characteristic of many in Europe."[138] Nevertheless, Mendeleev was disappointed to find that in their research American scientists had largely ignored geology and oil chemistry. In his detailed report, Mendeleev wrote: "I approached many scientists with a request for the most recent information about the scientific analysis of the oil question in America and was greatly surprised to learn that neither from the standpoint of chemistry, nor from that of geology, have Americans yet found the answers to the most basic scientific questions relating to oil."[139]

132. Mendeleev, "Journey," 96.
133. Ibid.
134. Ibid., 97.
135. *Proceedings of the American Philosophical Society* 94, no. 6 (1950): 582; 109, no. 1 (1965): 56.
136. MMA, record group 1, list 21, 20.
137. Mendeleev, "Journey," 108.
138. Ibid., 96.
139. Ibid., 97.

[2] Clearly bewildered, Mendeleev wrote in his diary:

> It can be said that in the last ten years hardly any progress has been made with regard to the scientific aspect of the oil question. . . . [3] If any other country had an industry that was as advanced and productive as the oil industry here, many people would be working on its scientific aspects. But in America they are only interested in extracting the largest possible amount of oil, with no thought for the past or the future, no desire to find a better and more rational way of approaching this task; they are concerned with the exigencies of the narrow present and rely on primary conclusions drawn from the aforementioned activities. Such a procedure is always fraught with unforeseen consequences and could cost the country dear.[140]

The Russian scientist quite reasonably believed that "spending on research pays for itself, because science can foresee much beforehand, it can warn, show what is possible, and separate the essential from the mass of practical details. . . . Science in the United States is yet to attain such a level of development in the oil question. That is why the oil business there suffers from a lack of confidence."[141]

From the practical and scientific point of view, the most productive part of the visit by Mendeleev to America was his sojourn of several weeks in the Pittsburgh area. He was accompanied everywhere by Valerii Gemilian, who acted as his interpreter and later acquired a distinguished reputation as a professor of chemistry at the Universities of Kharkov and Warsaw.[142] After he returned from the United States in September 1876, Gemilian presented a scientific paper at a congress of natural scientists in Warsaw.

While in Pittsburgh Mendeleev and his companion witnessed the celebrations of the centenary of the independence of the United States. As in other American towns, throughout the night bells peeled, steam sirens sounded, guns roared, and rockets and multicolored fireworks lit up the sky to the rapturous shouts of the crowd, which made merry all night long and began to disperse only at the break of dawn. Mendeleev wrote in his notes, "One must have a special predilection for the kind of amusements that people indulged themselves on that day."[143]

Mendeleev again noted with regret the lack of scientific research relating to the oil business, but every practical innovation, whether the original design of some mechanical component or the solution of a problem involving a technological process, won the Russian scientist's enthusiastic appreciation. At the same time Mendeleev rejected and condemned the rapaciousness of American businessmen and their methods of oil extraction. Later he wrote in one of his scientific tracts that the methods used in the exploitation of American oil fields led to their quick depletion.[144]

140. Ibid.
141. Ibid.
142. *Novyi Entsiklopedicheskii Slovar'* (The New Encyclopedic Dictionary), Brockhaus-Efron (St. Petersburg, 1890–1907), vol. 12, 926.
143. Mendeleev, "Journey," 113.
144. See Mendeleev, "Po neftianym delam" (Travels in Connection with the Oil Business), in *Works,* vol. 10, 400.

It is interesting to note that three years before the creation of the Standard Oil Company, the first oil monopoly in the United States, the Russian scientist's keen insight detected the tendencies in the industry that were to lead to that development. He wrote that the American oil producers planned "to conspire with each other to establish a monopoly, as a result of which they would have no special and urgent interest in increasing production, but rather would strive to keep the price high or even to raise it."[145]

Mendeleev and his companion were traveling in the United States when the industrial recession that followed the financial panic and crisis of 1873 reached its lowest point. [1] This was bound to create an unfavorable impression. Discussing the changes that had taken place in the country's sociopsychological circumstances since the abolition of slavery, Mendeleev noted that the spirit of the courageous struggle for human freedom and equality had been crushed by the mercenary spirit of capitalism.[146] In his travel notes Mendeleev on several occasions declared that "the desire for money has contributed to greed, deceit, and bribery," as a result of which America had become the land of "the all-mighty dollar, of a reigning and all-pervading philistinism."[147] Reflecting upon what he saw and heard in the United States, he wrote that, as far as "the idea of freedom" was concerned, Americans had "marched forward and come to a wall and turned back."[148]

During their travels in the United States, the two Russian scientists came across a large number of abandoned farms, prompting the following observation from Mendeleev:

> The fields show signs of considerable neglect; even the central provinces of Russia are hardly inferior in their level of cultivation to these areas of America. . . . [4] Since there are many empty and uncultivated areas even in the vicinity of the railroads, it is obvious that the migration to the western states is caused by the greater fertility of their soil.[149]

During the return trip from New York to Le Havre, standing on the deck or sitting in the passengers' lounge of the steamship *America,* Mendeleev and Gemilian exchanged impressions with Russians of their acquaintance who had been to the Philadelphia Exhibition. "On the voyage back everyone was sad, because they had lost their ideal image of America: they did not find what they had expected in that country, and they are happy to return to Europe."[150] The Russian visitors to the land beyond the ocean had thought they would see a new kind of society, one founded on the principles of justice and respect for human dignity, and free of all forms of tyranny. "Even after 100 years the ways of man in the New World remain the same—they are the ways of the Old World," wrote a disappointed Mendeleev. "It seems that the briny waters of the

---

145. Ibid.
146. MMA, record group 1, list 21, 25.
147. Mendeleev, "Journey," 91, 150.
148. MMA, record group 1, list 21, 25.
149. Mendeleev, "Journey," 112–13.
150. MMA, record group 1, list 21, 33.

ocean and the free institutions in the States have failed to renew man, have failed to refresh his thinking. Problems that should preoccupy the mind are not being solved there."[151]

But the disenchantment felt by the Russian scientist when contemplating the general picture of American life in the 1870s did not prevent him from noticing much that was in his opinion "extremely instructive and worthy of admiration and emulation."[152] [2] As a result of his extensive contacts in different parts of the country with Americans from various walks of life, he felt great sympathy for the ordinary people of the country: "I am simply delighted by the individuals I have met here, as well as by American nature and American ability to perform complicated practical tasks."[153] At the same time, Mendeleev's musings aboard the steamship led him to write in his journal, "I should not recommend to anyone who has progressed to an understanding of the problems facing society to live there. I think they would find America a frightening place. That country is meant for people of a different kind."[154]

In his journal Mendeleev summed up the impressions and opinions of America of many Russians who were sailing with him back to their native land. He was apparently expressing his agreement with them when he wrote:

> The exhibition itself, the quality of the Government, the absence of any idealistic strivings, the utterly repulsive and fruitless political squabbles, the treatment of the Negroes, the mutual hostility of the parties and nationalities that comprise the Union, all this, taken as a whole, affected many of my companions in such a way that they decided that America provides an excellent example of the flaws in contemporary culture.[155]

He also concluded that it was not the most attractive qualities of European civilization that the United States had assimilated and developed, but rather those that were mediocre or bad. The Russian scientist ended his account of his American visit on a pessimistic note:

> The vaunted system of universal suffrage, the desire to gain riches through political machinations, social intrigue, and the use of all kinds of foul methods, the exploitation of the defenseless multitudes who have no capital, and a boundless determination to preserve these practices no matter what the cost—all this is no different from what one sees in Europe. There is no new dawn across the ocean.[156]

Mendeleev's visit to the United States was of great practical benefit to him. It broadened his research interests, introduced him to the latest technological developments, and helped him to pursue his scientific investigations, which were to prove most productive.

151. Mendeleev, "Journey," 26.
152. Ibid., 150.
153. Ibid., 26.
154. Ibid., 151.
155. Ibid.
156. Ibid.

On the basis of his study of the American oil industry Mendeleev was able to confirm the correctness of his scientific hypotheses, substantiate his theory of the origin of oil, and develop a series of practical proposals relating to the business in Russia. He insisted that the Russian government should prohibit the export abroad of crude oil and advised that by-products of the oil-refining process should be used as fully as possible. Acting on this recommendation, the government abolished the tax on oil wells. This and some of his other proposals had a major impact on the development of the oil industry in Russia, which by the end of the nineteenth century was to become the largest oil producer in the world.[157]

Intellectual Exchanges in the Field of Military Technology

In 1871 Russia regained the right to maintain a navy in the Black Sea and naval fortresses on its coast. The country was now faced with the task of ensuring the defense of the Black Sea coast. This led Russian scientists to take a strong interest in torpedoes and mine warfare. At the Ministry of Navy a special team of experts led by I. F. Aleksandrovskii studied the problem of underwater navigation and worked on the development of self-propelled torpedoes. The ministry decided to send a group of scientists to America for the purpose of studying the torpedo systems being developed there. In order to secure the cooperation of the Americans, the Russian admiralty unofficially approached Admiral David Porter, who occupied an important position in the Department of Navy and was personally involved in research on the use of mines and the development of a doctrine of naval mine warfare. Porter indicated his readiness to introduce Russian naval officers to the latest American theories of mine warfare, and in an unofficial letter to Admiral Stepan Lesovskii declared that "all the Russian officers dispatched to America will be received with great hospitality and will be provided with every opportunity for pursuing the investigations they have been charged with."[158]

Naturally, the Russian navy decided to take advantage of "this amicable attitude on the part of the senior admiral of the American navy, who in view of the importance that submarine mines are presently acquiring in naval warfare was one of the outstanding figures in the war waged by the Northern states with those of the South."[159] Two men were chosen to go to America: Commander A. P. Novosil'skii, captain of the frigate *Admiral Lazarev,* and Aleksandrovskii. The official document describing their mission stated that they were being sent to the United States "to study, with the help of Admiral Porter, the design of submarine mines in America, as well as the views on their use that have been developed there."[160] The Russian legation in Washington was requested "to assist the officers in communicating with Admiral Porter."[161]

---

157. S. and L. Pershke, *Russkaia neftianaia promyshlennost', ee razvitie i sovremennoe polozhenie v statisticheskikh dannykh* (The Russian Oil Industry, Its Development, and Its Current State, As Reflected in Statistical Data) (Tiflis, 1913), 55–56; E. A. Godzishevskii, *Russkaia neft' na mirovom rynke* (Russian Oil in the World Market) (Moscow, 1924), 9.

158. Porter to Lesovskii, November 26, 1872, TsGAVMF, KMM, record group 410, inventory 2, list 3613, 5–6.

159. Report of Director of Naval Ministry, January 15/27, 1873, ibid., 3.

160. Ibid.

161. Krabbe to Offenberg, January 16/28, 1873, ibid., 16.

Americans not only showed their Russian visitors the types of mines and torpedoes used by the navy but also supplied them with the most recent technical literature and data,[162] took them to factories and design offices, and enabled them to be present at trials of new types of weapons. Porter even expressed his regret that the Russian naval ministry had sent them to the United States for such a short period—two and a half months.[163] The two Russian representatives made an excellent impression on their American colleagues. Their wide-ranging expertise, the originality of their ideas in the area of technology, and their elegantly simple approach to solving technical problems that arose won them the respect and genuine friendship of American officers and designers. The Russian minister to Washington reported that Novosil'skii and Aleksandrovskii "in fulfilling the task assigned to them showed excellent tact and exemplary diligence." The envoy stressed that "the favorable attitude of Admiral Porter, who showed himself to be a true friend of Russia, contributed to their success."[164]

Intellectual exchanges and cooperation between Russia and the United States in the field of military technology continued. At the Philadelphia exhibition of 1876 Russian naval officers were the only foreigners to receive permission from the Secretary of Navy "to acquaint themselves more closely with the design and controls of a new type of torpedo—Leigh's self-propelled mine" and to observe its tests.[165]

There were many interesting episodes in the history of the scientific and technological cooperation between Russian and American inventors in the development of new infantry weapons. Having suffered defeat in the Crimean War, the Russian government was forced to modernize its military equipment. After studying the state of the weapons industry in the economically developed countries of the world, the authorities in St. Petersburg decided "to use the enormous resources and experience of the American factories."[166] Naturally, friendly relations then existing between the two countries were also a factor in this decision.

In the late 1860s two officers of the Chief Directorate of Artillery, Colonel Aleksandr Gorlov and Captain Konstantin Gunnius went to the United States on a secret mission. They were given the task "not only to study the various types of American rifles and cartridges, but actually to design the model of a small-caliber rifle with a metal cartridge."[167] On the advice of members of the Russian legation, the two officers visited the Connecticut firm founded by the celebrated weapons manufacturer Samuel Colt. At the invitation of the American government they observed trials of rapid-firing rifles conducted in St. Louis.[168] After carefully inspecting the latest models of infantry

162. Porter to Lesovskii, April 21, 1873, ibid., 11–12.
163. Instructions of Krabbe to Novosil'skii and Aleksandrovskii, January 16/28, 1873, and Porter to Lesovskii, April 3, 1873 (6–7), ibid., 7–10, 13–14.
164. Offenberg to Krabbe, April 8/20, 1873 (52), ibid., 22.
165. W. N. Irffer to Semechkin, TsGAVMF, record group 22, inventory 1, list 99, 32; Semechkin to Lesovskii, July 12/24, 1876, TsGAVMF, KMM, record group 410, inventory 2, list 3713, 45.
166. M. Portnov, "K istorii priniatiia na voorushenie russkoi armii 4.2-lineivoi vintovki obraztsa" (Concerning the History of the Adoption by the Russian Army of the 1868 model of the 0.525 caliber rifle), *Ezhegodnik Gos. Istorich. Muzeia za 1961 g.* (Yearbook of the State Historical Museum for 1961) (Moscow, 1962), 64.
167. *Oruzheinyi Sbornik* (The Almanac of Weapons) 1 (1869), sect. 1, 76.
168. Gorlov to Katakazi, n.d. [late December 1869], AVPR, record group pos. Vash., inventory 512/3 (1869), list 99, 344–45.

weapons, Gorlov and Gunnius chose the breech-loading rifle designed by an American inventor, General Hiram Berdan.

Berdan had a sweet tooth; he first invented a mechanical device that made it possible to make candy without a human hand ever touching either the ingredients or the finished product. Berdan's invention was adopted in five American cities, but soon the intervention of a group of powerful confectionery manufacturers led to the imposition of a ban on its use. And so this attempt to create one of the first production lines in the history of world technology ended in failure.

During the Civil War Berdan fought on the side of the North, commanded a regiment, and attained the rank of general. The exigencies of war made this talented inventor turn his attention to improving the design of infantry weapons. He was also the author of inventions in the fields of torpedo warfare and naval shipbuilding.[169] General Berdan was a sincere friend of Russia and always stressed the importance of the help it had given the United States during the most difficult period of the internecine conflict. In December 1870 he visited Russia and was received by officials of the War and Foreign Affairs Ministries.[170]

Gorlov and Gunnius adopted a creative approach to solving the problem. They took as their starting point the design of Berdan's rifle. According to Vladimir Fedorov, an expert on the history of Russian infantry weapons, tests showed that the rifle had serious flaws; its bolt was not strong enough and the gun itself lacked accuracy.[171] The two Russian designers, in collaboration with the American inventor, began work on correcting these flaws.[172] They used the latest achievements of Russian technology (for instance, the superior design of certain parts of N. M. Baranov's rifle), making a number of significant improvements in Berdan's rifle. In addition, they produced an original design for a metal cartridge. The result of these improvements was a new type of rifle that at the American factories where the first orders for it were placed came to be known as the "Russian musket." "Russian muskets" were manufactured at the factories of the Smith and Wesson Arms Company in Springfield, Massachusetts, while a $7.5 million order for metal cartridges for these rifles was placed with the Union Metallic Cartridge Company of Bridgeport, Connecticut.[173]

To take delivery of rifles that had been ordered and check their quality, the Russian authorities sent to the United States Staff Captain Vladimir Buniakovskii. Upon his return a proud Buniakovskii wrote:

> In America Russian weapons and cartridges, the ones which in Russia we call "Berdan's," are considered to be superior to any others. This model is known in

---

169. *Voennaia Entsikopediia* (The Military Encyclopedia), 18 vols. (Moscow, 1911–1915), vol. 4, 480.

170. Reports of V. I. Westman to Alexander II, December 5/17, 1870, and December 27, 1870/January 8, 1871, AVPR, record group kants., inventory 470/4 (1870), list 43, 425, 439–40.

171. V. G. Fedorov, *Evoliutsiia strelkovogo orushiia* (The Evolution of Infantry Weapons) (Moscow, 1938), vol. 1, 117.

172. Fedorov, *Vooruzhenie russkoi armii za XIX stoletie* (Weapons of the Russian Army in the Nineteenth Century) (St. Petersburg, 1911), 225.

173. L. G. Beskrovnyi, *Russkaia armiia i flot v XIX v.* (The Russian Army and Navy in the Nineteenth Century) (Moscow, 1973), 305, 325.

America as the "Russian musket" and enjoys enormous popularity there, which extends to the names of the Russian officers who were chiefly responsible for its design. . . . In terms of its ballistic qualities our rifle is superior to any other infantry rifle in existence.[174]

In the early 1870s Berdan again visited Russia. He suggested replacing the folding bolt in the "Russian musket" with a sliding one. Russian inventors once again applied themselves to the task of improving the rifle's design. Fifteen changes to it were made before the Russian army added the second model to its armory. "Thus, it is Berdan who should be profoundly grateful to Russia for the opportunity to implement these changes, rather than Russia to Berdan," wrote Gorlov.[175] But the War Ministry refused to acknowledge the preeminent role played by Russia's weapons specialists in designing the rifle, giving the first and second models the names "Berdan No. 1" and "Berdan No. 2." In the Russian army and among the Russian people they were known simply as the *berdanka*. The rifle bearing the American name was successfully used during the Russian-Turkish War. A distinguished historian of the Russian army and navy, Liubomir Beskrovnyi, writes that by the end of the war the Russian field army was fully equipped with rifles of this type.[176]

A Messenger from the "People's Will"

The ideologists of revolutionary populism in Russia understood that the political system in the United States was dominated by the exploiter classes. It is true that before the Civil War Michael Bakunin had believed that the North of the United States possessed "the best political organization in history."[177] But after visiting the United States in 1861 and closely examining the workings of American political structures,[178] he concluded that in America "popular self-government, even though outwardly appearing to make the people omnipotent, almost always remains a fiction," and that it would take "a far more radical revolution than any that have until now shaken the Old and the New Worlds" for the principle of government by the people to become a reality.[179]

Lavrov also spoke highly of the American Constitution.[180] But he was far from idealizing the United States and its ruling class: "Venality, fraud, and indifference to the general good, jobbery of every kind, hypocrisy in the political programs and declarations," he wrote in 1875, "are more noticeable in this 'model republic' than even in the decrepit states of Europe. . . . Today no political idealist could honestly say that the United States of North America represent a political ideal."[181]

174. *Voruzheinyi Sbornik* 4, sect. 1 (1869): 1; Fedorov, *Vooruzhenie,* 225.
175. Portnov, "K istorii priniatii," 70.
176. Beskrovnyi, *Russian Army and Navy,* 310.
177. Bakunin, *Poln. sobr. soch.* (Complete Collected Works), vol. 1 (St. Petersburg, 1907), 57.
178. Oscar Handlin, "A Russian Anarchist Visits Boston," *New England Quarterly* 15, no. 1 (March 1942): 104–8; David Hecht, " 'Laughing Allegra' Meets an Ogre," *New England Quarterly* 19, no. 2 (June 1946): 243–44.
179. Bakunin, *Works,* vol. 1, 154–55.
180. Lavrov, *IS* 1: 336.
181. Ibid., 4: 34.

In the newspaper and journal published by Lavrov in the 1870s under the title *Forward!* much attention was devoted to chronicling the workers' movement in Europe and America, the latter based on information from two American workers' newspapers, *The National Labor Tribune* of Pittsburgh and *The Socialist* of Milwaukee.[182] *Forward!* printed articles about the condition of the working class in the United States[183] and its political and economic struggle.[184] Sometimes the newspaper published reports from New York,[185] which may indicate that the Russian revolutionaries grouped around *Forward!* were trying to establish contacts with members of the American labor and socialist movement. There is evidence that *Forward!* circulated not only in Europe but also in the United States.[186]

One may speak with certainty of the existence of contacts between the populists and the American workers' movement only after the middle of 1881, when the Executive Committee of the "People's Will" sent Lev Gartman [Leo Hartman] to New York as its representative. Gartman brought with him an appeal to the American public. Before joining the "People's Will," he had been an active member of the "Land and Freedom" and "Black Partition" secret societies and had taken part in the unsuccessful attempt by populist terrorists to blow up the tsar's train on the Moscow-Kazan railway. Gartman managed to flee abroad, but early in 1880 he was arrested in Paris. The authorities in St. Petersburg demanded his extradition, applying strong diplomatic pressure on the French government. Diplomats at the Russian embassy in Paris and even agents of the Okhrana [Russian secret police] joined the effort to bring Gartman back to Russia. Lavrov, who was in Paris at the time, and a number of French democratic organizations led by Victor Hugo mounted a campaign against Gartman's extradition. In March 1880 he was able to go to London.[187] There Gartman had several meetings with Karl Marx and Friedrich Engels, informing them of developments within the Russian revolutionary movement.[188]

The Russian revolutionaries believed that the task of liberating the people that they had set themselves "would be made significantly easier if we enjoyed the sincere sympathy of the free peoples."[189] Wishing to win the support of public opinion in the United States, the Executive Committee of the "People's Will" addressed an appeal

---

182. See the list of foreign socialist newspapers received by the editors of *Vpered!* ibid., 4: 417–20.
183. Ibid., 3: 29, 153, 349; *Vpered!* 2 (1875): 6, 13.
184. *Vpered!* 2 (1875): 4, 6–8, 13; Lavrov, *IS* 3: 32, 62, 83, 181, 221, 254, 285, 413, 443.
185. *Vpered!* 20 (1875): 23; Lavrov, *IS* 3: 636–37, 732–33.
186. See *"Vpered!: Sbornik statei, posviazhchennykh pamiati P. L. Lavrova* ("Forward!": A Collection of Articles Dedicated to the Memory of P. L. Lavrov), edited by Vitiazev (Petrograd-Moscow, 1920). This question requires special study of archival documents in the United States.
187. Lavrov, *IS* 1: 467; A. Z. Manfred, *Obrazovanie russko-frantsuzskogo soiuza* (The Formation of the Franco-Russian Alliance) (Moscow, 1975), 156.
188. S. S. Volk, *Karl Marks i russkie obshchestvennye deiateli* (Karl Marx and Russian Political Figures) (Leningrad, 1969), 196–202.
189. "Pis'mo Ispolnitel'nogo komiteta sotsial'no-revoliutsionnoi partii v Rossii K. Marksu" (Letter from the Executive Committee of the Socialist Revolutionary Party in Russia to Karl Marx), October 25/November 6, 1880, in *K. Marks, F. Engel's i revoliutsionnaia Rossiia* (K. Marx, F. Engels and Revolutionary Russia) (Moscow, 1967), 428.

to the American people, in which it painted a "picture of the real situation in Russia, with its absolute monarchy and its outrageous despotism." The populists described their relentless struggle against the tyranny of the tsars, a tyranny that was destroying "the flower of Russian society, the very elements that should truly be the pride of the country and the nation."[190]

The Executive Committee concluded its appeal to progressive America with this ringing declaration:

> Citizens and Democrats! Where do your sympathies lie? We already know the answer to this question. The country which at the dawn of its history sent phalanxes of its sons to march in defense of its independence, which received with open arms all the victims of persecution on the Continent of Europe, which even waged an internecine, fratricidal war to free millions of slaves cannot but sympathize with us, who have raised the banner of the struggle for the liberation of the Russian people from the chains of political and economic slavery. The abolitionists were your best sons, your favorite sons. They were true servants of Humanity. We are the Russian abolitionists! All your sympathies should belong to us! All your contempt and indignation should be directed toward our enemies! We treasury your sympathy, as we do the sympathy of all peoples. We ardently desire to strengthen it![191]

The representative of the "People's Will" came to the United States in order to develop and strengthen support among the American people for the revolutionary movement in Russia. He was given the task of setting up a permanent office of the party in the United States. The purpose of the office would be to keep American public opinion fully informed about the real situation in Russia by means of political meetings, lectures, and newspaper articles. [3] "Having decided to wage an active struggle against the Russian government by availing ourselves of the forces and resources of the Russian people," stated the Committee in its instructions to Gartman, "we authorize you, Comrade, to accept monetary assistance 1) for conducting 'foreign' propaganda locally; 2) to support humanitarian causes inside Russia; 3) and—from [American] workers—to help striking Russian workers."[192]

At the same time it issued its appeal to the American people, the Executive Committee addressed a letter to Karl Marx. The Committee expressed the deep respect "of the entire Russian social-revolutionary party" for the leader of the international workers' movement and asked for his help in achieving the aim of Gartman's mission, whose aim, according to the Committee, was "to find the means for informing England and America about current events in the political life of our country. . . . Filled with resolve to smash the fetters of slavery, we are certain that the hour is at hand when our suffering country will occupy a place in Europe that is worthy of a free nation."[193]

The events that followed, the assassination of Alexander II in March 1881 and the attempt in July on the life of President [James] Garfield, as a result of which he was

190. *Byloe* 1 (July 1917): 51–52.
191. Ibid., 52.
192. Ibid., 53–54.
193. *Marx, Engels and Revolutionary Russia,* 428.

mortally wounded, led the U.S. Senate, the New York legislature, a number of political organizations, as well as the American press, to condemn terrorist acts against heads of state and governments and, by implication, the activities of the "People's Will." Under the circumstances the populists thought it necessary to explain their position to public opinion in the United States. They composed an open letter-cum-declaration, in which they drew the attention of the American people to the difference in the political situation in the two countries. The Executive Committee declared that it was opposed to acts of violence like the attempt on the life of the American president. At the same time the populists defended the use of terror tactics in the struggle against the tyranny of the Russian tsars. Their credo was: "Violence is justified only when it is directed against violence."[194]

Before Gartman left England for the land beyond the ocean, Marx and Engels supplied him with letters of introduction to Friedrich Zorge, one of the leaders of the Socialist Workers' Party of the United States, and John Swinton, editor of the *New York Sun*.[195] After his arrival in New York in July 1881 Gartman began to write articles about the political situation in Russia and the struggle of the populists against the autocracy, which appeared in the city's newspapers (*New York Tribune* and *New-Yorker Folkszeitung*). He also published the address of the Executive Committee of the "People's Will" to the American people and its letter to Marx,[196] and appealed to Americans to show solidarity with the populists. [5] In his propaganda tour of the United States Gartman was accompanied by another Russian émigré, who hid his identity under the initial "P."[197] They visited several cities in order to lay the groundwork for the establishment of local branches of the "People's Will" in the United States. Their main task would be to keep the American public informed about the condition of the revolutionary movement in Russia.

The friendly relations that existed between Russia and the United States in the period under consideration were bound to influence the development of Russian-American contacts in various areas. During the years that followed the Civil War in the United States and the program of socioeconomic reforms in Russia, the relationship between the two national cultures grew in intensity. This was reflected in the growing desire in both countries for scientific cooperation and the exchange of data in the fields of natural science and technology, the interest that Russians and Americans showed in each other's literature and music, the joint Russian-American effort to set up an agricultural commune in Kansas, and the first contacts between the "Will of the People" and the American workers' movement.

---

194. *One Hundred Years: Documents Relating to the History of Political and Social Movements in Russia between 1825 and 1896,* compiled by V. L. Burtsev, edited by S. M. Kravchinskii (Stepniak) (London, 1897), vol. 1, 180.
195. See Marx and Engels, *Soch.* (Works), vol. 35, 157–58.
196. *Marx, Engels and Revolutionary Russia,* 448–49.
197. A. Ia. Kiperman, "Glavnye tsentry russkoi revoliutsionnoi emigratsii 70–80-kh godov XIX v.," (The Main Centers of the Russian Revolutionary Émigré Community of the 1870s–1880s), *Istoricheskie Zapiski* (Historical Notes) 88 (1971): 292.

Comment
by Ronald J. Jensen

The American Civil War aroused the interest of Russians as it did other Europeans. The prospect of a conflict in a large nation on the shores of the Atlantic naturally compelled attention. Besides the inherent drama of war, the struggle carried serious implications for international commerce and the potential for diplomatic confrontation. Then there was the moral question posed by slavery. Although Russia's economic and diplomatic interest in the United States was marginal, war would certainly complicate the congenial relations that the tsar's ministers had cultivated over the years. For Russian intellectuals, the Civil War reawakened the dialogue about the meaning of America that they had engaged since the very earliest days of the Republic. The political ideals and personalities of the Revolutionary Republic drew praise from progressives like Nikolai Novikov and Alexander Radishchev, while liberal Decembrists found American institutions appealing enough to serve as models for Russia. Yet the institution of slavery and materialist aspects of American economic life repelled Russians at the same time. By raising the prospect of the elimination of slavery, the Civil War restored the promise of 1776, at least briefly, for some of Russia's radical democrats. The present articles from prominent members of the Soviet historical establishment bear witness to that ambivalence about America. They also illuminate some little-known aspects of Russian-American relations on a personal as well as public policy level.

Nina Kiniapina revisits the political and diplomatic history of Russia's relationship with the United States during the Civil War in the most traditional Soviet manner. The objective here is to update and correct certain errors of emphasis found in M. M. Malkin's book, which has been the Soviet standard since 1939, and contribute insights from Russian sources that American scholars neglected. The earliest American scholars who treated this period, such as Albert Woldman (*Lincoln and the Russians*), were "insufficiently familiar with Russian sources," as Dr. Kiniapina charges, but that is no longer the case when one considers the work of John Gaddis, Hans Rogger, and, especially, Norman Saul. Of course she wrote the article a decade before Saul published *Distant Friends.*

She takes issue with Malkin for exaggerating contradictions in Russian policy and minimizing the impact of the Russian fleet visit. Therefore, in her presentation, Russian policy appears more consistently sympathetic to the Washington government than Malkin alleged. In amending Malkin's treatment, Kiniapina makes convincing use of Russian archives, especially Gorchakov's papers, and offers a more extensive treatment of the Russian fleet issue than her predecessor. These are, however, rather minor additions. For the most part Kiniapina's article follows the contours of Malkin's study and arrives at virtually the same conclusions. She agrees that Great Britain was the key factor in determining Russian-American relations and that Russian support contributed only marginally to the Union victory, for example. Her version of the *Trent* affair and the abortive Anglo-French plan to mediate the Civil War cites the same sources Malkin used and reaches similar conclusions. Nor does Kiniapina deviate from the conventional theoretical perspective that Malkin elucidated. For both, the Civil War was simply a socioeconomic clash between free and servile labor. This analysis serves reasonably well as a generalization, but the rigid class categories to which conventional Soviet historiography has reduced American society produce unfortunate contradictions. The author describes Abraham Lincoln as a representative of the bourgeoisie, for example, yet later credits him with implementing the policies of the working masses.

Within the ideological context in which it is framed, the essay provides a valuable amendment of Malkin's standard work and a more accurate summary of the facts than the older American works she cites. Yet from its opening quotation of Marx to the closing reference from Lenin, Kiniapina demonstrates how little Soviet historical scholarship changed between 1939 and 1980.

In contrast, Gennady Kuropiatnik's survey of cultural and social relations following the Civil War abandons overt Marxist-Leninist analysis in favor of narrative. His descriptions of utopian settlements, literary connections, and scientific contacts appear without any significant interpretive framework. Indeed, the only connection between these elements is chronological and the assumption that the history of political cooperation during the 1860s facilitated broader contact between members of Russian and American society generally. Directly and indirectly this was true. Flattering descriptions of America in Russian journals stimulated curiosity and enthusiasm that drew Frey and others to America in the 1870s much as it did Owenites in the 1830s.

Coincidentally, Russian-American literary relations, especially the American discovery of Ivan Turgenev, depended directly upon Civil War relations. When Admiral Lesovsky's Squadron sailed into New York harbor, Eugene Schuyler was a young lawyer with literary pretensions and a taste for exotic cultures. He met some Russian officers at a reception and immediately sought instruction in the Russian language from an Orthodox priest in the city. Soon after he applied for appointment as United States Consul in Moscow and, while in route to his post, presented Turgenev with the translation of *Fathers and Sons* that Kuropiatnik mentions.

Schuyler's awkward translation merely introduced Turgenev to a few American readers, but his subsequent writings acquainted Americans with Russian life more broadly. During the decade of his diplomatic career in Russia, Schuyler wrote dozens of articles about Russian customs, politics, society, and culture that were published regularly in national journals and New York newspapers. His generally sympathetic presentation of the Alexandrine reform era contributed to the good feelings of the 1870s that Kuropiatnik describes from the Russian side.

While the mutual admiration of Russian and American writers demonstrates genuine cultural interaction, the author's brief commentary on Russian music hardly qualifies as a parallel experience. Americans merely served as a passive, but appreciative, audience for Rubinstein and the others with no discernible consequences. Did America's introduction to Russian music bear any fruit beyond the personal distress of Rubinstein at his exploitation by promoters? Here and elsewhere in the essay the author leaves the reader to draw his own conclusions and jumps to another category of contact.

Kuropiatnik's article overflows with information about a surprising variety of Russian experiences in post–Civil War America and it is refreshingly free of dogmatism, yet the virtue of breadth carries with it the danger of thematic ambiguity. Relationships between the various categories of contact are sometimes hard to see, and the conclusion does little to tighten the connections. It merely restates the opening premise that the political friendship reinforced by the Civil War led to deeper contact in nonpolitical spheres. The theme that most consistently runs through the piece is the intriguingly contrary one of increasing disillusionment with America on the part of Russians. Frey was disappointed that American freedom did not nurture his commune, Rubinstein soured by greedy promoters, Mendeleev put off by the prevailing materialism in American life. Radicals like Michael Bakunin condemned American democracy as a fiction, after first praising American ideals. With some exceptions, the Russians Kuropiatnik describes came away from the United States disenchanted and hostile. It is not an unfamiliar theme, indeed it appears prominently in I. K. Malkova's study of populist editorials, and this essay provides telling examples of it. This nineteenth-century Russian critique of America deserves more explicit discussion and further analysis. The suggestion that the United States might serve as a model for post-Soviet Russia has provoked a strikingly similar critical reaction on the part of many Russians.

Although Kuropiatnik's subject is cultural and intellectual relations rather than political, he assumes that political relations were consistently positive in the 1870s. Outwardly this seemed the case, but government relations were not as harmonious as this piece suggests. The question of religious discrimination against Jews that later soured U.S.-Russian relations actually began in the decade after the Civil War. President Grant publicly condemned Russian policies toward Jews and in 1869 instructed the secretary of state to try to persuade the tsarist administration to cancel anti-Jewish practices, but to no avail. During the pogroms of 1881 similar informal representations were made by Washington and rejected. It seems that on both sides of Russian-American relations familiarity strained friendship.

Abel' Startsev's topic is a far more limited one, but no less interesting. Ivan Turchaninov was one of those Russians drawn to the United States because of its reputation for democracy and freedom only to be disappointed. The author makes much of his bitter letter to Herzen in 1859. In his condemnation of the materialism he found here, especially "capitalist tricksters" and the tyranny of wealth, Turchaninov echoes the critique of other idealistic democrats of the 1860s. After three years in America he had failed in business, lost out in his bid for an appointment to the U.S. Coastal Survey, and planned to return to Europe. Yet unlike many others, Turchaninov stayed, volunteered for service in the Union army, and retired a general and a hero.

In the absence of any but the sketchiest biographical evidence, the author pieces together a plausible explanation for Turchaninov's contradictory career. Startsev identifies him as a political refugee who fled the Russian army because of his "democratic ideas," and proceeds to interpret his Civil War service in America as a revolutionary cause. In favor of such an interpretation is one letter to Herzen but little else. Although he reputedly adopted radical ideas as a youth, Turchaninov served fifteen years as an officer, asking for medical leave in 1856 as a colonel of the Guards General Staff. His memoirs, *Military Rambles,* outspoken and opinionated as they are, apparently make no reference to his Russian career or his political views.

Still, Turchaninov would not be the first career officer to adopt radical ideas, and he was certainly a militant abolitionist. His protection of runaway slaves in violation of the fugitive slave law led to trial by military tribunal in 1862 and a sentence of dismissal that was only overturned by President Lincoln. American sources (*Generals in Blue* by Ezra J. Warner) credit the pleas of Turchaninov's wife for Lincoln's action, but Startsev persuasively attributes it to Lincoln's decision to adopt a more aggressive policy against the Confederacy. Lincoln not only dismissed the charges but promoted the Russian to general as a symbol of the new policy.

Startsev stretches his evidence, however, when he attempts to identify Turchaninov's views with Marx's analysis of the Civil War and socialism. The fact that both Turchaninov and Marx advocated a more aggressive military and political strategy against the South hardly proves that the Russian was familiar with Marx's writings, as the author suggests. Nor does Turchaninov's assertion that planter estates be divided among Union soldiers and freed slaves make him a socialist. Turchaninov's advice, written late in the war, sounds more like that of a vengeful abolitionist than a political ideologue. Despite a tendency to overinterpret, Startsev has made a sound contribution to the biography of a major Civil War figure.

8

Leo Tolstoy and Social Critics in the United States at the Turn of the Century, by I. P. Dement'ev

At the turn of the twentieth century Leo Tolstoy was the most famous and influential writer in the world. People everywhere listened to his voice. His estate, Iasnaia Poliana, was a place of pilgrimage for admirers from every country. Vladimir Lenin proudly observed that "no one" could be compared with Tolstoy the artist. According to Lenin, who called Tolstoy "the mirror of the Russian revolution," one of the most important reasons for his international fame was the social commitment, to which he gave expression in his works. Lenin wrote: "His global prominence as a writer and his international fame as a thinker and preacher reflect the global importance of the Russian Revolution."[1]

By the early twentieth century, Russia had become a web of economic and social contradictions. The tension between capitalist development and the many vestiges of serfdom was growing more acute. The agrarian question, which would determine the fate of a majority of the country's population, was the most urgent of the issues that confronted the approaching bourgeois-democratic revolution. Nevertheless, unlike the West European bourgeois revolutions of the eighteenth and nineteenth centuries, in the Russian revolution of 1905–1907 the proletariat acted as an independent political force, while Lenin's Bolsheviks assumed the role of organizers and leaders of the struggle. [3]

The great Russian writer felt himself bound to the Russian peasantry by indissoluble ties. "Tolstoy is great," wrote Lenin, "because he expresses the ideas and aspirations of millions of Russian peasants on the eve of the Russian bourgeois revolution."[2] On another occasion, Lenin declared that "Tolstoy's teachings have fused the protest of

---

1. V. I. Lenin, "L. N. Tolstoi" (November 1910), in *Polnoe Sobranie Sochinenie* (Complete Collected Works), 5th ed., 55 vols. (Moscow, 1960–1965), vol. 20, 19.

2. Lenin, "Lev Tolstoi kak zerkalo russkoi revolutsii" (Leo Tolstoy as a Mirror of the Russian Revolution) (September 1908), vol. 17, 210.

millions of peasants with their despair."[3] Indeed, Tolstoy was proud to call himself "the advocate of the one hundred million people who till the land."[4]

The great change in Tolstoy's views, which led to his decision to take the radical side, occurred in the late 1870s and early 1880s. Soviet scholar Mark Shcheglov notes that the writer's crisis as an artist was the result of a spiritual crisis he had experienced.[5] For a while only the voice of Tolstoy-the-preacher, who addressed himself to man's religious conscience, was heard. But then his creative powers brought forth new artistic achievements, among them *The Death of Ivan Ilyich, The Kreuzer Sonata, The Dominion of Darkness, The Fruits of Enlightenment, Resurrection, Hadji-Murad,* and *The Living Corpse.* Tolstoy, who suffered from a terrible feeling of guilt because of his membership in the privileged class of the nobility, renounced his status as a landowner and a proprietor of an estate, and gave up the copyright to his works. The writer's actions produced conflict within his family, which in the end led to his departure from Iasnaia Poliana and to his tragic death.

Tolstoy felt that his duty as a writer and publicist was to criticize the existing social order and, in the words of Lenin, "to tear away all masks of all kinds." He depicted the evils of Russian society: the poverty and back-breaking labor that were the lot of the peasants, the parasitical way of life of the upper classes. He was fearless in his condemnation of the autocracy and directed the main force of his protest against "the slavery of the modern age" and the ideology of capitalism, which he called a "pseudo-Christian civilization." [2]

The writer tried to find his own answers to the problems posed by the development of society. "The existing social order has had its day and will inevitably have to be rebuilt according to new principles," he wrote.[6] In 1895 Tolstoy expressed himself yet more forcefully:

> The existing social order should be destroyed. Both those who want to destroy it and those who defend it agree about this. The social order based on competition must be dismantled and replaced by a communistic one; the capitalist order must be dismantled and replaced by a socialist one . . . coercion must be abolished and replaced by a free and fraternal communion of people.[7]

Of course, Tolstoy was not a proponent of the principles of scientific socialism. He had developed his own interpretation of the social realities his contemporaries knew so well. In many ways, however, he was continuing an old Russian tradition of peasant radicalism. One of the most important elements in the writer's worldview was the belief that

---

3. Lenin, *Works,* vol. 20, 40.
4. L. N. Tolstoi, *Polnoe Sobranie Sochinenii* (Complete Collected Works), 90 vols. (Moscow-Leningrad, 1928–1958), vol. 76, 45.
5. Tolstoy, *Works,* vol. 88, vii–viii (Introduction by Shcheglov). The list of eminent Soviet scholars who studied Tolstoy's writings also includes N. N. Gusev, N. K. Gudzii, B. M. Eikhenbaum, A. A. Shifman, B. S. Meilakh, K. N. Lomunov, T. L. Motyleva, and V. F. Asmus.
6. Tolstoy, *Works,* vol. 28, 289.
7. Tolstoy, *Works,* vol. 68, 64.

the Russian people, instead of submitting to proletarianization like the peoples of Europe and America, must solve the agrarian question by abolishing the ownership of land and show other peoples the path to a rational, free and happy life without industry and without the violence and factory slavery of capitalism.... That is its great mission.[8]

Like the Russian populists, Tolstoy thought that the ancient institution of the peasant commune offered the country a means of escape from the socioeconomic developments that were beginning to affect it. In an age that saw the rise of the theory of scientific socialism, his search for a utopian and patriarchal solution to Russia's problems seemed particularly anachronistic. During this period the writer began to state his views on the way in which the kingdom of oppression and injustice could be overthrown. Having only an imperfect understanding of the role of the proletariat and being opposed to the revolutionary methods of struggle, Tolstoy formulated a religious-philosophical doctrine of "non-participation in evil" and "self-perfection." He preached that in one's life one should strive for simplicity, declaring that true happiness was not related to material things.

Tolstoy's belief that it was moral self-improvement rather than the class struggle that would lead to the restructuring of society was utopian. Lenin, who analyzed Tolstoy's legacy from the perspective of the class struggle of the proletariat, pointed out the "glaring contradictions" in his views:

On the one hand, he was uncompromising in his criticism of capitalist exploitation, exposed government violence, depicted the grotesque spectacle of the political system and of the courts, and revealed the profound contradiction between the rise in affluence and the advances of civilization—and the increase in the poverty, privations, and ignorance of the working masses; on the other hand, like a crack-brained preacher, he would preach sermons about "non-resistance to evil" by violence.[9]

Although he claimed to stand aloof from the political scene, Tolstoy reacted to all the important social events of the day. As a result, his pronouncements became a major revolutionizing factor, despite the fact that subjectively Tolstoy was trying to achieve something entirely different. George Plekhanov wrote: "He preaches non-resistance to evil, [but many of his sermons] infuse the reader with a sacred desire to oppose reactionary violence with revolutionary force. He suggests that we should limit ourselves to the weapon of criticism, but these powerful passages in his works undoubtedly justify the harshest *criticism by force of arms.*"[10] Later Stefan Zweig developed Plekhanov's idea:

We should not be misled by the evangelic meekness in his sermons of brotherhood, the Christian humility that colors his language, and his references to the rejection of

---

8. Tolstoy, *Works,* vol. 36, 230.
9. Lenin, *Works,* vol. 17, 209.
10. G. V. Plekhanov, *Izbrannye filosofskie proizvedeniia* (Selected Philosophical Works), vol. 5 (Moscow, 1958), 637.

social criticism directed against the state contained in the Gospels.... More than any other Russian, Tolstoy pointed and paved the way for a violent explosion.[11]

The contradictory nature of Tolstoy's actions and views became startlingly clear during the revolution of 1905–1907. Tolstoy hoped the revolution would be bloodless and peaceful. Basing himself on his doctrine of nonresistance to evil, he spoke out against the activities of the revolutionaries, and yet he believed that the revolution would bring about the liberation of the Russian people. Writing to the American writer Ernest Crosby, Tolstoy declared, "I am firmly convinced that the results of this revolution will be of greater benefit and importance to mankind than those of the French Revolution."[12]

Tolstoy owed his influence and worldwide popularity to the fact that he discussed the most urgent problems of the age: social injustice, national and racial discrimination, militarism, colonial oppression, the collapse of the family and morality, and the need for the reorganization of society.[13] Lenin wrote that Tolstoy "with tremendous force, conviction, and sincerity *posed* a whole series of questions relating to the fundamental features of the contemporary political and social order."[14]

Tolstoy became internationally famous in the mid-1880s, when his novel *War and Peace* appeared in translation in France. Ivan Turgenev's efforts to popularize the works of his fellow-writer and the publication of *The Russian Novel,* a book by the French critic Eugene-Melchior de Vogue,[15] also enhanced Tolstoy's popularity abroad. De Vogue wrote, "If one is to regard the books that describe the life of mankind at a particular moment in history as being the most interesting, then our age has produced nothing more interesting than the works of Tolstoy."[16]

During this period the American public also became acquainted with Tolstoy's writings. In 1885–1890 several of his works were published in the United States, including the trilogy *Childhood, Boyhood, Youth,* the novel *The Cossacks,* the *Sevastopol Sketches, Anna Karenina, War and Peace,* and *The Kreuzer Sonata.* In 1898–1900 a twelve-volume edition of Tolstoy's collected works appeared in America.[17]

American writer William Dean Howells wrote in his 1887 introduction to the *Sevastopol Sketches*: "I regard this Russian aristocrat, who lives somewhere at the

---

11. Quoted from K. N. Lomunov, "Vsemirnyi avtoritet" (A World-Respected Authority) *Literaturnoe Nasledstvo* (Literary Heritage), vol. 75: *Tolstoi i zarubezhnyi mir* (Tolstoy and the Outside World), pt. 1 (Moscow, 1965), 24.

12. Tolstoy, *Works,* vol. 76, 5.

13. Lomunov, "A World-Respected Authority," 8.

14. Lenin, *Works,* vol. 20, 38.

15. *Literary Heritage* 75, pt. 1, 44 (introductory article by T. L. Motyleva).

16. *L. N. Tolstoi v perevodakh na inostrannye iazyki: bibliografiia* (Foreign Translations of L. N. Tolstoy: A Bibliography) (Moscow, 1961), iv.

17. Ibid., 3. When Tolstoy's works were published in America, one of them was bowdlerized. For the first English translation of *Resurrection* the editors of *Cosmopolitan Magazine* altered its text, deleting a number of scenes they considered "indecent" and replacing them with passages of their own composition. Tolstoy declared this edition of his novel to be unauthorized. Tolstoy, *Works,* vol. 72, 115. In this connection, Ernest Crosby asserted, "The tyranny of the Russian censors was surpassed not by Western Europe, but by America, that land of false freedom." *Literary Heritage* 75, pt. 1, 398.

end of the world, as the human being who is closest to me.... This is because he helped me to learn about myself and because no one among the writers I know has described so accurately the life of man in the universal sense and also in its most intimate and private aspects."[18] Commenting on Tolstoy's popularity in the United States, the British journalist William Stead noted: "His works were translated in America earlier than in England and met with greater admiration in the land beyond the ocean than in this country."[19] Ivan Ianzhul, a professor at the University of Moscow, who took with him letters of recommendation from Tolstoy when he traveled to the United States in 1893, recalled that, like a magic key, these letters opened every door to him.[20]

It should be noted that the rise in Tolstoy's international fame coincided with the dramatic change in his worldview. His philosophical-spiritual and polemical works of the 1880s and 1890s, which marked a departure from his earlier style of writing, drew the attention of American readers. The campaign by the tsarist government against Tolstoy and his excommunication by the Russian Orthodox Church served only to increase their interest.[21] Sergei Stepniak-Kravchinskii (1851–1895), a member of the Russian revolutionary movement of the 1870s who had emigrated to America, wrote (although, perhaps, with some exaggeration): "Everyone knows that the special fame that now surrounds Tolstoy's name began after he published his *Confession* and the pamphlet 'What Do I Believe In?' For every one who loves Tolstoy the writer there are twenty fervent admirers of Tolstoy the priest of a new religion."[22]

If many Americans regarded Tolstoy as a moral and even a political teacher, this was not only because of the influence of his social views, but also because of the growing spiritual ferment in the United States. At the turn of the century similar socioeconomic phenomena were taking place in the United States and Russia. In both countries capitalism had entered the monopolistic stage, which had led to an intensification of class conflicts. However, there were also important differences. While in Russia the process of the bourgeois-democratic transformation of society had yet to run its course and the land question continued to be a major obstacle to the country's development, in America these problems had already been resolved. By the early twentieth century the United States was a classic example of the capitalist state. The concentration of economic power and of the most important instruments of political control in the hands of the giant corporations profoundly affected the interests of the broad masses in society. That is why during this period all the major democratic movements in America were to a greater or lesser extent hostile to the monopolies.[23]

---

18. *Literary Heritage* 75, pt. 1, 85. For further details, see B. A. Gilenson, "U. D. Gouells and L. N. Tolstoi" (W. D. Howells and L. N. Tolstoy), in *Uchen. zap. Gor'k. un-ta* (Studies of Gorky University) 60, no. 5 (1963): 282–95.

19. *Literary Heritage* 75, pt. 2, 108.

20. *Literary Heritage* 75, pt. 1, 407.

21. For details, see G. I. Petrov, *Otluchenie L'va Tolstogo ot tserkve* (The Excommunication of Leo Tolstoy) (Moscow, 1978).

22. *Literary Heritage* 75, pt. 1, 546.

23. See I. A. Beliavskaia, *Burzhuaznyi reformizm v SShA (1900–1914)* (Bourgeois Reformism in the United States [1900–1914]) (Moscow, 1968); V. V. Sogrin, "Formirovanie antimonopolisticheskoi ideologii v SShA v kontse XIX v." (Formation of the Anti-Monopoly Ideology in the

Farmers formed the nucleus of these antimonopoly movements that reached their culmination in the phenomenon of populism; while the majority of them continued to believe in the ideals of "true capitalism" and supported the principles of laissez-faire, the left wing of the Populist movement was already proclaiming the need for the socialization of monopolies. The Populist Party thus became the center of attraction for a number of antitrust and reformist groups: the followers of Henry George, who demanded the abolition of the monopoly on the private ownership of land; the nationalizers; the early muckrakers, writers and journalists who campaigned against the abuses committed by the trusts and exposed the wide-ranging influence of monopolies in American society. In their search for a solution to these problems, some opponents of the monopolies were drawn to the idea of a utopian social order based on humane cooperation of people.

The most popular work in this vein was Edward Bellamy's novel *Looking Backward* (1888). The socialist society Bellamy believed in would not arise as the result of a struggle waged by a revolutionary class; rather, it would represent the triumph of abstract reason. Nevertheless, his scathing criticism of the power of the trusts in the United States and his striking vision of cooperation in a classless society attracted the attention of the readers. Also characteristic of this period was the appeal exercised by the ideas of Christian socialism. The Society of Christian Socialists, founded in 1889 by William Bliss, demanded the nationalization of some industries as a first step toward the socialization of the entire economy. The movement of "anti-imperialists," which began during the Spanish-American War of 1898, was another important element in the social struggle. It represented one of the first attempts by democratic forces in America to oppose the imperialist expansion and aggression.

A number of writers reflected in their works the social ferment in the country and the deepening sense of disappointment with the reality of America felt by many of their contemporaries. In *Democratic Vistas,* Walt Whitman denounced the hypocrisy and money-grubbing of the capitalist speculators, while Mark Twain's novel *The Gilded Age* gave its name to that entire period of American history when big business flourished and dominated the country. Hamlin Garland and Frank Norris described the tragic lot of American farmers who had found themselves in the grip of all-powerful corporations, while Harding Davis and Stephen Crane depicted poverty in the big cities. Howells, shocked by the violent suppression in May 1886 of the [Haymarket] demonstration in Chicago, openly declared his sympathy for socialism. At the beginning of the twentieth century Jack London, Upton Sinclair, and Theodore Dreiser spoke out against the "iron heel" of the monopolies.

These were some of the ways in which American democratic thought developed during this period. Americans, who were acutely aware of the growing social antagonisms in their country, were moved by Tolstoy's cry, "one cannot live this way!" Many in the United States were influenced by his condemnation of capitalism and his calls

---

United States in the Late Nineteenth Century) *Vestnik MGU* (Herald of Moscow State University), History Series, 1970, no. 3; Kuropiatnik, *Fermerskoe dvizhenie v SShA: ot greindzherov k Narodnoi partii, 1867–1896* (Farmers' Movement in the United States: From Grangers to the Populist Party, 1867–1896) (Moscow, 1971).

for a reform of social relations and for social justice.[24] Of course, some of Tolstoy's American followers tried to create a dogma from the weaker elements in his teaching, like his emphasis on humility and biblical homilies.

Many years later, in the foreword to an English edition of Tolstoy's works, Hamlin Garland recalled:

> In those days almost all of us were to a greater or lesser degree reformers. Bellamy had just completed his novel *Looking Backward*; Henry George's *Progress and Poverty* continued to be the subject of passionate debate; Howells was writing his very serious novel *The Search for a New Happiness,* and in *A Connecticut Yankee at King Arthur's Court,* Mark Twain, inspired by the general desire for social justice, wielded his saber with elegant ease, inflicting telling blows on both present and ancient cruelties and injustices. The entire nation discussed the problems of impoverishment and ways of solving them.

And Garland continued: "His [Tolstoy's] appeal, 'Let us be just,' so majestic in its simplicity, was consonant with my own mood and the mood of my reformist friends. . . . In demanding the transformation of society, we turned to Tolstoy."[25]

It is important to note that in the mid-1880s, under the influence of Tolstoy, Howells's views underwent a significant change. In his letter to Tolstoy of December 10, 1898, the Russian writer's friend and translator, Aylmer Maude, described a meeting he had with Howells in New York: "He told me about the deep impression your works had made on him and said he was trying to change his life according to your example. However, he fears he will not be able to realize his wish."[26] Other American writers also felt the powerful impact of Tolstoy's realist style. Upton Sinclair wrote that *Resurrection* helped him understand the approaching Russian revolution. Tolstoy's words "echoed like thunder all over the world,"[27] he wrote. Dreiser remarked that the works of the great Russian writer had stirred the public's consciousness.[28]

Among Tolstoy's American correspondents were prominent figures in the various democratic movements of the period like Henry George; Benjamin Flower, editor of an influential journal, *Arena,* that supported the Populists; the Christian Socialist George Herron; Herbert Welsh and Ernest Crosby, who were anti-imperialists; and Booker T. Washington, the leader of the reformist wing of the Negro movement. Tolstoy also kept in touch with a community of Christian Socialists in Georgia. The well-known American Socialist, Frederic Heath, wrote to Tolstoy in August 1908: "Dear Comrade. I address to you the following request: 'Would you be so kind as to send me a few words about Labor Day for a special issue of the *Social Democratic Herald.'* "[29]

---

24. For details, see M. D. Lutskii, D. D. Stoliarov, *L. N. Tolstoy—oblichitel' kapitalizma* (L. N. Tolstoy as an Exposer of Capitalism) (Tashkent, 1961).

25. *Literary Heritage* 75, pt. 1, 162. The library at Iasnaia Poliana contains Garland's book, *The Main Travelled Roads* (1894), with an inscription by the author, "To Leo Tolstoy from his admirer Hamlin Garland, Chicago, 1897."

26. *Literary Heritage* 75, pt. 1, 87 (Commentary by B. A. Gilenson).

27. Ibid., 287.

28. Ibid., 148.

29. Ibid., 467.

Americans knew Tolstoy, but he in turn knew a great deal about contemporary America. First of all, he was familiar with nineteenth-century American literature and had a high opinion of it. Stead recalled that Tolstoy once remarked to him, "Turgenev . . . would tell me that Americans had written nothing worth reading. In this he was wrong. I like American literature, it is very good."[30] Not only did Tolstoy have many American correspondents who belonged to a variety of social classes, but Iasnaia Poliana was visited by dozens of Americans. Among these visitors to Tolstoy's estate were the leader of the Democratic Party, William Jennings Bryan; the pacifist poet Ernest Crosby; the writer and great-grandson of the millionaire Vanderbilt; the Socialist Robert Hunter; Henry J. Raymond, who was a professor of sociology; the son of Henry George; and the editors and correspondents of the largest American newspapers—the *New York Tribune,* the *New York Times,* and *New York World.* Tolstoy learned much about the United States from the American journals he would regularly or periodically receive. They included leading sociopolitical publications like *Forum, Harper's Magazine,* the *Independent, Review of Reviews,* and radical and religious journals such as *Arena,* the *Nationalist, Dawn, Social Gospel,* and *Christian Science.*[31]

In 1886 Tolstoy met the American journalist George Kennan, who in his book of sketches, *Siberia and the Exile System,* would describe the harsh conditions endured by political prisoners in tsarist Russia. Later Tolstoy wrote approvingly to Kennan: "Like all living Russians, I am very, very grateful to you for publicizing the horrors taking place during the present reign."[32] It would not be an exaggeration to say that Tolstoy was one of the best-informed people in Russia on the subject of America.

Tolstoy's attitude toward America cannot be summed up in a single sentence. Sometimes he would call it an "advanced country." He recognized that Americans enjoyed considerable freedom of conscience (one recalls that he did much to make possible the emigration to the United States and Canada of the members of the Dukhobor religious sect, who were persecuted by the tsarist government), and he referred to their relatively high standard of living. Yet it was not these features that defined America in the eyes of Tolstoy. Above all else, he regarded the United States as the embodiment of the principles of industrial capitalist civilization and believed that the socioeconomic developments taking place in that country represented a warning to Russia. In 1900, *Harper's Magazine* asked the writer to compose an address to the American people. Tolstoy declined, but in his letter to English journalist Edward Garnett he discussed certain aspects of the spiritual and literary development of the United States:

> If I were to address the American people, I should try to thank it for the great help those of its writers who flourished in the 50s gave me. I would mention Garrison, Parker,

---

30. Ibid., pt. 2, 108.
31. Ivan Gorbunov-Posadov, a frequent visitor to Iasnaia Poliana, wrote: "Among the piles of correspondence there are always a number of letters from England and America. . . . In the daily package of newspapers, journals, and books there is always a bunch of English and American (particularly American) newspapers, journals, and books devoted to religious issues or the problems of reforming life." Gorbunov-Posadov, "Ernest Krosbi, poet novogo mira" (Ernest Crosby, Poet of the New World) in *Tolstoi i ego zhizneponimanie* (Tolstoy and His Worldview) (Moscow, 1911), xi.
32. Tolstoy, *Works,* vol. 65, 138.

Emerson, Ballou, and Thoreau, not as its greatest writers, but as authors who had exercised a particular influence on me. I would also mention some other names, those of Channing, Whittier, Lowell, and Walt Whitman—a brilliant constellation, the like of which it is difficult to find in world literature. And I should like to ask the American people why it does not pay more attention to these voices (which I doubt the voices of Gould, Rockefeller, and Carnegie could replace), and why it is not continuing the good work they began so successfully.[33]

In this passage Tolstoy refers to the writers with whose philosophical, religious, and ethical ideals he felt the greatest affinity. Raising the banner of the antislavery struggle, Garrison, Parker, Emerson, and Thoreau had declared their belief in the supreme importance of the public exposure of injustice and had proclaimed the doctrine of "passive disobedience." Moreover, Tolstoy discerned a connection between the intellectual and spiritual achievements of these American writers and social thinkers, and their search for a solution to the grave social problems their country faced. He saw that there was a growing realization in the United States that radical changes in the life of the people had to take place. Tolstoy drew a parallel between the moral pathos of the American writers of the 1840s and 1850s and the social protest that found expression in Russian literature in the period preceding the Great Reforms of the 1860s. He said to his British translator, Maude:

Great literature is born only when an elevated sense of morality appears. Let us take, for example, the time of the liberation movements—the struggle for the abolition of serfdom in Russia and for the emancipation of Negroes in the United States. Look at the writers who emerged at that time in America: Harriet Beecher Stowe, Thoreau, Emerson, Lowell, Whittier, Longfellow, William Lloyd Garrison, Theodore Parker, and in Russia—Dostoevsky, Turgenev, Herzen, and others.[34]

Tolstoy thought it obvious that neither the abolition of serfdom in Russia nor the liquidation of slavery in the United States had brought the two peoples real freedom. He wrote that "the abolition of serfdom and slavery merely meant the abolition of an obsolete form of servitude that had outgrown its usefulness, and its replacement by a harsher form of slavery to which a larger number of slaves than before was subjected."[35] It was not the differences but the similarities in the actual condition of the working masses in various countries that he regarded as important, for everywhere he looked he saw the oppression of the people and political tyranny. Tolstoy, who had denounced Russian autocracy in stronger terms than almost anyone else, was surprised to find that many of its foreign critics failed to see similar evidence of glaring injustice in their own countries.

In England, America, France, Germany the government masks its evil character so well that some among their peoples point to events in Russia and naively imagine that

33. Tolstoy, *Works,* vol. 72, 397.
34. E. Mood [A. Maude], "Razgovory s Tolstym" (Conversations with Tolstoy), in *L. N. Tolstoi v vospominaniiakh sovremennikov* (Tolstoy in the Reminiscences of his Contemporaries), vol. 1 (Moscow, 1960), 437.
35. Tolstoy, *Works,* vol. 34, 169.

what is happening in Russia is happening only in Russia, while they enjoy perfect freedom and do not need to improve their situation; and so they live in a state of hopeless slavery—the slavery of slaves who do not understand that they are slaves and are proud of their status as slaves. In this respect, our situation as Russians is both worse (in the sense that the violence here is more brutal) and better, in that it is easier for us to understand what is taking place.[36]

Judging historical developments primarily from a moral perspective, Tolstoy believed that contemporary America had abandoned the high spiritual ideals of its recent heroic past (Tolstoy had great respect for Benjamin Franklin and Thomas Jefferson) and was experiencing the triumph of selfish interests—the deleterious consequence of relentless pursuit of wealth. In an interview in June 1903 with James Creelman, a correspondent of the *New York World,* Tolstoy declared: "America is no longer young.... You only produce rich men. In the years before and after the Civil War the spiritual life of your people flourished and bore fruit. But now you have become miserable materialists."[37] Tolstoy, however, was far from condemning the whole American nation. During a conversation with the French journalist Georges Bourdon he said, "I know what Americans are always reproached for and I know that to a degree they deserve these reproaches. Indeed, an American businessman acts only out of love for money, lives only for his billions. But does the entire people resemble him, and can one place on the people the burden of responsibility for the cupidity of the propertied class?"[38]

As a humanist Tolstoy was most interested in the problems of ethics and morality, which he always approached from a position of common sense. That is why he spoke of the power of the Goulds, Rockefellers, and Carnegies in the United States. When in 1903 Rockefeller, responding to Tolstoy's articles, declared that the accumulation of wealth did not contradict the teaching of the Gospels, the Russian writer mocked America's oil king, pointing out that the possession of vast wealth in a country where the masses lived in terrible poverty was an affront to simple justice. In "The End of the Century" Tolstoy wrote that American law allowed Rockefeller "to make and keep his billions at the expense of the interests of the masses."[39] In another article, "To All the Same" (1905), he compared the oppression of the people by the Rockefellers and Rothschilds to slavery in the Egypt of the pharaohs.

Tolstoy's views on the state reflected the influence of anarchist ideas, particularly those developed by representatives of the anarchist current of the Russian populist movement. Like them, Tolstoy believed that the most important function of the state was the exercise of violence. Like them, he felt that the nature of a country's political system was a matter of small importance. Whether the state in question was a monarchy or a parliamentary democracy, his attitude to it remained the same. About the democracy of contemporary America, which Russian liberals regarded as exemplary, he had this

36. Tolstoy, *Works,* vol. 36, 162–63.
37. *Literary Heritage* 75, pt. 1, 430.
38. Ibid., pt. 2, 57.
39. Tolstoy, *Works,* vol. 36, 270.

to say: "In the United States swindlers spend millions to elect a president, for they know that the one chosen to be president will support those fiscal policies and those monopolies which are advantageous to them, and that the money they spent on the election will be repaid to them with interest."[40]

Tolstoy was curious about the "workers' question" in the United States. His remarks concerning this issue reveal the direction in which his views were developing. Having received information about the relatively high standard of living enjoyed by American workers in comparison with their counterparts in Europe, Tolstoy concluded that in terms of their status and interests they "continue to be the slaves they were before."[41] Tolstoy, who was familiar with the reality of capitalism, had no doubt that "in England, in America, in France, in Italy millions of jobless people are dying of starvation just like in our country."[42] Several years later he found confirmation of his ideas in Upton Sinclair's *The Jungle*: "An amazing book. The author has expert knowledge of the life of workers. He reveals the flaws of the entire American way of life. One cannot say where things are worse."[43]

The great Russian writer and humanist could not but condemn one of the most appalling features of American reality—anti-Negro racism. In this, Tolstoy was continuing the noble tradition of Radishchev, Herzen, and Chernyshevsky. Many Americans saw Tolstoy as a natural ally. In 1903 American journalist Theodore Stanton wrote to Tolstoy at Iasnaia Poliana: "It is essential . . . that you should raise your authoritative voice against this injustice."[44] In 1909 Tolstoy received a letter whose authors, Lizzie Walker and Martha Tyler, writing in the name of the three thousand Negroes of New Albany, Indiana, begged him for help in connection with the racist persecutions in that city.[45] Tolstoy corresponded with Booker T. Washington and was familiar with the activities of the Tuskegee Institute.

Tolstoy condemned racism and anti-Negro discrimination, particularly in his sociopolitical writings. In his foreword to a biography of William Lloyd Garrison, a prominent fighter against slavery, Tolstoy wrote that the Negro question "now confronts the people of the United States."[46] He condemned the "immorality of a government" that permitted racist crimes to take place.[47]

We have noted that the writer disagreed with the revolutionary democrats on some issues and that he spoke out against revolution. But Tolstoy's "moujik" (peasant) democratism had just as little in common with the aspirations of the liberal reformers, which he characterized as the desire "without changing the existing order, to take from the upper classes, who have power and wealth, a minute proportion of that wealth and

---

40. Ibid., 326.
41. Tolstoy, *Works*, vol. 34, 171.
42. Tolstoy, *Works*, vol. 36, 401–2.
43. N. N. Gusev, *Letopis' zhizni i tvorchestva L. N. Tolstogo* (A Chronicle of the Life and Writings of L. N. Tolstoy) (Moscow, 1936), 573.
44. *Literary Heritage* 75, pt. 1, 491.
45. See Tolstoy, *Works*, vol. 79, 196.
46. See Tolstoy, *Works*, vol. 36, 97.
47. See Tolstoy, *Works*, vol. 79, 196.

throw it into the bottomless pit of poverty."[48] Tolstoy believed that the world could be changed through the moral self-improvement of man and a peaceful revolution of the spirit. He rejected capitalism and judged social critics and radical-democratic movements in the United States in the light of his beliefs, exhibiting a preference for vaguely socialist ideals that often had a religious coloration.

Tolstoy was interested in the Shakers, a religious sect originating in the mid–eighteenth century that preached communal ownership of property. The writer's interest grew in the late 1880s, when he was completing the *Kreuzer Sonata* and was actively corresponding with a number of leading Shakers.[49] And he referred approvingly to Adin Ballou, the founder of Christian communist colonies in the United States.

Tolstoy's attention was drawn to utopian socialist theories that had become quite popular in the United States in the 1880s and 1890s and to the movement for the creation of cooperative colonies that had been inspired by these ideas. Even the famous American Socialist, Eugene Debs, was influenced by the doctrines of utopian socialism. In a speech in June 1898 he declared: "Give me 10,000 men in one of the western states, give these 10,000 access to the means of production, and we will change its [the state's] economic conditions and capture the hearts and minds of the entire population."[50]

The Russian writer greeted with admiration Bellamy's *Looking Backward,* writing in his journal on June 30, 1889, "*Looking Backward.* An excellent work; must be translated," and the following day restated his opinion of the novel: "*Looking Backward* is superb."[51] Soon Bellamy's book was translated into Russian and was being avidly read by members of the workers' revolutionary circles together with Chernyshevsky's *What Is To Be Done?*[52] Tolstoy also found "much that is good" in Laurence Gronlund's book *Our Destiny.* Gronlund was another well-known American utopian socialist and author of *The Co-operative Commonwealth* (1884). In August 1891 Tolstoy wrote Gronlund that he "quite agreed" with the ideas expressed in *Our Destiny* and that he was trying to arrange for it to be translated into Russian.[53]

Tolstoy hailed the numerous attempts to set up cooperative colonies in the United States, viewing them as a source of moral education. He wrote about one of them: "Two days ago I received an American publication, *Social Gospel.* This is the organ of a group of people—they number about 100—who have formed colonies in Georgia in order to lead a life that is Christian even in the economic sense. This is difficult, but it is impossible not to sympathize with such attempts."[54]

At the same time the writer was skeptical about many aspects of these utopian projects, particularly the methods that were used to carry them out. We have noted that

---

48. See Tolstoy, *Works,* vol. 51, 36.
49. See Tolstoy, *Works,* vol. 50, 64.
50. Quoted in B. D. Kozenko, *Iudzhin Debs, sotsialist* (Eugene Debs, Socialist) (Saratov, 1967), 21.
51. Tolstoy, *Works,* vol. 50, 101.
52. B. A. Gilenson, *Sotsialisticheskaia traditsiia v literature SShA* (Socialist Tradition in the Literature of the United States) (Moscow, 1975), 50.
53. Gusev, *Chronicle,* 18; Tolstoy, *Works,* vol. 66, 33.
54. Tolstoy, *Works,* vol. 71, 288. [*Social Gospel* was published for only a few years, 1898–1901—ed].

Tolstoy's own views on the way in which the struggle with the evil of capitalism was to be conducted were wrong, but this did not prevent him from persuasively criticizing the ideas of reformers. While he accepted Bellamy's vision of a utopian society in America in the year 2000, where the "struggle for survival" would be replaced by a life based on the principles of "social cooperation," the Russian writer found it hard to believe that this happy state of affairs would come about as the result of the simple evolution of various elements in capitalist society. In his journal he commented on the mechanical nature of Bellamy's concepts and offered an ironic summary of the American's ideas: "Capital flows into a small number of hands, and finally will belong to a single individual. The worker's unions will also coalesce into a single union. And capital and labor shall be separate. Then the government or the revolution will bring them together, and all will be well."[55]

In similar vein, after commenting favorably on the principles of Christian socialism advocated by the journal *Dawn* and on the demands for the nationalization of various branches of industry made by Bellamy's followers in *Nationalist,* Tolstoy remarked, "All this is very good. But the methods proposed by them to this end are ill-defined and vague, and cannot be otherwise. They deliver all kinds of sermons and want to replace competitiveness in business and life with the principle of fraternity. But how are these principles to be applied in the world of struggle?"[56] Returning to the subject a year later, Tolstoy compared the methods favored by *Dawn* and *Nationalist* to an attempt "to persuade particles of air not to rise as they are being heated."[57] He saw only one solution to these problems: "[One must] plug the hole of worldly desires."[58]

Of the numerous sociocritical doctrines advanced in the United States in the late nineteenth and early twentieth centuries, Tolstoy was most impressed by those of Henry George. In his chief work, *Progress and Poverty* (1879; Russian translation, 1896), George painted a vivid picture of the poverty in which masses of people lived and proposed the introduction of a single progressive tax on land as a means of nationalizing it. He thought that in this way all the contradictions of the capitalist order could be resolved. Tolstoy was attracted to George's idea of nationalization of land that echoed his own beliefs. "The aim of those who are on the side of progress is one which the Russian people has in my opinion always tried to achieve; it is the abolition of the institution of private land ownership."[59] In February 1885, after reading George's book, Tolstoy wrote to Vladimir Chertkov: "I was ill for a week and was absorbed by George and his latest—and first—book, *Progress and Poverty,* which made a very strong and happy impression on me."[60] Thereafter, whenever the Russian writer expressed support for the idea of nationalization of land, he invariably referred to George, who had "destroyed all the sophistic arguments with which religion and science have defended the ownership of land."[61] It is interesting that the first draft of *Resurrection* ended

55. Tolstoy, *Works,* vol. 50, 101.
56. Ibid., 128.
57. Ibid., 36.
58. Ibid., 37.
59. Tolstoy, *Works,* vol. 73, 229.
60. Tolstoy, *Works,* vol. 85, 144.
61. Tolstoy, *Works,* vol. 67, 105.

with Prince Nekhludov becoming a follower of George, giving away his lands to the peasants, marrying Katiusha Maslova, and settling with her on the outskirts of a city in Siberia.

With the approach of the first Russian revolution the land problem became more acute. In 1905 Tolstoy published articles, "To the Working People," "A Great Sin," and "The Only Possible Solution of the Land Question," in which he defended George's program. At the height of the revolution the writer voiced the hope that Russia would show the world the path it should follow in solving the land question.[62] Tolstoy remained a staunch supporter of land nationalization until the day he died. In March 1909, he wrote:

> The realization of Henry George's teaching, that is, the abolition of the institution of private land ownership or, to be more precise, the abolition of the slavery in which people live because of the private ownership of land, is as urgently necessary today as the emancipation of people in America and Russia from actual slavery was fifty years ago.[63]

Tolstoy's demand that the land be nationalized without compensation appeared to contradict his doctrine of "non-resistance to evil."

Although he was persistent in his calls for the abolition of the private ownership of land, Tolstoy did not share George's conviction that the nationalization of land was a panacea for all evils. Writing to him, Tolstoy cautiously remarked, "We are following different paths."[64] On another occasion, Tolstoy expressed himself more emphatically: "My demands go much further than his; but this is the first rung on the ladder that I am climbing."[65] Paradoxical as it may seem, the Russian writer, while supporting George, rejected an essential part of his theory—the proposal for a single tax on land. William Stead recalled that Tolstoy once told him: "The transfer of the land to the commune is better than nationalization. . . . Naturally, I cannot agree with George that the land must be taxed. Only if the angels in heaven were in charge of collecting the tax would this be done justly and without any abuses. Personally, I am opposed to taxation in any form."[66]

This is an interesting passage in several ways. First, it clearly shows Tolstoy's opposition to any additional taxation of the peasants, who were already obliged to pay high taxes to compensate the powers-that-be for the abolition of serfdom. The writer's semi-anarchist hostility to the state was also a factor. Finally, in proposing the transfer of the land to peasant communes Tolstoy was to some extent expressing the views of the Russian populists, who combined elements of utopian socialism with the peasants' demand for the breakup of the estates of the landowners. Continuing his criticism of

62. Tolstoy, *Works*, vol. 36, 143.
63. Tolstoy, *Works*, vol. 79, 137. In 1896 George and Tolstoy exchanged friendly letters and planned to meet at Iasnaia Poliana, but George's death in 1897 made this impossible. *Literary Heritage* 75, pt. 1, 456; Tolstoy, *Works*, vol. 67, 77.
64. Tolstoy, *Works*, vol. 67, 77.
65. Tolstoy, *Works*, vol. 83, 481.
66. *Literary Heritage* 75, pt. 2, 103.

the proposal for a single national tax on land, Tolstoy wrote in "The Slavery of Our Times" (1900) that this would "inevitably create a new form of slavery, because a man who is obliged to pay rent or a single tax, would be forced, if he suffered a bad harvest or some misfortune, to borrow money from those who had it, and would again fall into slavery."[67]

Tolstoy lived in an age of constant wars. With the dawning of the modern age they became a horrible daily reality for millions and millions of people. "Open the newspapers and, whatever their date of publication, you will always, immediately, find some black spot, a possible cause of war: this might be Korea, or the Pamir Mountains, or the African territories, or Abyssinia, or Armenia, or Turkey, or Venezuela, or the Transvaal. The evil work does not cease for a minute."[68]

Tolstoy's condemnation of war was based on moral principles. While working on *War and Peace* he had considered defensive wars to be just. Later, as a prophet of nonresistance, he came to reject all wars, including revolutionary ones. Tolstoy's statements as a social commentator are of enduring importance because of his strong and uncompromising opposition to the rising tide of militarism, which was such a characteristic feature of the modern age. His antimilitarist and antiwar statements, based on passionate commitment and irrefutable logic, were among the supreme examples of anti-imperialist protest.[69] For example, Rosa Luxemburg spoke of the strength with which Tolstoy denounced militarism.[70] His stand on this issue was of particular importance, for the whole world listened to the voice of the great Russian writer.

One of Tolstoy's first major statements as a thinker was his sociophilosophical pamphlet, "The Kingdom of God Within You" (1890–1893), in which he formulated the main tenets of his antimilitarist doctrine. Tolstoy stressed that militarism was a distinguishing characteristic of "modern civilized countries" and discussed its pernicious consequences. He wrote that "newer and newer methods of killing large numbers of people in the shortest time are being devised"[71] as the nations of the world devoted huge portions of their resources to military spending.

In the late nineteenth century, doctrines of imperialist expansion were formulated in the leading capitalist countries. Tolstoy criticized these ideas. He spoke of the danger presented by the ideologies of pan-Germanism, pan-Americanism, and pan-Slavism.

---

67. Tolstoy, *Works,* vol. 34, 177. Gusev (*Chronicle,* 321) refers to an interesting detail pertaining to Tolstoy's attitude toward George and Marx:

Once in conversation Tolstoy expressed the idea that "even very eminent individuals" often display a lack of respect for others. For example, in Henry George's *Progress and Poverty,* Marx's name is not mentioned at all, and in his recently and posthumously published work [*The Science of Political Economy* (New York, 1898)] Marx is dismissed in just eight lines.

68. Tolstoy, *Works,* vol. 90, 47.

69. For further details, see S. N. Chubakov, *Lev Tolstoi o voine i militarizme* (Leo Tolstoy on War and Militarism) (Minsk, 1973).

70. Luxemburg, *O literature* (On Literature) (Moscow, 1961), 100.

71. Tolstoy, *Works,* vol. 28, 103. Tolstoy subsequently developed the antimilitarist ideas of this pamphlet in an article, "Carthago delenda est," and in "Advice for a Soldier" (1901) and "Advice for an Officer" (1901) that were meant to counteract the militaristic indoctrination of army personnel.

He condemned the exponents of these views, figures like Kaiser Wilhelm II, the "divine mikado," and Nicholas II.[72]

Tolstoy wrote in his journal, "First one must discover the lock and its mechanism, and then find the key. The lock that would keep the spirit of war imprisoned."[73] The path Tolstoy followed in his search for a solution to this problem was the right one. "States and governments intrigue and fight for possession of the banks of the Rhine, territories in Africa and China, land on the Balkan Peninsula. . . . The evil is rooted in the notion of property: almost the entire world is engaged in distributing and defending property."[74] Tolstoy's first antiwar pamphlet contains this passage: "The army has always been and continues to be the foundation of authority. Power has always been in the hands of those who command the army, and the chief concern of all rulers—from the Roman Caesars to the emperors of Russia and Germany—has always been the army."[75]

Tolstoy continued to develop and express forcefully the idea that armies cause wars and that they are to blame for the repressive nature of the state, "be it the government of the Russian tsar, or of the Turkish sultan, or the British government with its Chamberlain and its colonial policy, or the government of the North American United States with its support for trusts and its imperialism."[76] He may have expressed this most clearly in his letter to Prince Grigorii Volkonskii of December 1899. "The causes of modern war are these," he wrote: "First, the unequal distribution of property, that is, the robbing by some people of other people; second, the existence of a military caste, that is, of men selected and trained for murder; and third, an impotent, and largely false, religion."[77] The concept of war and peace that Tolstoy developed toward the end of his life received perhaps its fullest and most vivid expression in his short novel *Hadji-Murad*.

Tolstoy's antiwar statements were never abstract in character. His protests against Italy's war with Abyssinia ("To the Italians," 1898), the Boer War (Letter to Volkonskii, 1899), the Russo-Japanese war ("Think Again!" 1904) were tremendously moving and powerful. In "Think Again!" the writer condemned the Russo-Japanese war as a terrible "evil," describing it as the murder of thousands and thousands of "deluded Russian working men." One of the "criminal wars of the modern age" denounced by Tolstoy was the Spanish-American war of 1898. His article, "Two Wars," condemned those responsible for starting the conflict. Tolstoy wrote it after receiving a letter from an American woman, Jessie Gladwin, who had asked him to comment "on the noble role of the American nation and the heroism of its soldiers and sailors in the war now taking place."[78] Tolstoy's indignant response was: "The Spanish-American War is a cruel and

72. Ibid., 180. Tolstoy was one of the first to understand that the "Nietzschean obsession" was a reactionary phenomenon. After reading *Thus Spake Zarathustra,* he remarked: "Imagine the state of society, if a madman like this—an evil madman—is recognized as a teacher." Tolstoy, *Works,* vol. 54, 77. [1]
73. Tolstoy, *Works,* vol. 57, 85.
74. Tolstoy, *Works,* vol. 25, 397–98.
75. Tolstoy, *Works,* vol. 28, 132.
76. Tolstoy, *Works,* vol. 36, 180.
77. Tolstoy, *Works,* vol. 72, 255.
78. *Literary Heritage* 75, pt. 1, 474.

stupid, untimely, primitive, pagan war."[79] Noting that America enjoyed a reputation as the most developed and democratic of countries, Tolstoy concluded: "It would seem that never has any nation fallen into such a state of base bestiality and intoxication."[80] [1] Reacting to the suppression of the national-liberation movement in the Philippines, he wrote in his diary on January 8, 1900: "I am reading about the wars in the Philippines and the Transvaal, and I feel horror and revulsion."[81]

The aggressive foreign policy of the United States at the turn of the century, and particularly the Spanish-American War of 1898, also aroused the indignation of democratic forces in America. Their protest against the policies of their government resulted in the emergence of an antiwar and anticolonial movement. This movement was composed of a variety of disparate elements and was led by the anti-imperialist leagues, in which petty-bourgeois intellectuals played the chief role.

The press was not Tolstoy's only source of information about the antiwar protests in America. Many Americans, including members of the anti-imperialist coalition, asked him for help and advice.[82] Mary Thayer stated that *War and Peace* had instilled in her high moral principles and had helped her realize the gravity of the crimes committed in the Philippines by the government of the United States.[83] Montague Leverson, a member of the anti-imperialist movement, sent Tolstoy the text of a speech he had given at an anti-imperialist rally in Philadelphia in February 1900 and asked the Russian writer to compose an appeal to the American people that would "stir the sleeping conscience of the American people."[84] In 1902 Herbert Welsh, a writer and political figure who was also active in the anti-imperialist movement, sent Tolstoy his antiwar book, *The Other Man's Country,* and a number of anti-imperialist pamphlets. In a letter to Tolstoy he described the torture used by the American army in the Philippines. Before the war Welsh had spoken out in defense of the rights of Native Americans and had taken part in the civil rights movement, then becoming the publisher of an antiwar newspaper, *City and State.* Tolstoy replied, "I cannot but admire your actions, but the crimes being committed in the Philippines are precisely those that will always take place in states governed by violent methods or which tolerate violence and employ them as necessary and legal instruments."[85]

Of all members of the anti-imperialist movement, Tolstoy was closest to the American poet, publicist, and social activist Ernest Crosby, addressing him as "My very good friend Crosby" in 1903.[86] Under the impact of Tolstoy's philosophy, Crosby resigned his seat on the International Court, where he had represented the United States, and renounced his political career. In 1894 he came to see the Russian writer at Iasnaia

79. Tolstoy, *Works,* vol. 31, 97.
80. Ibid., 250.
81. Tolstoy, *Works,* vol. 54, 7.
82. The question of Tolstoy's relations with the anti-imperialists was first explored by American historian D. B. Schirmer, "American Anti-Imperialism and the Russian Revolution," in *For Dirk Struik,* edited by R. S. Cohen et al. (Dordrecht, 1974), 605–16.
83. See *Literary Heritage* 75, pt. 1, 347.
84. Ibid., 475.
85. Tolstoy, *Works,* vol. 73, 338.
86. Tolstoy, *Works,* vol. 74, 143.

Poliana. Later the novelist recalled that he had been struck by the purity and sincerity of his American visitor. When Crosby asked Tolstoy for advice about the kind of political activity he should engage in, the writer suggested he should support the cause of Henry George.[87]

Upon his return to the United States, Crosby became an active propagandist of Tolstoy's teaching. He wrote "Count Tolstoy's Philosophy of Life" (Russian translation published in 1911), founded the League for Social Reform, which consistently defended the interests of the workers, and then assumed the leadership of the Anti-imperialist League of New York. During this period he wrote antimilitarist pamphlets and satirical poems in which he attacked the war fever in his country and the colonial policy of the United States in Cuba and the Philippines. His satirical novel *Captain Jinks, a Hero* became one of the most popular works of anti-imperialist literature. A poem, "The New Liberty," contained these lines: "Grab Cuba, Hawaii, seduce Canada, occupy the great Southern hemisphere from one end to the other. But do these countries want to belong to you?"[88] Tolstoy approved of what Crosby was doing, noting that he and the American "think and feel the same."[89]

Tolstoy's ideas, his antimilitarist views, and his statements condemning the aggressive war waged by the United States against Spain made such a strong impact on public opinion that the American proponents of expansionism tried to neutralize his influence. One of the most extreme ideologues of American expansionism, Josiah Strong, who combined a belief in America's Christian mission with a Social-Darwinist justification of Anglo-Saxon racism, called the opponents of colonial expansion "philosophical anarchists" and "pupils of Count Tolstoy."[90] A few years later President Theodore Roosevelt, a "pragmatic expansionist," offered his own response to the Russian thinker. In his article "Tolstoy," which appeared in *Outlook,* Roosevelt acknowledged Tolstoy's stature as a "great writer" and a "great artist" but attacked the main principles of his moral and philosophical teaching, declaring that it was a "poor guide" for "men of action."[91] It is interesting that some time later Tolstoy happened to read Roosevelt's article, which had been reprinted in the newspaper, *Russkoe Slovo* (Russian Word).[92] The essay by the American president inspired this brief comment in Tolstoy's journal, "The article is silly."[93] Earlier Tolstoy had said about Roosevelt: "I only know that he is a militarist and an imperialist."[94]

Fate introduced Tolstoy to another American politician, William Jennings Bryan, a complex and contradictory figure, who to a large extent expressed the interests of rural America. In the elections of 1896 and 1900, in which he was the presidential candidate

---

87. Tolstoy, *Works,* vol. 40, 339–40. See Crosby's description of his visit to Iasnaia Poliana in "Two Days with Count Tolstoy," *Progressive Review* 2 (1897).
88. Gorbunov-Posadov, "Ernest Crosby," xxv.
89. Tolstoy, *Works,* vol. 77, 22.
90. J. Strong, *Expansion under New World Conditions* (New York, 1900), 212, 276.
91. *Outlook* 92 (1909): 103–5.
92. See V. Krugliak's essay, "Rusvel't o Tolstom" (Roosevelt on Tolstoy) *Russkoe Slovo* (Russian Word), May 19, 1909.
93. Tolstoy, *Works,* vol. 57, 70.
94. *Literary Heritage* 75, pt. 1, 479.

of the Democratic Party, Bryan put forward a series of proposals that reflected the farmers' opposition to the power of the railroad companies and the dominant influence of the banks. He criticized the trusts, yet he was a typical bourgeois politician. During the Spanish-American War, Bryan, in order to acquire the aura of a patriot, joined the American expeditionary force as a volunteer and subsequently spoke out in favor of the Paris peace treaty, which turned the Philippines into a colony of the United States. In the election of 1900, however, Bryan, in an attempt to gain the support of the broadest sections of the American people, made "anti-imperialism" the central issue of the campaign and strongly criticized the policy of colonial conquest. "The farmers and workers form the vast majority of the American people. What will these annexations bring it?" he asked. "Higher taxes, Asian immigration, and the prospect of sending its sons to serve in the army."[95] In January 1901, Bryan's newspaper, *The Commoner,* referring to a statement supposedly made by Tolstoy, declared: "You, Americans, are worse than the Muslims. They preach war—and fight, you preach peace—and undertake wars of conquest." And Bryan added, "The Russian philosopher is wise enough to know that commerce is the motive force of imperialism, while the phrases about 'destiny and the obligations of the United States' are no more than a smokescreen."[96]

In 1903 Bryan, while traveling in Europe, requested a meeting with Tolstoy. Petr Sergienko, one of the people close to Tolstoy, writes that the meeting, which took place on December 5, 1903, at Iasnaia Poliana, was very friendly. Unfortunately, the text of the conversation has not survived, although the American reporter Harry Flynn, who was present, made a shorthand record of what was said. According to Sergienko, Tolstoy and Bryan "discussed religion and economic and other matters that affect the life of mankind today. And the more they spoke, the clearer it became that they understood and respected each other."[97] When the Russian writer stated that the independence of Cuba, which the United States had described as its war aim, had been no more than a pretext, and that in fact the American government had been motivated by entirely different considerations, Bryan fully agreed with him.[98] The American visitor spent such a long time at Iasnaia Poliana that he postponed his departure for St. Petersburg for his scheduled audience with Nicholas II.[99]

Under the impact of his meeting with Tolstoy, Bryan wrote an article, "The Apostle of Love," while in his reply to a letter from Bryan Tolstoy stated: "I wish you with all my heart success in your efforts to destroy the trusts and to help the working people enjoy the fruits of their labor."[100] And later Tolstoy remembered him warmly as "an intelligent and progressive American."[101] In a letter to Randolph Jennings in September 1908 he wrote, "I have great respect and sympathy for Mr. Bryan and know

95. *Congressional Record,* 56th Cong., 1st Sess., 33, pt. 8, 451.
96. Schirmer, "American Anti-Imperialism," 607–8.
97. P. Sergienko, "Tolstoi i Brian" (Tolstoy and Bryan), in *Tolstoi i ego sovremenniki* (Tolstoy and His Contemporaries) (Moscow, 1911), 249.
98. P. E. Coletta, *William Jennings Bryan,* vol. 1 (Lincoln, 1964), 318; Schirmer, "American Anti-Imperialism," 608.
99. Sergienko, "Tolstoy and Bryan," 249.
100. Tolstoy, *Works,* vol. 75, 17.
101. Tolstoy, *Works,* vol. 36, 97.

that the principles, on which he bases his activities, coincide with mine in regard to the working masses, anti-imperialism, and recognizing the ashes spread by capitalism."[102] Even though these words did not exactly describe Bryan's goals, they vividly illustrate how Tolstoy wanted to see the American politician.

It is difficult to compare the antimilitarist and antiwar views of Tolstoy and the American anti-imperialists. Their beliefs had been formed in two very different political environments and spiritual climates. Moreover, the movement of the anti-imperialist leagues was markedly heterogeneous in its social composition, reflecting a spectrum of American opinion, for the leagues included reform-minded intellectuals and representatives of the Populist opposition, as well as the supporters of dollar expansionism whose isolationism was merely a modified version of the same imperialist foreign policy.[103]

Nevertheless, there was clearly much in common between Tolstoy's views and the views of those whom Lenin described as "the last Mohicans of bourgeois democracy."[104] Both criticized militarism and war from humanistic positions; but if the American anti-imperialists used arguments that were largely constitutional in character, Tolstoy's reasoning reflected his concerns as a moral philosopher. Both realized that the pursuit of an imperialist foreign policy abroad entailed repressions and the violation of democratic freedoms at home. Tolstoy and the left wing of the anti-imperialist movement showed some understanding of the connection between the policies of expansionism and the interests of the trusts. The Russian writer and the American anti-imperialist coalition undoubtedly made a major contribution to the humanist tradition of antimilitarism in the new and cruel age.

There were also important differences. The anti-imperialists believed in the ideals of bourgeois democracy and the principles of "free competition." They did not attempt to bring about radical change in the socioeconomic system of the United States, but instead tried to prevent their country from conducting colonial conquests and waging wars of aggression, hoping to save it from corruption by these two evils, which were among the most repulsive manifestations of imperialism. The anti-imperialists treated the question of expansion narrowly as one of direct colonial expansion, and by and large would only employ legal methods in their struggle.

This was not so in the case of Tolstoy. Living and fighting for justice in a country where the forces of political and social oppression were particularly brutal and brazen, he proceeded from the assumption that the sociopolitical system existing in Russia must be destroyed. He refused to limit himself to the advocacy of half-measures. In this respect Tolstoy's views reflected the scale and power of the Russian revolution. Tolstoy's convictions shaped his approach to foreign policy issues, even though his religious doctrine was based on the principle of "non-resistance to evil by violence." In an unpublished article, "To the Italians" (1895), the writer stated:

102. Tolstoy, *Works,* vol. 78, 231.
103. See Dement'ev, *Ideinaia bor'ba v SShA po vosprosam ekspansii (na rubezhe XIX–XX vv.)* (The Ideological Struggle in the United States on the Issue of Expansion [at the Turn of the Century]) (Moscow, 1973).
104. Lenin, *Works,* vol. 27, 409.

Consider: the time will come, and very soon, when after enduring terrible misfortunes and bloodshed the tired, maimed, suffering peoples will say to their rulers: just go to the devil or go with God, go to whoever sent you, put on these silly uniforms yourselves, fight and blow each other up in any way you like, carve up Europe and Asia, Africa and America on the map, but leave us, the people who worked this land and fed you, in peace. . . . Is it not clear that they are planning and preparing a terrible crime and that if we do not stop them now, this crime will take place—if not today, then tomorrow.[105]

Tolstoy's views on the methods to be used in the struggle against war were interesting. He observed the proceedings of the various international conferences with close attention and considerable distrust, believing that the speeches made at these gatherings merely masked the preparations for war. When in 1899 a conference on disarmament was organized in The Hague at the instigation of, among others, Nicholas II, the *New York World* asked Tolstoy for his opinion on this subject; he replied: "The Hague conference is merely a repulsive manifestation of Christian hypocrisy." The draft of his response contained the statement that the problem of preserving the peace "can be solved by people who not only chatter, but who (are obliged to fight) have to go to war themselves."[106]

That same year, in a letter, "To a Group of Swedish Intellectuals," the writer again declared that The Hague conference was an attempt to draw attention away from preparations for new wars. He appealed to those who were subject to conscription to refuse to perform their military service. He reported with great satisfaction that he had received an important piece of news from the theatre of operations in the Philippines: "An American regiment refused to go to Ilo-Ilo" to fight the Filipinos. Tolstoy continued: "All Americans going to Manila know what Bryan said about the American government's mania for conquest. They have heard that he called this an evil, immoral act. And every reasonable man must know that it is wrong to oppress morally the freedoms of peoples."[107]

Tolstoy viewed the soldiers' refusal to fight as a concrete example of the kind of passive opposition to evil he called "resistance by non-resistance." The only anti-imperialist in the United States who had advocated similar methods of struggle was Edward Atkinson. In his pamphlets, "The Cost of War and Warfare," "The Hell of War," and others, he called on the country's youth to refuse to fight. This caused such alarm to the American authorities that they demanded Atkinson's arrest. In the end it was decided that his works would be removed from the mail being delivered to the field forces in the Philippines. In the interviews he gave to the press Atkinson said that he was acting in the spirit of Tolstoy.[108]

In spite of the differences in the historical experience and traditions of Russia and America the best minds of the two countries attempted to tackle similar ethical and social problems. Their approach to these problems was often the same. There

---

105. Tolstoy, *Works,* vol. 31, 195–96.
106. Tolstoy, *Works,* vol. 72, 116–17.
107. Tolstoy, *Works,* vol. 9, 12–13.
108. Schirmer, "American Anti-Imperialism," 606.

was thus a great deal in common between Tolstoy, who reflected the strengths and weaknesses of the first Russian revolution, and the American social critics who were his contemporaries. The views that Russia's great novelist and the American social critics shared, the relations between them, and the way in which they influenced each other at the turn of the century form a vital chapter in history that continues to be of relevance today. Like every other important element in their heritage, their socioethical pathos, exposé of capitalism, denunciation of militarism and war, and support for the ideals of international peace and cooperation live on in the world of the late twentieth century.

9

American History and Policy on the Pages of *Delo* [Cause] and *Slovo* [Word], by I. K. Mal'kova

Starting in the late 1860s, a number of factors led to a marked increase in the interest that the history and modern political development of the United States inspired among the progressive elements in Russian society. The analysis of the results of that development not only provided them with a means for criticizing the semifeudal conditions in tsarist Russia, but also encouraged them to compare the ideas they had conceived about a just solution to the grave problems of Russian life with the actual results of bourgeois progress in its purest form.

It should be noted that the union of the North American states had drawn the attention of progressive Russian thinkers as early as the end of the eighteenth century, during the War for Independence and establishment of the Republic.[1] Democratic circles in Russian society felt sympathy for the just struggle for the elimination of slavery in the United States.[2] On the whole, however, the response in Russia to the events taking place in the Republic beyond the ocean was by and large sporadic, comprising, as it did, reports of an informational nature. With the outbreak of the Civil War, America began to

---

1. The few studies by Russian scholars on the early period in the relationship between Russian society and America (eighteenth and early nineteenth centuries) are discussed by N. N. Bolkhovitinov in *Stanovlenie russko-amerikanskikh otnoshenii* (The Establishment of Russian-American Relations) (Moscow, 1966) [English edition—*The Beginnings of Russian-American Relations, 1775–1815* (Cambridge and London, 1975)]. This article by I. K. Mal'kova was first published in *Amerikanskii Ezhegodnik* (Moscow, 1971), 169–82.

2. See I. P. Dement'ev, "N. G. Chernyshevskii i konstitutsiia Dzhona Brauna" (N. G. Chernyshevsky and John Brown's Constitution), *Voprosy istorii* (Problems of History) 12 (1959): 137–44; I. Ia. Levitas, "Grazhdanskaia voina v Soedinennykh Shtatakh (1861–1865 gg.) i russkoe obshchestvo" (The Civil War in the United States [1861–1865] and Russian Society), diss. abstract (Moscow, 1965); R. F. Ivanov, *Linkol'n i grazhdanskaia voina v SShA* (Lincoln and the Civil War in the United States) (Moscow, 1964); *K 100-letiiu grazhdanskoi voiny v SSha* (In Honor of the Centenary of the Civil War in the United States) (Moscow, 1965).

attract the attention of progressive Russians in what one journal, *Delo* (Cause), termed its "more serious and instructive" aspects.³ Year after year democratically oriented Russian journals like *Sovremennik* (Contemporary), *Russkoe Slovo* (Russian Word), *Otechestvennye Zapiski* (Fatherland Notes), and *Cause* remained loyal to the best traditions of the 1860s in the new historical situation that had arisen, continued to participate actively in the struggle against autocracy and the vestiges of serfdom, and provided the Russian reader with ever more comprehensive accounts of the socioeconomic experience of the advanced countries of Western Europe and America.

The extraordinarily rapid economic progress of the American nation, which with one mighty revolutionary effort had eliminated slavery—the chief obstacle on the path of capitalist development—attracted the attention of the entire Russian public, but the economic upsurge in America was characterized by a number of contradictions. Immediately, it had won the United States a place among the advanced industrialized countries of the world, but it had also brought the nation face to face with the inevitable consequences of the concomitant outburst of capitalist rapaciousness—crises of overproduction, unemployment, corruption among the elite, and the intensification of social conflicts. The Russian democratic movement was, as it were, discovering America for a second time—as a country of popular revolutions and of merciless oppression (and even extermination) of national minorities, a country that enjoyed a relatively high degree of democracy in its system of government yet suffered from patriarchal barbarism in the various spheres of social life, a country where the most advanced forms of education had been widely spread but large sections of the population (Negroes, women, immigrants) had no social rights. Of the Russian periodicals of the period, the journals *Cause* and *Slovo* (Word) offered the fullest and most profound analyses of the processes that took place in the course of America's socioeconomic and political development after the Civil War.

The literary-political journal *Cause* (1866–1888) was a direct successor to the progressive traditions of *Contemporary* and *Russian Word,* which had been suppressed by the tsarist government in 1866, the same year *Cause* commenced publication in St. Petersburg. After *Fatherland Notes, Cause* was the most popular journal among the non-noble sections of society, as well as among Russian youth. For many years (1866–1880) it was edited by Grigorii Blagosvetlov, the former editor of *Russian Word,* and after his death by Nikolai Shelgunov (until his arrest in 1881). The nucleus of the journal's editorial board was composed of distinguished publicists and prominent figures of the Russian and foreign revolutionary movements, such as Dmitri Pisarev, Shelgunov, Petr Tkachev, Afanasii Shchapov, Vasilii Bervi-Flerovskii, Lev Mechnikov, Aleksandr Sheller-Mikhailov, Serafim Shashkov, Veniamin Portugalov, and Elie Reclus—*Cause's* foreign commentator, who most often wrote under the pseudonyms Jacques LeFrene and Trigot. In the later years the editorial board included figures like Konstantin Staniukovich, Sergei Stepniak-Kravchinksii, Peter Lavrov, Lev Tikhomirov, Victor Jaclard (Reclus's successor as commentator on events abroad), and many others.⁴

---

3. *Cause* 4 (1872), pt 2: 63.
4. For more details, see B. I. Esin, *Demokraticheskii zhurnal "Delo"* (The Democratic Journal "Cause") (Moscow, 1959); Esin, *Russkaia zhurnalistika 70–80-kh veka* (Russian Journalism in

Word commenced publication in St. Petersburg in 1878, but after receiving several warnings from the tsarist authorities, it was suppressed in April 1881. Among the writers whose articles appeared in it were Maksim Antonovich (the former editor of *Sovremenik*), Semen Vengerov (the future editor of the populist journal *Ustoi* [Foundations]), Nikolai Ziber, B. Lenskii (B. P. Ongirskii), and others. Jaclard—a close friend of Paul Lafargue, a prominent figure in the international revolutionary movement, and an active member of the Paris Commune—also wrote for the periodical. He acted as an intermediary when the editors of *Word* invited Karl Marx and his daughter, Jenny, to become contributors to the journals.[5]

The attention devoted by these two journals to America constantly grew. The publicists of *Word* wrote: "The more closely a thinking individual looks at America, the more his thoughts tend to dwell on her."[6] In 1870 the journal declared, "We have a particular point in common with America—namely, economic reform, which was carried out there by means of the emancipation of Negroes and in our country by means of the abolition of serfdom. For the Russian reader the consequences of these two events, which took place in parallel, are very interesting in terms of their significance and character."[7] Later Lenin also commented on the concurrence of these two major events in the history of the two countries.[8]

During its twenty-odd years of existence, *Cause* published many articles and reviews concerning the history and political life of the American nation. Considerable space was devoted to the problems of history of civil society in America, including those relating to bourgeois democracy and economic policy of the United States.[9] The journal informed its readers about the state and scale of the women's movement in that country, popular education,[10] the religious question,[11] the problems of emigration and the new phenomenon of immigration,[12] and other subjects.[13]

---

the 1870s and 1880s) (Moscow, 1963); V. G. Serebrennikova, "Demokraticheskaia zhurnalistika perioda vtoroi revoliutsionnoi situatsii" (Democratic Journalism during the Second Revolutionary Situation), *Obshchestvennoe dvizhenie v poreformennoi Rossii* (The Social Movement in Post-Reform Russia) (Moscow, 1965), 344–65.

5. See *K. Marks, F. Engel's i revoliutsionnaia Rossiia* (K. Marx, F. Engels and Revolutionary Russia) (Moscow, 1969), 343–44. [Charles-Victor Jaclard, a follower of Auguste Blanqui and Bakunin, was married to a Russian, Anna Korvin-Krukovskaia, a close friend of Dostoevsky and also a writer. See I. S. Knizhnik-Vetrov, *Russkie deiatel'nitsy pervogo internationala i Parizhskoi kommuny* (Russian Activist Women of the First International and Paris Commune) (Moscow-Leningrad, 1964), 137–216—ed].

6. *Cause* 6 (1872), pt 2: 50.

7. *Cause* 5 (1870), pt 2: 45.

8. See Lenin, *Poln. sobr. soch.* (Collected Works), vol. 22, 345–46.

9. See L. I. Mechnikov, "Khlebnyi vopros v Amerike i Evrope" (The Grain Problem in America and Europe), 5 (1880), pt. 1: 49–87; 6, pt. 1: 133–75; and "Protektsionizm v Amerike," 7 (1880), pt. 1: 299–335; 8, pt. 1: 86–119. In "Odno-storonmost' promyshennogo progressa" (The One-Sided Nature of Industrial Progress), Shelgunov devoted a number of pages to the rapidly growing economy of the United States; 4 (1869), pt. 1: 274–303.

10. While harshly criticizing the policies of the tsarist government in the area of popular education, the journal informed its readers about those of other countries, particularly the United States. In the opinion of the contributors to the journal, in this respect the young Republic had left the most advanced countries of Western Europe far behind. The writers for *Cause*

Among the contributors to *Cause* who devoted particular attention to these topics was Nikolai Shelgunov. In the first issues of the journal he had already noted the growing interest toward the United States in Russia, declaring that America was a mass of astonishing and supremely fascinating mysteries. He was the author of full-length articles ("Studies in the History of the North American Union"[14] and "American Patriots of the Last Century"[15]), the notes on America in the section "News about Life Abroad," and miscellaneous items that were included in articles on contemporary problems of Russian life.

The two articles by Shelgunov treat the period from the establishment of the first settlements in the recently discovered lands of the New World to the end of the War of Independence and the election of George Washington as the first president of the Republic in 1789. Shelgunov discusses in some detail the history of the colonization of America, showing that economically it was to a considerable extent dependent on the labor of white slaves. The appearance of the institution of white slavery and its rapid spread had led, in his opinion, to the result that, "when the first ship carrying blacks arrived, public opinion was already completely in favor of slavery."[16]

---

argued for the complete separation of school and church, expressed the belief that interference by the church had had a pernicious effect on the schools for children of the common people, hailed the democratic character of American schools, and pointed out that the American school system (from elementary to high school level) was subjected to no other influence than the secular. See V. V. Bervi-Flerovskii, "Ne luchshe le molchat' po etomu voprosu?" (Would It Not Be Better to Keep Silent on This Question?), 2 (1871) pt. 3: 307–30, and "Pravo na vospitanie i obuchenie" (The Right to Instruction and Education) 3 (1871), pt. 2: 104–20. Shelgunov, in "Zemstvo samoupravlenie i narodnaia shkola" (Zemstvo Self-government and the Popular School), devoted considerable attention to the "free American school" and described the advantages of the American system, 12 (1870), pt. 2: 1–38. See also *Cause* 7 (1867), pt. 2: 84–103. In 1873 the same journal carried a lengthy and very interesting article by Mikhailov (A. K. Sheller-Mikhailov), "Pervonachal'noe obrazovanie v Severo-Amerikanskikh Shtatakh" (Primary Education in the North American States), 9, pt. 2: 1–36; and 10, pt. 2: 36–84. [3]

11. The history of the church in the United States and its current status were discussed by Elie Reclus in "Religioznye sekty v Amerike" (Religious Sects in America) 2 (1876), pt. 1: 260–95; 3, pt. 1: 247–355; 5, pt. 1: 115–42; by S. S. Shashkov, "Tsarstvo mormonov" (The Kingdom of the Mormons) 12 (1871), pt. 1: 97–118; and by Shelgunov and Reclus in articles and notes they wrote for the section "Political and Social Chronicle" (see, for example, 5 [1872], pt. 2: 28–33).

12. The issue of emigration to the United States was the subject of the following articles: "Emigratsiia v Severo-Amerikanskie Soedinennye Shtaty" (Emigration to the North American United States) by B. Ongirskii [B. Lenskii] in 11 (1871), pt. 2: 60–83; "Emigratsiia v Ameriku" (Emigration to America) by an anonymous author (probably, L. I. Mechnikov) in 10 (1876), pt. 2: 88–101; "Kolonizatsiia v Avstralii i v Amerike" (Colonization in Australia and in America) by Mechnikov in 11 (1880), pt. 1: 60–93 and 12, pt. 1: 105–39; and others (see *Cause* 4 [1873], pt. 2: 432–48; and 2 [1876], pt. 2: 88–89). The main thrust of these articles was that immigration was a blessing for the United States and one of the main sources of its rapidly growing prosperity. [3]

13. Thus, *Cause* published a long article by Tkachev, "Amerikanskie tiur'my" (American Prisons) in 3 (1867), pt. 2: 137–50. The considerable amount of information it contains about the American system of justice in the nineteenth century in all its negative aspects is still of interest to the modern reader.

14. See *Cause* 11 (1867), pt. 1: 95–137; 12, pt. 1: 60–99.
15. *Cause* 1 (1868), pt. 1: 57–117; 2, pt. 1: 42–91.
16. *Cause* 11 (1867), pt. 1: 108.

Shelgunov was interested in the history of the colonization of America and the conditions in which the rudiments of the internal political organization of the country took shape because it was these inchoate political structures that eventually provided the basis for the constitutional system of the United States. The American Constitution, as Shelgunov wrote, was the product of the entire previous history of the people, it was nothing but the external form of their internal existence, a reflection of the people's world outlook including their prejudices and misconceptions.[17] His second article contains a comprehensive evaluation of the Constitution itself and a detailed analysis of that document, and describes the intense struggle surrounding its adoption, how executive and judicial authority was organized after the achievement of independence, and the role of the president and his prerogatives and duties.

In his "Studies," Shelgunov devoted considerable attention to the genesis of many of the states and the ways in which they developed and offered an analysis of the internal logic of the independence movement, which turned the persecuted into persecutors. The intolerance of the supporters of independence, he observed, had led in turn to the establishment of new colonies, where the main principles of social relations were civil equality and freedom of conscience. The contribution of these communities to the judicial institutions of the United States was, in the author's opinion, extremely important. At the same time, he believed that the growing acceptance of the principle of individualism was the most important feature of the entire social life of the United States and that this principle had to a considerable degree shaped the country's internal political system.

The very structure and tenor of Shelgunov's articles were meant to convince the Russian reader of the advantages offered by the republican system of government and comparatively well-developed democracy. It is, therefore, easy to understand why his evaluation of the Constitution was by and large so positive. Today's reader might find many lacunae and questionable assertions in Shelgunov's articles, but these deficiencies are compensated by the author's revolutionary-democratic party spirit, his civic passion, the commendable vigor and the depth of his thinking, and finally, by his immaculate style.

Only a short period of time had passed since the great acts of emancipation that had concluded the Civil War, since the United States, as Shelgunov put it, had emerged victorious from "its recent difficult internal struggle."[18] The progressive circles in Russian society were almost unanimous in their opinion: America has a shining future, which will open up new vistas for mankind. The Americans' industriousness, inventiveness, and entrepreneurial spirit, and the relatively high degree of democracy in the government institutions they had created, would serve as a guarantee.[19] "Before us stands America," Portugalov echoed. "More than that, before us stands the New World.... America! This word expresses something so good it can be found nowhere else. The whole of mankind hopes that America will fulfill all the best dreams, all

---

17. Ibid., 96.
18. *Cause* 7 (1867), pt. 2: 84.
19. Ibid., 97–102; 6 (1872), pt. 2: 49.

the cherished desires and aspirations of the noblest friends of mankind."[20] In another article ("On Degeneration") he stated that, because America was not fettered by social despotism, was not constrained by class interest, "did not hold in her grip a single enslaved nation, condemned by her to immolation,"[21] it was "immune from and uncontaminated by the process of degeneration."[22]

Nevertheless, in the early 1870s several of the foreign reviews that appeared in *Cause* described the evidence of demoralization and corruption in the political institutions of the United States, developments that had a deleterious effect on the nation's entire social structure. In this connection, the view expressed by the author of the lengthy "Political Chronicle," which appeared in the July issues of the journal for 1872, is particularly interesting. Despite his appreciation of the achievements of the republican system in general, he wrote:

> But if, as the proverb says, one should not excessively indulge one's vices; and there is no doubt that in a community of states, just as in a community of individuals, the one that is the most immoral is the one that will suffer the most. Of course, at present it is impossible to find any sign of moral decay in the United States, but one must not forget that the Americans tend to advance in positive, as well as in negative, ways incomparably faster than other nations, and who knows what will happen to them if they do not take decisive measures against the terrible evil that is demoralizing their administration!
>
> This is what the United States is being told by its true friends, who see the looming danger and wish to prevent it. There is no doubt that should the people of the United States desire, they could easily carry out a radical reform of their corrupt administration because of holding power in their own hands; but it is necessary that they should decide to do this earnestly and before it would be too late.[23]

The mid-1870s in a sense marked a watershed in the evolution of the views of the publicists of *Cause* regarding bourgeois democracy in the United States and the nature of the socioeconomic relations that had emerged in American society as it marched along the path of capitalist progress. This was undoubtedly nurtured by the analysis of prospects for the development of Russian society that democratic thinkers as a whole had typically

---

20. *Cause* 7 (1870), pt. 2: 23.
21. *Cause* 3 (1871), pt. 1: 186. It is doubtful that writers of *Cause,* such as Shelgunov, Reclus, and others, would have agreed with Portugalov's views on this question. They had repeatedly stressed the mercilessness with which the Yankees had carried out the extermination of the entire people. "The Indians were not only everywhere forced out, they were massacred and, moreover, the Europeans endeavoured to justify this violence by employing a variety of legal sophisms" (11 [1867], pt. 1: 110). "This is how civilization acts in the forests of America," Reclus exclaimed (2 [1867], pt. 2: 87). The systematic extermination of the Native Americans, the establishment of reservations where their shameless exploitation was encouraged by the pastors, Quakers, and Methodists, who by the will of the government had become their guardians, was described by V. A. Timiraizev, "Severo-Amerikanskie Soedinennye Shtaty posle stoletnego sushchestvovaniia" (The North American United States after One Hundred Years of Existence) 3 (1876), pt. 2: 323–36.
22. *Cause* 3 (1871), pt. 1: 182.
23. *Cause* 6 (1872), pt. 2: 46–47.

come to offer. The revolutionary movement thus concentrated on defining the problem of capitalism, which Lenin considered to be its great historical achievement.[24] The publicists based their search for its solution in Russia on materials and conclusions that not only accumulated initial data about capitalist tendencies in the country's economy but also shed light on the relevant experience in Europe and America. Soviet scholars have paid little attention to the attitude of the "men of the 1860s" and the "men of the 1870s" toward the American experience, although it has been recognized that "representatives of the populist generation of the 1870s became extremely 'anxious' about the problem of capitalism in Russia before the end of that decade."[25]

In the 1870s *Cause* failed to develop a unified position on this problem, though the approach adopted by some of its contributors may be recognized as realistic, since they questioned the populist thesis that Russia would be able to avoid the capitalist stage. Indeed, on the pages of the journal are statements to the effect that Russia would go through the same stages of development as countries of the West.[26] This may explain why *Cause* began to devote greater attention to an American theme in general and to contemporary tendencies in the economic and political life of the United States in particular, and why the attitude of those of its contributors who wrote about America grew comparably more critical.

The orgy of enrichment fed by financial speculations and swindles of various kinds, the concentration of capital achieved at the expense of the ruin of small owners, and of the pauperization of certain strata of the working population provoked condemnation and moral protests on the part of these writers. It also led them to revise, on the basis of a more profound study of economic factors, several earlier interpretations of the basic trends in the historical development of the United States. The country that, in the words of one of *Cause's* contributors, had given "so many great examples of incorruptible honesty and heroic nobility,"[27] suddenly showed a different side—one that until then had remained hidden. A lengthy article by "Ia. L. P-r," "The American Plutocracy," manifests this new approach perhaps for the first time.

"The unflattering reports concerning the present state of affairs in the United States," wrote the author, "grow more numerous by the day; they arrive from every direction, but all of them testify equally to the profound corruption of the legislative and every other branch of the American government and to the spirit of exploitation that reigns in that society."[28] This moral deterioration, he observed, had taken place unexpectedly and in a precipitous fashion which was characteristically American.[29] "Ia. L. P-r"

---

24. Lenin, *Works,* vol. 2, 531.
25. *V. I. Lenin i russkaia obshchestvenno-politicheskaia mysl' XIX-nachala XX v.* (V. I. Lenin and Russian Sociopolitical Thought in the Nineteenth and Early Twentieth Century) (Leningrad, 1969), 145.
26. B. P. Kozmin, *Iz istorii revoliutsionnoi mysle v Rossii* (From the History of Revolutionary Thought in Russia) (Moscow, 1961), 678–80; V. A. Tvardovskaia, *Sotsialisticheskaia mysl' v Rossii na rubezhe 1860–1870-kh godov* (Socialist Thought in Russia in the late 1860s and Early 1870s) (Moscow, 1969), 76–77.
27. *Cause* 11 (1876), pt. 2: 173.
28. Ibid., 146.
29. Ibid., 148.

dwells on the demoralization of political life in the United States, the corruption of its administrative system, instances of the abuse of authority, and the process that led to the estrangement of the legislative bodies from the masses of the people. "In every sphere of government the popular representatives are men who were not really chosen by the people but were rather imposed upon them by means of open deceit, clandestine intrigues, and bribery," he wrote.[30] Government authority in the United States is increasingly concentrated in the hands of the plutocrats, those "knights of speculation, who have a direct and personal interest in governing the country."[31] All these shameful developments are the result of "the factor that dominates our age,"[32] namely the feverish desire for a quick and easy profit.

The publication in August 1879 in *Word* of Nikolai Ziber's article, "The Fiasco of National Liberalism,"[33] was also highly significant. Its author devoted special attention to the impact of the rapid development of new forms of capitalist enrichment on every sphere of the spiritual and political life of American society. The propositions advanced by Ziber and the evidence on which he based them would have been impossible to find in any article published in the 1860s or even the early 1870s. With unconcealed irony the author acknowledged that "in the 1820s and 1840s, and even to a certain extent until very recently, the republic of the United States was a kind of political Eldorado . . . a state that was exemplary in every way."[34] But such idealization of the conditions reigning in America had prevented a sober examination of the reality of that country.

> What has our public been told by the organs of national liberalism, in whose interest it is to conceal all this, about the financial-legislative thread that runs through these endless bank peculations, the pernicious gambling with shares, the serious crimes in the field of government finance, the cases of the million-dollar embezzlers . . . the unbecoming conduct of the boards of the banks and the railroads, the immorality of the highest-ranking government officials and representatives of the people, the venality of the judges, etc.? Nothing or very little.[35]

Ziber agreed fully with a statement by a New York newspaper that he thought necessary to make known to his Russian readers. The passage quoted is, despite its length, extraordinarily pithy and, we venture to say, retains its relevance even today.

> America, the land of contradictions and impossibilities, of prudery squared and unbridled free-thinking, obligatory freedom and humiliating tyranny, is, whatever the names chosen for all these contradictions, the very same republic which homegrown orators and incorrigible idealists willingly cite as a paragon of the form of government; in a word, America, the land of liberty, regards herself with respect . . . . The times

30. Ibid., 157.
31. Ibid., 172.
32. Ibid., 158.
33. *Word* 8 (1879), pt. 1: 45–33.
34. Ibid., 45.
35. Ibid.

of popular prosperity have long passed, the courageous honesty and open character of the rulers of our destiny have become a myth, throughout the country the craftsman finds himself suffocated by the weight of taxes, duties and exactions of every kind. Yet none of this prevents our propertied classes from living supremely luxurious lives, squandering their fortunes, and holding intoxicating feasts. . . . The hankering after money and riches, the need to accumulate more and more wealth, which is then frittered away, in order to pay for the luxuries of dishonestly won fortunes, boundless political ambition, and the desire to rise above others—this is what has given modern American society such an unpleasant ambiance. The power of moral ideas is unfortunately bankrupt and at present stands before the world, which points its finger at it, like the knight of the rueful countenance.[36]

The author has no illusions that the legislative bodies of the United States would be able to prevent the depredations of the monopolies. "Free economic development," meaning capitalism, is in his opinion helpless in the face of such abuses, and he finds proof of this in the conditions prevailing in America, which "reveal a whole mass of rotten elements" and "lead one to fear the worst for the future."[37] The author concludes that, owing to the usually free development of capitalism and general worship of the cult of profit in the United States, the type of civilization that was evolving in that country was about to "end in universal demoralization wrought by the rule of money and to turn the absolute veneration of the 'Golden Calf' into a state religion."[38]

Subsequent developments, such as the growth of the power of corporations and the social consequences of that process, continually offered new evidence of the validity of these "worst fears." The country was being turned into a vast domain of the capitalist oligarchy, which dominated all things and imposed its will on the state, the Congress, and the government. In a series of articles published between 1880 and 1886, both *Word* and *Cause* offered a serious analysis of these phenomena. Among them were two articles by Tsakni (who used the initials T. and T-ni) that bore the same title, "Letters from America,"[39] and another, entitled "The Growth of Oligarchy in the United States and Its Political Influence," written by an anonymous author who used the initials "E. I."[40]

In the first of his articles Tsakni laid particular emphasis on the usurpation of all "economic and political functions" in the country by big business and the many-tentacled corporations. The central thesis of his article was the following:

These corporations which exercise unbridled control over all means of communication and possess huge amounts of capital, naturally strive to monopolize other areas of economic activity in the understandable belief that the wider the sphere of economic domination, the greater and more effective their power over the people. In that view, it is not surprising that the United States represents the worst kind of oligarchy, that which has not precedent in history in terms of its power and influence. . . . [4] what is at fault here is, of course, not political liberty as such, but the structure of society,

36. Ibid., 46–47.
37. Ibid., 47, 49.
38. Ibid., 50.
39. *Word* 11 (1880), pt. 2: 37–49; 1 (1881), pt. 2: 116–30.
40. *Cause* 1 (1886), pt. 1: 231–55.

which under conditions of political freedom merely serve to untie the hands of the might and gives them an even greater advantage over the weak.[41]

Tsakni stressed that it would be more difficult to overcome the despotic power of economic oligarchy of the United States than that of any other country. He believed that the reason for this was the existing historical conditions in the country and, above all, the fact that the economic and social guarantees rooted in the structure of American society were far less developed than their equivalents in Europe. Tsakni thought that the oligarchy's particularly strong hold on power in America was due to the excessive predominance of the private over the public, the personal over the communal, class self-interest over broad political and state solidarity, as well as to a strong devotion to the morality of the marketplace.[42]

The author of "The Growth of Oligarchy in the United States . . ." appearing in 1886, drew the conclusion that the United States was no longer "the promised land, where the mass of the destitute and hungry European proletariat could find refuge and sustenance."[43] On the basis of a considerable quantity of factual evidence, the writer traced the process whereby large capital had penetrated the fabric of the social organism of the United States. The following passage from "E. I.'"s article may be regarded as a summary of his arguments:

> The principle of the deeply understood solidarity and association of entrepreneurs and their supplies of capital dominates all branches of industry and commerce and creates a highly cohesive plutocracy which has a profound understanding of its class importance; and has no parallel in history in terms of the power and influence it wields in the political and economic life of the country. Because of the existence of this oligarchy the democratic system in the United States, with its universal franchise and broad popular representation in every branch of government, amounts to a fiction which conceals the unlimited dominion of a single class.[44]

No one should be fooled by the visible attributes of American democracy, writes the publicist. The electoral struggle and the constant clashes between the bourgeois parties have but a single purpose—that is to determine which of the two factions of the ruling class will take power and beat a path to the government feeding trough. These truths were demonstrated in vivid journalistic language by Jique (Jaclard) in "Political Parties and the Presidential Election in the United States" (1880).[45] Tsakni was no less categorical in his conclusion: "Whether it is the Democrats or the Republicans who win a victory, the practice of government changes little, since the struggle between them is waged not on the basis of political principles but for the sake of power, the source of influence and wealth."[46]

41. *Word* 1 (1881), pt. 2: 120.
42. Ibid., 126–27.
43. *Cause* 1 (1886), pt. 1: 232.
44. Ibid., 237.
45. See *Cause* 12 (1880), pt. 2: 175–213.
46. *Cause* 1 (1886), pt. 1: 242.

As in the case of several other issues, the views of the publicists of *Word* and *Cause* on possible solutions to the Negro question in America also changed considerably in the period after the end of the Civil War. From the very beginning all their sympathies were on the side of the oppressed Negro people. At the same time, the legislation pertaining to the civil rights of American citizens, which Congress had adopted after the war, filled these writers with the earnest hope that the Negro minority would be made in every way equal with "full-fledged" citizens of the United States. A number of articles conveyed a sense of optimism regarding future prospects for the social and material well-being of Negroes.[47]

Eventually the journals' contributors realized, however, that progress in this area was extremely slow, hindered as it was by the prejudices of the more ignorant sections of the white population, and by the deliberate actions of the opponents of Negro equality who played on these prejudices as well. *Cause* started to publish accounts of the orgy of bestial terror against the Negroes carried out by the Ku Klux Klan and its open sympathizers, both among the Democrats and within the former abolitionist party, the Republicans.[48] The antiracist position of the Russian democrats was also reflected in the fact that *Cause* sharply attacked the proponents of the concept of "white superiority" that at the time was extremely popular among American sociologists. The publication of a number of works bearing the imprint of these views met with harsh rebuke from the journal.[49]

Ten years after the end of the Civil War, the time was ripe for a review of the first results of the attempt to solve the race problem in America. Such a review was carried out by "Ia. L. P-r" in 1876. In particular, he stated, "the Act of Emancipation naturally could not atone for all the miseries of the former oppressed condition of the Negroes."[50] He further noted that "even now the mass of blacks continue to live in terrible poverty; there are places where their life is harder than it was during the time of slavery, if one excludes the planter's whip."[51] In the cities, Negroes had become a "class of pariahs" to whom the path to economic advancement was in effect closed and who could not "emerge from the state of subjugation and misery created by centuries of slavery. Let us add to this the contempt generally felt toward Negroes by the white population as a whole, including the emancipators." This contempt "makes the lot of the black particularly hard."[52] Exposing the hypocrisy and sanctimoniousness implicit in the conduct of those emancipators who were bourgeois liberals, among whom "there is scarcely a single person who does not share the Democrats' views concerning the legal capacity, or rather the legal incapacity of Negroes,"[53] he noted that all this was quite natural and in full accord with the "morbid symptoms" manifested by social organs in the United States.

47. *Cause* 2 (1869), pt. 2: 86–88; 4, pt. 2: 134–36.
48. *Cause* 1 (1876), pt. 2: 33; 3, pt. 2: 349–50; 11 (1887), pt. 2: 387–95.
49. *Cause* 10 (1871), pt. 2: 67–70.
50. *Cause* 11 (1876), pt. 1: 164.
51. Ibid., 165.
52. Ibid.
53. Ibid., 165–66.

The upsurge of the Russian labor movement during the second revolutionary stage led the legal populist press to begin systematic publication of articles on the labor question. [2] The articles on this subject dealt with the situation of the workers not only in Russia but also abroad—in England, in France, in Germany, and in America. In 1880–1881 *Cause* published two articles by Tsakni (T-ni) on the situation of the American working class under the same title, "Scenes of the Condition of Labor in the United States."[54] The author used government statistics and press reports, statements by various labor societies, and "declarations of various official and unofficial figures who would accidentally stumble upon this or that abnormal phenomenon." The writer discussed the material conditions of the life of workers and farmers against the backdrop of the rapid growth of capitalism in the United States, with its characteristic attributes of centralization of production and capital and all related developments engendered by this process. [2] "The free soil of America," wrote Tsakni in the second article, "is the soil on which capitalism, unconstrained here by any limitations and penetrated [into] all spheres of the life has attained its highest degree of development."[55] He continued:

> Capitalism, which has taken over the whole sphere of production and which little by little is gradually spreading its tenacious grasp over huge areas of useful land, threatens to place the life of the free American in fetters that are so strong that it would be harder to break them than in any of the most capitalistic countries of Europe. . . . In spite of theoretically free conditions of labor supply and demand, in spite of the freedom to strike and existence of all kinds of labor organizations, labor in America cannot prevail in the struggle against organized forces of capital.[56]

No large, historically established aristocracy had arisen on the democratic soil of America, but large capitalist companies, having become a powerful sociopolitical force, had taken over key positions in society, while "American capitalists, who have grasped the principle of class solidarity better than their European counterparts, have joined forces in order to wage, and with great success, their struggle against labor, reducing its share in the process of production to a minimum."[57]

After editing the data collected by the statistical bureaus of Missouri, Massachusetts, Pennsylvania, and other states, Tsakni concluded that the steady decline in the living standards of the "hired class" on the one hand, and the growth of affluence and luxury on the other, indicated that

> in this "paradise" there is a mass of discontented people whose discontent is rooted in an organization of society that controls the [country's] natural riches, the insufficiency of which in relation to the density of the population some economists ascribe all the misfortunes of Europe. . . . Like England, France, Belgium, etc., the United States has its own proletariat, whose size may be ascertained from the fact that in the entire Union there are some two million who constantly lack work and who depend on organized social charity.[58]

54. *Word* 2–3 (1880), pt. 2: 23–35; 10, pt. 2: 18–31.
55. *Word* 10 (1880), pt. 2: 19.
56. Ibid., 18.
57. *Word* 1 (1881), pt. 2: 118.
58. Ibid., 116.

Wage cuts particularly affected the stratum of unskilled workers that had grown noticeably over the years as large industry continued to squeeze out the small workshops that "30 to 40 years ago were the dominant feature of American industry."[59] Those in this numerous segment of the population, Tsakni wrote, were forced to send their wives and children to perform "exhausting work in the factories" and were reduced to starvation during periods of unemployment.

The terrible consequences of economic problems—poverty, despair, suicide, and crime—whose most pernicious impact fell on the mass of "working folk," forced the workers to resort to an active form of protest, namely strikes. According to Tsakni, "the years 1872 and 1873 may be said to have inaugurated the era of unemployment and strikes, which recur with systematic regularity and which are caused by the succession of industrial crises that has afflicted the United States during this period."[60] But strikes were merely "the worst kind of palliative and, if successful, can ensure a higher wage for only a short time, while the fundamental conditions of labor are left quite unchanged."[61]

Years passed, but the publicist's views on the effectiveness of the strike movement remained the same: "Strikes seldom help the workers," Tsakni wrote in 1881, "and cannot withstand the organized resistance of the capitalist."[62] He regarded the emerging national movement for an eight-hour working day as a far more promising development. Stressing its political character,[63] he felt that workers' demands signified the awakening of a new consciousness among them and the beginning of new possibilities for the labor movement in the United States.[64]

Particularly interesting is Tsakni's analysis of the general strike of railroad workers in 1877. It is not possible to reproduce all his arguments, but the author's sympathy was clearly with the workers who had risen up against oppression. He showed a clear understanding of the reasons for the workers' defeat, which was due, he believed, to

---

59. *Word* 10 (1880), pt. 2: 21.
60. Ibid., 22.
61. Ibid., 25.
62. *Cause* 1 (1881), pt. 2: 117.
63. *Word* 10 (1880), pt. 2: 26; 11, pt. 2: 41.
64. Tsakni also commented on the formation of a political party for workers in California. He wrote:

> Nowhere else in America has the semi-socialist working-class movement attained such scope and influence as in San Francisco, where the so-called Labor Party has won several important political victories in the state. We know that recently, the last few years, this party has grown so strong and has acquired such a cohesive organization that some time ago it was able to secure the adoption of a new constitution for the State of California—one which largely reflected the party's program. As a result of the elections of May 1879, which were conducted in accordance with the new constitution, Labor candidates were elected to almost every important position in the city and the state. "The workers were becoming the masters of the city, causing panic in the ranks of the capitalists and affluent classes, and from the very beginning suggested to many the ideas of moving away and transferring their capital to a more favorable environment." *Word* 11 (1880), pt. 2: 42–46.

the strength of resistance of the ruling class and to the organizational and ideological immaturity of the labor movement.

> In itself this major and significant move by a group of American workers was unsuccessful and indeed could not be successful—first, because the united and organized plutocracy had all public powers on her side . . . , second, because this was an action carried out by a single, albeit numerous, group of workers, an action which was as yet unorganized, lacked a thought-out plan and a well-defined and well-understood goal [3] . . . Strikes and riots cannot improve the situation, and so we must try to devise methods of self-defense that are more rational and effective.[65]

Tsakni clearly saw that the intensifying class conflict between capital and labor shaped, in a broad sense, the performance of the bourgeois-democratic institutions, resulting in an extension of the punitive functions of the bourgeois state and a strengthening of its mechanisms of coercion.[66]

A survey of Russian observations on the labor problem in America in the late 1870s and early 1880s would not be complete without a discussion of several other pieces that appeared in *Cause*. Of particular interest are the "Letters from America" by P. P. (P. I. Popov)[67] and his "The Growth of the Oligarchy in the United States and Its Political Influence." In the first of these articles, considerable attention was devoted to a discussion of the strike movement and of the economic and social position of the working class in relation to the rapidly advancing process of monopolization in American industry. In the section "The Most Difficult Points of the Labor Question in America," Popov argued that "the vaunted capitalist competition" had tied all the major tension in American society into a tight knot, had created two classes that were hostile to one another, had given complete freedom of action to only a few individuals, and had turned millions of people into slaves. Economic polarization had led to the appearance of an elite composed of "monopolistic millionaires," as well as of a "redoubtable proletariat."[68]

---

65. *Word* 1 (1881), pt. 2: 129. [3] In the immediate aftermath of the strike, a commentary appeared in the "Chronicle" section of the journal (*Cause* 1 [1878], pt. 2: 68–70). In underground publications, where revolutionaries could be frank and outspoken in stating their views, the 1877 strike was described as an important indication of the awakening socialist consciousness of the American workers. The newspaper *Nachalo* (Beginning) declared:

> This was the first event to prove that the social question does exist in America, that it has advanced far along the path of the systematic exploitation of the working people, in some ways even surpassing Europe in this regard. . . . It left its mark on the life of America: it roused the minds of Americans and forced them to think about the existing order in the social life of the country.

Revoliutsionnaia zhurnalistika 70-kh godov (The Revolutionary Journalism of the 1870s) (Paris, 1905), 23–24.
66. *Word* 1 (1881), pt. 2: 129–30.
67. *Cause* 10 (1883), pt. 2: 120–47.
68. Ibid., 142.

Popov demonstrated a clear understanding of the general features of the social consequences resulting from the growth of large industry, mechanization of labor processes, and centralization of capital.[69] These developments, controlled as they were by the monopolies that had arisen "on the free soil of America" and had no equivalent anywhere else in the world, were a source of profit for the monopolists and spelled enormous danger for the workers. "Of course, one should not lose sight of the fact that the condition of the workers in this country—as compared with the condition of the workers in Europe—is brilliant, but this is of little concern to the Americans: they are only interested in the position of the American worker in relation to his American masters."[70] After examining the situation from this perspective, the author concludes that conditions in the United States are approaching a "critical" point as a result of the "spirit reigning in modern industry and in the economic system."[71] Tensions between poverty and affluence have led to a sharpening of a political division between the two major classes. One pole is occupied by the capitalists, who are well organized and "a terrible force that imperiously dictates its terms to millions of workers and the public . . . a party that is cohesive, intelligent, energetic."[72] The other pole is occupied by workers who are only beginning to awake to the need for active struggle, who are organizing themselves but who are "as yet insufficiently advanced to be able to unite in pursuit of their interests. Therefore, the workers are the second party—one that is strong in numbers but still weak in development and organization."[73]

Popov considered the possible outcome of the struggle between workers and capitalists in America. His conclusion is entirely in keeping with the spirit of romantic socialism and of utopian projects to cure the social evils of capitalism—projects that were very popular among democratically minded American intellectuals with whom, it would appear, the publicist had had close contacts.

> I am convinced (as much as a man who has personally studied America for twelve years is capable of being convinced) that the labor question in this country will be solved, not on the streets nor in the factories, but in Congress. . . . The representatives of a free people vested with supreme authority will cut the Gordian knot that entangles the labor question, and no blood will be spilled.[74]

Not all Russian publicists, however, had such a rosy view of the way in which the central social conflict in bourgeois society would be resolved. The more protracted and bitter the clashes between workers and capitalists became, the more these writers were inclined to believe that the end result would probably be quite different. The May issue

---

69. Ibid., 143.
70. Ibid., 145.
71. Ibid., 146
72. Ibid.
73. Ibid.
74. Ibid., 146–47. Popov's article offers a detailed discussion of the activities of a Senate committee that for the first time had undertaken an investigation of the labor question in the United States. The author quotes statements by members of the committee who spoke of the growing feeling of discontent and anger among the workers that was fraught with the danger of a revolutionary explosion, a "bloody revolution."

of *Cause* for 1886, appearing when America was stirred by a nationwide strike for the principle of the eight-hour working day, contained the following:

> The civilized countries of Europe and America are at present going through a serious sociopolitical crisis, a stage of intense struggle among the various elements in society, a stage of major problems in their political and economic life, a stage which in the more or less near future threatens *major shocks and upheavals*. And the more advanced the social development of the country, the more broadly and comprehensively it has employed in the sphere of practical life the achievements of science, civilization, and culture, the more striking and intense are the manifestations of the *class struggle* and, consequently, of social discord, as may be seen in the case of the most industrial and capitalistic countries, such as England, Belgium, and America. Indeed, in America this discord and these problems are even deeper.[75]

According to the writers of *Cause*, with the abolition of slavery the chief issue facing the internal political life and the cultural development of the United States became the women's rights problem. That question provided them with a useful platform for agitation against all forms of oppression, against all forms of the denial of rights, and in favor of the general democratization of Russia. It is, therefore, understandable that the contributors to the journal made wide use of data that shed light on the program put forward by the movement for the unconditional emancipation of women that was unfolding, not only in Russia but also in almost every country of Western Europe as well as the United States, where it was particularly strong. Shashkov's article, "The Cause of Women in America,"[76] several pieces by Elie Reclus, among them "Women in the United States,"[77] an article by N. Lunin (Blagosvetlov) entitled "Women's Labor and Its Renumeration,"[78] Mariia Tsebrikova's "The Struggle of American Women for Emancipation,"[79] and several articles and statements by Shelgunov[80] were all devoted to the feminist movement in America.

The journal presented the Russian reader with a comprehensive (and in some ways even contradictory) picture of the situation of American women in society. On the one hand, it emphasized that "nowhere else do women enjoy the same respect as in the American Republic"[81] and pointed out the profound differences between the position of women in America and in Europe; on the other, the contributors to the journal,

---

75. *Cause* 1 (1886), pt. 1: 231 [author's italics].
76. *Cause* 1 (1872), pt. 1: 34–59; 2, pt. 1: 152–84.
77. *Cause* 2 (1869), pt. 2: 1–32; see also 8 (1867), pt. 2: 108–13; 4 (1869), pt. 2: 136–40. [For a biography of Reclus, who resided in Zurich during most of this period, see Paul Reclus, *Les Frères Elie & Elisée Reclus, ou du Protestantisme á l'Anarchisme* (Paris, 1964)—ed].
78. *Cause* 2 (1870), pt. 1: 243–80.
79. *Cause* 3 (1883), pt. 1: 304–38.
80. *Cause* 3 (1867), pt. 2: 75–88; 2 (1871), pt. 2: 1–20.
81. *Cause* 2 (1869), pt. 2: 2. Shelgunov, for example, thought that the difference in the status of women in America and Russia was that "American women are to a greater extent the product of a new environment that placed American settlers in new, non-European conditions, and the roots of the American sense of freedom are also to be found in this social and economic organization, in these conditions of soil and geography." Ibid., 2 (1871), pt. 2: 13.

basing themselves on statements by prominent advocates of the cause of women such as John J. Curtis, B. Penney [probably Virginia Penney—ed], Susan B. Anthony, and Elizabeth Cady Stanton, adopted an increasingly critical view of the political and social status of American women. "While ideas, political institutions, and all social conditions quickly changed after the republic seceded from the mother country," wrote, for example, Reclus, "the law always being conservative and habit-bound tended to avoid any changes where the woman was concerned. As a wife, widow, or mother nowhere is she recognized as an individual in full possession of her rights."[82]

The publicists of *Cause* pointed out that the legal position of the American woman, who was precluded from participating in political activities and deprived of the right to vote, placed her in the same category as the insane, the criminal, and individuals who were under guardianship or had been found guilty of bribery. As Shashkov explained, "the boy grows up to be a man and a voter; the madman may recover his sanity and his rights; the criminal whose hands are covered in the blood of his country and its liberty may be forgiven and his rights restored; but neither age, wisdom, special talents, public service, nor ardent desire—nothing can free the woman of this abnormal and extreme disqualification."[83] Echoing the opinion of the "American emancipators," Shashkov and Reclus asserted that working women were far more interested in gaining political rights than were women who belonged to the upper classes, since the right to vote would allow the former to take part in governing the Republic and, through their chosen representatives, to carry out reforms that could improve their economic position.[84]

Cause commented in most favorable terms on the energy with which the leaders of the suffragette movement (Stanton, Anthony, Penny, Olympia Brown, and others) pursued their goals, on the establishment and activities of women's congresses and conventions, as well as on the work carried out by the Women's Labor Society and the American Association for the Voting Rights of Women and its many branches—organizations that published women's journals and brochures and held rallies in support of their cause.[85]

The reader could find on the pages of *Cause* accounts of the oppressed status of working women and of their ever-growing immiseration. The economic inequality between men and women with regard to their wages had led to the appearance of a large army of female proletarians. "Poverty, shameful poverty," Reclus wrote, "is already creeping into many cities of the free American republic. Hunger and cold have also become common in America, and it is the women who suffer from them."[86] By using statistical data the contributors to the journal (Blagosvetlov, Shashkov, Reclus) laid bare the phenomenon of prostitution—America's "social ulcer"—particularly in the country's "most important" city, New York. "There are few cities in the world where

82. *Cause* 2 (1869), pt. 2: 9–10.
83. *Cause* 2 (1872), pt. 1: 169.
84. *Cause* 2 (1869), pt. 2: 31–32; 1 (1872), pt. 1: 58.
85. See *Cause* 4 (1869), pt. 2: 137–40; 2 (1870), pt. 1: 243–45; 1 (1871), pt. 2: 58–59; 2, pt. 3: 1–20; 2 (1872), pt. 1: 165–67, 179–84.
86. *Cause* 2 (1869), pt. 2: 13.

vice devours its victims more quickly and greedily than in New York. This is because in the United States, where everything takes an extreme form, public opinion does not admit the existence of intermediate degrees of vice and virtue."[87]

The journal's reporters did not limit themselves to informing the Russian public about the current situation of American women. They commented in a thoughtful and original manner on the future prospects of the campaign for women's equality and on its role in the political life of the United States. They pointed out that the working women's movement was beginning to enjoy the broad support of organized labor, the American trade unions. These unions, as Reclus noted, "have become quite numerous and very strong in the big cities and industrial districts of America. . . . Thus, thanks to the coalition it has formed with male workers, the union of women will add enormous extra support to its present strength."[88]

At the same time, these writers noted the difficulties encountered by the democratic movement in its quest for unity. Quoting Reclus,

> Negroes and women who were equally denied the protection of universal rights, wanted to fight for them together, wanted to act in concert both during the struggle and after victory was achieved. Of course, their triumph would not have been long in coming if there were sincere and unshakable agreement between these allies; but very often lingering prejudices of race and petty factional intrigues would lead to quarrels and mutual hostility. Thus, in Kansas many voters who were sympathetic to the idea of extending the franchise to women voted against the enfranchisement of Negroes, and the New York ladies who edit with such tact and audacity the newspaper "The Revolution" have recently drawn closer to the Democratic party which is ill-disposed toward the Negroes, in the hope of inducing it to adopt a program that would be favorable to women.[89]

The lack of unity among the different currents in the democratic movement was apt to retard seriously social progress in America. This was in fact the conclusion reached by Reclus in his analysis of the women's movement in that country.

Finally, a brief discussion is warranted on certain problems of the ideological and intellectual life of American society that were also examined on the pages of these two journals. In this connection, three full-length articles are of particular interest: "A Historical Sketch of American Journalism" by K. Gardner,[90] which appeared in the first two issues of *Cause*, "The Development of Philosophical Ideas: The Experience of the United States" by "N. F-skii,"[91] and "American Types" by "P. P." (Popov).[92]

87. *Cause* 2 (1869), pt. 2: 14; see also 1 (1872), pt. 1: 57–58.
88. *Cause* 2 (1869), pt. 2: 31.
89. *Cause* 4 (1869), pt. 2: 136. In the same article Reclus discussed the position of the Republican Party, which passionately spoke out in Congress and in the press in defense for the right of Negroes to vote but which argued against "women's franchise" at meetings and rallies. He believed that by "wishing to sacrifice one form of progress for another" the Republicans had in the end sacrificed both (ibid., 136–37).
90. *Cause* 4 (1877), pt. 1: 186–216; 5, pt. 1: 139–73.
91. *Cause* 8 (1878), pt. 1: 278–312.
92. *Cause* 2 (1884), pt. 1: 138–63.

The first of these articles is a comprehensive study of the history of the American press as the collective exponent of political ideas and social relations in different periods of the country's history—from the colonial era to the one of which the writer himself was a contemporary. The quality of this article is such that even today it has still not lost its relevance for the study of the history of American thought. The author points to the tremendously positive influence exercised by the "fledgling" periodicals published by supporters of independence that prepared Americans for the reformation period and inspired them to join the struggle for national and political freedom. The liberal press, which had largely remained faithful to the traditions of the struggle for independence and in many cases continued to act as the bearer of Thomas Jefferson's ideas, was able to give considerable help to the abolitionists by demonstrating to the people the justice of the struggle for racial equality. But after the age of the great revolutionary events had passed into history, many of the exalted ideals of the fighters for independence lost their importance for America. In Gardner's opinion, the evolution of the dominant tendency in American political thought reflected this retrograde process. He concluded,

> The first great champions of American liberty, however, have passed from the scene; a crowd of dwarfs, possessed neither of a particular Weltanschauung, nor of any convictions, clambered onto their empty pedestals; in place of the true politicians, who were able to combine the high sentiment of patriotism with universal human principles, appeared a host of petty political intriguers who reduced the struggle of the parties to a parochial squabble and the clash of mercantile interests. . . . The exalted honesty that had been the mark of such champions of liberty as Franklin, Jefferson, Harrison, and others was reduced to base bribery, and vigor of thought and unbending conviction were frequently replaced by meretricious public and external effects designed to appeal to the stupidity of the mob. In a word, the press, educated in the noble school of struggle and great national ferment, on the whole ceased being the rostrum occupied by the publicists of the past and became a shopkeeper's desk; it could no longer adequately reflect the new conditions and supreme demands of life; it failed to express fully either the public's consciousness, or its conscience, or its aspirations.[93]

The main propositions advanced by "N. F-skii" echoed Gardner's arguments. He believed that the spread of money-grubbing concepts among the American people was the fault of the bourgeois intelligentsia, which had forgotten its own history and had degenerated into a "squalid tribe of political hacks and pedants."[94] Both the slave-owning planters and the bourgeoisie of free states had availed themselves of its services in order to maintain among the people "those false sentiments and views which led to discord within it and enabled them to govern on the basis of Machiavellian principles." In a veiled fashion the writer gave his readers to understand that in order for a society that regarded the welfare of the people as its chief concern to develop harmoniously, it was necessary for it to overcome the ideology of bourgeois success, to infuse the

---

93. *Cause* 5 (1877), pt. 1: 149.
94. *Cause* 8 (1878), pt. 1: 310.

masses with "the correct fundamental philosophical idea," and to develop "systematic thinking."[95] Clearly, the author was referring to the ideals of socialism. The negative aspects of the history of the United States offered, in his view, "tangible proof" of the need for such a spiritual revolution.

---

95. Ibid., 311–12.

10

Chekhov and America, by A. N. Nikoliukin

In the spring of 1890, Anton Chekhov set off on a journey to the island of Sakhalin. On his way there he stopped at Krasnoiarsk, where earlier in the century Nikolai Rezanov, the head of the Russian-American Company who did much to further the Russian settlement of North America, had died on his journey back from Russian America (California). Chekhov was to mention Rezanov in his book, *The Island of Sakhalin*.

On May 28, 1890, Chekhov wrote to his relatives from Krasnoiarsk that he intended to return to Russia via America. Nothing came of this plan, however. Chekhov's hopes of traveling with Leo Tolstoy's son to the Chicago World's Fair of 1893, which he mentioned in his letters to Aleksei Suvorin of October 18, 1892, and Ilia Repin of January 23, 1893, were also never realized.

Krasnoiarsk occupies a memorable place in Chekhov's writings owing to another circumstance that until now has escaped the attention of scholars. The city, or, to be more precise, its natural setting, made a tremendous impression on the writer. "I should be happy to live in Krasnoiarsk," he wrote in the same letter to his relatives. In his travel sketches, which he entitled *From Siberia,* Chekhov declared that he had never seen a river more majestic than the Enisei. Life on the banks of the Enisei began with a moan, but will produce exciting achievements beyond our wildest imaginings, he wrote. "Krasnoiarsk, the best and most beautiful of all the cities in Siberia, is on this bank, and on the bank opposite I saw mountains which reminded me of the Caucasus, for they are as smoky and dream-like. I stood there and thought: one day these shores will be illuminated by a life that is vigorous, intelligent and bold!"

Ten years later, Chekhov wrote *Three Sisters*. The action in the play, as the text makes clear, takes place in a provincial capital on a river. One of the characters, Prozorov, says that the city has existed for two hundred years. So, what is the name of this town? There were no provincial capitals in European Russia that were two hundred years old. However, there was one in Siberia. The town of Krasnoiarsk on the Enisei was founded in 1628, and became the capital of Enisei Province in 1822. Moreover, why should someone living in one of the provincial capitals of Central Russia, none of which was farther than a day's journey by train from Moscow, dream, like the three sisters in Chekhov's play, of "going to Moscow," and say, "I felt such a longing to get back to Moscow"? But the picture changes if we imagine that the play is set in Krasnoiarsk, a remote Siberian town that, when Chekhov visited it, still lacked a railway link to the outside world.

We may, therefore, conclude that the setting of *Three Sisters,* schematically drawn though it is, was in some ways inspired by Chekhov's memories of Krasnoiarsk. Such a conclusion is confirmed by a statement Vershinin repeats twice in the play, which echoes Chekhov's opinion of Krasnoiarsk in *From Siberia* quoted above. In act 1, Vershinin says, "In two or three hundred years life on this earth of ours will have become marvelously beautiful." In act 3, he exclaims, "And before very long, say, in another two or three hundred years, people may be looking at our present life just as we look at the past now, with horror and scorn. Our own times may seem uncouth to them, boring and frightfully uncomfortable and strange . . . Oh, what a great life it'll be then, what a life!" Indeed, in the letters Chekhov wrote en route to Sakhalin he several times emphasizes how much he had been impressed by the Enisei and the Amur.

"The Amur area is fascinating," wrote Chekhov in one of his letters. "It is fiendishly original. It teems with the kind of life that in Europe they cannot even imagine. The things I have seen here remind me of the stories about life in America."[1] Chekhov's comment was above all else an allusion to the stories of Bret Harte, which were regularly published in the major Russian journals and also appeared in separate editions. The characters in Chekhov's story "The Boys" (1887) decide to run away to America after reading their fill of Mayne Reid and Fenimore Cooper.

It was during this period that Chekhov's works first attracted the attention of the American reading public. In the 1890s translations of his stories began to appear in American journals. In 1891 Isabel Hapgood, the well-known translator of Russian literature, published a translation of "At Home" in *Short Stories: A Magazine of Fact and Fiction,* a New York journal. But it was the publication of the thirteen-volume edition of Chekhov's *Collected Works* (1916–1922) in Constance Garnett's translation that firmly established the Russian writer's reputation among English-speaking readers.

Late in life, Garnett, who had done much to popularize the Russian classics in the English-speaking world (her translation of *The Brothers Karamazov* was a momentous event in the history of English and American literature), recalled that she "took far more time over my translations of Turgenev and Chekhov than over any of my other translations because their Russian is so beautiful."[2]

One of Chekhov's contemporaries, the American writer William Dean Howells, spoke of the enormous impression the works of Russian writers—first Turgenev's

---

1. Chekhov, *Sobranie Sochineniia* (Collected Works and Letters), 30 vols. (Moscow, 1976), vol. 14–15, 35; vol. 4, 124–25. This article by A.N. Nikoliukin first appeared in *Vzaimodeistvie Kul'tur SSSR i SShA xviii–xx vv.* (The Cultural Interactions of the U.S.S.R. and the U.S.A., Eighteenth-Twentieth Centuries), edited by O. E. Tuganov (Moscow, 1987).

2. Garnett, "The Art of Translation," *The Listener* 37, 942 (January 30, 1947), 195.

and Tolstoy's, and later Chekhov's—had made on him. "They opened to me what seemed to be a new world—and it was only the real world. There is Tcheckoff—have you read his 'Orchard'? What life, what colors, what beauty of truth are in that book!"[3]

Theodore Dreiser's published diaries reveal that he read Chekhov with great interest.[4] Sherwood Anderson, whose library contained three English-language collections of Chekhov's stories and plays, wrote in his posthumously published memoirs: "It was a good deal later that I began to read the Russians, Tolstoy, Chekhov, Dostoevsky, Turgenev. I think that then, when I came to them, that I did feel a kinship. . . . I felt brotherhood with Chekhov."[5] Virginia Woolf sensed the artistic kinship between the two writers when she read Anderson's stories. She observed that Anderson's novellas recall the feelings "with which we read Chekhov for the first time."[6] T. S. Eliot, the leading modernist poet and literary theorist, believed, however, that the world of Chekhov's plays was "simplified universal."[7]

In the years after World War I, Chekhov's reputation became firmly established in the United States. The great American playwright Eugene O'Neill thought that the best plotless plays ever written were Chekhov's. Discussing the genre of the short story, F. Scott Fitzgerald named as his models "The Overcoat" by Nikolai Gogol and "The Darling" by Chekhov. The power of these stories, said the American writer, has nothing to do with "plot for shocks."[8] Upon reading Chekhov's letters on literature,[9] Fitzgerald wrote to his editor, "God, there's a book."[10]

As a young man, Thomas Wolfe, another prominent American writer, wrote plays that found their inspiration in the dramatic works of O'Neill, Tolstoy, Chekhov, and Andreev.[11] In Wolfe's novel, *Of Time and the River,* the protagonist reads aloud a passage from the book he has written, whereupon one of his listeners remarks, "It is as good as 'The Cherry Orchard.'"[12] Chekhov had now become a standard and a criterion of artistic merit.

American writers learned from Chekhov to be laconic and expressive. He also taught them the importance of civic responsibility in a writer. Sinclair Lewis was referring to the artist's sense of duty toward society in one of his last articles, written shortly

---

3. Howells, " 'War Stops Literature,' says William Dean Howells," in Joyce Kilmer, *Literature in the Making by Some of Its Makers* (New York, 1917), 7.

4. Dreiser, *American Diaries, 1902–1926,* edited by T. P. Riggio (Philadelphia, 1982), 239, 242–43. Dreiser included Chekhov's plays among "real literary achievements." Dreiser, *Letters: A Selection,* edited by R. H. Elias (Philadelphia, 1959), vol. 1, 188.

5. Anderson, *Memoirs: A Critical Edition,* edited by R. L. White (Chapel Hill, 1969), 451.

6. Quoted from Dorothy Brewster, *East-West Passage: A Study in Literary Relationships* (London, 1954), 211.

7. Eliot, *The Sacred Word: Essays on Poetry and Criticism* (London, 1960), 69.

8. Fitzgerald, *The Letters,* edited by A. Turnbull (New York, 1963), 116.

9. The work in question was Chekhov's, *Letters on the Short Story, the Drama and Other Literary Topics,* edited by L. S. Friedland (New York, 1924), vol. 12, 346.

10. Fitzgerald, *Letters,* 202.

11. Wolfe, *The Notebooks,* edited by R. S. Kennedy and P. Reeves (Chapel Hill, 1970), vol. 1, 13.

12. Wolfe, *Of Time and the River* (Harmondsworth, 1971), 633.

before his death, when he advised aspiring writers to read "such novelists as Tolstoy, Dostoevsky, Chekhov."[13] Ernest Hemingway confessed that he, too, had learned from Chekhov, and recalled the first impression the stories of the Russian writer had made on him:

> In Toronto, before we ever came to Paris, I had been told Katherine Mansfield was a good short-story writer, even a great short-story writer, but trying to read her after Chekhov was like hearing the carefully artificial tales of a young old-maid compared to those of an articulate and knowing physician who was a good and simple writer.[14]

During his visit to the Soviet Union, William Saroyan declared that he felt "infinite sympathy and respect for the great Chekhov," who had taught him "how shall I put it, something like intellectual refinement." "He has been my companion all my life," said Saroyan about Chekhov. "I often re-read him even now. Everything in him inspires envy, in the good sense of the word.... He has a delicate soul, a delicate lyricism, and a delicate sincerity, and even Chekhov's courage and firmness of principle are delicate."[15]

When as an old man William Faulkner was asked which short-story writer he esteemed most highly, he named Chekhov. "Can't think of some of the others,"[16] he added. Where Faulkner-the-storyteller was concerned, other writers had not influenced him as much. Explaining how he wrote his stories, Faulkner turned to Chekhov's works: "The first job the craftsman faces is to tell this as quickly and simply as I can, and if he's any good, if he's of the first water, like Chekhov, he can do it every time in two or three thousand words to do this, but if he is not that good, sometimes it takes him eighty thousand words."[17]

There were two American editions of Chekhov in Faulkner's library: a collection of plays ("The Seagull," "Uncle Vanya," "Three Sisters," "The Cherry Orchard") and a book of stories and tales (New York, 1932), which included "The Steppe," "The Hollow," "Kashtanka," "A Day in the Country," "Old Age," "The Enemies," "On the Way," "Little Vanka," "La Cigale," "Grief," "An Inadvertence," "The Black Monk," "The Kiss," "In Exile," "A Work of Art," "Dreams," "A Woman's Kingdom," "The Doctor," "A Trifling Occurrence," "After the Theatre," "The Runaway," "Vierochka," and "Rothschild's Fiddle." Chekhov said that art should show the absolute truth of life. Using his own methods, Faulkner tried to follow that dictum.

In defining the special characteristics of the genre of the short story, Faulkner used the example of Chekhov's writing technique:

---

13. Lewis, *The Man from Main Street: A Sinclair Lewis Reader* (New York, 1953), 187.
14. E. Kheminguei [Hemingway], *Sobranie Sochineniia* (Collected Works), 4 vols. (Moscow, 1966), vol. 4, 471.
15. Saroian [Saroyan], "Iablochn'—Zvezdy . . . Eto Velikolepno!" (The Apple-Trees Are Stars . . . and That's Wonderful!), interview in Armenia, *Literaturnaia Gazeta* (Literary Gazette) 15 (November 17, 1976).
16. *Faulkner in the University: Class Conference at the University of Virginia, 1957–1958,* edited by F. L. Gwynn and J. L. Blotner (New York, 1959), 24.
17. Ibid., 48.

> In a short story that's next to a poem, almost every word has got to be almost exactly right. In the novel you can be careless but in a story you can't. I mean by that the good short stories like Chekhov wrote. That's why I rate that second—it's because it demands a nearer absolute exactitude. You have less room to be slovenly and careless.[18]

Shortly before Chekhov's death, Faulkner listed him among the writers whose books he reread every year.[19] Continuing the esthetic and literary traditions of Faulkner, who had a great respect for Russian literature, the American realist writer John Gardner, in his programmatic book *On Moral Fiction,* which is directed against those writers who express a lack of faith in man and his achievements, turned to Chekhov in order to show that "art tells the truth."[20]

The debate about Chekhov's artistic legacy has continued to this day. His international reputation grows with every decade. In his article, "Chekhov's Drama—A Challenge to Playwrights," the well-known American dramatist and Marxist critic, John Howard Lawson, spoke out against the idea, which has gained widespread currency since the time of Lev Shestov, that Chekhov was a pessimistic writer who "killed people's hopes."[21]

> Chekhov has exerted a considerable influence on theatre development in the United States. However, this influence has been based, in no small degree on a one-sided and essentially false interpretation of Chekhov's art. It is ironic that Chekhov, the prophet of a new era, has been eulogized as a prophet of doom! The man who hated pessimism, who mocked the inertia of the intellectuals and derided false sentiment, is called the father of the drama of decadent moods, pretentious intellectualism and false sentiment.... From an historical point of view, it is essential to place Chekhov's work in its proper perspective.... But the rediscovery of the real values of Chekhov is above all necessary *for ourselves*—so that these values may serve and enrich our contemporary American theatre.[22]

Literary scholars and critics in the West were unable immediately to understand everything in Chekhov's esthetic and artistic heritage. Professor Thomas G. Winner of the University of Michigan has this to say about Chekhov's popularity in the United States after World War I:

> Although during that period the number of editions of Chekhov's works that was published increased sharply, and his best-known plays were for the first time performed

---

18. Ibid., 207.
19. Faulkner, *Lion in the Garden: Interviews with William Faulkner, 1926–1962,* edited by J. B. Meriwether and M. Millgate (New York, 1968), 284.
20. Gardner, *On Moral Fiction* (New York, 1978), 150. Almost all contemporary American writers have paid tribute to Chekhov's artistic achievements. The veteran American writer Robert Penn Warren described Chekhov as the author of short stories that were unsurpassed in the history of the genre. *Interviews, 1950–1978,* edited by F. C. Watkins and J. T. Hiers (New York, 1980), 134.
21. Shestov, "Tvorchestvo iz nichego" (Creation from Nothing), in *Nachala i kontsy* (Beginnings and Endings) (St. Petersburg, 1908), 3.
22. J. H. Lawson, "Chekhov's Drama: Challenge to Playwrights," *Masses and Mainstream* 7, no. 10 (October 1954): 11.

on the American stage, American critics failed at the time to offer a serious critical assessment of Chekhov's writings. Chekhov was still a mystery to American critics, and one that they found more difficult to understand than Tolstoy, Turgenev, or Dostoevsky, with whom the American reading public was much more familiar. It was for this reason that many critics confined themselves to an attempt to explain Chekhov by using the method of comparison.[23]

This observation, which was made more than a quarter of a century ago, is still valid today, as may be seen from some of the articles on Chekhov by American writers and critics published in the last decade.

In her article, "Chekhov and the Theatre of the Absurd," Joyce Carol Oates, who is well known in Russia, tries to present the Russian playwright as the precursor of the theatre of the absurd in the West. She believes that in those passages in his works where he combines symbolism with the depiction of "that which is strange, absurd, and paradoxical in people's lives" Chekhov anticipated the methods of the theatre of the absurd:

> Much of what seems stunning and avant garde in the last two decades of the theater has been anticipated in both theory and practice by Chekhov. For instance, one has only to examine the central issues *The Cherry Orchard* and *The Three Sisters*—the hopeless, comic-pathetic loss of tradition and the futile longing for Moscow—to see how closely Chekhov is echoed in Beckett's *Waiting for Godot* and other works.[24]

While conceding that Chekhov's art was based on the traditions of nineteenth-century realism (which Oates, like other American critics, calls "naturalism"), she argues that "his technique is only apparently naturalistic: it is fundamentally symbolic."[25] Oates believes that Chekhov's plots, his manner of depicting events, the devices he uses, and the linguistic structure of his works all reflect the absurdity of being (she is referring to lines like "I suppose down there in Africa the heat must be terrific now" and "Balzac's marriage took place at Berdichev" [*Plays*, 244, 282]). According to Oates, Chekhov's characters have lost the ability to express themselves. They no longer know how to live and how to have a clear understanding of their environment.

To prove the "absurdity" of Chekhov's plays, Oates gives the example of the final scene in *The Cherry Orchard,* where Feers, the old servant, is left behind when the other characters leave the house. According to her, although this event symbolizes the

---

23. T. G. Vinner [Winner], "Chekhov v Soedinennykh shtatakh Ameriki" (Chekhov in the United States of America), *Literaturnoe Nasledstvo* (Literary Heritage) 68 (Moscow, 1960): 783. Soviet scholars have also studied the various attitudes toward Chekhov's literary legacy in the United States; see Iu. I. Sokhriakov, "Traditsii A. P. Chekhov v amerikanskoi novellistike XX veka" (The Tradition of Chekhov and the American Short Story in the Twentieth Century) in *Tvorchestvo A. P. Chekhova: Osobennosti khudozhestvennogo metoda* (The Writings of Chekhov: Features of His Artistic Method) (Rostov on Don, 1979), vol. 4, 106–13; and "Traditsii A. P. Chekhova v dramaturgii SShA XX v." (The Tradition of Chekhov in Twentieth Century Drama in the United States) in *Khudozhestvennye metod A. P. Chekhova* (The Artistic Method of Chekhov) (Rostov-on-Don, 1982), 129–38.

24. Oates, "Chekhov and the Theater of the Absurd," in *The Edge of Impossibility: Tragic Forms in Literature* (New York, 1972), 118.

25. Ibid.

end of the "old order," so that the audience does not know whether to laugh or cry, from another point of view, a purely theatrical one, the scene creates an impression of absurdity and distracts one's attention from the main themes and ideas in the play, which have to do with the reactions of the main characters to the sale of the family estate.

And yet Oates concedes that in Chekhov's plays the dramatic action unfolds according to the precepts of realism; his characters speak a language that reflects everyday reality. "In essence his conception of drama is more complex and more iconoclastic than that of the absurdists, whose revolt is chiefly in terms of a simplification of life and an attendant exaggeration of limited experiences."[26]

In traditional drama the central theme is always well developed. It determines the nature and pace of the stage action: the hero kills the king, or ends by marrying his beloved, or, on the contrary, frees himself of the social and family ties binding him. Oates believes that Chekhov and the absurdist playwrights either do not reveal their central theme, or do not develop it. As a symbol, the cherry orchard has so many meanings that it represents completely different things to different people. Yet in itself the orchard does not exist, for it lacks artistic content. No one sees the cherry orchard as it actually is. Some of the characters regard it as a lost source of revenue, while others consider it an embodiment of the serfdom of the past, or think it hides the spirits of their deceased ancestors. Each character sees his own reflection in it, as in a mirror. That is why Gaev is so happy it will be sold: "Indeed, everything's alright now. Before the cherry orchard was sold everybody was worried and upset, but as soon as it was all settled finally and once for all, everybody calmed down, and felt quite cheerful, in fact."[27]

Oates writes that Chekhov's plays, like the plays of the modern absurdists, cannot be reduced to a single emotion or idea. She believes that the multidimensional approach to reality Chekhov shares with the modernists amounts to a hidden connection between them. Oates tries to show that there are further similarities between the artistically disparate works of Chekhov and the modernists by referring to the "antihumanism" supposedly professed by the Russian writer who, she says, had an absurdist worldview: "Humanism is a failure, the absurdists say, because man is not 'human,' cannot know himself, therefore cannot control himself, and, above all, cannot control his world."[28]

Noting the similarity in the depiction of the degradation and dehumanization of society in Chekhov and the theatre of the absurd, Oates concludes that "the vision of man in absurdist drama and in Chekhov is similar, if not identical."[29] She thus ignores completely the sociopsychological and historical motivation of the characters in *The Cherry Orchard* and the other works by Chekhov she analyzes.

Responding to the American writer, the Russian scholar Iurii Sokhriakov subjected her theory to deserved criticism: "Chekhov was not the predecessor of Beckett and Ionescu, but a great realist who long before the appearance of the theatre of the

---

26. Ibid., 123.
27. Chekhov, *Collected Works and Letters*, vol. 13, 247.
28. Oates, "Chekhov," 124.
29. Ibid., 125.

absurd had explored in his plays (and not only in his plays) themes to which the modernists would lay an exclusive claim."[30] In her introduction to the American edition of Chekhov's letters, Lillian Hellman discussed the social dimension of his characters. "There can be no doubt, on the evidence, that Chekhov was a man of deep social ideas and an uncommon sense of social responsibility."[31]

Chekhov's drama has attracted the attention of American writers who disagree with the attempt by Joyce Carol Oates to draw a parallel between the poetics of Chekhov's plays and the theatre of the absurd. One of the critics of her approach is the playwright Edward Albee. He concedes that the absurdists have changed our views on modern drama, but thinks that the national tradition of the theatre in America has little in common with the theatre of the absurd. "And it is my guess that the theatre in the United States will always hew more closely to the post-Ibsen/Chekhov tradition, than does the theatre in France, let us say."[32] In his article "Which Theatre Is the Absurd One?" Albee conclusively demonstrates that "the theatre of the absurd (or the avant-garde theatre or whatever you want to call it) as it now stands is on its way out."[33]

In his memoirs, Tennessee Williams describes how many years earlier he fell in love with Chekhov's books, and particularly his plays.

> They introduced me to a literary sensibility to which I felt a very close affinity at that time. Now I find that he holds too much in reserve. I still am in love with the delicate poetry of his writing, and *The Seagull* is still, I think, the greatest modern play, with the exception of Brecht's *Mother Courage*. It has often been said that Lawrence was my major literary influence. Well Lawrence was, indeed, a highly *simpatico* figure in my literary upbringing, but Chekhov takes precedence as an influence.[34]

It is worth noting that in a letter written during World War II, Tennessee Williams mentions a portrait of Chekhov that hangs in his study.[35]

Chekhov's plays have been staged by every major American theatre. In an article he wrote about the American tradition of drama, Arthur Miller said that playwrights cannot read Chekhov without envying his mastery of harmony and the balance that exists among the elements in his plays. "In this, I think, he is closer to Shakespeare than any dramatist I know."[36] And Miller adds that in his opinion not just Chekhov, but all Russian writers are distinguished by the ability to reveal the psychology and

---

30. Iu. I. Sokhriakov, "Chekhov i 'teatr absurda' v istolkovanii D. K. Outs" (Chekhov and the "Theatre of the Absurd" in the Interpretation of J. C. Oates), in *Russkaia literatura v otsenke sovremennoi zarubezhnoi kritiki* (The View of Russian Literature in Contemporary Foreign Criticism) (Moscow, 1981), 87.
31. Hellman, "Introduction," in Chekhov, *Selected Letters,* edited by by L. Hellman (New York, 1955), xxiii.
32. Albee, "Which Theatre Is the Absurd One?" *New York Times Magazine,* February 25, 1962.
33. Ibid.
34. Williams, *Memoirs* (New York, 1976), 51.
35. Williams, *Letters to Donald Windham, 1940–1965,* edited by D. Windham (New York, 1977), 82.
36. Miller, "The Shadows of the Gods: A Critical View of the American Theater," *Harper's Magazine* (August 1958), 38.

the entire inner world of the characters. Indeed, the impact that Chekhov's plays have had on the literature of the English-speaking world forms cannot be separated from the more general influence exercised by Russian writers and playwrights on English and American literature.

More recent studies of Chekhov published in the United States attempt to combine an analysis of the ideas and themes in his works with a close examination of the artistic qualities of the Chekhovian narrative. In April 1975, a Chekhov conference was held at the University of North Carolina. Its proceedings were published in book form under the title *Chekhov's Art of Writing*. The papers presented reflected the various views on Chekhov current in contemporary American literary criticism. In the introduction to the collection its editors, the eminent American Slavicists, Paul Debreczeny and Thomas Eekman, attempted to explain why many of the studies in the book were formalist or structuralist in character: "The preponderance of formal studies in the volume is not an indication of a 'trend,' less even of a fad; it simply shows that impressionist criticism, or thematic criticism, not rooted in the intricate structure of the text itself, are things of the past."[37]

In 1980, Professor Peter Stowell of Florida State University published a monograph entitled *Literary Impressionism, James and Chekhov*, in which he compares the Chekhovian narrative with the impressionism of Henry James. The two writers belonged to entirely different literary worlds and were not familiar with each other's works, although James's novels were translated into Russian and were published in Russian journals at the end of the nineteenth century, at a time when Chekhov's stories began to appear in British and American journals.

Stowell believes that Chekhov and James embraced the technique of impressionism when they realized that they needed to purge their prose of the qualities of descriptiveness and authorial omniscience. "Both broke from the transcendent subjectivity of realism to forge the subjective objectivism of literary impressionism." The American scholar believes that the austere architectonics of Chekhov's plays, and the depiction of different points of view, the "multilayered consciousness" in the novels of James, provided the basis for the "new prose" that the two writers created. "Time becomes irrevocably tied to space through prose that compresses time into spatialized moments and space into blurred shards of frozen time."[38] This new way of looking at reality switches the attention of the author and the reader from the invention of images and plots to other literary categories, those of simultaneity of action, repetitiveness, plurality, and the phenomenological perception of reality.

To substantiate his thesis about Chekhov's impressionism, Stowell cites the well-known statements by Tolstoy concerning Chekhov's style of writing: Chekhov and modern writers in general display an unusually developed technique of realism. Everything in Chekhov is so believable it is almost an illusion, his works create the impression of a sort of stereoscope. He juggles words in seeming confusion and, like

---

37. *Chekhov's Art of Writing: A Collection of Critical Essays,* edited by Debreczeny and Eekman (Columbus, Ohio, 1977), 7.

38. Stowell, *Literary Impressionism, James and Chekhov* (Athens, Ohio, 1980), 4.

an impressionist painter, achieves the most surprising results with his brush strokes.[39] Stowell attempts to prove that the stories "The Lady with the Little Dog," "The Bishop," and "The Bride" are largely impressionistic in character by suggesting that it is impossible for the reader to know whether Gurov loves Anna, whether the bishop is a bishop, and whether Nadia really changes her life.

In 1984 a collection of articles entitled *Chekhov: New Perspectives* was published in the United States. In his introduction, Rene Wellek notes that no other event contributed as much to the understanding of Chekhov in the United States as the American tour of the Moscow Art Theatre in 1923, when it performed *The Cherry Orchard* and *Ivanov*. Wellek recalls the words of the distinguished American poet Conrad Aiken (1889–1973), who in 1921 said, "Anton Chekhov, possibly the greatest writer of the short story who has ever lived."[40]

Chekhov's drama and prose are the subject of increasingly detailed study by American Slavicists. Nonetheless, America is yet to arrive at a genuine understanding of Chekhov's literary legacy. The great American realist writers of the twentieth century, who felt the power of Chekhov's realism and its importance for their own artistic development, were the first to attempt to do that. American literary scholars have so far failed to follow their example.

---

39. *Lev Tolstoi ob iskusstve i literature* (Leo Tolstoy on Literature and Art) (Moscow, 1958), vol. 2, 143–44.

40. *Chekhov: New Perspectives,* edited by Rene Wellek and Nona Wellek (Englewood Cliffs, N.J., 1984), 28.

Comment
by Richard M. Abrams

Americans have usually had enormous respect for the Russian intelligentsia, and especially for Russian literary figures. Tolstoy, Chekhov, Turgenev, and Dostoevsky appear to Americans as giants, all-time greats among the world's intellectuals. Their durable influence testifies to a common ethical theme that Americans and Russians share.

In other respects, Americans have had a lesser regard for Russian culture. The regime of Imperial Russia contained nearly all that Americans most despised. That included the tsar's unrelenting oppression and the often government-inspired pogroms, the complicity of the Russian Church in the prevailing brutality, the stifling social structure, and the often stolid, retrograde attitudes of the peasantry. The Soviet regime that succeeded the reign of the tsars presented a hardly more attractive face. Quite apart from its other transgressions against humanist values, the Soviet state's controls on the Russian intelligentsia made Russian scholarship highly suspect. And amid the anxieties of the Cold War, it was all too easy for Americans to reject anything that Russians might offer in the way of social criticism.

But not that Americans are not required as a national security matter to see only virtue in the price-and-market system of resource allocation (capitalism), it may be possible for them to find some value in what Soviet-era scholars have said about United States history. No one doubts, I think, that Soviet scholars operated under fairly rigid constraints to exalt socialism and find fault with American liberalism; and that those constraints gave a one-dimensional cast to their accounts. And yet, with ideological blinders off, it may now be possible for Americans to see past those constraints to how much of the Soviet critique of American industrial capitalism rested on traditionalist, as opposed to Marxist, foundations, and found important expression moreover among contemporaries in the United States. In other words, it may now be easier to accept at least the part of the socialist argument that suggested how nineteenth-century liberalism probably went too far in its rejection of traditionalist economic regimes, too far in its rejection of age-old state and community limits on private individual ambition.

Liberalism, as a system of social organization that placed individual liberty at the center of state policy, emerged in the eighteenth century mainly in the northwestern extremity of Europe and in North America. It directly challenged the traditionalist presumption that individual needs and ambitions always must stand subordinate to the purposes of the community and the state. In contrast to the prevailing despotisms throughout the world, it had heralded for some—for those whose hearts went out to the long-suffering masses of humankind and who believed that something could be done about suffering—the promise of liberation from the dual oppressions of poverty and tyranny.

Liberalism transformed the status of individuals from subjects to citizens. It empowered them with substantial measures of immunity from state and community dictates in their private contractual arrangements among themselves and in their use of property for private gain. It was this empowerment over contracts and property that underwrote the price-and-market system of economic organization. And the individualistic energies that liberalism released served well to produce a remarkable rise in material well-being. Especially in the United States during the early nineteenth century, at least in those regions where slavery did not exist, the promise of a broad liberation seemed to be approaching some substantial fulfillment. An increasingly permissive legal structure amidst ample natural resources had provided exceptional opportunities for individuals from diverse class backgrounds to improve the quality of their lives. In such a favorable environment the marketplace appeared to provide direct rewards to personal merit, defined in terms of talent and diligence. The ending of slavery in the 1860s gave the liberal promise still greater respect.

But the liberation of citizens in the nineteenth century from what historically had been oppressive requirements of state and community had a serious downside. That included a spreading inequality of wealth—even as aggregate wealth grew—resulting in profound social resentment. It included, too, the brutalization of masses of people whose different temperaments, talents, and skills sold for low prices in the unforgiving marketplace. And it included the exaltation of a social ethic that, as the Social Christian Walter Rauschenbusch put it, appeared to raise selfishness to the status of high moral principle. The wholesale rejection by liberalism of traditionalist social controls on individual appetite, in other words, had brought about long-term and progressive economic growth, but at substantial short-term human and social costs. It also induced a longer-term sense of moral desolation, especially among the many who retained a traditionalist passion about social responsibility.

Surely it was that sense of moral desolation that helps account for the extraordinarily broad influence of Anton Chekhov on American literature, which A. N. Nikoliukin describes. No doubt there were elements of style, especially in his short stories, that—in Nikoliukin's account—attracted American writers as diverse as William Dean Howells and Tennessee Williams. But it must also be the theme of *decline,* of *boredom,* of *purposelessness,* down to utter *despair* and *depravity* that unites Howells, Williams, Faulkner, Hemingway, the "theater of the absurd," and all the others who, as Nikoliukin shows, acknowledged their heavy debt to Chekhov. The sources of the problem differed greatly. For Chekhov, it was the decay of the old order in Russia under the load of an anachronistic state and social structure, and the ineffectuality of the custodians of Mother Russia's moral order—from the church and aristocracy down through the bemused gentry—for salvaging the still-cherished spiritual elements of the old order. For the Americans, it was the sense that the achievement of material abundance through industrialism, and over the bodies of too many uncompetitive souls, had left a great hole in the nation's character; that the pot at the end of the rainbow was empty.

American reformers noted the costs of industrialization, and strove to reduce them, but their progress was slow—partly because the aggregate economic growth associated with the release of individualistic energies had mitigating effects of its own. Two of the historians in this section of Dialogues focus on the costs, making use of the American reformers' own writings. I. K. Mal'kova's 1971 article on U.S. history and politics during the late nineteenth century, as viewed through the lens of two Russian magazines, gives the critique of the American industrial revolution summary treatment:

> The orgy of enrichment fed by financial speculations and swindles of various kinds, the concentration of capital achieved at the expense of the ruin of small owners and of the pauperization of certain strata of the working population provoked condemnation and moral protests on the part of these [American] writers.

"Pauperization" may be too strong a word for most of the "working population" since real wages rose significantly throughout the last quarter of the nineteenth century; that is, throughout the most tumultuous stages of the American Industrial Revolution. But it is certainly true that there were many temporary and some permanent losers in the transformation of the U.S. political economy. And what was lost was more than income; traditionalist artisans, farmers, and shopkeepers lost their way of life as machines and factories displaced artisanal producers, large-scale commercial agriculture made family farming a dwindling vestige of a bygone social order, and large interstate and international corporations drove independent merchants and shopkeepers from local economies.

Furthermore, as the state relaxed its controls on constructive energies, it unfettered destructive energies as well. Freedom provided the opportunity and the incentive for the economic innovations that generated an affluence unprecedented in world history. The same freedom also opened possibilities for cheats, predators, and schemers. As the scale and scope of enterprise grew, along with the wealth of those who commanded the strategic economic junctures, so too did the dimensions of business corruption. The incidence of corruption could not have been new, but its extent and notoriety probably was. And so Americans' scramble for material wealth offended traditionalist sensibilities everywhere, including that of the Russian reformers who strained against tsarist oppression.

"The hankering after money and riches," Dr. Mal'kova tells us one such critic wrote in the journal *Slovo* (Word) in 1879, "the need to accumulate more and more wealth, which is then frittered away, in order to pay for the luxuries of dishonestly won fortunes, boundless political ambition, and the desire to rise above others—this is what has given modern American society such an unpleasant ambiance. The power of moral ideas is unfortunately bankrupt and at present stands before the world . . . like the knight of the rueful countenance." There are many Americans today, as there were in the 1870s and 1880s, who would echo such sentiments about the "Robber Barons" in what Mark Twain dubbed "The Gilded Age." It appears, moreover, to be the judgment made by Dr. Malkova. She concludes her article with an endorsement of the idea that "it was necessary to overcome the ideology of bourgeois success," and substitute a "spiritual revolution," which by implication she equates with the ideals of socialism.

But of course not all fortunes were dishonestly won, nor all wealth frittered away. A great deal was invested in further economic development, the benefits of which spread quite extensively throughout the society. Much was also spent on education, on health care, on scientific research, on the arts, and on sustaining democratic institutions. One has to wonder, indeed, if socialism's objective widespread human welfare could have been achieved as quickly, or at all, without "the ideology of bourgeois success" and "the desire to rise above others" that it sometimes has seemed so easy to deplore. Walt Whitman—not exactly a model of bourgeois culture, and whom Igor Dement'ev cites in his essay on Tolstoy as an example of an American who attacked the "money-grubbing" capitalists—seems to have believed otherwise. In *Democratic Vistas,* he wrote (beginning with phrasing not unlike that in *Word*'s commentary): "The extreme business energy, and this almost maniacal appetite for wealth prevalent in the United States, are parts of amelioration and progress, indispensably needed to prepare the very results I demand. My theory demands riches and the getting of riches. . . . Upon them, as upon substrata, I raise the edifice designed in these Vistas."

There are similar problems with Tolstoy's critique of American society, as presented in Dement'ev's fine article. Tolstoy's disapproval of Americans is that of a traditionalist committed to nonmaterialist objectives, and to a village ethos that deplores the seeking of wealth and perhaps ambition itself. Like many of those who wrote for *Delo* (Cause) in its radical period (up to c. 1882) and *Word,* Tolstoy tended to exaggerate the virtues of a peasant and preindustrial society, while engaging in hyperbole to attack the evils of the U.S. Industrial Revolution. Not unlike John C. Calhoun, the fiery American advocate of chattel slavery who made the same dubious analogy decades earlier, Tolstoy professed to see no moral difference between slavery and wage labor. Dement'ev himself, committed to Marxian materialism and to the Bolshevik Revolution, cannot accept either Tolstoy's rejection of violent class struggle or his spiritualism—what he calls "the weaker elements in his teaching, like his emphasis on humility." But he uses Tolstoy to emphasize liberalism's spiritual weaknesses by noting what Tolstoy had in common, or seemed to, with some literary critics of U.S. society.

One problem with the Dement'ev essay is his and Tolstoy's eccentric interpretation of the American writers whom Tolstoy apparently admired. Their extravagant approval of Edward Bellamy's utopian novel, *Looking Backward,* for example, suggests a remarkable ability to take whatever one wants from a document for one's own uses, even when it renders the document otherwise unrecognizable. How could this man whom Dement'ev describes as close to an anarchist, and who was almost certainly a complete pacifist, find so much of value in a work that exalted the military organization of society? Bellamy's utopia required children to spend years in a military school, as preparation for their recruitment into what is in fact described as an industrial army. Workers were to be trained in methodical labor and strict obedience. Nor did they participate equally in the political process. Workers were trained to obey, not to vote. "The [industrial] army is not allowed to vote for president?" asks the incredulous time-traveler in a crucial passage that Tolstoy took no note of. "Certainly not," answers the novel's, and Bellamy's, voice. "That would be perilous to its discipline, which it is the business of the president to maintain as the representative of the nation at large."

One can perhaps understand why that might not be disturbing to someone committed to the Soviet political system. And if neither Tolstoy nor Bellamy found it objectionable, that must be attributed to the greater value that they placed on traditionalist presumptions about the virtue of order and social obligation beyond all else. Bellamy, however, assumed that one could have military discipline for the masses and material affluence, too. Tolstoy's traditionalist sensibilities, on the other hand, like that of the many Russian populists who contributed to journals like *Cause* and *Word*, rejected material things altogether.

Through it all, what these articles reveal is a common ethical background among Russian and American humanists and scholars. The work of Mal'kova, Dement'ev, and Nikoliukin underlines the value of historiographical exchanges to which this volume makes an important contribution.

11

Some Questions on American Foreign Policy in 1898–1914 in the Russian Bourgeois Press, by A. F. Tsvirkun

In the early years of the twentieth century, as the United States began to carry out its expansionist designs in the world arena, the Russian press kept its readers informed about the internal situation in that country and its foreign policy. [2] At the turn of the century the bourgeois-liberal press in Russia was largely represented by three publications: *Vestnik Evropy* (European Herald), *Mir Bozhii* (World of God), and *Russkaia Mysl* (Russian Thought). These monthly journals were widely respected among broad sections of the Russian public and influenced to a considerable degree the formation of its views on foreign policy issues. Each enjoyed a stable circulation, never exceeding fifteen thousand copies (*World of God*).[1] All three journals devoted their main attention to historical, political, and literary topics.

The publications in question were chosen as a subject for this study for the following reasons. While functioning within the mainstream of Russian bourgeois liberalism, they exemplified three of its major currents. *World of God* occupied a position on the left, *Russian Thought* on the right, and *European Herald* was centrist. Describing the political platforms of these journals, Vladimir Lenin wrote:

> *European Herald* has its orientation—one which is wrong, vapid, witless, but which serves a certain element, namely, certain strata of the bourgeoisie, and which also unites certain sections of the so-called intelligentsia that are comprised of professors, civil servants and "decent" (or rather, would-be decent) liberals. *Russian Thought* has

---

1. Each journal printed its annual circulation figures in the last issue of the year. This article by A. F. Tsvirkun originally appeared as "Nekotorye voprosy vneshnei politiki SShA v 1898–1914 gg. v osveshchenii russkoi burzhuazno-liberal'noi pechati," in *Amerikanskii Ezhegodnik 1986* (Moscow, 1986), 169–92.

an orientation that is contemptible but of great service to the counter-revolutionary liberal bourgeoisie. The *Modern World* [*World of God*—author] has its orientation— one that is Menshevik-Kadet (with a current bias towards ideological Menshevism), but an orientation nonetheless.[2]

European Herald was one of the oldest periodicals in Russia, first appearing in 1866. Its centrist position among the Russian journals of the bourgeois-liberal variety owed much to the continuing adherence of its publishers to some of the traditions of the Russian enlightenment of the 1860s.[3] The journal approached historical and social issues from the perspective of moderate Russian "academic" liberalism. It was no accident that the public figures whom *European Herald* brought together later became the organizers of the party of democratic reforms. Among the contributors were prominent Russian writers, eminent scholars, and important public figures of the late nineteenth and early twentieth century, such as Mikhail Stasiulevich, Konstantin Arsen'ev, Aleksandr Pypin, and Dmitrii Ovsianiko-Kulikovskii.

From 1866 until October 1908 the editor and publisher of the journal was Stasiulevich.[4] In 1908 Maksim Kovalevskii took over the position of publisher,[5] and Arsen'ev and Ovsianiko-Kulikovskii assumed the editorship. The general orientation of *European Herald* was not affected by the change in editorial control. In spite of the journal's politically moderate character, the censors regarded it with suspicion. Its editors, particularly Stasiulevich, were warned on a number of occasions that they should soften the tone and critical content of the articles they published.

As was already mentioned, the position on the left flank of the bourgeois-liberal press was occupied by *World of God,* published between 1892 and 1906. In 1902 M. K. Kuprina-Davydova, the wife of the well-known Russian writer Aleksandr Kuprin, became its publisher. Lenin placed *World of God* in the category of periodicals that displayed a sympathy for Marxism "out of considerations of fashion."[6] The journal printed articles by well-known Menshevik writers like Paul Axelrod and Nikolai Iordanskii. Among its permanent contributors was George Plekhanov. In 1898 *World of God* published Lenin's review of Aleksandr Bogdanov's book, *A Brief Course of Economic Science.*[7] The shift to the left that *World of God* effected under the impact of the revolutionary events of the period led to its suppression in 1906. The journal resumed publication that same year, however, as *Contemporary World.*

2. V. I. Lenin, *Polnoe Sobranie Sochineniia* (Complete Collected Works), 5th ed. (Moscow, 1960–1964), vol. 48, 3–4.

3. Lenin, *Works,* vol. 2, 543.

4. Mikhail Matveevich Stasiulevich (1826–1911), historian, publicist, and public figure of bourgeois-liberal views. In 1858 he became a medieval history professor at the University of St. Petersburg.

5. Maksim Maksimovitch Kovalevskii (1851–1916), historian, jurist, sociologist, and bourgeois-liberal political figure. In 1905 he was a professor at the University of St. Petersburg, where he taught a course on medieval history; in 1906 he was elected to the First State Duma; in 1907 he was appointed to the State Council.

6. Lenin, *Works,* vol. 46, 23.

7. Lenin, *Works,* vol. 21, 168.

The most reactionary of the bourgeois-liberal periodicals in Russia was the journal *Russian Thought*. From being a publication that was Populist in orientation, it evolved in the course of its existence into a defender of the principles of bourgeois progress, subjecting Marxism and its adherents in Russia to vicious attack. After the revolution of 1905–1907 *Russian Thought* became the organ of the right wing of the Kadet [Constitutional Democrat—ed]. Party and a mouthpiece of the counterrevolutionary bourgeoisie. The journal's publisher and editor was Vukol Lavrov.[8]

The above-mentioned journals devoted considerable attention to international issues, particularly to the foreign policy of the United States and Russian-American relations. The period in question was rich in major international events, with the great powers waging a struggle for the final partition of the world. The United States was becoming an increasingly active player on the international scene. That country was beginning to pay close attention to the situation in Europe, although the thrust of American expansionism remained directed at Latin America and the Far East. In these circumstances the United States and Great Britain began drawing closer, while American-German antagonisms grew more acute. Relations between St. Petersburg and Washington had traditionally been friendly, and remained so, although Russia was beginning to be concerned about the United States as a new and powerful rival, especially in the Far East.[9]

Among these Russian periodicals, most attention was devoted to international relations and the foreign policy of the United States by *European Herald,* reflecting the character of the publication. *Russian Thought* printed informative articles on foreign policy matters that dealt with a variety of topics, although fewer articles of this kind appeared in it than in *European Herald*. *World of God* also devoted attention to American foreign policy. Each journal included a section entitled "Foreign Review," which contained information on the most important events that had taken place in the world. In addition, these publications were represented by permanent correspondents in a number of foreign countries. As a result, they were able to offer their readers detailed reports on important international events.

The articles and reports pertaining to American foreign policy in these journals fall into three major categories: 1) foreign reviews; 2) articles by permanent correspondents in the United States; 3) travelogues and essays by Russians traveling abroad or by individuals who visited foreign countries on official business. In addition, these journals published scholarly studies of U.S. foreign policy.

Articles belonging to the first category were most numerous, the most interesting appearing in *European Herald*. Between 1883 and 1918 the "Foreign Review" section was edited by Liudvig Slonimskii,[10] and every issue contained a "Foreign Review." Of 198 "foreign reviews," 43, or one-fifth, dealt with various aspects of American foreign

---

8. Vukol Mikhailovich Lavrov (1852–1912), prominent publicist and translator.

9. Interesting in this regard is the directive of January 29/February 10, 1898, sent by Mikhail Murav'ev, Russia's minister of foreign affairs, to Ambassador Artur Cassini in Washington, *Krasnyi Arkhiv* (Red Archive) 52 (1932): 133–38.

10. Leonid Liudvig Zinov'evich Slonimskii (1850–?), jurist, public figure, contributor to several newspapers and journals, and author of articles on history, jurisprudence, economics, and political affairs.

policy. Obviously, a considerable amount of space was devoted to American subjects. Among the issues discussed were the events in Cuba and the Spanish-American War and its aftermath; the colonial policy of the United States in the Philippines and Puerto Rico; the rise of American expansionism in different parts of the world; the Venezuelan crisis; Russian-American relations; and disputes over foreign policy within the American government.

Virtually all the pieces dealing with these subjects were written from the perspective of bourgeois pacifism and, as might be expected, reflected a liberal position on international issues. The naïveté and idealism that were so characteristic of Russia's liberals became particularly noticeable when the author of these pieces attempted to address the problem of preserving and guaranteeing international peace. Slonimskii's article, "Pacifism and War," provides a clear illustration of his foreign policy views.[11] Idealizing the practice of arbitration, he expressed the belief that agreements providing for the binding arbitration of international disputes, signed by almost every state in the "civilized" world, guaranteed that the danger of armed conflict had disappeared forever. It is interesting to note that this article was written exactly a year before the outbreak of World War I.

Unfortunately, little is known about Slonimskii's life. Still, an analysis of his articles in *European Herald* suggests that he was a talented and original writer who had an excellent understanding of the details of American foreign policy. In his contributions to "Foreign Review," he made wide use of foreign and Russian press reports, the cables of the Russian Telegraph Agency (RTA), and official government statements. Slonimskii engaged in sharp polemics on international issues with right-wing newspapers and journals, particularly *Novye Vremeni* (New Times) and *Moskovskie Vedomosti* (Moscow Gazette). Despite the methodological flaws evident in his writings, which were due to his bourgeois-liberal and pacifist outlook, his articles sounded a powerful note of protest against the expansionist colonial policies of the imperialist powers, including the United States. In his surveys of the international scene, Slonimskii emphasized the way in which the aspirations of the United States had assumed an increasingly aggressive character during the Spanish-American War. His articles of this period are full of criticism of the American administration for its abandonment of a "peaceful" foreign policy.[12] The behavior of American troops in the Philippines and Puerto Rico especially provoked his indignation.

> Having taken the path of foreign war, Americans, in spite of all their political traditions, unwittingly found themselves in the unaccustomed role of military entrepreneurs and gradually came to act like ordinary conquerors who had forgotten the original motives and aims of the enterprise. What are the Americans on the island of Luzon if not the bearers of crude and unvarnished destructive force?[13]

As this passage shows, Slonimskii had an idealized view of the foreign policy of the United States before 1898. With regard to the question of Russian-American relations,

---

11. Slonimskii, "Patsifizm i voina" (Pacifism and War), *European Herald* (1913), no. 8.
12. "Inostrannoe obozrenie" (Foreign Review), *European Herald* (1898), nos. 5, 7, 8.
13. *European Herald* (1898), no. 4: 216.

Slonimskii called for a strengthening and deepening of friendly relations between Russia and America and criticized the *"New Times* patriots" who advocated declaring a "tariff war" on the United States.[14]

The "Foreign Review" section of *Russian Thought* was edited by Viktor Gol'tsev,[15] a talented journalist who was in effect the editor of the periodical but who died in 1906. After his death "Foreign Review" experienced a number of problems. It was edited in quick succession by several different figures, as a result of which its structure and the way in which the materials in it were presented underwent frequent changes, making a study of the articles in it difficult. Compared with the "Foreign Review" section of *European Herald,* the range of issues covered in *Russian Thought* was narrower. As a rule, only key issues of international relations of the period were discussed. Thus, the journal paid particular attention to such major aspects of American foreign policy as the Spanish-American War and its consequences, the foreign policy debate in the United States, Russian-American relations, and problems in the Far East.

If Slonimskii's outlook was heavily influenced by pacifism, Gol'tsev's was far less so. While the former traced the causes of the Spanish-American War to the liberating mission of the United States, Gol'tsev's view was more skeptical: "The United States would be happy to annex Cuba as a new state or, should she declare independence, to derive every advantage from her new situation."[16] There can be no doubt that Gol'tsev's position on this question was a reflection of his bourgeois-liberal objectivism, an attitude that could not provide the basis for a correct understanding of the roots of the conflict between the United States and Spain. Nevertheless, in his approach to international issues, Gol'tsev displayed greater realism than Slonimskii.

A second feature of Gol'tsev's review writing, and one that was far more characteristic of his articles than of Slonimskii's, was a guarded attitude toward—indeed almost a fear of—the growing military and economic power of the United States. Almost every article on the United States in this section of *Russian Thought* contained warnings about the rise of American power. Gol'tsev devoted particular attention to analyzing the state of the American army and navy and to discussing the prospects for their future development.[17]

Gol'tsev and the other contributors to *Russian Thought* displayed an equivocal attitude to the colonial policy of the United States. On the one hand, Gol'tsev hailed the transfer of sovereignty over the Philippines from Spain to the United States, declaring that "the American flag will protect the freedom of conscience and sanctity of private property both in Cuba and in the Philippines";[18] on the other hand, he was alarmed by the rapid extension of American influence, particularly to areas where Russia also had interests, such as China and Korea. These concerns may explain the

---

14. *European Herald* (1903), no. 6; (1912), no. 11 [pages not indicated in original—ed].
15. Viktor Aleksandrovich Gol'tsev (1850–1906), well-known publicist; received a legal education. He contributed articles to *European Herald, Russkoe Bogatstvo* (Russian Wealth), and many other journals. In 1885–1906 he was the de facto editor of *Russian Thought.* In his writings Goltsev advocated a moderate constitutional-democratic program of change.
16. "Inostrannoe obozrenie" (Foreign Review), *Russian Thought* (1898), no. 4: 179.
17. *Russian Thought* (1899), no. 5: 185.
18. *Russian Thought* (1898), no. 12: 199.

critical statements about the actions of the American colonial army in the Philippines, which in 1898–1902 frequently appeared in the foreign review section of *Russian Thought*.[19]

Although *World of God/Contemporary World* devoted comparatively little attention to the activities of the American government in the field of foreign policy, the journal published several interesting articles on this topic. Naturally, the marked shift to the left of *World of God* in the course of the revolution of 1905–1907 influenced its treatment of foreign policy matters. Initially, the journal's foreign news section, which appeared under the rubric "Abroad," differed little in style and presentation from its counterpart in *European Herald*. After K. L. Veidemuller began to edit this section, the tenor of the articles became very different. This may be clearly seen in his own article about the Mexican Revolution of 1907–1911 and the foreign policy of the United States toward Mexico during that period.[20] The author employed concepts like the class struggle, the labor movement, and the national liberation struggle that were not found in any other bourgeois-liberal publication. Veidemuller was unequivocal in his condemnation of the armed intervention by the United States in Mexico's internal affairs. This long article also contained an analysis of the activities of American trusts in that country. "No branch of the economy is free of the involvement of American capital, no enterprise is immune from cruel and systematic exploitation by it," he writes.[21] Elsewhere in the piece Veidemuller describes the influence of American trusts on the formation of foreign policy.

In another of his articles Veidemuller harshly criticizes America's ambitions in China:

> Among the civilized newcomers to that country who, like birds of prey, have swooped upon the ancient land of China, which they thought would lie quiescent forever, among these rapacious colonizers the Americans occupy a special place. It goes without saying that the motives that lie behind the foreign policy of the North American United States are no different from those that drive other countries to action. Here, too, greed has led to imperialism and a colonialist policy.[22]

He emphasized the sophisticated methods used by the United States in pursuit of its goals.

Before considering the second category of published materials, it is necessary to point out that of the three journals only *European Herald* had its own correspondent in the United States. Their man in America was Petr Tverskoi, a Russian nobleman who was a permanent resident of the United States.[23] Tverskoi was a prolific writer, publishing in

---

19. *Russian Thought* (1902), no. 9: 233–35; (1899), no. 1: 155; (1899), no. 3: 190.
20. "Za rubezhom" (Abroad), *Sovremennyi Mir* (Contemporary World), (1911), no. 4.
21. Ibid., 329.
22. *Contemporary World* (1911), no. 11.
23. Petr Alekseevich Tverskoi (real name Dement'ev [but known in America as Peter Demens—ed] [1850–1923]), landowner, zemstvo activist, journalist and publicist. In the 1880s he emigrated abroad (for nonpolitical reasons) [and became a successful businessman and developer (lumber and citrus) in Florida and California].

European Herald twenty-four major articles on foreign policy during this period. Leo Tolstoy and Vladimir Korolenko both expressed a high opinion of Tverskoi's reports from the United States, although Korolenko also referred in uncomplimentary terms to his personal character.[24] Lenin also cited one of Tverskoi's pieces about America in an article, "On the So-Called Question of Markets."[25]

Tverskoi was a close observer of the political life of his adopted country, and his reports from the United States were invariably distinguished by a comprehensive approach to the various problems and developments in American foreign policy. Of particular interest are the articles he wrote in the last years of the nineteenth century, when the United States was beginning to embark on a broad course of imperialist expansion. While being generally critical of the actions of the American administration, he, nevertheless, tried to defend President McKinley himself. Tverskoi's views on these subjects frequently led to polemics with Slonimskii.[26]

In his dispatches Tverskoi dealt with the events of the Spanish-American War, providing vivid character sketches of the president and his generals and admirals.[27] He wrote much and in detail about the conflicts within the American government concerning foreign policy matters.[28] Several articles dealt with these disagreements and the political struggle between the United States and Britain over the issue of the Panama Canal.[29] Between 1905 and 1907 Tverskoi devoted a great deal of attention to Russian-American relations and to President Roosevelt's activities as mediator during the Russo-Japanese War.[30] Despite certain flaws, Tverskoi's articles and letters are a valuable source for students of the history of American foreign policy.

Although he was on occasion critical of the American government, there can be no doubt that for Tverskoi the United States represented the ideal political system. He believed it to be the most democratic country in the world and thought that all other countries, including Russia, should aspire to emulate it.[31] Tverskoi was blind to the hidden imperialist designs that lay behind Roosevelt's offer to act as mediator during the Russo-Japanese War. He sees the president as a peacemaker with an olive branch in his hand, a man who would spare no effort to reconcile the two warring nations. Yet Tverskoi was inconsistent in his views: he lurches from pacifism to a defense

24. Tolstoi, *Polnoe sobranie sochinenii* (Complete Collected Works), 90 vols., vol. 69, 43; Korolenko, *Izbr. pis'ma* (Selected Letters), 2 vols. (Moscow, 1932), vol. 1, 124–25.

25. Lenin, *Works,* vol. 1, 95–96.

26. "Inostrannoe obozrenie," *European Herald* (1898), no. 7: 9.

27. Tverskoi, "Bor'ba na ostrove Kuba i iz-za Kuby" (Struggle on the Island of Cuba and for Cuba), *European Herald* (1898), no. 5; "Mir—ili novaia voina?" (Peace—Or Another War?), *European Herald* (1898), no. 11.

28. Tverskoi, "Noiabr'skie vybory v S. A. S.-Shtatakh" (November Elections in the North American United States), *European Herald* (1899), no. 1; "Velikaia bor'ba v Soedinennykh Shtatakh" (The Great Struggle in the United States), *European Herald* (1899), no. 5; "Amerikanskaia 'zloba dnia' " (The American "Topic of the Day"), *European Herald* (1901), no. 9.

29. Tverskoi, "Amerikanskaia 'zloba dnia'," *European Herald* (1906), no. 4; "Predstoiashchee otkrytie Panamskogo kanala" (The Forthcoming Opening of the Panama Canal), *European Herald* (1913), no. 7.

30. Tverskoi, "Amerikanskaia 'zloba dnia,' " *European Herald* (1906), no. 4.

31. "Pis'mo iz Ameriki," (Letter from America), *European Herald* (1909), nos. 3 and 11.

of American aggression, and in some of his reports he expresses unapologetically racist views.[32]

Between 1898 and 1914 Tverskoi moved to the right. If at the beginning of this period he still criticized the actions of the American government, by 1906 he had become a staunch defender of American expansionism, and in articles of 1911–1913, he openly called on the United States to intervene militarily in the internal affairs of Mexico.[33]

A third category of published materials are the notes and sketches written by Russian travelers and citizens who went abroad on official business. This category comprises fewer items than the first two, but it represents an important resource for scholars working on the history of the United States. Between 1898 and 1914 three pieces of this type appeared in *European Herald*.

For historians studying American foreign policy, the most interesting is an article by Fedor Martens.[34] He had personally met and held discussions with President Roosevelt and other prominent American social and political figures. The author offers a thoughtful analysis of the economic and political situation in the United States at the turn of the century. Martens is full of admiration for American "democracy" and for the economic and cultural achievements of the United States, but when he turns to foreign policy issues, his tone changes. The author calls on the Americans to renounce the pursuit of military power. "Modern American imperialism will inevitably act as a stimulus for the emergence of the most unforeseeable political complications," he writes. Further in the article he says, "The role of 'world citizen' does not come cheap. That is why the military budget of the United States is growing at such a prodigious rate and why it is impossible to predict when that growth will cease."[35] Clearly these views have not lost their relevance even today.

Of considerable interest are Martens's views on the Monroe Doctrine and its relation to the spread of American expansionism to other continents:

> One needs only to recall the phases that the famous Monroe Doctrine has gone through over the last few years. Originally this doctrine was a protest by the United States against the desire of the great European powers to intervene in the struggle of the peoples of Central America to gain their liberty. It put an end to such intervention and insured the free development of the Central American states in the form of endless revolutions, assassinations, and feuds. Thereafter, the Monroe Doctrine served as the

---

32. "Amerika i Iaponiia," (America and Japan), *European Herald* (1906), no. 9; "Razlozhenie partii i noiabr'skie vybory v Amerike" (The Disintegration of the Parties and the November Elections in America), *European Herald* (1907), no. 2.

33. "Pis'mo Iz Ameriki," *European Herald* (1910), no. 1; (1911), no. 8; (1913), no. 11.

34. Martens, "Amerikanskie vpechatleniia: Ocherki i zametki" (American Impressions: Notes and Sketches), *European Herald* (1902), no. 11. Fedor Fedorovich Martens (1845–1909), Russian diplomat and jurist, expert on international law, president of the European Institute on International Law, took part in almost all the major international conferences of the period, played an important role at The Hague conferences, and was a permanent member of the international arbitration tribunal in The Hague. He was made an honorary doctor of jurisprudence by a number of foreign universities, including the University of Pennsylvania.

35. Ibid., 324.

foundation for the claim by the United States to act as the supreme protector over the whole of America, for "America must belong to Americans." It was also seen as supporting the right of the Washington government to interfere even in relations between the countries of Europe—who held parts of the American continent—and their own subjects or neighboring American peoples. Finally, in recent times the Monroe Doctrine was even used to justify the conquest of the Philippine Islands, for as an eminent American diplomatist recently remarked, "We Americans have almost grown into citizens of the entire Universe."[36]

An article published in *European Herald* in 1898 was signed "P. S-ov."[37] The initials concealed the identity of Petr Strel'tsov, a man who had lived a very interesting life. As a young man he went to Cuba to join the local insurgents, becoming in 1896 a member of the detachment commanded by General Maseo, "the Bronze Titan," and took part in the fighting against the Spaniards in the province of Pinar del Rio. Some time after he returned to Russia, he was subjected to persecution by the police for his links with Social-Democrats [Marxists].[38] Strel'tsov's article is a useful source for scholars specializing in American history, for the author writes at some length about the attitude of the United States toward the revolt in Cuba. As is to be expected, Streltsov, being a supporter of Cuban independence, was critical of the annexationist policies of the United States.[39] He writes:

> With a few minor exceptions, the American people as a whole merely limit themselves to expressing a somewhat platonic sympathy for the freedom fighters in Cuba, whereas the government, placing its commercial interests above all others, follows an uncertain course of action, in the apparent hope that a Spain weakened by the conflict would cede the rebellious island to the United States, even though this does not accord with the wishes of the majority of the insurgents.[40]

Next the author points out the following curious detail:

> The influence of the United States in Cuba is noticeable in many ways. At present the role of carriers and communicators of American culture is played by Florida and New York pharmacists, cigar-makers, and barbers (the children of Americanized Cubans), who come here as officers and would-be saviors of a homeland they have never seen. The influence of these typical representatives of American civilization can only be

---

36. Ibid.
37. P. S-ov, "Dva mesiatsa na ostrove Kuba" (Two Months on the Island of Cuba), *European Herald* (1898), no. 5.
38. Strel'tsov is identified as the author on the basis of the similarity between the events it describes and the facts of his life (see P. A. Mironchuk, "Istoricheskii ocherk otnoshenii mezhdu Kuboi i Rossiei i Kuboi i SSSR" [Historical Sketch of the Relations between Cuba and Russia and Cuba and the U.S.S.R.], Ph.D. diss. abstract [Moscow, 1979], 10, as well as on the basic congruence between the initials "P. S-ov" and the name).
39. A. S. Trofimov, *Proletariat Rossii i ego bor'ba protiv tsarizma, 1861–1904* (The Russian Proletariat and Its Struggle against Tsarism, 1861–1904) (Moscow, 1979), 90.
40. P. S-ov, "Two Months," 130.

described as pernicious. They behave arrogantly toward their dark-skinned fellow-countrymen, as if they do them honor by the very fact of their presence.[41]

A third article was by the Russian traveler F. Knorring,[42] who focused on the attitude of American public opinion toward the foreign policy of the United States. After citing concrete examples of the chauvinistic fervor imbuing certain segments of American society after the Spanish-American War, he describes a performance entitled "The Battle of Manila," full of pretentious stage effects. The show concluded with the singing of the national anthem. "A great rush of patriotic enthusiasm, many have tears in their eyes. The production, accompanied throughout by a stentorian commentary from a lecturer, ends with the audience offering thunderous applause and emitting bellicose cries."[43]

Of four travel pieces in *Russian Thought,* the first two were by Anna Cherevkova, a Russian woman doctor who had visited the United States in 1900.[44] Travelogues written by visitors to America are particularly interesting because of the references in them to specific foreign policy actions by the United States. Cherevkova, for example, discusses the manifestations of American economic expansion in Europe. She relates the story of an American dentist of her acquaintance who had decided to extend his practice to Europe. On the basis of this seemingly insignificant fact the author, quite correctly, draws the following conclusion: "America, as we know, has opened a fully-fledged offensive against the industries of the Old World, sending her products to the four corners of the earth and winning one market after another. Dr. K.'s enterprise appears to be part of this *Drang nach Osten,* which forms such a characteristic feature of recent American history."[45] But on the whole Cherevkova's two articles are full of admiration for America's economic might and its impact in the Old World. One curious aspect of her writings merits particular attention. She describes the perception that Americans have of Russia and Russians, and records her impressions of a play she had seen at a Chicago theatre, in which Russia and its inhabitants were presented in a completely ridiculous light.[46]

The other two travel pieces were written by Vladimir Korsakov, a physician at the Russian embassy in Peking, who had worked there for a number of years and had survived the siege of the embassy during the Boxer Rebellion. In his travelogue, "Along the Korean Shore," Korsakov refers to certain issues pertaining to the policy pursued by the great powers, including the United States, toward Korea, and hails the "civilizing" influence of these countries on the Korean people. In his other article, "A Year in Peking," the author describes the activities of the foreign expeditionary forces

---

41. Ibid., 143.
42. F. I. Knorring, "Mesiats v Amerike: Iz dorozhnykh zapisok" (A Month in America: A Selection of Travel Sketches), *European Herald* (1901), nos. 10 and 11.
43. *European Herald,* no. 10: 749.
44. A. A. Cherevkova, "Chikago (Iz puteshestviia po Amerike)" (Chicago: [From an American Journey]), *Russian Thought* (1902), no. 11; "Niagara-N'iu Iork (Iz puteshestviia po Amerike)" (Niagara-New York), *Russian Thought* (1902), no. 12.
45. "Niagara-N'iu Iork," *Russian Thought* (1902), no. 12: 121.
46. Ibid., 135.

in Peking and discusses their attitudes toward one another, as well as their relations with the local population. Korsakov reserves particular praise for the American contingent, whose discipline he finds to be admirable.[47]

In addition to the three categories of materials we have analyzed, the journals printed a number of theoretical articles by different authors, which were either entirely devoted to the subject of American foreign policy, or which touched upon it to some degree or other. Thus, an article in *European Herald* by P. A. Nadin[48] is of interest because it discusses aspects of American foreign policy in the Far East; an article by Slonimskii entitled "Pacifism and War," because it dealt with the question of international arbitration and analyzed the activities of Andrew Carnegie;[49] and, finally, a lengthy article by Maksim Kovalevskii.[50] This last piece contains much valuable information on the problem of the Far East as a factor in the foreign policy of Russia, the United States, and Japan. Kovalevskii describes in detail the course of the Russian-Japanese negotiations, President Roosevelt's actions behind the scenes, and his "contribution" to the conclusion of the peace treaty. We have not been able to identify the informant who supplied Kovalevskii with the intelligence for his article. The author himself states that he "does not believe he has the right to name the source of his information and takes full moral responsibility for its accuracy."[51] An analysis of the contents suggests that Kovalevskii received his information from a member of the Russian delegation at Portsmouth.

It appears that lack of detailed knowledge about the negotiations was the reason why all the contributors to *European Herald,* including Kovalevskii, described Roosevelt as a friend of Russia and a disinterested peacemaker. The journal continued to express this profoundly erroneous view in later years, although in 1911 it published an article whose author wrote: "We may say with complete confidence that however much he [Roosevelt] tried to pretend that at a difficult moment for our country he acted out of friendship toward Russia, it is now a secret for no one that he continues to hate Russia, even after realizing the short-sighted and pernicious nature of his Japanophile policy."[52]

Two treatments of American foreign policy appeared in *World of God.* The author of the first of these, on the history of the Monroe Doctrine, was D. Netochaeva.[53] She discusses at length its genesis and analyzes its application throughout the entire course of the nineteenth century. Netochaeva invests this document with a content very different from its real one, and draws her readers' attention to "Monroe's great principle—defense of one's own freedom and refusal to encroach on anyone else's."[54]

---

47. V. V. Korsakov, "Po beregam Korei" (Along the Korean Shore), *Russian Thought* (1904), nos. 4–7; "God v Pekine" (A Year in Peking), *Russian Thought* (1905), no. 1.
48. Nadin, "Piatidesiatiletie Amurskogo kraia" (Fiftieth Anniversary of the Amur Province), *European Herald* (1905), no. 5.
49. Slonimskii, "Pacifism and War."
50. Kovalevskii, "Portsmut," *European Herald* (1908), no. 6.
51. Ibid., 98.
52. "Outsaider," "Konets Ruzvel'ta," *European Herald* (1911), no. 1: 225.
53. Netochaeva, "Doktrina Monro" (The Monroe Doctrine), *World of God* (1899), no. 2.
54. Ibid., 51.

The author concludes by expressing regret, as was now usual for a bourgeois writer, that the United States, by annexing the Philippines, had violated Monroe's principles and had embarked on a dangerous course of foreign conquest.

> But now the United States itself is setting off on a perilous path, violating the second part of the Monroe Doctrine, which forbade interference in the affairs of other continents and the pursuit of foreign conquest outside the American continent. The conquest of the Philippines, whose inhabitants do not wish to submit to American rule, threatens the hitherto brilliant progress in the internal life of the United States with huge complications and may embroil it in international difficulties that may disrupt for a long time the regular course of American life.[55]

The second article, by Emiliia Pimenova, contains an analysis of the foreign policies of President Roosevelt.[56] In her discussion of the president's actions, the author displayed some of the same misconceptions that have already been described. Pimenova placed particular emphasis on the peace-loving pronouncements that Roosevelt was in the habit of making. She repeatedly declares, "Aimless, senseless war does not find an advocate in him.... Several times he proclaimed himself a supporter of peace and in Washington he has mediated treaties by the dozen."[57] Unlike some other writers, however, Pimenova points out the contradictions between the president's pacific statements and his simultaneous demands for an increase in American naval construction.

Many notices on U.S. foreign policy appeared in *Russian Thought*. The most important of these were the articles "Sakhalin as a Colony" by A. Seich and "Why Is America Advancing So Rapidly?" by Ivan Ozerov, a bourgeois economist who was a professor at the universities in Moscow and St. Petersburg.[58] Seich's article is largely devoted to the rivalry between Russia and the United States in the Far East, particularly on the island of Sakhalin.[59] The island's riches had long excited the appetites of American businessmen. Seich describes the attempts made by the Americans in the late nineteenth century to take over the Sakhalin coalfields.

As noted above, the rapid rise of the United States as an economic power and the intensification of its expansionist activities in various parts of the world created serious concern in Russia. Ozerov analyzes the reasons for the impressive economic growth of the United States and discusses the penetration by American capital of the European market. His essay reflected the anxiety felt by Russia over the increasing economic might of the United States: "The industrial development of the United States threatens the whole world with major perturbations."[60] And further in his article he declared:

55. Ibid., 54.
56. Pimenova, "Teodor Ruzvel't—XXV prezident Soedinennykh Shtatov" (Theodore Roosevelt—25th President of the United States), *World of God* (1905), no. 2.
57. Ibid., 305, 309.
58. Ibid., 309.
59. Seich, "Sakhalin kak koloniia" (Sakhalin as a Colony), *Russian Thought* (1904), nos. 6, 7, 9–11; Iv. Ozerov, "Otchego Amerika tak bystro idet vpered?" (Why Is America Advancing So Rapidly?), *Russian Thought* (1903), no. 10.
60. Ozerov, "Why Is America Advancing So Rapidly?" 186.

"Europe is faced with a grave test, and victory will belong to the one who possesses the superior culture."[61] To illustrate his inferences, the author offered a table in which he compared the incomes of the five largest economic magnates in America and the five most powerful European monarchs. The comparison was clearly not to Europe's advantage. [2]

The journals *European Herald, Russian Thought,* and *World of God/Contemporary World,* representing three central strands in the Russian bourgeois-liberal press of the period, to a certain extent differed in their treatment of American foreign policy between 1898 and 1914. These differences were in fact those of representatives of the same political camp—that of the liberal bourgeoisie. That is why, despite the divergence in the journals' attitudes toward the foreign policy actions of the United States, the positions taken by the three Russian journals on the fundamental issues of American history and politics clearly have much in common.

Thus, all three periodicals idealized the American political system. This is true even of Veidemuller, who held Social-Democrat views and among the writers we have discussed was most critical of the United States. For example, in one of his pieces he declares, "The United States is a country where the people enjoy full sovereignty."[62] It goes without saying that this idealization of the internal political structures of the United States could not but affect the authors' analysis of that country's foreign policy. Of course, they wrote many critical things about the American government in general and about the presidents in particular. Yet as a rule their criticism was inconsistent and, owing to its methodological inadequacies, could not identify the true causes of the imperialist policies of the United States. Thus, whilst denouncing the colonial policies of the United States, the contributors to *European Herald* and *Russian Thought* condemned not the goals of the government, but only the cruel methods Americans used to pursue those goals. Only *World of God* made a half-hearted attempt to criticize the colonial aspirations of the European powers and the United States. In discussing American colonial policy as a whole, *European Herald* and *Russian Thought* referred to what they considered its benign influence on backward peoples.

When analyzing the growing aggressiveness of the United States, its decision to pursue colonial expansion beyond the American continent, and the consequences of this for Russia, which was now faced with a new rival, particularly in the Far East, the bourgeois-liberal authors expressed fears of a possible military conflict between the United States and the European powers. In response to these developments the contributors to *European Herald* set all their hopes upon the long history of friendly relations between Russia and the United States and closed their eyes to the very real antagonisms existing between the two countries, particularly in the Far East. *Russian Thought,* however, was more skeptical in its evaluation of the tradition of cooperation between the United States and Russia and in its attitude toward future prospects for such cooperation.

In any discussion of the way in which the Russian bourgeois-liberal press informed its readers about aspects of American foreign policy, the following fact must be mentioned.

61. Ibid., 187.
62. "Za rubezhom" (Abroad), *Contemporary World* (1912), no. 1: 328.

Whilst criticizing the growing aggressiveness of the United States, all bourgeois-liberal authors idealized that country's foreign policy prior to the Spanish-American War, describing it as "peaceful" and "idyllic." Thus, the materials on the foreign policy of the United States during 1898–1914 in these Russian journals should be approached critically. The factual statements in the texts in question should be verified by means of an analysis of other types of sources. There can be no doubt, however, that as a source in their own right these materials are of considerable interest, which is why they deserve the attention of scholars specializing in American history.

Comment
by Norman E. Saul

It is interesting to contrast the views of the United States depicted in a liberal journal of the 1820s (Bolkhovitinov) and those of the 1870s (Mal'kova) with what A. F. Tsvirkun finds represented in key periodicals at the turn of the century. America is no longer a distant model to be praised, contrasted, or critiqued with Russian reform and progress in mind. This is partially the result of the fading of radical-liberal idealism in Russia, and also of a rise in self-conscious Russian nationalism. Most of all, the shift represents the "coming of age" of the United States, its rise in status to that of a world power, actually or at least potentially greater than that of the Russian Empire.

Tsvirkun stresses that *even* liberal journals in the early twentieth century, those that one might expect to be sympathetic to the United States, the chief proponent of a democratic, progressive way of life, contained sharply negative views. Evidently, the writers and editors of these publications were reacting to a disappointment that the United States, in their and many others' eyes, had "betrayed the cause" and had become imperialistic, self-centered, a class society like that of the much-disparaged old Europe. The idealistic hopes of the "communists" and populists of the 1870s, discussed by Kuropiatnik, have been dashed to pieces by rising internal social conflict and international military and economic rivalry.

The author, however, treats the subject from a one-dimensional, traditional Russian perspective, one that could be just as easily representative of pre– or post–Soviet Russia as in the days of the Cold War. What is missing then is any analysis of why the United States might be perceived as an increasing threat, a country to be watched with care and concern. There is no mention of why the United States might be taking a more aggressive, hostile stance in world affairs, and especially toward Russia. To cite just two relatively new factors: the perception of Russian expansionism in the Far East with reluctant and unsatisfactory responses to the "open door," sponsored by the United States, and leading to strong initial American support for Japan, much resented by all shades of Russian opinion, in the Russo-Japanese War that resulted. American public opinion and official policy toward Russia had also shifted considerably as a result of Russia's obvious and official anti-Semitism and the increasingly bloody pogroms that were an indirect result. This led to the "passport question," strong public opposition to denying visas to American citizens on religious grounds, and the subsequent abrogation of the commercial treaty of 1832.

On the other hand, American economic penetration of Russia was relatively modest, but perhaps more visible, than that of European states. The Singer Sewing Machine Company, for example, not only saturated the countryside but also dominated the landscape of Nevsky Prospect in St. Petersburg with its largest office building. But much of it was supported and encouraged by the government and most of Russian society in the interests of development and progress. Tsvirkun's mention of an American dentist in Russia is interesting but hardly demonstrates a new economic imperialism. Americans had dominated high-quality dentistry in that country for most of the nineteenth century, but this was obviously a rather small "market" in any event.

P. A. Tverskoi (Peter Demens) is an interesting figure, a comparatively rare example of a successful Russian immigrant, who deserves a careful study in his own right [personal papers in Library of Congress]. As a wealthy California businessman, he took on various causes—including settlement of the Dukhobor and Molokan religious sects—and wrote extensively about Russia for American publications. That he was the only—or at least one of the few—resident Russian correspondents in the United States may indicate one of the problems in Russian appraisals of that society.

Fedor Martens also deserves more attention. Though a learned scholar of international law, he was no diplomat and won no friends among Americans for his cantankerous and obstructionist behavior in the Treaty of Portsmouth negotiations and at The Hague peace conference. That he would have a negative view of America is not surprising but is hardly representative of the Russian diplomatic corps. He, too, however, is worthy of additional study.

What Tsvirkun has contributed is nonetheless important as a study of liberal attitudes in turn-of-the-century Russia. While not fully representative—omitting Americanophile Paul Miliukov—they do reveal a nationalist, unpragmatic bent that very much affects the liberal failure in Russia: the inability or refusal to deal with the nationality problem in 1917, or in the 1990s. They presage the bedeviling resentment of American "intrusions" and international influence by "the good democrats" of recent Russian history. A similar article might be written about the American theme in post-Soviet liberal journals. But Americans, too, can learn from seeing themselves in the Russian mirror, warts and all.

Postscript
Past, Present, and Future
by N. N. Bolkhovitinov and Norman E. Saul

In recent decades the understanding of international relations and, in particular, the relations between Russia and the United States and the interaction between their peoples, including the whole complex of trade, diplomatic, scientific, cultural, and other contacts, has been very productive. In this tradition Nikolai Bolkhovitinov as well as many others developed their scholarly works. Highlights included the basic Soviet-American joint publication of documents: *The United States and Russia: The Beginning of Relations, 1765–1815,* the monographs of Gennady Kuropiatnik, Aleksandr Nikoliukin, and Norman Saul.[1] Many special studies appeared devoted to different aspects of Russian-American relations, for example, literary, social, and economic contacts, and also trade connections on Northwest America.[2]

---

1. N. N. Bolkhovitinov, *Stanovlenie russko-amerikanskikh otnoshenii, 1775–1815* (The Beginnings of Russian-American Relations, 1775–1815) (Moscow, 1966), and *Russko-amerikanskie otnosheniia, 1815–1832* (Russian-American Relations, 1815–1832) (Moscow, 1980); *The United States and Russia: The Beginnings of Relations, 1765–1815* (Moscow and Washington, 1980); G. P. Kuropiatnik, *Rossiia i SShA: ekonomicheskie kul'turnye i diplomaticheskie sviazi, 1867–1881* (Russia and the U.S.A.: Economic, Cultural, and Diplomatic Connections, 1867–1881) (Moscow, 1980); Norman E. Saul, *Distant Friends: The United States and Russia, 1763–1867* (Lawrence, Kans., 1991), and *Concord and Conflict: The United States and Russia* (Lawrence, Kans., 1996).

2. N. N. Nikoliukin, *Literaturnye sviazi Rossii i SShA: stanovlenie literaturnykh kontaktov* (The Literary Connections of Russia and the United States: The Beginnings of Literary Contacts) (Moscow, 1981), and *Vzaimosviazi literatur Rossii i SShA: Turgenev, Tolstoi, Dostoevskii i Amerika* (Interrelations of Russian and American Literatures; Turgenev, Tolstoy, Dostoevsky and America) (Moscow, 1987); Walther Kirchner, *Studies in Russian-American Commerce, 1820–1860* (Leiden, 1975); Howard I. Kushner, *Conflict on the Northwest Coast: Russian-American Rivalry on the Pacific Northwest, 1790–1867* (Westport, Conn., 1975).

Serious attention was given to scholarly ties, the position of Russian publicists, and, especially, the attitude toward America of Russian writers and public figures, beginning with Mikhail Lomonosov, Nikolai Novikov, and Alexander Radishchev, and ending with Ivan Turgenev, Fedor Dostoevsky, Lev Tolstoi, and Vladimir Korolenko, who had American interests and connections.

The articles included in the present volume offer proof of the usefulness of such broad complex approaches to the study of the history of relations between Russia and the United States. Indeed these articles differ from each other, according to the importance of the proposed goals, embracement of documentary sources, and depth of their analysis, but all contribute to an understanding of the cultural, scientific, literary, and personal ties between Russia and the United States, enrich perceptions on the interdependence of the cultures of peoples, and, in the end, contribute to change mutual ignorance to mutual knowledge and respect. Their significance increases because all of them were published during the Cold War, when the image of "enemy" was created in the U.S.S.R., and the American perception of Russia was far from the ideal, especially considering such references as "evil empire."

An example of the difficulty of pursuing serious scholarship on Russian-American relations during the Cold War is the article "The American Theme in the Journal *Dukh Zhurnalov* (Spirit of Journals)," published in 1972. It is now difficult to believe, but at that time its publication was not a simple affair, as it might seem today after the collapse of the Soviet system. It was sent out for review for publication more than ten times. And its appearance in press to some extent was a fortuitous accident. The question arises—why? This article pertained to events of 150 years ago! But some rather cautious editors understood that the journal examined and its editor, Iatsenkov, passionately defended the political composition of the United States and its constitution in the Russia of autocracy and despotism. The article proved that *Spirit of Journals,* which was mistakenly considered reactionary, was in reality closed for being politically unreliable, especially for publication on its pages of American materials and, in particular, the introductory remarks to the "State Calendar of the American United States" (*Spirit of Journals* 42 [1820]: 18).

But after that breakthrough, the American theme on the pages of the Russian press became quite popular as a subject for research. In addition to articles in this present edition, dissertations by Iaroslav Ivanchenko, Levon Arustamian, and others appeared.[3] But much more remains to be done, especially on the corresponding image of Russia in American journals.

Even more productive has been the study of attitudes of leading Russian public figures and men of letters toward America. The pioneer in this field before World War II was the prominent Soviet philologist Dr. Abel' Startsev, and in the 1980s appeared the works of Aleksandr Nikoliukin, one of which, the article on Anton Chekhov, is included

---

3. For example, Ia. A. Ivanchenko, "Amerikanskaia problematika v Russkoi peridicheskoi pechati (1825–1841 gody)" (The American Problem in the Russian Periodical Press [1825–1841]) (University of Moscow diss., 1982); L. R. Arustamian, "Amerikanskaia probelmatika v russkoi periodicheskoi pechati (1841–1856 gody)" (The American Problem in the Russian Periodical Press [1841–1856]) (University of Moscow diss., 1992).

in this volume. It is necessary to say that for the eighteenth century this subject has been explored nearly exhaustively, but much more research is needed on the nineteenth century and beginning of the twentieth century. There are, for example, a number of references to "American models" in the research on Russian economic and institutional development under Sergei Witte and Petr Stolypin but no thorough study of their roles in shaping Russian policies and institutions.

Even such a well-known theme as "Tolstoy and America," which is the subject of a series of in-depth studies and documentary publications, including the article of Igor Dement'ev, is far from being comprehensively investigated. The same conclusion applies to other Russian men of letters, including Chekhov and the Ukrainian Vladimir Korolenko, who, as is known, had already visited the United States before the end of the nineteenth century.

Although the majority of articles in this collection have no particular political coloring, in some cases and especially in the article by Vladimir Moriakov one can see a strong influence of orthodox Marxism. Even very radical heroes of his essay—Paine, Raynal, and Radishchev—sometimes are characterized as "inconsistent" and full of "class-based limitations." Paine, for example, "hailed the Constitution of 1787," was "against the revolutionary terror of the Jacobins," was "unable to comprehend fully the complex situation" during "the last stage of the revolution in France."[4] "As the revolutionary struggle unfolded," Moriakov concludes, "Paine's lack of consistency, Raynal's desire for a compromise with the monarchy, and Radishchev's dissatisfaction with the results of the revolutions in America and France all became clear."[5]

In his evaluations Moriakov followed the traditional views of Soviet historiography, which in more recent years have been the object of major revisions. For example, the old evaluation of the Constitution of 1787 as "Thermidor," the stress on the conservatism and limitation of the American Revolution in comparison with the French, to say nothing about decisive reappraisal of Jacobin terror as the highest stage of the Revolution in France, have now been rejected.[6]

The articles represented in this collection in their majority relate to the period before "perestroika," when there were many "blank spots" in Soviet historiography, that is, themes or subjects that practically were omitted from the attention of researchers. Such closed or semi-closed subjects existed also in Russian-American relations, and among them we first of all may mention the Jewish question. Beginning in 1864, this

4. Vestnik *MCU* [Herald of the University of Moscow], Series 8 (History), 1984, no. 5: 72–74.
5. Ibid., 76.
6. Bolkhovitinov, "'Belye piatna' v izuchenii istorii SShA" (Blank Spots in the Study of American History), *Obshchestvennye nauki* (Social Sciences), 1989, no. 2: 151–59; "Revoliutsiia 1789 g.: gil'otina i termidor" (The Revolution of 1789: Guillotine and Thermidore), *Vstrechi s istoriei* (Encounters with History), vol. 3 (Moscow, 1990): 3–16; and "La Révolution Française et la Révolution Americaine: experience nouvelle d'une étude comparative," in *L'Image de la Révolution Française,* edited by M. Vovelle, vol. 2 (Paris 1989): 1203–7; "New Thinking and the Study of the United States in the Soviet Union," *Reviews in American History* 19, no. 2 (June 1991): 155–56. For additional details on radicalism in the American Revolution, see Gordon S. Wood, *The Radicalism of the American Revolution* (New York, 1991).

question occupied a position of increasing importance in the relationship up to 1917 (to say nothing about in the relations between the U.S.S.R. and the United States in the second half of the twentieth century). But still relatively little has been done by Russian scholars on "the Jewish Question" in Russian-American relations.

It is probably impossible to ignore that even in such serious works as the monographs of Kuropiatnik and Rafail Ganelin the Jewish question was practically ignored, and only in recent years has a decisive breakthrough occurred.[7] Serious attention to the attitude of the American public to the situation of the Jews at the end of the nineteenth century is given in the dissertation of Viktoria Zhuravleva, and recently Valerii Engel' devoted a special study to the history of the passport conflict (1864–1913).[8]

The general backwardness in the study of these problems in Russia has still not been overcome, while the clear priority of the study of the Jewish question has belonged to American historians, as in the monograph by Naomi Cohen, the book of Hans Rogger, and many scholarly articles in historical journals. It is also true that little attention has been devoted to the anti-Russian influence of the many Polish and Ukrainian immigrants to America on Russian-American relations in the early twentieth century.

Little work has been done on the activities of American businessmen in Russia. Even such well-known American firms as McCormick-Harvesting Machine Company and Singer Sewing Machine Company, though studied by Americans, have been neglected by Russian scholars. These two firms employed as many as sixty thousand Russians just before World War I, and how many other Russians used their products? Also important in cultural interaction are the operations of American insurance and electric companies and mining enterprises. Special investigations in the future could reveal much on the cultural impact of these Americans in Russia, and much material on them should now be available in Russian archives.

Similarly, little work has been done on the presence and contacts of American travelers throughout the period but especially at the end of the nineteenth and early twentieth centuries, when the Trans-Siberian Railroad attracted a host of adventurers from America and when disastrous famines drew American relief efforts. Thorough studies are also waiting on the impact of the Russian revolutionary movement and in particular the Revolution of 1905 on the American Socialist movement.

Much should be expected also from investigations of Russian contributions to American culture and science, especially to music, literature, art, even folk art, and history in the twentieth century. More liberal access to Russian archives, including documents of the Communist Party and the Foreign Ministry, offer grounds to improve and broaden the study of the relations between Russia and the United States. Of course,

---

7. Kuropiatnik, *Rossiia i SShA . . . 1867–1881;* R. Sh. Ganelin, *Rossiia i SShA, 1914–1917* (Leningrad, 1969).

8. V. I. Zhuravleva, "Probelmy politicheskoi i sotsial'noi zhizni Rossii kontsa XIX veka v obshchestvennom mnenii SShA" (Problems of Political and Social Life of Russia at the End of the Nineteenth Century and Public Opinion in the U.S.A.), University of Moscow diss., 1992; V. V. Engel', "Amerikanskii pasport i russko-evreiskii vopros v kontse XIX-nachala XX veka" (The American Passport and the Russian-Jewish Question at the End of the Nineteenth–Beginning of the Twentieth Centuries), *Amerikanskii Ezhegodnik 1991* (Moscow, 1992), 104–20.

this relates primarily to the Soviet period, to the history of World War II and the Cold War, but we can expect many new possibilities for the study of the eighteenth and nineteenth centuries too.

There was a time when even the use of the word "colonization" aroused opposition from vigilant Russian publishers. This term was changed for the word "acculturation" (*osvoenie*). It was practically impossible to write objectively on negative aspects of Russian colonization of Siberia and the Northwest coast of the American continent, exploitation of native population, the cruelty toward Aleuts by Grigorii Shelikhov, Alexander Baranov, and other pioneers of Russian expansion on the North Pacific, and about armed conflicts of Russian fur traders with native Tlingits on the territory of Russian America.

In regard to the Russian presence in Northwest America, it is also important to study the impact of the Orthodox Church from its beginnings in the eighteenth century through the twentieth century. The ties between the Russian Orthodox Church and other denominations contributed to mutual understanding between the peoples, but there was also rivalry and conflict. And Orthodoxy had an impact not only in Alaska but also in a number of locations in the continental United States.

The area of comparative history is very promising for future study, for example, in regard to frontier history. A mutual fascination existed in each country: Russians with the American West, Americans with the settlement and development of Siberia. On this, as well as other topics such as policies toward native peoples, joint Russian-American studies and conferences could be quite fruitful, spark new perspectives, and provide for a continuing dialogue.

Many obstacles and limitations to study and research are now lifted, and it is possible to hope that a future history of Russian America in three volumes, which is now in preparation by the Center of North American Studies at the Institute of General History, with the cooperation of scholars in St. Petersburg, Barnaul, Fairbanks, and Toronto, will be free from the burdensome legacy of the past and will become a starting point for all who are interested in the history of Alaska. It is also possible to expect an improvement in the professional level of future documentary publications, such as in the continuation of "Russian Exploration on the Pacific Ocean." A new third issue of this publication, under the title "Foundation of the Russian American Company and the First Round the World Voyages, 1799–1815," is soon to appear. It is hoped that the considerable new Russian publishing on Russian America, omitted from this volume, can also be translated and made available to American scholars.

Serious work is being conducted on Russian-American relations during the American Civil War and the liberal reforms in Russia in the 1860s. Perhaps one can finally hope that after M. M. Malkin's groundbreaking book, *Tsarist Russia and the Civil War in the U.S.A., 1861–1865*, published in 1939, a new serious step forward will be made in the study of this major period in the history of relations between our two countries.

It is necessary to note, however, that new difficulties for publication of scholarly work in post–Soviet Russia are now being encountered. Russian and American scholars and archivists succeeded in the preparation of the joint basic documentary publication covering the years from 1765 to 1815, which appeared simultaneously in Moscow and Washington in 1980, but now the work on its sequel "Russia and the United

States: The Development of Relations, 1815–1865" is dormant because of financial difficulties on both the Russian and the American sides. Severe economic hardships born by researchers and teachers in institutes and universities of the former Soviet Union have impeded scholarship in recent years. Many scholars have been forced to turn to other pursuits to survive, and the existence of journals such as *Amerikanskii Ezhegodnik* (American Annual) has been threatened. Increases in support programs in both countries and special initiatives, such as those undertaken by the Soros Foundation, are badly needed.

In conclusion, it is necessary to note that the articles included in the present collection, though varying in professional and scholarly levels, in general reflect both the positive and negative aspects of the study in Russia of the history of the broad cultural relations between the two countries and contribute to the mutual understanding between the Russian and American peoples. They provide the foundation for what we may expect to be important new studies by both Russian and American scholars in the future.

Contributors

Russian and Former Soviet Contributors

Nikolai Nikolaevich Bolkhovitinov is Director of the Center for North American Studies of the Institute of General History and Academician of the Russian Academy of Sciences.

Igor Petrovich Dement'ev is Professor of History in the Department of Modern and Contemporary History of the University of Moscow.

Iaroslav A. Ivanchenko was a candidate of historical sciences, University of Moscow, now in international business.

Nina Stepanovna Kiniapina is Professor in the Department of Modern and Contemporary History, University of Moscow.

Gennadyi Petrovich Kuropiatnik is Chief Researcher in the Institute of General History, Russian Academy of Sciences.

Irina Konstantinova Mal'kova is managing editor of *Vestnik Drevnei Istorii* (Journal of Ancient History) of the Institute of General History, Russian Academy of Sciences.

Vladimir I. Moriakov is Professor in the Department of Modern and Contemporary History, University of Moscow.

Aleksandr Nikolaevich Nikoliukin is Doctor of Philology in the Institute of Information on the Social Sciences, Russian Academy of Sciences.

Abel' Isaakovich Startsev is Professor Emeritus, Institute of World Literature, Russian Academy of Sciences.

Aleksandr F. Tsvirkun is Associate Professor of History, University of Odessa, Ukraine.

American Contributors

Richard M. Abrams is Professor of History, University of California–Berkeley.

John T. Alexander is Professor of History, University of Kansas–Lawrence.

Dane Hartgrove is Senior Editor, National Archives Publications Office, Washington, D.C.

Ronald J. Jensen is Professor of History, George Mason University.

Richard D. McKinzie was Professor of History, University of Missouri–Kansas City.

Norman E. Saul is Professor of History, University of Kansas–Lawrence.

Select Bibliography

In Russian:

Al'perovich, M. S. *Rossiia i Novyi Svet (posledniaia tret' XVIII veka)* (Russia and the New World [last third of the eighteenth century]). Moscow, 1993.

Arustamian, L. R. "Amerikanskaia tema na stranitsakh *Otechestvennykh Zapisok* (1841–1856)" (The American Theme in the Pages of *Fatherland Notes*, 1841–1856). *Amerikanskii Ezhegodnik 1991* (Moscow, 1992), 93–103.

Bogina, Sh. A. *Immigrantskoe naselenie SShA, 1865–1900 gg.* (Immigrant Population of the U.S.A., 1865–1900). Leningrad, 1976.

Bolkhovitinov, N. N. *Rossiia otkryvaet Ameriku, 1732–1799* (Russia Discovers America, 1732–1799). Moscow, 1991.

———. *Russko-Amerikanskie otnosheniia, 1815–1832 gg.* (Russian-American Relations, 1815–1832). Moscow, 1975.

———. "U istokov pravoslaviia v Severnoi Amerike (seredina XVIII veka–1794 god)" (The Origins of the Orthodox Church in North America [mid–eighteenth century to 1794]). *Amerikanskii Ezhegodnik 1993*, 127–32. Moscow, 1994.

Bolkhovitinov, N. N., et al., eds. *Istoriia vneshnei politiki i diplomatii SShA, 1775–1877* (The History of the Foreign Policy and Diplomacy of the U.S.A., 1775–1877). Moscow, 1994.

Chistiakova, E. V. *Russkie stranitsy Ameriki* (The Russian Pages of America). Moscow, 1993.

Dolgova, S. R. *Tvorcheskii put' F. V. Karzhavina* (The Creative Voyage of F. V. Karzhavin). Leningrad, 1984.

Engel', V. V. "Amerikanskii pasport i russko-evreiskii vopros v kontse XIX–nachale XX veka" (The American Passport and the Russian-Jewish Question at the End of the Nineteenth and Beginning of the Twentieth Centuries). *Amerikanskii Ezhegodnik 1991* (Moscow, 1992), 104–20.

Evseeva, M. "Russkie muzykanty i russkie muzykal'nye traditsii v ispolnitel'skoi kul'ture SShA" (Russian Musicians and Musical Traditions in the Development of American Culture). In *Vzaimodeistvie kuo'tur SSSR i SShA: XVIII–XX vv* (The Interaction of U.S.S.R. and U.S.A. Cultures, Eighteenth to Twentieth Centuries), edited by O. E. Tuganova. Moscow, 1987.

Iazkov, E. F., ed. *Istoricheskii obraz Ameriki* (The Historical Image of America). Moscow, 1994.

Ivanov, Robert F. *Diplomatiia Avraama Linkol'na* (The Diplomacy of Abraham Lincoln). Moscow, 1987.

Korshunov, Iu. L. "Pervyi vizity flotov Rossii i SShA" (First Visit of U.S. and Russian Fleets). *Probl. Dal. Vostoka* (Problems of the Far East) 4 (1991): 90–100.

———. "Amerikanskie eskadryna Kronshtadskom reide" (American Squadrons at Kronstadt). *SShA—ekonomika, politika, ideologiia* 4 (1991): 55–63.

Kuropiatnik, G. P. *Rossiia i SShA: Ekonomicheskie, kul'turnye i diplomaticheskie sviazi, 1867–1881* (Russia and the U.S.A.: Economic, Cultural, and Diplomatic Relations, 1867–1881). Moscow, 1981.

Lapitskii, M. I. "Tokvil' i Rossiia: uroki demokratii" (Tocqueville and Russia: Lessons of Democracy). *SShA—ekonomika, politika, ideologiia* (U.S.A.—Economy, Politics, Ideology) 7 (1993): 22–44.

Melamed, E. I. *Dzhordzh Kennan protiv tsarisma* (George Kennan against Tsarism). Moscow, 1981.

Nikoliukin, A. N. *Literaturnye sviazi Rossii i SShA: stanovlenie literaturnykh kontaktov* (Literary Relations of Russia and the U.S.A.: The Beginnings of Literary Contacts). Moscow, 1981.

———. *Vzaimosviazi literatur Rossii i SShA: Turgenev, Tolstoi, Dostoevskii i Amerika* (Interrelations of Russian and American Literatures: Turgenev, Tolstoy, Dostoevsky, and America). Moscow, 1987.

Petrov, A. Iu. "Rol' klana Shelikhovykh pri formirovanii Rossiisko-Amerikanskoi kompanii v kontse XVIII v." (The Role of the Shelikhov Clan in the Formation of the Russian America Company at the End of the Eighteenth Century). *Amerikanskie Ezhegodnik 1994*, 137–52. Moscow, 1995.

Petrov, Viktor. *Russkie v istorii Ameriki* (Russians in the History of America). Moscow, 1991.

Ponomarev, V. N. *Krymskaia voina i Russko-Amerikanskie otnosheniia* (The Crimean War and Russian-American Relations). Moscow, 1993.

———. "Polveka za okeanom: rossiiskii diplomat and literator Aleksei Evstaf'ev" (A Half Century Overseas: Russian Diplomat and Publicist Aleksei Evstaf'ev). *Amerikanskii Ezhegodnik 1990* (American Annual) (Moscow, 1991): 191–205.

Sokolov, A. S. "Rossiia na vsemirnoi vystavke v Chikago v 1893 g." (Russia at the 1893 World Exhibition in Chicago). *Amerikanskii Ezhegodnik 1984* (American Annual 1984) (Moscow, 1984): 152–64.

Sokolov, V. "Sibirskii sled v sotrudnichestve Rossii s Amerikoi" (The Siberian Traces in the Cooperation of Russia with America), *Mezhdunarodniaia Zhizn'* 4 (1993): 139–47.

Sol [Saul], N. E. "Predstavleniia russkikh ob Amerike" (Russian Perceptions of America), *Amerikanskii Ezhegodnik, 1990* (Moscow, 1991): 166–90.

———. " 'Prostaki za granitsei', ili Kak amerikantsy i russkie otkryvali drug druga, 1867–1881" ("Innocents Abroad," or How Americans and Russians Discovered Each Other, 1867–1881). *Amerikanskii Ezhegodnik 1993* (Moscow, 1994): 80–95.

Startsev, A. I. *Russko-Amerikanskie etiudy* (Russian-American Studies). Moscow, 1995.

Tudorianu, N. L. "Sotsial'no-ekonomicheskie polozhenie Rossiiskikh emigrantov v SShA v kontse XIX-nachala XX veka" (Socioeconomic Situation of Russian Emigrants to the U.S. at the End of the Nineteenth and Beginning of the Twentieth Centuries), *Istoriia SSSR* (History of U.S.S.R.) 3 (March 1986): 146–55.

Tuganova, O. E., et al., eds. *Vzaimodeistvie kul'tur SSSR i SShA, xviii-xx vv.* (The Cultural Interaction of the U.S.S.R. and U.S.A., Eighteenth to Twentieth Centuries). Moscow, 1987.

Zhuravleva, V. I. "Kogo demokraticheskaia Amerika vydavala Tsarskoi Rossii? (russko-amerikanskaia konventsiia 1887 goda o vzaimnoi vydache prestupnikov)" (Who Did Democratic America Surrender to Tsarist Russia? [the Russian-American Convention of 1887 about Extradition of Criminals]). *Amerikanskii Ezhegodnik 1993* (Moscow, 1994), 116–26.

In English:

Allen, Robert V. *Russia Looks at America: The View to 1917.* Washington, D.C., 1988.

Bashkina, N. N., et al., eds. *The United States and Russia: The Beginning of Relations, 1765–1815.* Washington, D.C., 1980.

Best, Gary Dean. *To Free a People: American Jewish Leaders and the Jewish Problem in Eastern Europe, 1890–1914.* Westport, Conn., and London, 1982.

Blakely, Allison. *Russia and the Negro: Blacks in Russian History and Thought.* Washington, D.C., 1986.

Bolkhovitinov, N. N. *The Beginnings of Russian-American Relations, 1775–1815.* Cambridge, Mass., 1975.

Bradley, Joseph. *Guns for the Tsar: American Technology and the Small Arms Industry in Nineteenth Century Russia.* DeKalb, Ill., 1990.

Carstensen, Fred V. *American Enterprise in Foreign Markets: Studies of Singer and International Harvester in Russia.* Chapel Hill and London, 1984.

Cassedy, Steven. "Chernyshevskii Goes West: How Jewish Immigration Helped Bring Russian Radicalism to America." *Russian History* 21, no. 1 (spring 1994): 1–22.

Dmytryshyn, Basil, et al., eds. *The Russian American Colonies, 1798–1987: A Documentary Record.* 3 vols. Portland, 1989.

Dubie, Alain. *Frank A. Golder: An Adventure of a Historian in Quest of Russian History.* Boulder, Colo., 1989.

Gaddis, John Lewis. *Russia, the Soviet Union and the United States: An Interpretive History.* 2d ed. New York, 1990.

Good, Jane E. " 'I'd Rather Live in Siberia': V. G. Korolenko's Critique of America." *The Historian* 44, no. 2 (February 1982): 190–206.

Guttridge, Leonard F. *Icebound: The Jeannette Expedition's Quest for the North Pole.* New York, 1988.

Hardwick, Susan Wiley. *Russian Refuge: Religion, Migration, and Settlement on the North American Pacific Rim.* Chicago, 1993.
Hasty, Olga Peters, and Susanne Fusso. *America through Russian Eyes, 1874–1926.* New Haven and London, 1988.
Healy, Ann E. "Tsarist Anti-Semitism and Russian-American Relations." *Slavic Review* 42, no. 3 (fall 1983): 408–25.
Jensen, Ronald J. "The Politics of Discrimination: America, Russia and the Jewish Question, 1869–1872." *American Jewish History* 75 (March 1986): 280–95.
Karlowich, Robert A. *We Fall and Rise: Russian-Language Newspapers in New York City, 1889–1914.* Metuchen, N.J., and London, 1991.
Kasinec, E. "L. B. Khavkina (1871–1949), American Library Ideas in Russia, and the Development of Soviet Librarianship." *Libri* 37, no. 1 (1987): 59–71.
Laserson, Max M. *The American Impact on Russia, 1784–1917.* New York, 1962.
Nikoliukin, Alexander, comp. *A Russian Discovery of America.* Moscow, 1986.
Prince, Nancy. *A Black Woman's Odyssey through Russia and Jamaica: The Narrative of Nancy Prince.* Introduction by Ronald G. Walters. New York, 1990.
Rogger, Hans. "America Enters the Twentieth Century: The View from Russia." In *Felder und Vorfelder Russischer Geschichte: Studien zu Ehren von Peter Scheibert.* Freiburg, 1985.
———. "*Amerikanizm* and the Economic Development of Russia." *Comparative Studies on Society and History* 23, no. 3 (July 1981): 382–420.
Saul, Norman E. *Concord and Conflict: The United States and Russia, 1867–1914.* Lawrence, Kans., 1996.
———. *Distant Friends: The United States and Russia, 1763–1867.* Lawrence, Kans., 1991.
Schrier, Arnold, and Joyce Story, eds. *A Russian Looks at America: The Journey of Aleksandr Borisovich Lakier in 1857.* Chicago, 1979.
Shavit, David. *United States Relations with Russia and the Soviet Union: A Historical Dictionary.* Westport, Conn., and London, 1993.
Travis, Frederick F. *George Kennan and the American-Russian Relationship, 1865–1924.* Athens, Ohio, 1990.
Walker, Dale. L. *Januarius MacGahan: The Life and Campaigns of an American War Correspondent.* Athens, Ohio, 1988.
Weeks, Charles J., Jr. *An American Naval Diplomat in Revolutionary Russia: The Life and Times of Vice Admiral Newton A. McCully.* Annapolis, Md., 1992.
Williams, Robert C. *Russian Art and American Money, 1900–1940.* Cambridge and London, 1980.
Yoffe, Elkhonon. *Tchaikovsky in America: The Composer's Visit in 1891.* New York and Oxford, 1986.

Index

Abbe, Cleveland, 10
Academy of Sciences, Moscow (Soviet), 1, 90
Academy of Sciences, St. Petersburg (Russian), 4, 7, 9, 10 passim, 43
Adams, John Quincy, 7 passim, 54
Adelung, Friedrich, 6
Aepinus, F. U. T., 3, 5, 43
Agrenev-Slavianskii, Dmitri, 145–46
Akademicheskie Izvestii (Academic News), 4
Albee, Edward, 219
Aldridge, Ira, 21
Aleksandrovskii, I. F., 159 passim
Alekseev, Mikhail, 18
Aleuts, treatment of by Russians, 247
Alexander I: speech by, 59, 63, 64; liberal views by, 64, 68, 74, 75, 90 passim
Alexander II, 129, 164
American Academy of Arts and Sciences (Boston), 4, 6
American Association for the Voting Rights of Women, 208
American Constitution, 45, 49, 69 passim, 196, 245
American Enlightenment, 31, 43
American Historical Review, xiv
American Industrial Revolution, 224
American Philosophical Society (Philadelphia), 4, 6, 44, 155
American Revolution: impact on Russian-

American cultural relations, 5, 26; impact in Russia, 32, 35, 85, 98, 128, 192, 195
American Weekly Mercury, 2
Amerikanskii Ezhegodnik (American Annual), 248
Amur River, 213
Anaconda plan, 118
Anthony, Susan B., 208 passim
Arakcheev, Aleksei, 45, 68
Army of the Cumberland, 113, 114.
Army of the Ohio, 112, 113, 114.
Atkinson, Edward, 190

Bache, Alexander, 7
Baer, Karl, 7
Baird, Spencer F., 10
Baku, refineries of, 153
Bakunin, Michael, 162, 168
Ballou, Adin, 181
Balmont, Konstantin, 145
Bancroft, George, 7
Battle of Chattanooga, 114
Battle of Chickamauga, 114
Beasley, E. S., 133
Belinsky, Vissarion, 15, 88, 91
Bellamy, Edward, 142, 175, 181–82 passim, 225
Bellini, Carlo, 6
Bel'skii, Martin, 1
Bennett, Arnold, 139
Berdan, Hiram, 161

Bestuzhev, Nikolai, 14
Biblioteka dlia chteniia (Reading Library), 19
Bilie, Ia. V., 6
Bogdanov, Aleksandr, 228
Bolkhovitinov, Nikolai, 32, 33, 34, 43, 89, 93
Bolshevik Revolution, 225
Bond, George, 10
Bond, Thomas, 4
Bortnianskii, Dmitri, 145
Boston Evening Journal, 12, 152
Boston Gazette, 2
Boston News Letter, 2
Botanical Gardens, 9
Boxer Rebellion, 236
Brandt, Johann, 9, 10
Braun, Joseph-Adam, 4
Briggs, Stephen, 134
Bryan, William Jennings, 177, 187–88 passim
Buell, Don Carlos, 112, 113, 114, 120, 123
Bulgarin, Faddei, 86, 91
Burke, Edmund, 73
Butler, Benjamin, 125

Calhoun, John C., 225
Caspian Sea, 8
Catherine the Great, 5, 42, 43 passim, 98
Caucasus, farming in, 7
Cedar Vale commune, 134–38
Centennial Exhibition (1876, Philadelphia), 11 passim
"Chaikovskii Circle," 131, 135, 136
Chaikovskii, Nikolai, 135
Chekhov, Anton, 212, 213–14
Chekhov Conference, University of North Carolina, 220
Cherevkova, Anna, 236
Chernyshevsky, Nikolai, 100 passim, 102, 117, 119
Chicago Tribune, 111, 120, 123
Chikhachev, Platon, 9
China, relations with Russia, 66
Christian socialism, in America, 175. *See also* Society of Christian Socialists
Chukovskii, Kornei, 145
Churchman, John, 7
Cincinnati Gazette, 120, 121
Civil War: Soviet historiography of, 93; American historiography of, 94; the beginnings, 96, 108, 192
Civil War Dictionary, 115
Clay, Cassius, 103
Cloots, Anacharsis, 37
Coffin, James, 149

College of William and Mary, 6
Collins, Edward, 7
Common Sense, xiii, 27, 28 passim, 40
Confederate Congress, 96
Confederate States of America, establishment of, 96
Continental Congress, 6
Convention on Maritime Rights, 102
Cooper, James Fenimore, 14, 15, 25, 78–79 passim, 81, 85, 91
Corps of Mining Engineers, contacts with America, 7
Cotton loan, 103
Crimea, farming in, 7, 8
Crimean War, Russian defeat in, 95, 98, 107, 110, 160
Crosby, Ernest, 173, 177, 186–87 passim
Cuba, 1, 187, 230, 235

Dardanelles, seizure of, 94
Dashkova, Princess Ekaterina, 6
Davis, Jefferson, 96, 114
Dawn, 182
Debogorii-Mokrievich, Ivan, 131
Debs, Eugene, 181
Decembrist uprising, defeat of 78, 167
Declaration of Independence, 36
Delo (Cause), 192–211, 225; editorial board of, 193; on American affairs, 194, 197–98; on development of Russian capitalism, 198; on capitalist oligarchy, 199–200; on negro question, 202; on American working class, 203, 205; on women's rights, 207; on prostitution, 209, 225
Demens, Peter. *See* Tverskoi, Petr
Dement'ev, Igor, on historiography of Civil War, 93, 225
Dickens, Charles, 139
Dobell, Peter, 52, 53
Don Cossacks, 109
Don River, 1
Donkov, Russia, 1
Dorogobuzh, Russia, 1
Dostoevsky, Fedor, 139, 141
Dukh Zhurnalov (Spirit of Journals), 14, 45–76, 244; summary of American Constitution, 45; first publication of, 46–47; on American slavery, 48; criticized in Russian press, 50; on farming and manufacturing in Russia, 55; on European peasant serfdom, 62
Dukhobor, settlement of, 242

Eclectic, 23

Index

Emerson, Ralph Waldo, 142
Emigration: to America, statistics, 129; reasons for, 129
Engels, Friedrich, 41, 93, 97, 116, 118, 163
Enisei Province, 213
Enisei River, 213
Euler, Leonard, 4, 7
European Enlightenment, 28
European Herald, 50, 51
Everett, Alexander Hill, 12
Evstaf'ev, Aleksei, 12, 13

Fabian strategy, 126
Farming Journal, 7
Faulkner, William, 215; collection of Chekhov's works, 215, 223
Fearon, Henry B., 65–66 passim
Federalists, 3, 6
Fischer, Gotthelf, 6–7 passim, 9
Fitzgerald, F. Scott, impressions of Chekhov, 214
Flugel, Johann (Leipzig), 9
Fonvizin, Denis, 5–6
Fort Sumter, 96
Fox, Charles, 72
France, intervention in Mexico, 97
Franklin, Benjamin, 3–6, 33, 179, 210
Fraser's Magazine (London), 23
Free Economic Society, 4
Fremont, John, 112, 114
French Enlightenment, 35
French Revolution, as seen in Russia, 39
Frey, William. *See* Geins, Vladimir
Fuss, Nicholas, 6 passim

Galich, Russia, 1
Gardner, K., 209–10
Garfield, James, 164, 165
Garibaldi, 122
Garland, Hamlin, 175, 176, 177
Gartman, Lev (Hartman, Leo), 163
Geins (Heinz), Vladimir K., 132, 133, 136, 138
Gemilian, Valerii, 156
George III, King of England, condemnation of, 72, 73
George, Henry, 142, 175, 182
Glinka, Mikhail, 146
Golitsyn, Alexander, 56, 61, 65, 72, 74
Golitsyn, Dmitrii, 8
Golitsyn, Iurii, 145
Gol'tsev, Viktor, 231
Gorchakov, Alexander, 97, 102, 103, 105
Gorlov, Aleksandr, 160, 161

Gould, Benjamin, 7, 10
Great Britain: growing tensions with Russia, 94; assistance to the South, 97
Grech, Nikolai, 51
Grek, Maksim (Mikhail Trivolis), 1
Gronlund, Laurence, 181
Gulf of Finland, 110
Gunnius, Konstantin (Captain), 160, 161

Hague Conference, 190
Hall, Asaph, 10
Hapgood, Isabel, 213
Harrison, Joseph, 8
Harrison-Smith, Mrs., 81
Harte, Bret, 142
Harvard Observatory, opening of, 10
Hawthorne, Nathaniel, 142
Hayes, Isaac, 111
Haymarket Riot, 175
Heath, Frederic, 176
Heckewelder, John, 5
Henry, Joseph, 11
Herzen, Alexander, 95; on Trent incident, 101, 107, 111, 168
Holbach, Paul Henri, 32
Holy Alliance, consolidation of, 45
Holy Synod, 56
Homestead Act, 97
Horsford, Eben Norton, 155
Howe, Elias, 12
Howells, William Dean, 142, 176, 177, 213, 223
Hungary, peasant serfdom in, 62
Hunt, Thomas Sterry, 155

Ianzhul, Ivan, 174
Iasnaia Poliana: Tolstoy's estate, 170; Bryan's visit to, 188
Iatsenkov, Grigorii, 46, 49; responding to criticism of *Spirit of Journals,* 50, 57; in dispute with Pravdin, 60; on liberal reformism in Russia, 64, 89
Imperial Guard, 75
Ioss, N. A., 12
Irving, Washington, 14 passim, 81, 85, 86, 91
Istoricheskie, Genealogicheskie and Geograficheskie Preimechanie (Historical, Genealogical, and Geographical Notes), 2
Istoricheskii Zhurnal (Historical Journal), 82, 84

Jackson, Andrew, 77, 92
Jacksonian Democracy, 77, 89, 91

James, Henry, recollections on Turgenev, 140, 141
Jamestown (Va.), 1–2
Jefferson, Thomas, 48, 89, 179, 210
"Jewish Question," in Russian-American relations, 246
Journal of the Ministry of Public Education, 83, 87

Kamchatka, 52
Kankrin, Egor, 8
Karzhavin, Fedor, 6 passim
Katkov, Mikhail, 95
Kennan, George, 177
Kherson, cultivation of tobacco, 8
Kirghizia (Central Asia), 9
Klingstadt, Timotheus, 4
Knorring, F., 236
Korsakov, Vladimir, 236
Kovalevskii, Maksim, 237
Kozodavlev, Osip, 57
Krabbe, Nikolai, 104
Kraft, Nikolai, 8
Krasnoiarsk (Siberia), Chekhov's stay in, 212
Kronstadt Cable Factory, 151
Kronstadt Steamship Factory, 151
Kruzenshtern, Ivan, 6
Krylov, Ivan, 52 passim
Ku Klux Klan, 202
Kunitsyn, Aleksandr, 52, 59
Kupffer, Adolph, 6, 10
Kurbskii, A. S., 129
Kushner, Howard, on Russian-American relations, 95

Lafayette College (Pa.), 149
Lavrov, Peter, 110, 132, 137–38, 143, 162
Lavrov, Vukol, 229
Lenin, Vladimir, 189, 195, 227, 233; on American Civil War, 93, 106; on Tolstoy, 170 passim
Lermontov, Mikhail, 15
Lesovskii, Stepan, 104, 106, 167
Leverson, Montague, 186
Lewis, William D., 15, 16
Liberalism, in America, 223 passim
Lincoln, Abraham, 96, 97, 102, 105, 108, 113, 118, 169, 202
Literaturnaia Gazeta (Literary Gazette), 13, 81, 91
Litke, Fedor, 9
Lomonosov, Mikhail, 2–3, 4, 244
Longfellow, Henry, 143–44
Louisville Journal, 120

Lovers of Russian Letters (Moscow), 9
Luxemburg, Rosa, 184

McClellan, George B., 114, 118, 124, 125
McCormick Harvesting Machine Company, 246
Machtet, Grigorii, 129, 132, 134
Madison, James, 53
Madison, James (Bishop), 6
Malikov, Aleksandr, 135
Malkin, M. M., 93, 166
Martens, Fedor, 234, 242
Martinique, 6
Marx, Karl: on War for Independence, 26; on Civil War, 93, 97, 101; on Lord Palmerston, 102, 116, 118; in support of Gartman, 163, 164, 169
Maseo, General, 235
Maury, Matthew, 7, 10
Medical-Surgical Academy, 9
Mel'nikov, Pavel, 8
Mendeleev, Dmitrii: visiting America, 11, 152; impressions of America, 153–54, 157, 158; elected society memberships, 155; interest in oil production, 155, 156
Mensheviks, 228
Mexican Revolution, in Russian press, 232
Mikhailov, Mikhail, 22
Mikhailovskii Artillery School, 110, 132
Military Rambles, 114, 116, 119, 127, 169
Miliukov, Paul, 242
Mineralogical Society, 9
Minor, The, 6
Mir Bozhii (World of God), 227, 228
Missouri, 111
Mochul'skii, Viktor, 8 passim
Molokan, settlement of, 242
Monroe Doctrine, 234, 237
Monroe, James, 48, 58, 66
Moreau, General, 53
Moriakov, Vasilii, 42 passim
Moscow Agricultural Society, 7
Moscow Art Theatre, American tour, 221
Moscow Gazette: on War for Independence, 33 passim. See also Novikov, Nikolai
Moscow Society of Natural Scientists, 7 passim, 9
Moscow State University, Fulbright program, x
Moskovskie Vedomosti (Moscow Gazette), 101, 230
Moskovskii Telegraf (Moscow Telegraph): publication of American novels, 14, 22;

on education in America, 78, 86; on relationship between Russia and America, 79, 80, 90; book reviews, 91
Murat, Achille, 82
Murat, Joachim, 82

Napoleon III, 102 passim; on intervention in Poland, 104
National Era, 20
National Union Catalog, xiv
Nationalist, 182
Native Americans: raids by, 2; language of, 5; treatment of, 66, 84, 189
"Nechaevites," 136
Nedel'ia (Week), 134, 144
New England Courant, 2
New York Daily Tribune, 120, 123
New York Gazette, 2
Newcomb, Simon, 7, 10
News Letter (Boston), 2
Nicholas I, 78 passim
Nicholas II, 185, 188, 190
North American Review, 13, 23, 66, 80 passim, 90
Novaia Biblioteka dlia Vospitaniia (New Educational Library), 19
Novikov, Nikolai, 33, 42, 166
Novosil'skii, A. P., 159
Novye Vremeni (New Times), 230, 231

Oates, Joyce Carol, 217–18
Obruchev, Vladimir, published in *Sovemenuik,* 100, 110
Obukhov Ordnance Factory, 151
Ogarev, Nikolai, 95, 99
Oneida, 133
"Open Door" Doctrine, 241
Ostrog, Russia, 1
Ostrogradskii, Mikhail, 6
Otechestvennye Zapiski (Fatherland Notes), 134, 193
Ozerov, Ivan, 238

Paine, Thomas, xiii, 26, 245; his position on French Revolution, 28, 37; on absolution, 29; on constitutional monarchy, 29, 30, 31; views of Raynal, 32; his republicanism, 37; on popular sovereignty, 37; elected to the French Convention, 37; on Girondins, 38 passim
Pallas, Peter, 6
Palmerston, Lord, 102 passim
Panama Canal, 233
Paris, 5–6 passim, 82

Paris Peace Treaty (1856), 94, 110
"Pauperization," 224
Pedagogical Institute, 9
Penn, William, 2
Peredvizhniki (wanderers), 151
Peter the Great, 2 passim
Petrov, N. N., 12
Philadelphia Exhibition, 150; Russian pavilion, 150–51, 152
Philadelphia National Gazette, 16
Philippines: national liberation movement in, 186, 188, 190 passim, 235; annexation of, 238
Phoenix, 84
Picture of America, 67, 70 passim, 89
Plekhanov, George, 172, 228
Pobedonostsev, Konstantin, 95
Poland, uprising in, 103, 106
Poletika, Petr, 12, 82
Polevoi, Nikolai, 14 passim, 78, 85, 87, 90, 91
Poliarnaia Zvezda (Polar Star), 108
Polish Seim, opening of, 59
Pope, John, 112
Popov, Andrei, 104 passim, 106
Popov, P. I., 205–6 passim, 209
Populism: Russian, 172; in America, 175.
Populist Party, 175, 176
Porter, David, 159
Pravdin, 59–60 passim, 63, 74
Priestley, Joseph, 37
Progressive Commune, 134, 135
Provisional Constitution, 21
Pugachev, Emelian, 5; rebellion led by, 33, 40
Pulkovo Observatory, 7, 9, 10, 132
Pushkin, Alexander, 16–19, 86, 91

Radishchev, Alexander: on American Revolution, 5, 27; on French Revolution, 28, 33, 39; on popular revolution, 34; on "new" despotism in France, 39; comparison between French and American Revolutions, 40
Raynal, Abbe Guillaume, 27, 28, 29, 30, 31, 39
Razumovskii, Count Aleksei, 46, 47, 51, 74
Reclus, Elie, 207–8, 209
Repnin, Nikolai, 61
Republican Party, 96
Review of Russian Journals, 52
Revolutionary populism, in Russia, 162
Revue Britannique, 83
Riabinin, Semen, 151
Richmann, Georg, 3

Richmond (Va.), capture of, 118
Rogger, Hans, 95
Rolleston, Thomas, 144
Roosevelt, Theodore, 187, 233
Rosecrans, William, 113
Rossiiskie Vedomosti (Russian Herald), 2
Rubinstein, Anton, 146, 147 passim, 168
Russell, John, 103
Russian Bible Society, 56
Russian colonists, in America, 129–30 passim
"Russian Enlightenment," 27, 35, 41, 43
Russian Invalid, 51
Russian musket, 162, 163
Russian opera, debut in America, 146
Russian Orthodox Church: in America, 130; against Tolstoy, 174
Russian-Swedish War, 2
Russian Technological Society, 153
Russian Telegraph Agency (RTA), 230
Russkaia Mysl (Russian Thought), 227, 229
Russkii Vestnik (Russian Herald), 21
Russkoe Slovo (Russian Word), 193
Russo-Japanese War, 185, 233, 242
Russo-Turkish War, 128; use of Berdan rifle in, 162

Quakers, 2 passim

St. Petersburg Conservatory, 146
St. Petersburg Gazette, 46
St. Petersburg Herald, 25
Sakhalin Island, 212
Saratov, 8, 151
Schubert, Friedrich, 6
Schultz, Theodore, 5
Schuyler, Eugene, 139, 141, 167
Semenovsky regiment, 75, 90
Serfdom, abolished in Russia, 94
Sevastopol, 110
Severnaia Pochta (Northern Post), 57, 63
Seward, William H., 98, 103, 104
Shakers, in Russia, 181
Shays's Rebellion, 36
Shelgunov, Nikolai, 102, 192, 195, 196, 207
Shelikhov, Grigorii, 247
Sherman, William T., 112, 113, 125
Shestov, Lev, 216
Siberia, 52, 148, 247
Sinclair, Upton, 175, 176; *The Jungle,* 180
Singer Sewing Machine Company, 246
Skal'kovskii, Konstantin, 12
Slavinskii, Nikolai, 129–30 passim
Slavinskii's Russian folk choir, 146
Slonimskii, Liudvig, 229

Slovo (Word), 193–211, 224; formulation of, 194; on capitalist oligarchy, 199–200; on negro question, 202
Smith, John, 1–2
Smithsonian Institution, 9, 11, 148
Society of Christian Socialists, 175, 176
Society of Literature and Art (Mittau), 9
Sogrin, Vladimir, 37
Sokhriakov, Iurii, 218
Somov, Orest, 81
Sovremennik (Contemporary), 20–22, 100, 117, 143, 193; publication of Uncle Tom's Cabin, 20; on events in America, 21–22
Spanish-American War, 175, 185, 188, 230, 240
Standard Oil Company, 156
Startsev, Abel', 244
Stasiulevich, Mikhail, 228
Stead, William, 174
Stiles, Ezra, 3–4 passim
Stoeckl, 98 passim, 102, 103, 105, 106
Stolypin, Petr, 245
Stowell, Peter, 220
Struve, Otto, 7, 10
Struve, Wilhelm, 6, 9
Svin'in, Pavel, 12, 13
Syn Otechestva (Son of the Fatherland), 14, 21, 48, 51, 59, 74 passim

Tartars, 5
Telegraph, between Russia and America, 99
Teleskop (Telescope), 81, 83, 91
Thackeray, William, 139
Thoreau, Henry, 142
Tilezius, V. G., 6
Timkovskii, Ivan, 47, 57
Tocqueville, Count Alexis de, 77
Todd, Charles S., 9
Tolstoy, Leo, 24, 139, 170–91; on peasant radicalism, 171; religious-philosophical doctrine, 172, 174; on the 1905 Russian Revolution, 173; international popularity, 173; publication of his works in America, 173; excommunication from Russian Church, 174; on America, 178–85; on Russo-Japanese War, 185
Transactions of the Royal Society, 4
Trans-Siberian Railroad, 246
Trent, incident of, 101, 102 passim, 167
Tribune, 21, 22 passim
Tsakni, Nikolai, 129, 130, 200–201 passim, 203–4 passim, 263
Turchaninov, Ivan, xiii, 101, 107–27, 169; in the Union army, 101; in correspondence

with Herzen, 107; views on America, 108; participation in Civil War, 108, 111–14; biography of, 108–9, 112; escape to America, 110–11; trial of, 113, 119–22; on slavery, 119, criticism of Union army, 124–26; on his role in Civil War, 127, 169. *See also Military Rambles*
Turchaninov, Nadezhda, 110, 111, 115
Turgenev, Ivan, 23, 24, 128, 139–40, 141, 167, 173
Tverskoi, Petr, 232, 223
Twain, Mark, 145, 175, 225

Ukraine, farming in, 7
University of Kazan, 9
Uvarov, Sergei, 9, 46, 56, 61, 65, 72

Van Buren, Martin, 77
Vedomosti (Herald), 2
Veidemuller, K. L., 232
Venezuelan Crisis, 230
Verstovskii, A. N., 146
Vestnik Evropy (European Herald), 227–40; first publication of, 228; on Russian foreign relations, 229; on American expansion, 230; on American foreign policy in the Far East, 237
Viazmitinov, Sergei, 46, 51, 74
Vladimirov, Mikhail, 129
Voeikov, Aleksandr, 11, 148, 149
Vremia (Time), 20

War of 1812, 98, 102, 128

Washington, Booker T., 176, 180
Washington, George, 5, 33, 53, 37, 85, 151, 168, 195
Welles, Gideon, 105
Welsh, Herbert, 186
Weniawski, Hendryk, 146, 147 passim
West Point Military Academy, 124 passim
Whistler, George, 8
Whitman, Walt, 141, 142, 175
Whittier, John Greenleaf, 142
Wilhelm II, 185
Williams, Tennessee, 219, 223
"Will of the People, The," 128, 163, 164–65 passim
Winans, William L., 8
Winthrop, John, 3, 22
Witte, Sergei, 245
Woldman, Albert, 95
Wolfe, Thomas, 214
Women's Labor Society, 208
World War I, 230
Wythe, George, 6

Zagoskin, Mikhail, 86, 91
Zhurnal Manufaktur i Torgovli (Manufacturing and Trade Journal), 14
Ziber, Nikolai, 199
Zommerfel'd, F., 8
Zorge, Friedrich, 165
Zweig, Stefan, 172